FILM REVIEW 1974-75

FILM REVIEW
1974-75

edited by F. Maurice Speed

W. H. Allen · London
A division of Howard and Wyndham Ltd
1974

Printed in Great Britain by Fletcher & Son Ltd, Norwich, for the publishers W. H. Allen & Co. Ltd, 44 Hill Street, London W1X 8LB

ISBN 0 491 01601 8

Designed by Lesley Banks

CONTENTS

INTRODUCTION

This has been the year of Kung Fu – or whatever – in the cinema and I'm pretty sure will be historically recorded as such. Starting with a somewhat tentative release of one of the Hong Kong productions from the Shaw Brothers, starring the redoubtable Bruce Lee, we were soon, thanks to the film's instant and considerable success, watching the trickle turn to a flood as various companies jumped on the band-wagon, gleefully conscious of the vast reservoir of such films. And for every one of the many shown there were always another half a dozen waiting in the wings, so to speak; some of them, I've been told, so bloody, brutal and beastly that in spite of the relaxed censorial standards prevailing they are unlikely ever to get a public showing in this country. But at the moment these "unarmed combat" movies are still coming, and in quantity. One can only sit back – by now a little bored perhaps? – and wonder when this cycle will tail off, and what other cycle will take its place!

It wasn't long before the Americans stepped in to make a Kung Fu movie and now the Italian celluloid sausage-makers, having just about scraped the *Decameron* and *Godfather* barrels dry, are turning to the new scene, and so with proliferation and quick-buck standards taking over, the demise of the cycle already appears inevitable.

Certainly the sex cycle has now exploited itself almost out of existence, for while there are still sex films being shown, and made, they are mainly minor and unimportant productions for the most part aimed at what I believe is called the Raincoat Trade. Sex in the more serious, major productions has veered away from the explicit and sensational and settled down to become increasingly used with good taste and balance. Of course we still have nudity and couplings on the screen, but they are no longer being arbitrarily introduced into almost every movie just for shock-effect – and for this small mercy, this resort to celluloid sanity, I think we should all be grateful.

Of course, the cinema being what it is, there have been other cycles during the year, some of them still going on, some of them already well past their peak. There was, for instance, the "Black" cycle, with American producers – suddenly realising the potential of the film aimed at their Negro market – producing a number of movies in which the cast was either wholly black, or in which the great majority of those taking part were of that colour, some also being directed by Negro moviemakers. A few of these were passably good, others shockingly cynical and, I would have thought, an affront to the very people at which they were aimed.

Perhaps the best judgement of these movies came from the man who produced what I think was the best of all of them, *Sounder*, a rather (in this country) sadly neglected minor screen classic with a magnificent black cast and presenting the Negro's case with artistry and understanding. Said Robert B. Radnitz during a flying visit to Britain in connection with his film: "They (the 'black' films) are phoney, not honest and that is the reason why black leaders do not endorse them. They are 'rip-offs' and nothing more." But if the sex and "Black" cycles are on the wane*, violence is one that is certainly not. The considerable cops and robbers cycle which waxed mightily during the period (and is still waxing, it appears, as I write these lines) included a number of productions in which there was a great deal of needless – and I am inclined to add, mindless – violence which did nothing for the film in question or the cinema in general.

And within this cycle has been a smaller one in which a number of movies contained a very disturbing implication. In these films the official forces of law and order, the police and the authorities controlling them, were shown to be "bent", to be unwilling or unable to control the crooks, the gangsters and the drug-traffickers, and it was left to the private citizen, or citizens, by the use of force, to obtain justice and defeat these villains, usually by means of a final bloodbath. Art mirrors life, it is said, and the cinema, as all other arts, reflects the times; if this is so, and we must presume that it is, the implication is a little short of terrifying, for what is being suggested is that the crust of civilised life, supported by the legal code and the forces to uphold it, is no longer to be relied upon. That way lies complete anarchy and some of these films were not reticent in suggesting that this in fact is the position.

In spite of all the signs we can only hope that this is not so: a hope strengthened perhaps by the knowledge that most if not all the films in this category were hardly likely to have been made with any great moral intention.

---

*A couple of interesting footnotes about this is that as I write United Artists have been told in the courts that they must defend a privately brought action claiming that *Last Tango in Paris* is obscene; and although banned in New York (where something like a £40,000 fine was chalked up against it) America's most way-out sex film yet, *Deep Throat* may be on the way here, even though censor Stephen Murphy has gone on record saying that as examiners who had seen the film had passed on the opinion that it was hard-core pornography it was unlikely that any British distributor familiar with his Board's views would submit the film for a certificate!

8

One of the remarkable points about this year in the cinema has been the cycle of Kung Fu films and the emergence in them of the first Asian super-star Bruce Lee, who died at the height of his career. Typical was the success of *The Way of the Dragon* which when premièred at the London Rialto broke all the cinema's attendance records, with fifteen of the first sixteen performances all of house capacity.

The Cinema – is it on the upward or downward plane? A tricky question, for it is always difficult at any one moment to get a clear idea of what precisely is happening in the film industry in view of the rapidly changing patterns and the many quite conflicting statements that are made by the people within it. But what does appear pretty evident is that the decline in the actual numbers of people going to the cinema continues, though at the decreasing rate which has emerged from the experience of the immediate past few years.
Some interesting figures published by that invaluable trade paper *Cinema TV Today* revealed that during the first quarter of 1972 some $44\frac{1}{4}$ million cinemagoers paid an average of 36.5p per seat while in the same period for 1973, 37,380,000 paid an average of 40.9p per admission. Taking that a bit further, admissions were more than $12\frac{1}{2}$ million down in the first five months of 1973 compared with the same period in 1972. So as seat prices rise the attendance figures fall, but the answer to the question as to whether one is the result of the other can only be guessed at.

A gloomy footnote to this was the same magazine's careful judgement that the final figure to emerge at the end of 1973 would be a slide of something like 21 million in cinema admissions in this country.

An interesting contrast to these figures were another set relating to the number of cinemas operating in Britain. At this point of time it appears there are actually something like a hundred more cinemas open – in spite of a number of closures – than there were at this time in 1973. And, it appears, they will go on proliferating at something like the same rate for some time to come. But there is something which must be taken into consideration in reading these figures and that is that the additional cinemas are often the result of "twinning" or even "tripling" old cinemas so that with several new mini-cinemas under the old one's roof the actual seating capacity may be the same or in some cases even less. On the other hand, experience shows that when a complex takes the place of one cinema the overall admissions increase, one obvious reason being that with three films showing where only one was shown before the appeal is widened to embrace a far greater potential audience taste.
Another interesting point to arise from this twinning and tripling is that whereas it would now cost something like £400,000 to build a cinema from scratch, one cinema could be converted into three for something like a quarter, or less of that amount.

A serial cinema story during this year has been the on-and-off sale of the famous (£6 million) Classic Group of cinemas by their owners the Laurie Marsh Group. Sold to

Price-Freezer (a pregnant trade name in these days if ever there was one!) the deal, after various swings and roundabouts, fell through completely at the beginning of 1974. The amusing point here is that while the alarums and excursions were going on the property scene changed so vitally that with the cinema values sliding down in terms of bricks and mortar and up in terms of film showing profitability, the potential sellers were probably quite happy to see the deal fall through!

The High Street cinema is, though, apparently fighting a losing battle. Value as site has become so high that a return on capital investment is very modest. At least one estate agent has prophesied it is only a matter of time before every High Street cinema will have been converted into some sort of flat or office building, the only hope then being that room will be found in the basement perhaps for a small cinema within the complex.

The Rank Group at any rate have no doubt about the future of the cinema, for in 1973 this consistently successful Group moved into Europe in a big way by taking over the twenty-three-cinema-owning Dutch Matubel Company.

The continuing story of film studio retraction in this country continues. At Shepperton, for instance, with only 20 of the original 60 acres retained (the rest having been scheduled for development) and a loss of something like half-a-million pounds during the year, the apparent intention seems to be to run down activity to probable final closure at the end of 1974.

There is a sadly similar story from the old

A complete paradox was that in a year when violence in all forms was regrettably prevalent on the screen, there was in contrast an obvious nostalgia for the past, illustrated by Gala's ambitious revival of a whole series of Mary Pickford's old silent films (and early talkies) such as *My Best Girl*.

MGM–EMI studios at Elstree, after MGM announced they were no longer prepared to pay an annual £170,000 a year into the kitty. Even without a film on the floor these studios were costing £15,000 a week to run and with British production in its present sorry state that loss appeared to be of indefinite duration. In fact it appears (with Ardmore Studios in Ireland – built during the boom period – to ease congestion – failing and going under the hammer) that soon only Pinewood will be left as the only major British studio complex – although one must not overlook Bray, where there is no depression in the house and the talk is even at this moment of future expansion.

Rationalisation of distribution goes on apace. We have Columbia and Warner in dual harness, Fox and Rank in collaboration, Universal with Paramount, and Cinerama closed down as a distribution company in 1973 after a six-year existence.* But a number of small distribution companies are springing up, mostly with minor programmes, though others like Scotia–Barber are expanding.

*In this connection a sad milestone was MGM's 1973 decision to sell the studios, and their cinemas – including the Empire in Leicester Square – and close down the distribution company. They say the company will continue to actually produce films, and so keep the old lion roaring, but one wonders on what scale this will be?

The ACTT (Union) managed to hit the headlines again this year with the old cry for nationalisation or worker-ownership of the film industry (an idea which fills a large number of people, including this writer, with some horror!) coupled with the public-ownership of cinemas, studios and all else concerned with the film industry. This was highlighted at a stormy union meeting in November last, when about a thousand more moderate members, including people like Ken Russell and Robert Bolt, turned down a suggestion that countries like Greece and South Africa should be blacked and that no productions should be made outside the walls of the British studios. The resultant uproar was interesting; so was the voting result.

Technically there is little to report. There are still whispers of new stereoscopic systems, of laser-beam developments and what have you. But nothing solid has emerged, though one significant story at the bottom of a column said that for a new film called *Wicked, Wicked*, the producers would be using "Duovision" by which two sides of the same story would be shown on the same screen, using a development of the highly heralded but since neglected (by the cinema, but television has used it more recently) split-screen technique.

I've no room left to detail the uproar about the proposed Indecency Bill (which, its detractors claimed, brought the threat of stricter censorship) that died on course with the coming of the Socialist government; or the cries in the Houses of Parliament for more cash for production; or Chancellor

Healey's finance bill which seemed likely to send nearly all the resident American moviemakers exiting to other countries; or the sensible limiting of time per week in which films can be shown on Italian and French television screens; or the optimistic predictions that 1974 was going to be a boom year for Hollywood, with more money likely to be invested in production, more people going to the movies, more work and profits all round (let's hope it will all be justified). Only just room, in fact, to close with what you might find a couple of memorable quotations. The first is from that great veteran director Frank Capra: "I made films to entertain, educate and inspire the individual in society – it never occurred to me I might be making a masterpiece along the way." The second quote comes from the loquacious (and successful) young British moviemaker Michael Winner: "If you want Art, don't muck about with movies – buy a Picasso." And with those pregnant thoughts I leave you until next year.

Another fascinating revival was that by Essential Cinema Ltd of fourteen Max and Dave Fleischer *Betty Boop* cartoons of the thirties (packaged as *The Betty Boop Follies*) given a fresh depth of entertainment by being electronically (and most successfully) coloured for their new lease of life.

IN MEMORIAM

It took just about two minutes with ANNA MAGNANI, Italy's most formidable female film-star, to realise the power of her personality (I once had lunch with her and it was an entirely unforgettable experience); and just about two minutes of screen time to realise what a great actress she was. In fact she was only half Italian, for her father was Egyptian. Born in Alexandria in 1908 (March 7), she was five before she came to Rome. Though she had made a previous film (*Cavalleria* in 1936, directed by her then husband, Godfredo Alessandrini) it was Rossellini's *Open City* which brought her world-wide acclaim. In the films that followed Miss Magnani's roles made her the epitome of Italian womanhood. *Love* brought her a Venice Festival and other Italian awards; the Hollywood film, *The Rose Tattoo* brought her an Oscar and the New York Critics' Award for 1955. Some of her other successes included Visconti's *Bellissima*, Renoir's *The Golden Coach*, *Wild is the Wind*, *The Fugitive Kind* and *Mamma Roma*. Her last screen appearance was a brief cameo in Fellini's *Roma*. Apart from all her films, Anna Magnani did a great deal of stage work and at the time of her death was about to embark on a television series. She died, aged 65, in a Rome hospital – "a tumour on the pancreas" – on September 26, 1973.

SESSUE HAYAKAWA, who died in a Tokyo hospital from pneumonia, the aftermath of a thrombosis attack, on November 23, 1973, was 83 and had been acting on stage and screen since around 1914. Destined for the Japanese Navy, he was turned down because of a defect in one ear and was sent by his father to Chicago to learn banking. Graduating with a degree, he went to Los Angeles and started helping the Japanese Theatre there (at which point he changed his real Christian name of Kintaro to Sessue). His first leading film role was in De Mille's *The Cheat*, soon after which he formed his own company. In the twenties he

toured this country (as well as France) in a series of plays but his film career slumped with the advent of the talkies, and he made only an occasional movie in the thirties. Trapped in France in 1939, he made a living by selling his paintings and it was not until ten years later that he went back to America, where after appearing in *Tokyo Joe* he was kept fairly busy in war films, including his superb performance in the British film *The Bridge on the River Kwai*. Latterly he had returned to his native country to devote himself to the teaching of acting.

LAURENCE HARVEY, a Lithuanian (born Larushka Mischa Skikne – October 1, 1928) who died of cancer in London on November 26, 1973, was always a controversial actor whose achievements for some reason – considerable though they were – never quite matched up to his promise. Educated in South Africa, his first professional stage appearance was at the

12 Johannesburg Little Theatre in 1943. He arrived in London in 1946 and after a brief spell at RADA joined the Manchester Library Theatre. But from the moment he made his first movie he seldom appeared on the boards, making a steady succession of varyingly successful pictures such as *The Good Die Young, The Alamo, Silent Enemy, Three Men in a Boat, Butterfield 8; Room at the Top* (which brought him a 1959 Oscar nomination); the strangely if muddily poetic *The Ceremony* (which he directed, partly wrote and produced as well as being the star); *The Manchurian Candidate* (one of his best performances); *I Am a Camera* and *Romeo and Juliet.* Harvey never lacked self-confidence and would attempt to play any kind of role. His last film was the recent release *Night Watch* in which he again co-starred with Elizabeth Taylor. (There is also, apparently, in existence an Orson Welles film starring him which has never been seen in public, having remained on the shelf since its completion some years ago!)

Between his first appearance in the Pearl White serials and his final performance in *Rosemary's Baby*, 78-year-old SIDNEY BLACKMER appeared in some 200 films (as well as forty plays on Broadway and numerous television films, ranging from hero to villain roles); on no less than ten occasions he played the role of Theodore Roosevelt on the screen! But apart from all his films and play appearances Blackmer was very much concerned with the politics of the theatre, was a founder of the American Equity organisation and worked on other similar bodies, leading the big struggle between the performers and managers that occurred in America just after the First World War. He died of cancer in a New York hospital on October 5, 1973.

LILA LEE, who died in New York at the age of 68 on November 13, 1973, as the result of a stroke, was once known as "Cuddles"; that was when she started her career in vaudeville. It was Gus Edwards who "discovered" her in her father's hotel. Her first film was for Jesse Lasky who signed her at the age of 13 for his Famous Players. She had roles in an early De Mille film and you'll see her name in the cast sheet of Valentino's *Blood and Sand.* Thereafter she made a number of films, of which probably the easiest recalled will be *The Unholy Three,* made in 1930 with Lon Chaney.

JOSEF SOMLO, the Hungarian-born producer who became one of the leading lights and a director of Two Cities films, started his film career way back in 1907 in Vienna, later becoming one of the most distinguished figures with UFA in Berlin. He soon made his mark when he came to this country in the early thirties and one of his finest credits was the production of the Olivier *Hamlet.* He died, on November 29, 1973, in his Locarno home at the age of 89.

Though it was with a Jean Cocteau film (*Les Enfants Terribles*) that he made his first real success, French director JEAN-PIERRE MELVILLE's (real name Grumbach) subsequent output was notable for the fact that his films were mostly American-style gangster pieces and the like: *Le Deuxième Souffle, Le Cercle Rouge, Le Samouraï,* etc. His admiration for the American film led to him always wearing a cowboy hat on the set! He died on August 2, 1973, at the age of 55 from a heart attack in his native Paris.

The generally moustached face of GUY MIDDLETON was for a long time a familiar one on the British screen where he more usually appeared as a sort of cad, even if a well-born one! A stage star of the 1930s, his biggest hit was in *French Without Tears,* with which he went to America, to make an equal success. His films include *Laughter in Paradise, The Happiest Days of Your Life* and *No Place for Jennifer.* He died, at the age of 65, on July 30, 1973, after a long illness which had kept him away from the screen for several years.

With LON CHANEY JNR. (real first name Creighton) it was a case of like father like son, for having started off using his own name he took his father's when he started to play similar horrific parts! Of all his many roles, ranging from macabre contributions to several "Frankenstein", "Dracula" and "Mummy" films, to the broad comedy in an Abbott and Costello opus (*Here Comes the Co-Eds*), his greatest impact was made as the pathetic half-wit Lennie in Lewis Milestone's memorable film of the Steinbeck story *Of Mice and Men*. After his initial screen appearance in 1932 (*Bird of Paradise*), Lon Chaney went into a Western serial called *The Last Frontier*, which led to type-casting as a villain for a while, until he turned to the horror roles which were to keep him busy for almost the whole of his career, and unfortunately inclined to hide his great versatility. Born in Oklahoma, raised in Hollywood, he had numerous jobs (including, apparently, that of a butcher's lad) before getting around to acting. He was 67 when he died last year (July 12, 1973) at his Californian home after a year's struggle against the liver complaint that killed him.

ROBERT RYAN had only just completed work on his 1974 release *The Outfit* when he died, of cancer, in a New York hospital on July 11, 1973, aged 63. Ryan came into the acting business in 1936 through working with an amateur group (after a variety of non-show-business jobs), from which he graduated to repertory and the little theatre scene. He finally made Broadway acclaim in 1941 in *Clash By Night*, a success which proved the key to films, his first starring role being in the socially conscious *Crossfire* in 1947. Though it was often as the villain of the piece that he made his impact, he could with success cross the line to give such memorably sympathetic performances as in *The Set-Up*, that great boxing film. Much of his best work came in Westerns, such as in *Bad Day at Black Rock*, *The Professionals* and *The Wild Bunch*. In-between films he returned to his first love, the stage, where he was allowed to be more versatile, ranging from Shakespeare and O'Neill to the musical *Mr President*.

The legendary JOHN FORD, director of some of the greatest Westerns ever made, including the classic *Stagecoach*, died on the last day of August 1973, at his Californian home, from cancer, at the age of 78, after some forty years of almost constant work in the cinema. His extremely large, always distinctive output (even when below his best) was in many cases a mixture of realism, sentimentalism and broad humour which few other directors could have got away with. It is interesting to note, by the way, that of the four films which brought him Oscars, none were theWesterns for which he will go down in the film history books. The team of director Ford and actor John Wayne resulted in some of his finest work; though other Ford favourites include Victor McLaglen (*The Informer*, perhaps Ford's greatest work) and Ward Bond. Even with a quick glance through the long list of his films, one immediately becomes aware of how many outstanding pictures he made; titles like *The Grapes of Wrath* (one of the greatest films ever made up to its time), *The Iron Horse*, *How Green Was My Valley* and *The Quiet Man*.

Although it was in the series of Hong-Kong-made Kung-Fu films such as *Fist of Fury*, *The Big Boss*, *The Chinese Connection*, *The Way of the Dragon* (which he also directed) that BRUCE LEE came to fame, he was in fact born in San Francisco and educated in Washington. Probably one of the world's greatest masters of the so-called art of self-defence, it was as a teacher of this in Los Angeles that he began his career, switching to an American television series and then

14 going to Hong Kong, where he quickly became one of Asia's most popular hero-stars in a rapid succession of movies notable mainly for their exploitation of unarmed – and sometimes armed – combat. It was just after completing his first American production, *Enter the Dragon*, for Warners that on July 20, 1973 he was found dying in his Hong Kong apartment: he was only 32.

In his long career as a film director, Basle-born, French-educated MARC ALLEGRET made something like fifty films, only a very few of which were ever shown in Britain and America. His best work was achieved in the thirties with such memorable pictures as *Lac au Dames*, *Gribouille*, *Orage*, *Les Beaux Jours* and *Fanny*. In some of these films he discovered such stars as Michele Morgan and Jean-Pierre Aumont and it is amusing to record that he used Brigitte Bardot before she became famous (Allégret's assistant for a while was Roger Vadim!). His first film was a documentary *Voyage au Congo* which he

made with his uncle André Gide, and one of his last completed movies was a feature-length documentary about the writer. Since the war Allégret had travelled, making films in Austria, Canada and this country (*Blanche Fury* in 1947) as well as his native France, but none of them achieved the status or popularity of his earlier work. He was 72 when he died in Paris on November 3, 1973.

Only 55 years old when she died of a brain haemorrhage in the hospital at Cape Cod on September 13, 1973, BETTY FIELD was stricken the day before she was due to join the cast of John Schlesinger's production of *The Day of the Locust* in Hollywood. Miss Field was a very versatile and brilliant player who was born in Boston and started her career by appearing in a school play. Even before she graduated from the American equivalent of our own RADA, she had won acclaim for a performance in a London play (*She Loves Me Not*, 1934). She quickly achieved Broadway stardom, making her first film *What A Life* in 1939. She was extremely impressive in *Of Mice and Men*

and thereafter made a great many movies of which her performances in *The Southerner*, *The Great Gatsby* (the Alan Ladd version), *Bus Stop*, *Picnic* and *Coogan's Bluff* all stand out, though only slightly so from many others almost as impressive. She was equally good in dramatic or comedy roles and she had a personality which stamped itself on every film in which she appeared.

With a name like VEDA ANN BORG, and with those very blonde good looks, one could be excused for thinking of this, in fact, Boston-born film star as Swedish, as she was in fact often called. Starting her film career in 1936, Miss Borg played both light comedy and heavy drama: among her films were *Mother Wore Tights*, *Guys and Dolls* and *Big Jim McLain*. She died, aged 58, on August 16, 1973, in Hollywood, after a long illness which had kept her off the screen for a number of years.

After a long and gallant fight against the cancer which had taken his voice away in an operation seven years previously, one of Britain's most British stars JACK HAWKINS died in a London hospital on July 18, 1973, at the age of 62. In his long career he made more than fifty films and appeared in about the same number of stage plays. A graduate from the famous Italia Conti school, Hawkins made his stage début in the London production of *Where the Rainbow Ends* in 1923. Nine years later, after appearing in the New York production of Sheriff's *Journey's End*, he made his screen début, in Maurice Elvey's *The Lodger*, starring Ivor Novello. But it was not until after the war that he began to make his

Carmichael as Bertie Wooster. Aged 58, Price died at his Guernsey home, where he had gone some years previously in order to try and repair his shaky financial situation.

VERONICA LAKE's story is a sad one. Brooklyn-born in 1919, she grew up in Miami with her real name of Constance Okelman, only switching to the movies – and a new name of Constance Keane – when she won a beauty contest success. After a few extra and bit parts she achieved a leading role in *I Wanted Wings* and immediately her peek-a-boo hair style, with the long, straight blonde tresses falling over one eye, stamped her individuality with the moviegoers. Thereafter she made a rapid succession of movies including *This Gun for Hire*, *The Glass Key*, *Slattery's Hurricane*, *The Blue Dahlia*, *So Proudly We Hail* and what most people would agree as being her best two performances, *I Married a Witch* and *Sullivan's Travels*. Then, suddenly, Miss

mark with moviegoers, in a series of rugged parts in war films like *Angels One Five*, *The Malta Story*, *The Cruel Sea* and, of course, his considerable contribution to *The Bridge on the River Kwai*. A notable performance was as General Allenby in *Lawrence of Arabia*; other films for which he will be recalled are *Lord Jim*, *Young Winston*, *Five Finger Exercise* and the crook comedy *The League of Gentlemen*, in which he gave one of his most polished performances. Even after he had lost his voice and his roles had to be dubbed in by another player, he was kept busy in the studios, appearing in such films as *Jane Eyre*, *Waterloo* and *Nicholas and Alexandra*.

Dennistoun Franklyn John Rose-Price, better known to filmgoers simply as DENNIS PRICE, the son of a Brigadier-General, was educated at Radley and at Oxford and always showed every moment of that background during his film career. Destined for the Army, or perhaps the Church

Dennis switched his sights after becoming a member of OUDS. He made his professional stage début at Croydon in 1937 and hit the West End the following year. Further progress was halted by the war, which he entered in 1940, but which ended for him two years later when he was invalided out of the Royal Artillery. He had appeared in a number of plays when he made his film début in 1944 in Michael Powell's production of *A Canterbury Tale*, after which he had a steady succession of both stage and film roles. His style was ideally suited to the old Ealing satirical comedies and one of his finest works was in that studio's *Kind Hearts and Coronets*. But he will also be recalled for his performances in *Private's Progress*, *I'm All Right Jack*, *School for Scoundrels*, all parts which suited his dry, cool style much better than productions like *The Bad Lord Byron* playing the poet. More recently he had achieved considerable success with TV viewers for his performance as that perfect butler Jeeves in the series with Ian

In Memoriam

16 Lake vanished from the screen to be discovered some years later working as a barmaid, admitting that part of the cause of her eclipse had been a drinking problem. In the 1960s Veronica Lake lived for several years in England, where she appeared with some success in a stage version of *A Streetcar Named Desire*. It was also while here that her autobiography was published: *Veronica*. She was still only 53 when she died in a Vermont hospital of acute hepatitis on July 7, 1973.

FAY HOLDEN, who died in Hollywood on June 23, 1973, of cancer at the age of 77, was a stalwart character actress whose high standard of performance in any role made every film in which she appeared at the very least interesting. English (real name Dorothy Hammerton Clyde), she had already established herself as a top-line actress (under the name of Gaby Fay) when she went to America in 1935. Her first films were made the next year (*I Married a Doctor* and *Polo Joe*) but it was her next movie, Hathaway's *Souls at Sea* which established her reputation and started the long succession of feature roles in films like *You're Only Young Once, Test Pilot* and *Guns of the Pecos*. But it was as Mickey Rooney's mother in the Andy Hardy family series (a role she played in fifteen films) which brought her the most public acclaim.

CONSTANCE TALMADGE, youngest of the Talmadge sisters trio, died in a Los Angeles hospital at the age of 73 on November 23, 1973. Following her sisters into the Vitagraph studios, she made a number of films before all of them moved to Hollywood in 1921. Of her many films perhaps one of the few titles familiar to today's moviegoers would be Griffith's *Intolerance*, but other films included *The Honeymoon, Her Sister from Paris, A Pair of Silk Stockings, East is West* and many others. When the talkies came Miss Talmadge quickly bowed out.

BILLY DE WOLFE, at one time one of Hollywood's most popular light comedians, and a contributor to the fun in some of Bing Crosby and Bob Hope's uproarious Paramount comedies, died this March (1974) of cancer in Hollywood, aged 67. He had in fact been around a long time (he started out as a cinema attendant) and made many screen appearances before hitting the public's fancy with his performance of a female drunk in 1946's *Blue Skies*. Some of his other films were: *Dear Ruth, Call me Madame* and *Billie*.

Familiar to television viewers as The Master in the Dr Who serial, ROGER DELGADO,

British-born (in 1918) though of Spanish and French parents, was educated at the London School of Economics but turned to the stage in the late 1930s and started with the Leicester Repertory, which he left in 1940 to join the Forces. Though concentrating on television after the war he did make a number of film appearances, including *Antony and Cleopatra, Star* and *Khartoum*. He was killed in a car accident in Turkey.

ERNEST TRUEX, the Kansas City-born comedian, died at the age of 82 at his Californian home on June 27, 1973. You could say his career began at the age of five, for that's when he played in the ghost scene in *Hamlet*! In 1924, after many stage successes in America, Truex came to England as star of *The Fall Guy*, in which he made an instant hit, staying here for the next five years before returning to Broadway with his new British stage success, *Many Waters*. It was his 1932 stage hit *Whistling in the Dark* which led him into making a movie adaptation of the play in 1933, after which he made a considefable number of films including *Adventures of Marco Polo, This is the Army* and *Life with Blondie*.

GEORGE MACREADY, who died at the age of 73 on July 2, 1973, in Hollywood, started his career as a New York newspaper reporter and it was only some years later that he switched to stage acting, soon making a name for himself in Broadway productions of plays like *Romeo and Juliet, The Barretts of Wimpole Street* and *Victoria Regina*, in which he made a big hit in 1937. He arrived in Hollywood for his first film, *The*

Commandos Strike at Dawn, in 1942, since when he made something like seventy or more movies as well as an even greater number of television shows and stage productions. His movies include *Wilson, Story of Dr Wassell, A Song to Remember, Gilda, Paths of Glory*, and *Vera Cruz*. His speciality was villains, especially of the smooth, sophisticated variety. His last film, made some three years ago with his son as producer, was the chiller *The Return of Count Yorga*.

That mouth, which was his trademark, helped to give JOE E. BROWN, who died at his home on July 2, 1973, after a protracted illness, his comic individuality. He was 82 and for seventy of those years he had been extremely active in the world of entertainment, doing everything from variety and the circus to stage, screen and television work. Like all great comedians he had the knack of mixing broad comedy with a certain underlying tragedy and he proved on many an occasion that he could swiftly switch the mood of his audience from laughter to tears. Although he didn't play the role in the film, his greatest and most consistent success was in *Harvey* and in his *Variety* obituary it was suggested he played the part some 10,000 times! His first job was with a trapeze act (he ran away from home to join it), which only folded with the advent of the 'Frisco earthquake in 1906. His first film was *Crooks Can't Wait* in 1927 and he then proceeded to make another seventy-five before taking his screen farewell in Billy Wilder's *Some Like It Hot*. Some of the titles of his films that will spring to mind

are *Hollywood Canteen, Fireman, Save My Child, The Circus Kid* and, of course, *Shut My Big Mouth*. Brown was universally loved, by the public, by most of the critics, and certainly by the people he worked with.

ALLAN (ROCKY) LANE, who died in a Californian hospital for the picture people, on October 27, 1973, was a Western hero who in both 1951 and 1953 appeared in the list of top money-making Western stars. Starting out as a professional footballer, he appeared on the stage prior to making his screen début. Latterly he was kept fairly busy by television and had not appeared on the screen for quite a while.

18 Born in 1912, ARLINE JUDGE had enjoyed quite a lot of stage success before she went to Hollywood and started her movie career in 1930. Small, dark and lively, she had the leading role in many thirties and forties films including *Are These Our Children?* (her first, in 1931), *Girl Crazy, Valiant is the Word for Carrie* and *Two Knights in Brooklyn* (1939). She died in her sixty-first year in her Hollywood home on February 7, 1974. Among her seven husbands – all divorced – were Wesley Ruggles and brothers Dan and Bob Topping.

The last job of MICHEL SALKIND, who died in Paris in February 1974 at the age of 83, was to assist his son Alexander and grandson Ilya with the production of the 1974 "Royal Film" *The Three Musketeers*. Born in Russia, he first came into prominence as manager of the Yiddish Theatre there, later moving to Germany and France to make films in those countries; he made Pabst's classic *Joyless Street* and in France he did a number of films starring Jean Gabin. He produced *The Trial* for Orson Welles and he also made Buster Keaton's last movie.

GINO CERVI, one of Italy's best-known international film-stars, died at the age of 72, from pneumonia, in a small town near Rome on January 3, 1974. To most moviegoers in this country he will always be associated with the role of the Communist Mayor, opposed to the local priest Fernandel, in five of the "Don Camillo" films. Gino entered films through dubbing in 1930 (something he continued to do on and off for all his career, the most outstanding effort being his "voice"

for Laurence Olivier in the Italian version of *Hamlet*), actually not making his visual appearance on the screen until four years later. But from then on he was always busy, making innumerable movies, only a small proportion of which have ever been seen outside Italy.

BETTY GRABLE, who died of lung cancer in Santa Monica on July 3, 1973, at the age of 56, will always be recalled as the girl with the "three million dollar legs", for that is the amount they were reputed to be insured for! Miss Grable came up the hard way; at one time signed for the chorus line for Fox musicals, switching to dance-band singer before appearing in a Wheeler and Woolsey musical: it was a stroke of luck – and ill fortune for Miss Faye – that set her on the road to film fame. When Miss Faye had to bow out of *Down Argentine Way* to undergo an operation, Fox appealed to Miss Grable to take her place and that was the start of a film career that between the years 1940 and the mid-fifties brought her some twenty-five features and earned her, so it is said, more than three million dollars. But it was all over by 1955 and from then on Miss Grable, who had a very sound idea of her own talent, lived in semi-retirement only accepting a few roles at intervals (one such foray was for the ill-fated 1969 London stage production of *Belle Starr*, which folded after running for only seventeen days!). Latterly she had been fighting cancer and several times had been hospitalised before finally succumbing. Some of her best-known films include *Moon Over Miami, Springtime in the Rockies, Wabash Avenue* and *My Blue Heaven*.

Sixty-seven-year-old MICHAEL O'SHEA, who died on December 4, 1973, was still in harness and was in fact about to join wife Virginia Mayo's touring company in Houston five days later when a sudden heart attack struck him down in Dallas, Texas. O'Shea's work embraced radio, television and the theatre as well as films, of which he made a considerable number including *Captain China, Jack London, Man from 'Frisco* and *Circumstantial Evidence*.

TEX RITTER, the Country & Western singer–composer–star, one-time among the ten highest money-making Western stars, performer of that famous *High Noon* title song, died from a heart attack – suddenly, while visiting a friend at Nashville's county jail – on January 2, 1974, at the age of 67. Texas-born Tex (born Woodward Maurice) made more than seventy-five films during his Hollywood career which began in 1936, with *Song of the Gringo*. Latterly he had appeared quite a lot on the small screen, made several recordings and actually ran for a US Senate nomination.

MARCEL PAGNOL, who died on April 18, 1974, in Paris, will always be associated with the great "Fanny" triology (*Marius, Fanny* and *César*, of which he himself only directed the last, though stamping his character, as producer, on the others). Born near Marseilles in 1895, Pagnol was a writer, teacher of English and dramatist before he started his film career with *Marius* (directed by Alexander Korda – 1931). He actually opened his own studios in Marseilles in the 1930s and turned out a whole string of movies based on his own and other writers'

work (producing, writing and directing, though not always all in the same film) which did not travel well and have seldom if ever been seen outside France. One of his greatest international successes, made just before the war, was *La Femme du Boulanger*, in which the magnificent Raimu gave one of his finest performances. Pagnol's great achievement was to put authentic Provence on to the screen in all its richness, character and humour.

BOBBY DARIN (real name, Robert Walden Cassotto) who started his career as a pop-singer, rising to the top before starting his film career in 1960 in *Come September*. He made a number of movies after that, in many of them playing straight, dramatic roles; films like *Pressure Point, Gunfight at Abilene, Cop-Out, The Happy Ending* and *Stranger in the House*. He wrote quite a lot of film music, including the entire score for *The Lively Set*. He also appeared in numerous TV shows and presented a very successful night-club act.

URSULA JEANS (real name Ursula McMinn) was primarily a stage actress but she did occasionally make an appearance in a film, including *Cavalcade, Dark Journey, The Weaker Sex* and *The Dam Busters*. Born in 1906 in Simla, India, she was a graduate of RADA, making her professional stage début at Nottingham in 1925.

ROBERT SIODMAK, the Tennessee-born (in 1900), German-educated director–producer–banker (yes, banker; he once owned five European banks!) was a writer and film editor for UFA in Berlin before becoming a distinguished director, with such films as *The Tempest* (starring Emil Jannings), *The Strange Affair of Uncle Harry, The Spiral Staircase, The Crimson Pirate, Dark Mirror, The Killers* and *Custer of the West* to his credit.

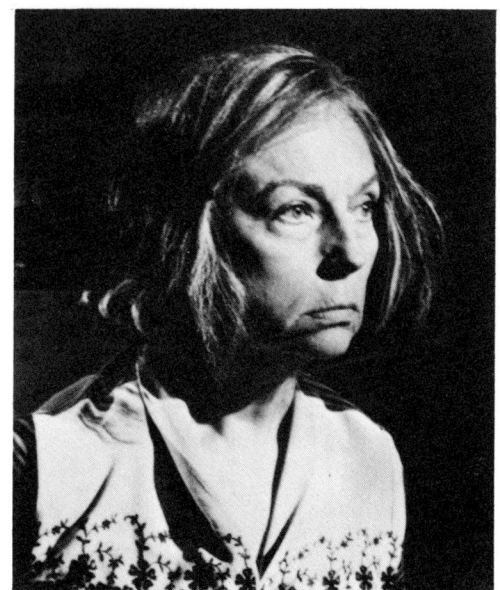

ANNA Q. NILSON is a silent screen star best recalled by older cinemagoers; she was busy in the twenties and made her final screen appearance in *Sunset Boulevard* in 1950. She was 85 when she died this year (February 11, 1974). She began her career as a stage actress in her native Sweden and her American screen début was in *The Love Burglar* in 1919.

BUD ABBOTT, the straight man half of the Abbott and Costello comedy team, who died in late April of this year, had been a sailor, box-office cashier and a radio comic before teaming with Costello and making that very successful series of comedies with him that included *Abbott and Costello Meet Frankenstein, Buck Privates, Pardon My Sarong* and *Jack and the Beanstalk*, etc.

AGNES MOOREHEAD, who died in early May, in Hollywood at the age of 67, had been an actress for half a century. A daughter of a Presbyterian Minister, the product of the American equivalent of our own Royal Academy of Dramatic Art, she made her screen début, after a lot of stage experience, in *Citizen Kane*, earning an "Oscar" nomination for her second appearance in a Welles film, *The Magnificent Ambersons*. That was the first of four subsequent nominations: for *Mrs Parkington, Johnny Belinda, All That Heaven Allows* and *Hush, Hush, Sweet Charlotte*, which was one of her last film performances. Recently she had been busy on TV and will certainly be best remembered in this field for her delicious playing of the sharp-tongued witch in the series *Bewitched*.

FRANÇOISE ROSAY, who died in Paris on March 28, 1974 at the age of 82, had been acting since she was 21 and during her long and distinguished international career had made more than 100 films, in her native country, in Britain and Germany. At one time a singer at the Paris Opera, she made her screen début in 1913. Married to director Jacques Feyder, she at one time worked on the set as his assistant. But it was in *Carnet de Bal* and, more especially, in her husband's masterpiece *La Kermesse Heroïque* that she won international acclaim. During the war she worked with the Free French and for her work on Radio Algiers was awarded the Legion of Honour. Latterly she had been busy appearing in plays in Paris, writing her autobiography, starring in television series and running her two drama schools, in Paris and Geneva. Her last film, yet to be seen here, was Maximilian Schell's *The Pedestrian*.

A FILM PIONEER

by John M. East

Seated in blissful comfort in the upholstered, double-sprung seats of a new triple cinema, do you ever stop to think what moviegoing was like for your grandparents, who saw the earliest motion pictures? How much do you know about the birth of the cinema trade; the struggles, triumphs, disappointments, comedies and tragedies of the pioneer days at the turn of this century? The stories are almost lost in the mists of the past, hidden under the crowding interests of the present. In the early 1890s moving pictures were considered a curiosity to be discussed by scientific societies. The first commercial run of a cinematograph show, at the Empire, in London's Leicester Square from March 9, 1896, was presented by the Lumière Brothers of Paris.

The bioscope, as the attraction was speedily called, soon found a place on music-hall programmes. The films themselves were little more than murky, flickering shadows. To see people and objects actually moving on a flat white screen was the marvel, and so real did these pictures appear to the audience of that time that on one occasion, when a scene had been obtained by placing a camera in front of an oncoming train, it looked as if the train was heading straight for the auditorium and as one, the entire audience rushed out into the street, terror stricken; vowing never again to waste money "on this nine days' wonder".

An uncle of mine, John Codman (1876–1935), started presenting his own programme of "animated pictures" on music-hall bills in the North Country in August 1896. His routine was all bustle; packing up the projector, dismantling the transparent screen of calico, (dampened by water and glycerine) and moving on to the next hall. Speed and organisation meant that John Codman projected his programme in several music halls in the course of an evening.

Codman found the music-hall business too competitive, and he switched careers by designing his own portable cinema, with shuttered sections of wood for the walls, a tarpaulin sheeting over the ground and a canvas canopy as the roof. Wooden benches were arranged in rows and, by the way, the centre was the best and safest place to seat one's anatomy – perched at either end, one was quite likely to be pushed off during the excitement!

The unit was hauled by a traction engine, which also served to generate sufficient power to operate the cinema projector and to light the booth, seating 600 people. A typical programme reads as follows:

JOHN CODMAN'S NEW EMPIRE & AMERICAN PICTURE COMPANY PRESENTS

Twice nightly. 6.40 & 8.30 p.m. Change of programme thrice weekly.

New pictures, brimful of humour and pathetic interest!

Extraordinary dissolving and dioramic effects!

FULL ORCHESTRAL BAND!

HIGH CLASS COMPANY OF EMINENT ARTISTS IN SUPPORTING VARIETY BILL!

ABSOLUTELY ROCK STEADY!

A Codman Daybill, dated 1915.

22 PROJECTED BY THE LATEST FIRE-
PROOF MACHINERY!

Read the Press! We proudly quote: "Mr
Codman's show gives to man an additional
faculty of recalling past and present events,
and clothing them with the charms of life
and movement" – "Cambrian News."

1. Overture.
2. Launching of His Majesty's Battleship
   "King Edward VII" by the King (FILM)
3. Refined serio (selected) from Miss
   Naomi Codman.
4. Soprano solo (selected) from Miss
   Florence Codman.
5. Grand reproduction of *The Battle of
   Trafalgar*, resulting in the loss of
   England's most successful Admiral
   (FILM)
6. Scenes from "The Passion Play at
   Ober-Ammergau" actually filmed by
   Mr Codman.
7. A trip to New York by liner, with views
   of New York. (FILM)
8. "Mr Hughes and His Christmas Turkey".
   Produced by John Codman (FILM)
9. Professor Richard Codman's ROYAL
   COMIC MANIKINS as given before
   Royalty.
10. Song (selected) from J. Tremain (the
    Cornish baritone)
11. Wonder movements from The Two
    Millers (duettists and dancers)
12. Harp solo from John Miller.
13. "A Tragedy in the Air" (FILM)
14. "The Coalman's Bath" (FILM)
15. "The Miner's Daughter" Produced by
    John Codman (FILM)
16. "Driven from Home" The story of a
    lonely father (FILM)

17. "A Tour of North Wales". Produced by
    John Codman (FILM)
18. COWBOYS AND INDIANS! a thrilling
    FILM.
          GOD SAVE THE KING.
THE VERY LATEST WONDERS OF
LIFE IN THE FORM OF MOTION
PICTURES BROUGHT TO YOU
THROUGH THE INDUSTRY AND
ENDEAVOUR OF JOHN CODMAN.
ADMISSION: 2/- : 1/- : 9d : 6d : 3d.
Two half-sovereigns will be given away as
prizes for the guess nearest to the amount of
money taken at the box-office on Monday.

The interior of the Picturedrome (formerly
the Victoria Hall) at Newtown,
Montgomeryshire, one of John Codman's
chain of cinemas.

John Codman's projector worked from early
morning to late at night. When matinées
were given, and before each evening showing,
he would stand outside his booth, hustling
the public with "Walk up!" "Walk up!" and
"See my stupendous attraction! See people
come alive in pictures!"
John Codman was not content to show other
people's efforts, and he produced many
short films, both comic and dramatic, in
addition to a series of travelogues. When
visiting a new town he always pursued the
same policy. Bill-posting and publicity had
already heralded the event. When he arrived

And here's a picture of John Codman himself, second from the left in the group posed outside his Picturedrome at Oswestry – *circa* 1910.

the natives knew all about him, and he took advantage of the interest by standing on the back of an open lorry and touring the main streets. A camera was fixed to the floor, and an assistant was seen vigorously turning the handle, appearing to take infinite pains to get all the onlookers "in shot". John Codman would shout: "Come and see *yourselves* on the screen tomorrow night! A handsome prize for those who claim to have recognised themselves!"

The excited public immediately rushed round to the advance box-office to book seats, never guessing that the camera was loaded with film only for the first few minutes, and their chances of "Immortality on Celluloid" – another of John Codman's pet expressions – was lost for ever.

Soon the public showed a desire to be told a story, and, as the "feature" or longer treatment came into being, so did the emergence of motion pictures as a separate art form.

The old time film showmen were shrewd in their dealings with companies that hired out the movies. Lt.-Col. A. C. Bromhead, the manager of the original Gaumont Company in Britain, remembered an old fairground woman who wanted to equip a travelling cinema. She bought all the apparatus, including a projector and some films, for £214, paid in pennies, half-pennies and threepenny bits!

Several companies that rented and sold films had offices in Cecil Court, off the Charing Cross Road, soon given the nickname, Flicker Alley. A number of dubious dealers actually sold films "on the street" – a wicker table, a chair and some canisters of films and they were in business, being given the title of "gutter distributors". Some unscrupulous operators made a living by manufacturing dupe prints of films, which they marketed at cut prices in Britain and abroad. There was a story related of one "duper" who contrived to have a printer in conjunction with his projecting machine, in a room immediately below it. While he and the seller innocently watched the film on the screen, it passed through to the printer before rewinding, and was then returned, intact to the seller and politely refused, the negative having already been taken while the picture was being shown! It was the custom of film-makers to send copies of new films to cinema booth owners on approval. Although most showmen dealt honestly with the print and returned it if it was not required, others showed it to a paying audience for some days before despatching the canisters to the manufacturer, as not wanted.

How many people realise there were talking films over seventy years ago? The idea of synchronising gramophone records with films dates back to about 1901, when a French invention, the Ciné-Phono-Matograph, was patented. Unfortunately, it

24 did not produce a harmonious combination of words and action on the screen.
In 1902 Messter of Berlin and Leon Gaumont of Paris jointly invented the chronophone, and their handout states: "The picture shows a performer rendering a song; the phonograph produces, at the same time, with the perfect system of synchronisation, the words and melody that flows from the singer's mouth.'
The chronophone comprised two synchronised motors, cine and gramophone, controlled by a third, the governing motor. The result, so far as synchronisation was concerned, was perfect, *when* running correctly. "When" was the operative word! If the needle jumped a line on the disc, or if the film broke, the fat was in the fire. Once the film broke, not a single picture could be cut out, otherwise the entire film fell out of synchronisation with the disc. The state of recording at that time rendered it impossible to make the film and the disc simultaneously. When recording, the artist had to stand immediately in front of the receiver, which only had a short range. Until the advent of the electric pick-up, the simultaneous recording of sound and action remained impracticable. The artist had to make himself letter perfect with the disc, which was played as he was being filmed. He mouthed the words, as nearly in synchronisation as he could get it. The electric gramophone was synchronised with, and controlled by the speed of the camera. Harry Lauder was one of many famous stars who made talking films. I interviewed an assistant on one of these movies. He told me Lauder said: "That wee camera, laddie, that's my audience. I don't see it though I

One of the earliest Portable Cinemas.

play to the thousands of people who will pay to see the film the world over." Strange to relate, a bogus producer distributed a "Harry Lauder singing film" which showed the great artist rendering "Stop Your Tickling, Jock" in long shot or, to be accurate, another actor, near enough his double, singing this ballad. It was Lauder's voice all right, and it deceived audiences all over the country. The first demonstration of the chronophone was at the Grand Theatre, Fulham, in 1904. It was so successful managements booked the attraction throughout Britain, and the London Hippodrome owners, Moss Empires Ltd., paid £300 a week for it for a run which extended from December 1906 until May 1907. It also received the honour of a Royal

Command at Buckingham Palace.
There were other passing fads in the trade. Early examples of colour films hardly matched up to their publicity: "Photographed in the exact colours of Nature." One caustic notice read: "What a pity the leading lady's arms were a leaden blue."
The cinema trade attracted some flamboyant showmen. About 1903 or 1904 it was announced that the Rt. Hon. Arthur Balfour, then Prime Minister, was to receive the freedom of the city of Edinburgh. A local film showman arranged for the Gaumont Company to send up a cameraman to cover the event. He was eventually posted at the head of the steps leading to the hall with

The side of the Electric Cinema in Ranger Road (since renamed Jasper Road) at Upper Norwood, as it survives today.

LOYAL GREETING TONIGHT, AN "EXCLUSIVE" ATTRACTION!

Portable cinemas were fire-traps, because the projector and the highly inflammable film was situated in an exposed position within the area where the public was seated. Occasionally there would be a bucket of sand handy, or possibly a tank of water, but foolhardy people often had no worry about precautions, soon forgetting an incident at a charity bazaar in Paris in 1897 when seventy-three visitors lost their lives in a fire. Later, portable projectors were invented, which had iron walls and measured about six feet by six feet, and it was in this confined space that the poor projectionist had to work. The first booth of this sort was purchased by the owners of the Balham Empire in 1897. Run as a music hall, in later years it became a cinema, and the building still stands in the High Road.

Travelling penny gaffs gave way to bijou picture palaces, and one of the first to open was a converted shop in Bishopsgate Street in London. Under the Gaumont banner, it seated about one hundred people. John Codman, the travelling showman I have already mentioned, leased some twenty halls in Wales and the border counties. He was soon to learn that films alone were not the attraction for, when he tried an experimental week at his cinema in Newtown with the lights *on*, the courting couples were outraged and with one voice demanded the privacy of darkness. Never slow in recognising the main chance, Codman later introduced *lovers' knot* seats in the back row for those more interested in romance than watching animated pictures.

Canoodling, a tinkling piano, cigarette

orders to start shooting when instructed. The showman was there, dressed for the occasion in his best frock coat and silk hat, and he stood alongside the camera. When the carriage and pair occupied by Mr Balfour arrived at the foot of these steps, the Lord Provost and other magnates were standing at the top to receive him. At the precise moment Mr Balfour descended from the carriage, the showman, having previously instructed the cameraman to start turning, stepped rapidly forward, keeping well in

frame, and became the first person to greet the astonished Mr Balfour. Mr Balfour, of course, grasped the proffered hand, and engaged the showman in conversation until the infuriated dignitaries arrived and pushed the usurper away. Fortunately, everything "was in the can", and that afternoon posters, previously prepared, were placarded all over Edinburgh:
LOCAL SHOWMAN WELCOMES
MR BALFOUR TO EDINBURGH.
COME AND SEE THE FILM OF HIS

The façade of the Globe Cinema at 311 Lavender Hill, Clapham Junction, which was in operation from about 1910.

smoke, and the flickering image on a screen, all contributed to the excitement of a visit to the movies. Derogatory descriptions like "A poor man's theatre" did not deter the thousands who enjoyed the thrill of stepping over mysterious cables, and seating their anatomy in a tip-up seat to watch moving pictures.

A Cinematograph Act, which became law in January 1910, empowered the Home Secretary to enforce safety regulations in cinemas and local authorities only granted licences to showmen who complied with the rules.

That was a serious blow to John Codman and other small-time proprietors. None of the buildings under Codman's control had been constructed for film-shows. In the main they were former drill halls, assembly rooms and temperance halls and until the Act there were no restrictions laid down for the safety and comfort of the public.

Anyway, these makeshift premises were being forced out of business by the construction of proper cinemas in key locations, designed solely for the exhibition of motion pictures; and an entry into the field in 1905 of two competing concerns, who vied with each other in the speed of building, accelerated the process.

John Codman's prosperity diminished as the circuits of cinemas developed. Companies with vast capital behind them built palatial fun palaces, with red plush, marble pillars and elaborate mirrors. Dark corners were ornamented with brightly polished brass pots sprouting glorious ferns. These thousand-seater Olympias and Electroscopes soon outpaced the Codman-style Picturedromes and, as the rental for a balanced programme of films rocketed upwards, John Codman's days as a cinema manager were numbered.

I interviewed another pioneer, J. Bannister Howard, who lost his fortune (made from being a theatre manager) by venturing into the cinema industry – he failed because he did not recognise that the exhibition of pictures needed fresh methods of promotion – it was a world apart from live entertainment. He told me:

"I bought a skating rink in Union Street, Aberdeen, for £1,000 and I converted it into a cinema. To get an afternoon audience essential to meet the cost of renting the films, I provided a free tea with the one shilling admission fee. I had to stop those free teas! How they ate, those canny Aberdonians! I should think they arrived without having their breakfasts and lunches. Many of them had tea twice over. It was an Aberdonian that explained matters to me: 'Why mon, we're so mean in Aberdeen, that we borrow money to put it in the bank.'

"I was forced to sell out, at a loss, and years later that building realised £20,000 and became one of Aberdeen's premier cinemas. In my day it was called the Electric and seated 600. For the evening programme in 1912 I charged 3d and 6d admission fees. My other venture, the New Electric Theatre, Nethergate, Dundee was another disaster – I lost a great deal of money there. At my bankruptcy hearing my liabilities amounted to £7,442 and my sole assets were £27 19s 9d."

To the general public anything concerned with movies spells glamour and the chance of making one's fortune. In my own experience I have seen as many film ventures fail as those which have passed muster, let alone make remarkable returns. I recollect a small distributor who got hold of a fairly old film which he decided to offer as a second feature. An actress who played a supporting role had, since the picture was made, become a major star. The distributor billed her name in big letters over a new and provocative title. All went well until this package was booked into a "flea-pit" cinema in Wales. By a million-to-one chance the same film, with its original title, had played at that cinema the previous week. Nobody had bothered to run it through first, and the audience, as one, gave vent to howls of disapproval, before rushing towards the terrified box-office clerk demanding the return of their ticket money.

Nowadays, cinemas are closing down with ominous regularity throughout Britain, and

The Lyric Picture Playhouse, Wandsworth – *circa* 1915.

Few people today who use the motor-cycle and cycle shop at 222 Battersea Road realise that it was one of the earliest cinemas opened about 1908.

Now a bingo hall, the old Majestic Cinema at Clapham has a narrow but fascinating façade.

interest in all aspects of cinema, past and present. Members go on organised visits to cinemas and there is a bimonthly bulletin. Anybody interested in joining should contact the Secretary: Marcus Eavis, 123B Central Road, Worcester Park, Surrey.

yet it is surprising the number of the very earliest electroscopes and picturedromes which have survived, and now fulfil a bewildering array of functions. A Codman "flicker palace" in Llanidloes in Wales, for instance, is now a hardwear store. Fabbro's Electroscope Palace in Falcon Road, Battersea, became a newspaper office, and a rival cinema, near the entrance to Clapham Junction Railway Station, was a furniture store.

It is an interesting pastime to seek out these places, and I have often discovered the remains of former glories in trimmings of Edwardian baroque, swags, egg and dart mouldings, elliptical windows and dumpy columns, sad reminders of the great days when cinemagoing was at the peak of its popularity.

The Cinema Theatre Association is an organisation with nationwide membership which has the object of promoting a serious

John M. East comes from a pioneering cinema family. His grandfather, also name of John M. East, was a well-known silent screen actor, who was also an executive with the Neptune Film Company, which built the first-ever film studios at Boreham Wood in 1914. His first wife, Leah Marlborough, was the wicked woman or vamp in some of the earliest British pictures.

The present John M. East, at thirty-seven, is an authority on show-business history. He has done over 450 radio broadcasts for this country and abroad, and he frequently prepares items, usually on entertainment, for London and Regional TV programmes. As an actor he has appeared a great deal in comedy programmes with Harry Worth, Tommy Cooper, Morecambe and Wise, Red Skelton and many other stars. His average Press output each week is 4,000 words, including features for London and Provincial papers and magazines. He writes weekly for the London Newspaper Group. In 1967 John East wrote the story of his family 'Neath the Mask (Allen & Unwin) and in addition to Film Review he is a contributor for the next Oxford Companion to the Theatre.

IN DEFENCE OF DUBBING

by Robert Rietty

The prejudice against dubbed films is very strong in Britain; perhaps with cause, for the few foreign films with superimposed English sound-tracks which reach our screens have – as often as not – been dubbed with an eye more to low cost than quality. The result displays bad direction, indifferent casting and poor performances.

But let us take the case of a well-dubbed film. How is it done?

An experienced writer sits at a moviola for hours on end for anything between two and five weeks, viewing each sequence of a film over and over again on a small screen, scrutinising the way the lips open, meet, spread or tighten, and attempts to write an English text which can fit those words spoken in Dutch, Italian, Russian, German, Swedish or Japanese. And these new words must not only appear to come from those lips, but must also make sense, phrased in precisely the same length and number of syllables where the labials (the Ms, the Bs, the Ps) plus the Fs and the Ws all occur at identical moments in a totally different language.

As a result, the new dialogue may bear little resemblance to the original and the final text itself becomes more an original work than a translation. These new words must rise and fall where the anger of the character on screen dictates, must match his gestures, his smiles, his grimaces, and must convince us that Mastroianni was born in Huddersfield or Bond Street and that Brigitte Bardot makes love in impeccable English.

Foreign faces unfortunately play havoc with that illusion. How do you make the tightening lips on "Je" sound like the opening and closing movement on "I"? How do you make the English "Me" come from lips which say "Moi" (phonetically pronounced mooahh)? Once the writer has completed his work, the client or distributor who is paying for the dubbing may dislike his text and change those words born with agonising labour into others he prefers but which will be impossible to synchronise.

Next, the director must find voices which match the personalities on the screen: voices which can imitate or improve, or at least serve the original artists. The actors then assemble in a recording theatre day after day until every syllable, sigh, grunt or wheeze is reproduced on magnetic tape or film. The ability of director and actors is taxed to the hilt. In the same breath, an actress may be requested to "expire like Bernhardt, stretch that 'Ah' and hit the labial two beats earlier".

After this, the sound editor takes over and lengthens or tightens vowels, cuts lingering consonants, creates or narrows down pauses and adds his vitally important contribution to the work. When this is completed, the new dialogue track is "mixed" with the sound-effects and music and sent away to the laboratory to be printed.

There, a tired or unskilful technician can easily print the track *out* of synch. and thereby utterly destroy an illusion painstakingly created over weeks of tough bargaining with unforgiving labials, relentless vowels and troublesome diphthongs.

Do you imagine that's all that can go wrong? Goodness, no. In the cinema or television transmission, the projectionist can "lace up" the film incorrectly – and again put the dialogue out of synch. with the action. A very high percentage of commercial advertisements and filmed news interviews on television are shown out of synch.! And the immediate reaction of a discerning spectator? – *bad dubbing*!

Aside from the complete revoicing of films from one language to another, a great deal more dubbing goes on today than the average member of an audience is aware. There is a growing tendency for co-productions to be made between companies of different nationalities. Each producer insists on a star whose selling powers will ensure profits in *his* country. Sometimes these stars speak no English at all and have learned their lines parrot-fashion, or it can happen that they speak with a strong accent and must afterwards be re-voiced by an actor attempting to justify agonising hesitations, impossible rhythms, illogical pauses, swallowed words and mangled phrases. After all, how do you make "Ai don' tink ai . . . ken chop to . . . to . . . to keel 'im dis Vensdi Torsday Fraiday Satdayorvikent ol poy" sound like: "I don't think I can hope to kill him this Wednesday, Thursday, Friday, Saturday or even this weekend, old boy?"

At times dialogue is changed or requires re-recording for technical reasons and the original artist is not available. This means the character must be revoiced entirely, or a

30 clever mimic must speak the new lines in a convincing imitation of the other's mannerisms, timbre and pitch.

In many English and American top feature films, several characters (often principals) are revoiced. And as for the Italian films we admire so much and think it would be "sacrilege" to dub – it is a fact that almost *all* have already been dubbed in Italian, seldom by the artists we are seeing and frequently with little regard for synchronisation. There is a complete industry of dubbing in that country and when shooting is finished, a "second eleven" team of actors moves into the studio and re-records the whole film. Moreover, the director frequently rewrites the script there and then. Perhaps the most famous of all Italian directors prefers to use non-professional actors who in some cases merely improvise mumbo-jumbo or mutter numbers from one to eleven – and the actual dialogue is invented in the dubbing studio.

In the make-believe world of cinema, the familiar actor portraying a character we know is not himself, the designer who suggests to you that the set built in the studio is actually the King of Naples' Palace, or that the backcloth really is the New York skyline, the composer who creates the right mood, the lighting expert, the photographer, the recording engineer, the editors, costume designer, hairdresser, the script girl, even the location caterers – all are generally given a credit on the screen. Not so the artist who provides those gaping mouths with new voices. He is forced to remain anonymous. His fee is low by any standards of art or craft: he may receive half a day's pay for completing vocally what the original actor has taken five weeks to perform visually.

In fact the entire economics of dubbing make eyebrows rise. As one writer remarked: "The logic of spending a few thousand dollars and taking six days or less to dub a film which took four months to shoot and cost in the millions of dollars . . . smacks of lunacy."

Professional critics loathe dubbed films – yet are often unaware of expert work. The principle: "if you notice it – it's bad dubbing" has been changed by them to "if it's dubbed – it's bad"! A good example of this is *The Red Tent* – an Italian–Russian co-production shot mostly in English and given an almost completely new sound-track afterwards. A foremost London film critic condemned the dubbing and singled out as an example the only sequence in the entire film where the original sound-track was used!

The dubbing director has to fight the strangest odds – not excluding the producers of the film whose ideas might at times show lack of knowledge of the problems involved. The director may know only two artists who are capable of revoicing a particular actor convincingly yet he is asked to supply at least twelve different tests on tape.

How do you cope with a Russian producer who tells you in his charming Slav accent: "Misterrr Rrrrietty, I don' want starrs. To me it would be rrridiculous to see the faces of Rrrussian actors on the screeen and to hear the voices of Olivier, of Gielgud or Rrrex Harrison coming frrrom their mouths. No – I don' want starrrs. Now, I want good actors who know their jobs but arre not famous. Now, I want Peter Ustinov, I want Laurence Harvey and . . . someone has suggested to me an actrrres here called Dame P . . . Peg . . ."

"Do you mean Peggy Ashcroft?"
"Yes – that's right!"
Could it have been a "dubber" who coined the phrase: "You can't win for losing?"

Jack Hawkins

Fernandel

Gérarde Philipe

Adolfo Celi

Marcello Mastroanni

Vittorio de Sica

32

... and the voice of them all, Robert Rietty, who has "dubbed" for all of them at one time or another. Here, by the way, he is shown as an actor in his own right, as the Chief of the Police in *The Italian Job*.

Robert Rietty was born in London in 1923. A writer, actor and broadcaster, he has become internationally famous for his ability to dub foreign films into English, sometimes just doing the dialogue for one character and sometimes directing the entire operation. Probably the greatest authority on the subject, his views on the business are amusing, authoritative and interesting.

NOVEL INTO FILM

by Gordon Gow

A scene from David Lean's *Doctor Zhivago*, the Robert Bolt adaptation of the Boris Pasternak novel (Carlo Ponti–MGM).

Film-makers are very much inclined to take books as their basic material rather more frequently than they adapt stage plays for the screen, and certainly far more often than they commission original movie scripts. After all, it is reassuring for them to know that they are dealing with stories which have proved successful on the bookstalls; and what's more, the flexibility of form in a novel or a biography allows readier changes of scene than the majority of works that the cinema adopts from the theatre.

There can be handicaps, though: sheer weight of substance for one. This is evident even in some of the best transitions from the printed page. Take, for example, Robert Bolt's carefully detailed screenplay based upon the very long Boris Pasternak novel, *Doctor Zhivago*. The process of compression, skilled as it is, nevertheless brings about a certain imbalance: the character roles are so varied and strong and so impressively cast (with Ralph Richardson, Alec Guinness, Rod Steiger and Siobhan McKenna, among others, bringing vivid life to the personages they depict) that the key figure of Zhivago himself, although well played by Omar Sharif, tends to be undermined.

The effect, upon me at any rate, was quite different from reading the book. There, because of the stress which Pasternak had time to give, the character of Zhivago predominated. But in a film, the straight man who carries the major burden of a plot can be swamped by the torrent of variegated performances that surround him. No fault of the leading performer: it is a hazard of the

34 game. One sees examples of it often in the theatre, too: a quiet and reliable leading man, who is probably well cast for his role, will hold the entire piece together, sometimes remaining on stage for the entire duration of a play, and yet a character actor can come on and give a showy display for no more than five minutes – perhaps a drunk scene, which is hardly ever really difficult – and go off to a vociferous round of applause. The public responds to flashy fireworks; the task of a lead player, unless he is an especially flamboyant star, can be rather thankless. In print, the true balance is easier to maintain.

Of course, the abridgement of *Doctor Zhivago* was adroitly managed by Bolt in respect of incidents, as distinct from that balance of character emphasis – a matter out of any writer's hands once filming has begun and the actors take over. But where incidents are concerned, condensation is usually a big problem if a book has been written at length. Bolt compressed Pasternak with subtlety. Trickier was the film of Henri Charrière's autobiographical *Papillon*, which occupied about 550 pages in its paperback edition and covered the author's nine prison escapes over a period of thirteen years, more than could reasonably be encompassed even by a movie that ran two and a half hours. Here we had the spirit and pace of the book, without the same amount of detail; and often this state of affairs is as much as we can expect. Considerably shorter as source material was James Leo Herlihy's novel, *Midnight Cowboy*. Yet in the film version nearly ten chapters of the book were omitted. They were vital ones, too, about formative influences that were brought to bear upon the central figure, Joe Buck, during his childhood and adolescence.

Out of those experiences grew his wishful attitude to life, together with his notion that he would be able to earn a handsome income as a hustler in New York.

To be sure, occasional incidents were plucked from those missing chapters and incorporated in the film as memory flashes. But they were cryptic in their impressions of little Joe's upbringing by a relative of easy virtue, and his sexual initiation by a voracious young girl who happened to be mentally retarded. The full significance of such points could scarcely have been comprehensible to any spectator who had not read the novel before seeing the film; and no film-maker can take it for granted that every single person in his widespread audience will have done this kind of advance homework.

Of course the idea of the cinematic memory-flash, no matter how succinct and mystifying, was so well established by the time *Midnight Cowboy* was shown that its hints were just accepted, presumably with a shrug, by those who were unacquainted with the novel. Yet readers of Herlihy were certainly able to appreciate every nuance set forth, however minimally, by the director John Schlesinger in his visual interpretation of this sleazy slice of life.

The vulnerability of Joe Buck drew fine acting from Jon Voight; he emanated the right charisma for anybody who knew the full nature of the character Herlihy had devised. Such an apt performance is an exception when a book is filmed, because it is difficult always to find a player who will embody the reader's imagined picture of a fictitious character, let alone the photographs we have seen when the subject is somebody who really existed. Steve McQueen, for example, good

as he is in *Papillon*, does not remotely resemble the likeness of Charrière himself on the back of the book's jacket.

On the other hand the film of Margaret Mitchell's *Gone With The Wind* could not be faulted in its casting of the two leads. Vivien Leigh, as the attractive and wilful Scarlett O'Hara, gave a portrait of total persuasion, her English accent modified to the near-drawl of a Southern American belle of Irish descent. And surely nobody could have made a more acceptable Rhett Butler than Clark Gable, at once virile and wry and muscular and dapper, his very presence suggesting the banked fires that would ultimately flare.

There are times when affection towards a specific artist will dissolve the critical instinct. And one such, for me, was the improbably American yet wholly delightful Micawber in the 1934 Hollywood treatment of *David Copperfield*. How could one possibly quibble at the wildly incorrect accent when the performer was that magnificent comedian W. C. Fields? In a cast that mingled its Americans with a goodly proportion of British actors (among them Frank Lawton, Hugh Williams, Basil Rathbone and Freddie Bartholomew), Fields won through, barely changing his familiar persona and yet seeming to inhabit the flesh and bones of that hapless optimist. More recently Micawber has been played on the screen by Ralph Richardson, English to the core and indubitably Dickensian in the role; yet to my mind it is with Fields that the palm rests for this specific character. His climactic denunciation of the villainous Uriah Heep (Roland Young) is one of the cinema's historic joys, Fields brandishing a weighty ruler all the while, as

W. C. Fields in the 1935 adaptation of the
Charles Dickens classic, *David Copperfield*
(Cukor).

if at any instant his hard-pressed moral
fervour will inflate to the point where he will
put this ordinary piece of office equipment
to a positively lethal purpose.

There are some prolific readers, chiefly of
venerable writers, who will adhere to the
opinion that the cinema should leave books
well alone and seek its drama elsewhere.
In English-speaking countries especially,
cinema is still looked upon by many as a poor
cousin of the arts, whereas a literary work
carries automatic prestige. In France it is
quite another matter: it was the French who
began using the word *auteur* to describe not
the writer of a film but its director, the
man who puts the visuals before us on the
screen. I believe there is a lot of
justice in this although, of course, it is a
generalisation and the truth of the matter will
vary from one film to another.

Film is a visual medium – but also, we must
remember, an aural one. And what is heard
in it will usually include words along with
other sounds. As distinct from that, literature
can be termed strictly a medium of words.
Yet words were used in films of the silent era.
Printed captions frequently interrupted the
visuals, not only to supply the necessary
snippets of dialogue, but also to stress certain
proclivities of the characters if these were
not regarded as adequately emphasised in the
mime of the actors.

History, it can be argued, is on the side of the
written word as something to be taken very
seriously. Literary criticism, after all, can be
traced back as far as Aristotle, more than
300 years B.C.; but the earliest flickerings of
film did not take place until less than 100
years ago. Some would claim that the cinema
medium has not existed long enough to

36 attain the status of art. With this, needless to say, I for one would disagree.

In materialistic vein, it is true that a writer can gain far more money when a book is sold for cinema, even if he doesn't work on the screen adaptation personally, but simply hands the story over. Some writers are said to be reconciled to the fact that they might not become best-sellers to the reading public, but that the rewards from movie versions of their work are decidedly consoling.

At the same time, a good many novelists will state emphatically that, glad as they are of the added income from cinema, they would never be able to create a story if they kept the possibility of an eventual film at the backs of their minds. In the opinion of Patricia Highsmith, for example, it would be "like an artist thinking of a statue while he's painting a picture". Yet her books can be converted into highly flexible movies with reasonable fidelity to the original writing: for example, there were Hitchcock's famous 1951 film of her *Strangers on a Train*, and René Clement's *Plein soleil* in 1959 (sometimes known as *Purple Noon*) which was taken from her brilliant psychological thriller *The Talented Mr Ripley* and proved a high point in the career of its leading actor, Alain Delon. Patricia Highsmith rates strongly with critics of the printed word, despite the fact that her stories adapt so easily to cinema, despite the occasional censor-wary alterations like the intimation at the end of *Plein soleil* that Ripley's crime would be discovered and justice would be done. In a superbly visual *risson*, the movie showed the body of a man he had killed and thrown overboard from a yacht (after the film's vivid central fight sequence) being hauled back to shore at the end attached to the vessel's keel while Ripley, all unaware of the fate in store for him, sat nearby in the sunshine with an expensive drink to hand. The irony was neat, but Patricia Highsmith's ending, with Ripley still at large and savouring his ill-gotten wealth and at the same time never being sure at what moment retribution would come, had both a freedom and a moral implication which the cinema, at least in 1959, had to eschew in obedience to a censorship code that wanted movie criminals to be seen to be brought down at the fade-out.

Today the cinema allows more freedom, but still not as much of it as the novelist can have. And equally there is a tendency for the cinema to simplify a novelist's work, sometimes purely on account of time, but often because a spectator in a cinema has to grasp a point more quickly than a reader who can set his own pace and even turn back the pages to check some detail that might be puzzling him.

Such things apart, the affinity between novel and cinema is really much closer than is generally conceded. It is part of the novelist's task to make us visualise as we read, picturing to ourselves the people and the places and the turn of events. There was no such thing as cinema in 1861 when Dickens wrote *Great Expectations*, yet its opening paragraphs might have been the first draft for the screenplay that was filmed by David Lean in 1946. What a startling impact Lean made when the small boy in the dark graveyard ran smack into the arms of the horrific-seeming convict. This, we felt as we watched, was a shock that only cinema could provide. Yet note how closely the effect adheres to what Dickens set down on paper:

". . . on a memorable raw afternoon towards evening . . . I found out for certain that this bleak place overgrown with nettles was the churchyard; and that the dark flat wilderness beyond the churchyard was the marshes . . . and that the small bundle of shivers growing afraid of it all and beginning to cry, was Pip. 'Hold your noise!' cried a terrible voice, as a man started up from among the graves at the side of the church porch. 'Keep still, you little devil, or I'll cut your throat!' "

No screenplay writer of today could possibly be more helpful to a film director.

By contrast, the novel *A Clockwork Orange* by Anthony Burgess had a cerebral appeal in print whereas the movie of it, directed by Stanley Kubrick, could be said to have made a greater impact upon the emotions than upon the intellect, although its messages – that brainwashing and scientific dehumanisation are bad things, and concomitantly that violence begets violence – were essentially the same as those of the book. The reason for this difference in effect upon reader and filmgoer can be traced, I think, to the inventive use made by Burgess of a slang known as "nadsat", a sort of amalgam of Russian and Cockney, used in a first-person narrative and so tricky to follow in print that one had continually to keep interpreting the sentences into normal terminology in order to follow the plot. This process, incidentally, seemed to me to buffer the shocks of the violence. But in the film the violence was graphic, and its visual strength impinged more fully, outweighing the curiosity value of the words.

The outcome, too, was a distinct case of the director taking *auteur* status as his right. The film was advertised as "Stanley Kubrick's

A scene from Stanley Kubrick's adaptation
of the Anthony Burgess novel *A Clockwork
Orange* (Warner).

38 *A Clockwork Orange*" and the credit for Burgess as creator of the initial novel was minimal by comparison. An even firmer instance was the Italian film of the *Satyricon* of Petronius, very idiosyncratically made, and to my mind brilliantly cinematic. The director Federico Fellini named his work quite boldly *Fellini Satyricon*: an Italian of today had adopted the work of an ancient Roman, converting it to another medium, and making what lots of us would consider a viable claim to authorship. Subsequently he made *Fellini Roma*, the naming of which was incontestably exact since it was a series of his personal impressions of Rome and his younger days in the city: virtually an autobiography conceived as a film rather than as a book.

Among *cinéphiles* of deepest dye, of course, you can find bigotry as fervent as that of the literary snobs. Thus, by some of Alfred Hitchcock's devotees, *Rebecca* (1940: his first Hollywood film) is reckoned to be poor stuff, simply because it sticks quite closely (although not entirely so) to the popular mystery novel by Daphne du Maurier. For me, however, it is exemplary both as story-telling and as cinema, not least because I consider it to hold the best film acting of Laurence Olivier in a "straight" and hellishly difficult role, but also because it makes one freshly aware at every viewing of how assuredly Hitchcock took to the efficiencies of Hollywood technique, creating his gently romanticised Cornish atmosphere in Californian studios, and building his suspense with the timing of a master.

The year before, in Britain, working on a different kind of subject by the very same novelist, he had indeed looked in dull form: *Jamaica Inn* was eighteenth century hokum with Charles Laughton's ham accentuated by manifestly false bushy eyebrows, and such other notable players as Robert Newton, Maureen O'Hara and Leslie Banks getting nowhere in the effort to inject just a nip of credibility into the pervading melodrama. *Rebecca* was a most satisfying contrast to this, beautifully detailed and polished, its refined melodrama presented with a restraint that carried persuasion.

Hitchcock's only other version of a Daphne du Maurier plot is his elaboration of her exceedingly short story, *The Birds*. The locale was shifted in this case, quite emphatically and photogenically, from the Cornish to the Californian coast, and a subject that had originated as neat and rather scientific, as well as hauntingly macabre, was engagingly stretched, at first with some light romantic humour and then with mounting suspense tactics that eschewed much scientific explanation for the menacing behaviour of the massed birds, a phenomenon since echoed in real life. Hitchcock chose to lace the yarn with moral and metaphysical implications, which he controlled superbly, treading the uncertain ground that lies between realism and fantasy.

Where fact is involved, it is dangerous for a film-maker to use a book merely as a springboard, although with good judgement he can still use the change of medium to advantage, as did Richard Fleischer in his gripping movie of that inevitably interesting but nevertheless gigantic tome of criminal reportage, *The Boston Strangler* by Gerold Frank. It was a case of thirteen murders by strangulation, of females whose ages ranged from 19 to 85, yet all regarded as the crimes of a single male, committed between the summer of 1962 and the winter of 1964. Albert De Salvo, who eventually confessed, was generally supposed but not actually proven to be guilty. De Salvo was played in the film by Tony Curtis who, for much of the first part of the narrative, was seen only as a fragmented and unidentified man. Shots of his hands and feet, moving in sinister fashion, were framed in variously shaped and sized rectangles, while other sections of the sizeable wide screen contained more rectangles that showed certain simultaneous action. Thus the strangler could be approaching a door, and at the same moment we could see inside the room where his potential victim was going about her housework unaware of the danger. It was Fleischer's way of giving back a measure of suspense to situations of which the outcomes were known to the bulk of the audience, since the case was a notorious one. Additionally this method could on occasion litter the huge overall frame of the screen with a multiplicity of images, set in different parts of the city of Boston, indicating that many things are happening at once: the police throwing out their dragnet, the women bolting themselves indoors as the reign of terror intensified. This was a remarkable and intelligent example of cinematic technique applied to a book that was packed with information so intricate and of such length that one was bound to put it down periodically, if only to eat. A film goes right on, and until we have the anticipated cassette age when we can show our moving pictures at home (and presumably make tea

Henry Fonda and William Marshall in Edward Anhalt's adaptation of the Gerold Frank novel *The Boston Strangler* (Fox).

40 breaks whenever we wish) it is important for directors to compensate somehow for the unbroken continuity of action. This Fleischer did, as well as dealing nimbly with the abridgement problem. If several things go on simultaneously before our busy eyes, time is being put to the maximum use. The cinema's technical resources, applied in that case to factual material, are given further range when fantasy prevails. But the printed word can go to greater extremes. A rather nice instance can be found in Graham Greene's short story *The Basement Room*, filmed by Carol Reed in 1948 as *The Fallen Idol*. A key incident concerned a child who was awakened in the night to find a woman he detested looming over him. In print, Greene built towards this moment by letting the child have a nightmare, quite a vivid one with "a bleeding head . . . in a basket" and "Siberian wolves . . . breathing heavily". Then he woke, and the woman was there: "A loose hairpin fell on the pillow . . .". This last detail, the hairpin dropping to the pillow beside the small boy's face, was the only visual effect that Reed kept. The remainder of that sequence, the entire nightmare, was omitted. Previously there had been a rather eerie game of hide and seek before bedtime, filmed in a vast but dimly lit room with the camera giving an oblique tilt to the image, suggesting a degree of disorientation. And presumably Reed felt that this was enough. Where the nightmare had merged into the reality of the face by the bedside – a superb effect, undoubtedly, in the written work – the cinema would have been going to melodramatic extremes had it indulged in the dream images, and would thereby have threatened the mood of a somewhat delicate story. But that small shock of the falling hairpin, before we saw the ensuing close-up of the woman's hate-ridden face, was a truly filmic *frisson* and an excellent piece of visual selectivity.

Such moderation is uncommon. More frequently the cinema will seek to "improve" upon a book by heightening it, and until fairly recently there was a preference for happy endings which had to be imposed where they had originally not prevailed. Even in a truly satisfactory film, like the tender sad-comedy of *Breakfast at Tiffany's*, directed by Blake Edwards, George Axelrod's splendid screenplay was permitted no truck with the doom decreed for the heroine Holly Golightly by the writer of the novel, Truman Capote. At the end it rained, as Capote ordained, but at the same time there were hugs and happiness for Holly – who was portrayed so charmingly by Audrey Hepburn that one really wanted her to come through smiling, anyway.

Novelists who sell a good deal of their work to the cinema are inured to having it changed. Wryly, Rumer Godden (*Black Narcissus*, *Greengage Summer*, etc.) recalls that when she returned to India to work with the great French director Jean Renoir on the screenplay of her book *The River* in 1951, he told her that they would "remember" what she wrote, and then he added, "But the first thing we'll do is put the book up on the shelf". What resulted, as Rumer Godden is the first to recognise, was a really beautiful essay in cinema, still reasonably related to her own touching account of the transition from adolescent idealism to adulthood and practicality.

Nevertheless changes for the worse are still too much with us. *Black Flowers for the Bride* (known in the United States as *Something for Everyone*) was transmogrified, to put it politely, from a brilliant if black satire by Harry Kressing called *The Cook*. In the novel, the leading character made such tempting dishes in his kitchen that he eventually dominated his employers by causing them to grow fat and powerless, until, in an epilogue, he was seen to have suffered almost fatally from an overdose of his own toothsome medicine. The film, which was the first to be directed by the well-known Broadway musical specialist Harold Prince, converted the whole thing into a matter of sex, giving the central role to personable Michael York and presenting the equivalent situation of power coming before a fall in terms which, in recent years especially, the cinema has rendered commonplace. Sexual gamesmanship hasn't anything approaching the novelty value of conquest by culinary prowess.

The late Spencer Tracy, who gave one of his finest performances in the John Sturges–Warner film of Ernest Hemingway's *The Old Man and the Sea*.

42 Adaptations that do their best to be faithful to books, even when the purchase of screen "rights" has given the producer a completely free hand, will still contrive as far as possible to favour the visuals above the words. An exception to this tight-minded rule was the contentious screen treatment of Ernest Hemingway's *The Old Man and the Sea*, which, by nature of its story, had only one human being on the screen for the greater part of its duration – Spencer Tracy as the gnarled and noble fisherman, catching his marlin, set upon by sharks, suffering but surviving; the tale is a testament to the resilience of human dignity.

All this could possibly have been made visual, like a silent movie with sea-sounds added. But in fact the screenplay by Peter Viertel used an abridgement of Hemingway's eloquently structured prose, and this was spoken as an off-screen narration by Tracy, not in the character of the fisherman but as a third person, a disembodied story-teller. Die-hards, believing strictly that talking pictures ought to say everything in dialogue (unless they are educational documentaries), waxed indignant. They considered it anti-cinematic. To me it seemed a fusion of beautiful pictures with spoken words of great philosophical strength. True, there were some technical deficiencies due to bits of faking in the scenes at sea, but these were minimal in a film of eye-filling splendour, photographed in colour by James Wong Howe with locations mainly off the Hawaiian Islands.

Exceptionally, the director of *The Old Man and the Sea*, John Sturges, took the view that "The words in the book are the thing. We used them simply to hear them: to let Spence say them. It seemed to me that what happened on the screen wasn't as powerful as what was said – literally, the words." Personally, I'd pay him the compliment of disagreeing. I think he had it both ways. For once, here was a film that brought the verbal and visual elements together in perfect harmony.

Gordon Gow is a film critic and radio broadcaster with an interest in virtually all the performing arts. He writes for Films and Filming, International Film Guide, The Guardian *and other publications on a freelance basis, and is the author of two paperback books*, Suspense in the Cinema *and* Hollywood in the Fifties. *His enthusiasm for ballet finds expression frequently in* What's On in London *and* Dancing Times, *and he sees this as the art most kindred to movies because they both deal in patterns of movement. The latter predilection would account as well for his keenness for swimming, which, second to eating, is his favourite sport.*

THE MARCH OF THE MOVIES

A Technical Review by E. Smith Morris

In the two years between *The Jazz Singer* in 1927 and the first MGM musical *Broadway Melody*, the weekly admissions to cinemas in the USA rose from sixty to a hundred and ten millions. The coming of sound had almost doubled the appeal of the cinema and producers could afford to be jubilant and confident in the future of the cinema industry.

The years that followed were to see many improvements in presentation and technical quality. Production companies vied with each other to attract the floating audience and their executives, not surprisingly, were ready to consider any idea which might repeat the box-office miracle of the late twenties.

Many of the developments were in the nature of refinements to the materials and mechanisms already vital to the process. The first sound films were photographed by cameras which, because of the noise they made, had to be enclosed in sound-proof booths large enough to accommodate the camera crew. These booths were airtight, uncomfortable and clumsy, and were soon to be abandoned in favour of quieter cameras enclosed in sound-proof "blimps". These were not much larger than the camera itself, and enabled the cameraman and director to return to the fluidity of camera movement which had characterised many of the silent movies. *Applause*, directed by Rouben Mamoulian in 1929, was the first sound film to have this freedom of movement.

The problems to be met in the making of a *quiet* motion-picture camera are great, and the attainment of maximum picture steadiness and consequent high image quality on the screen is much easier if the noise factor can be ignored. The major contribution was that of George A. Mitchell, whose high-precision camera continues to this day as the standard studio camera. First shown in 1920, the Mitchell camera was extremely quiet, even without a blimp. When sound came it it became the first choice of camera, displacing the popular Bell and Howell which, although noisy, remains unexcelled for the precision of its mechanism and is still in use today for critical work in animation and special effects.

The high standards of mechanical design were set by pioneers who were able to anticipate most of the subsequent requirements of cameramen, and techniques of film-making: but early cameras were cranked by hand and to do this without shaking the camera required a rigid tripod. For documentary and newsreel work the tripod was sometimes a hindrance, and a variety of lighter, portable cameras began to appear, driven by clockwork or electric motors. It was one of these, made by Arnold and Richter in Germany, which captured the world market. The Arriflex 35 mm was designed primarily as a hand-held reportage camera and embodied a mirrored reflex shutter which enabled the cameraman to view the action at the time of shooting and to focus and observe the set-up precisely as seen through the lens of the camera. The first Arriflex was delivered in 1938 but it was not until after the war that it could become widely known as the indispensable and versatile camera which gave a new freedom to the cameraman.

The reflex shutter was adopted in France by the Caméflex camera, and in Britain by the Newman Sinclair and Vinten cameras. Cinema Verité was invented and the freedom from the restraint of tripod or crane gave us some of the most exciting sequences, but also a surfeit of ill-considered and amateurish work where one became over-conscious of the camera at the expense of involvement in the subject or story.

Greater audience involvement was the motivation behind the use of Cinemascope, Cinerama, Vistavision, Todd A-O, Technirama, Techniscope, Panavision and many other presentation systems which sought to provide a more vivid contact between the audience and the action. In general, the wide screen has succeeded, and persists in those forms which are economic in production. Three-strip Cinerama, where three cameras and three projectors working in synchronism were required to fill the wrap-around screen, was used for two major films only – *How the West was Won* and *The Wonderful World of the Brothers Grimm*. Nowadays Cinerama is a single film system similar to others using 70-mm film. A three-strip system similar to Cinerama was used by Abel Gance in 1927 for *Bonaparte*.

Many attempts have been made to extend the screen around the full three hundred and sixty degrees. In the 1958 Brussels World Fair, Disney showed Circarama with a

44 coast-to-coast scenic coverage of the United States. This complete panorama was filmed by eleven synchronised 16-mm cameras mounted radially on a circular base which could be carried on a special camera car or slung on a retractable boom from below an aircraft. At the 1967 World Fair in Canada, Disney presented Circle Vision 360°, a similar system using 35 mm and providing higher image quality.

International Trade Fairs and exhibitions tend to be the show-places for cinematic ingenuity but the systems shown amount to thinking aloud, and are usually too complex or too expensive for general acceptance. At Expo 70 in Japan there were screens of every size and shape with sound and effects to match. In the pavilion of the Mitsubishi Group images were projected on to spherical screens from within, on to a walk-through screen of smoke retained by curtains of air, and on to the Hori-Mirror screens where the visitor was surrounded on all sides by a raging tempest extending as far as the eye could see.

The Australian pavilion presented the audience with simultaneous pictures on nine wide screens; others used dome screens and multi-screen arrays arranged for dramatic presentation effect. The largest motion picture format of all was Imax, where each frame on the 70-mm print was three times the size of the normal 70-mm frame, extending horizontally over fifteen perforations and measuring 2·74 in. × 1·91 in. This could fill a screen 85 × 120 feet with a high quality picture.

Cost and restricted application or camera mobility make these systems impractical, but there is one effect which still eludes the back-room boys – the true three-dimensional effect seen without the aid of special glasses. The use of red and green, or polaroid spectacles, makes a limited 3-D effect possible and there have been many attempts to persuade audiences to the new dimension, especially around 1953 when there was a rush into production of 3-D films. Eyestrain and technical difficulties for the cinemas in synchronising projectors, as well as poor story content and doubtful 3-D effect, led to the abandoning of these systems but the world and the film producer waits for true 3-D. Research now taking place with holograms may well in time make the illusion of reality almost complete.

A hologram is a photographic film or plate on which complex wave patterns form a record of the subject. This can be used subsequently to reconstruct an image of the subject in three dimensions. The effect of 3-D is complete – as the observer views the hologram from different positions he sees different aspects of the subject. To view it is necessary to look through the hologram, and it seems unlikely that projection on to a two-dimensional cinema screen will ever be possible. Television seems to offer better prospects, although the problems that exist of transmitting the vast amount of information in a hologram over the available transmitter bandwidths have yet to be solved. However, the three-dimensional effects already obtained are startling in their effectiveness, and it seems likely that rapid progress will be made, aided by parallel development of holographic and laser techniques for a multitude of industrial applications.

Sound is already stereophonic – it arrived in the cinema with Walt Disney's *Fantasia,* which in the original 1940 presentation used seven sound tracks and thirty loudspeakers. The version shown today has had its tracks dubbed for normal sound system presentation, but the impact of the original is something to be remembered. Wide-screen systems today use stereo by playing sound through a series of loudspeakers ranged across the width of the screen. Ambient or background noise is distributed by speakers around the auditorium. Normally four separate tracks are used on 35 mm and six tracks on 70 mm systems.

The improvement in the quality of recorded and reproduced sound since the advent of the talkies is remarkable, and is due to a great extent to the invention of magnetic tape recording and the very rapid progress in the radio and television industries, where the research in component and circuit design has been concentrated. The miniaturisation of electronics makes possible a top quality tape-recorder in the space of a slim paperback book, together with sound better than that obtained thirty years ago with several tons of equipment.

The mobility of modern recording equipment has been matched by the cameras now available which, using the latest 16 mm colour film emulsions, can produce images suitable for feature quality productions. These highly portable sound and picture cameras, developed initially for television and documentary or news work, are now used increasingly for feature film-making especially where locations are cramped and the smaller equipment is at an advantage. Over the years since 1929, technical progress has been towards perfection in the projected

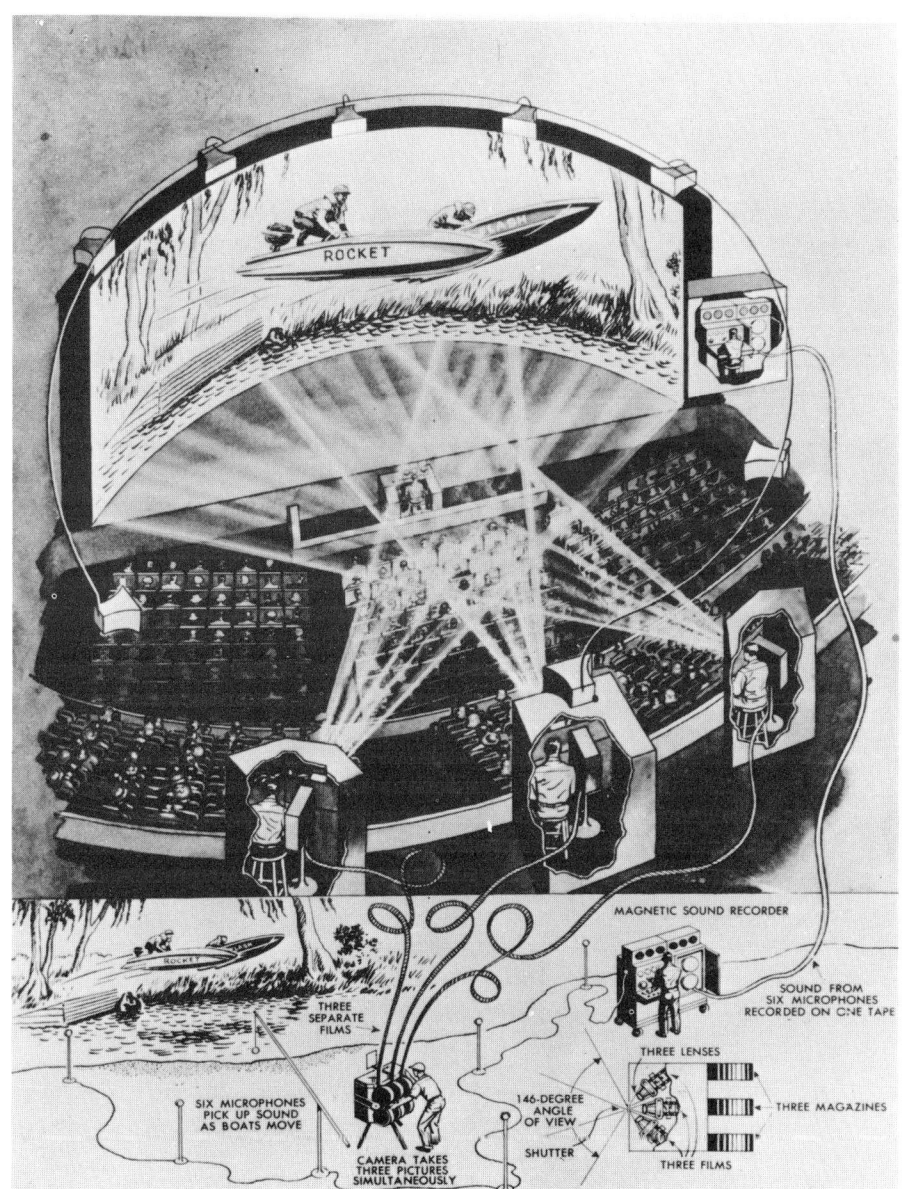

image and reproduced sound. To make the images three-dimensional, to be able to feel and smell, are effects which remain to be achieved, although the latter has been tried in a limited way. Will it come to be that one wall of our rooms will be a large television screen presenting the perfect visual, aural and tactile experience, or will we just don a headset with electrodes to communicate directly these impressions to our brains and provide the full impact of reality? There may well be those who think that the closer we come to real experience the more remote from art. Perhaps we may hope there is room for both.

A visual idea of the way that the original three-camera, three-projector Cinerama worked. The snag was always the edges of the three images and their occasional failure to quite match up.

ROCKET

MAGNETIC SOUND RECORDER

SOUND FROM
SIX MICROPHONES
RECORDED ON ONE TAPE

THREE
SEPARATE
FILMS

THREE LENSES

SIX MICROPHONES
PICK UP SOUND
AS BOATS MOVE

146-DEGREE
ANGLE
OF VIEW

THREE MAGAZINES

CAMERA TAKES
THREE PICTURES
SIMULTANEOUSLY

SHUTTER

THREE FILMS

46

E. Smith Morris has a vast knowledge of all facets of the motion picture. From 1937 until the war he was involved in a Ministry of Education pilot scheme to assess the use of films as an educational aid. During the earlier part of the war he was responsible for the film requirements of three Royal Ordnance factories and as such made many films for staff training, works relations and research and motion study. From 1941 to 1946 he was Editor, Director and Producer at Gaumont British Instructional and from the end of that period up till 1959 was Managing Director of Polytechnic Films Ltd, a major producer of short educational films. In 1967, after a period of working on the board of a number of film companies and acting as consultant to others, he joined the London Film School where for the last five years he has been a Vice Principal, lecturing, supervising the production of textbooks and acting as head of the Animation Department which he himself set up.

An artist's impression of Circlorama, a system of circular projection by which the audience were entirely surrounded by a circular screen in which they either watched standing or from swivel seats in order to keep track on what was happening on all sections of the screen. It ran for quite a while in a specially built circular cinema in Piccadilly Circus.

The stream of publications on films and film-makers continues in full flood. As the sale of admission tickets goes down, the sale of books goes up. It seems that the less often people go to the cinema, the more they want to read about it – a situation undoubtedly due in part to the reappearance of old (or often not so old) movies on television.

If only on account of the space available, therefore, the following review section cannot claim to be exhaustive. Technical textbooks have been excluded, as have most books in which the film has only a very marginal part. There are also, unavoidably, books that have escaped my net: it is impossible to keep track of everything that appears, and in this respect I am particularly grateful to all those publishers who have kept me regularly – if I may so put it – in the picture. Apart from these omissions I hope that the majority of film books of interest that have appeared during the period will be found in the following pages.

I have retained the same three-section classification as last year but, as indicated then, the divisions are inevitably somewhat arbitrary, and certain titles could reasonably be fitted into more than one category. Finally, it is unhappily necessary to mention that, as production costs continue to rise, book prices – like everything else – are subject to change.

BIOGRAPHY, MEMOIRS

Marion Davies: Fred Lawrence Guiles; W. H. Allen, £3.50

An enthusiastic, well-researched and engrossing biography of the ex-Follies girl who became equally famous as the mistress of newspaper tycoon William Randolph Hearst and as a film-star under his patronage. The author suggests, very persuasively, that this very patronage (Hearst's determined efforts to turn her into a white-flame-of-purity dramatic actress) may well have stifled an excellent comedienne. Mr Guiles is firmly and justly insistent that many of her films have been underrated. He is equally relentless in his depiction of the Movie Mecca in one of its least attractive aspects – filled, as Hearst himself said – with the "chowder crowd"; actors and actresses newly risen to great affluence, but with "the manners of boarders in an Irish rooming house". Also emphasised is the unfairness with which Miss Davies has been linked in the public eye with the Susan Alexander of *Citizen Kane*.

Here and there a certain infelicity of style clouds the author's meaning: e.g. on page 27 an unfortunate use of the word "disinterest" (for indifference or lack of interest) gives exactly the opposite impression to that which was apparently intended. All in all, however, this is compulsive reading for anyone captivated by the Hollywood legend. There is an excellent detailed filmography – together with a generous number of fascinating illustrations.

Dorothy and Lillian Gish: Lillian Gish; Macmillan, £6.50

A volume of sheer enchantment, recording the lives and careers of the two wonderful sisters in theatre and film. The brief text is warm, wise and humorous – but it is the illustrations that dominate. There are hundreds of them, stills, family photographs, press cuttings, many of great rarity and all of absorbing interest. An exceptionally full filmography and "stageography" has been compiled by James E. Frasher, of the greatest value to researchers. Miss Gish has put us all in her debt for preserving so unique a record of her and her sister's unforgettable careers, and the publishers are to be congratulated on having so worthily presented it.

Tallulah: Brendan Gill; Michael Joseph, £7.50

In last year's *Film Review* I somewhat rashly referred to Lee Israel's life of Tallulah Bankhead as "definitive", and now comes along this sumptuous volume to challenge me. In truth, however, the books do complement each other. Mr Gill's chronicle is briefer, concentrating on the professional side of his subject (though her private life is very adequately covered), and presenting a clear, concise, unintimidated picture. The illustrated section, comprising about two-thirds of the large book, is superb – a mass of private and professional photographs accompanied by full informative captions. Newspaper reviews are reproduced with sufficient clarity to be read complete, and there are splendid inclusions of pages from contemporary magazines. The extraordinary quality of the strange and unique personality that was able to initiate so broad a cult on so narrow a base comes clearly through these elegantly printed pages; and the distressing picture of her later years – foul-mouthed, hard drinking, toadied to by her "caddies", is not dimmed down.

On Cukor: Gavin Lambert, W. H. Allen, £3

One of the best "interviews with a director" books to appear for a long time. The subject is articulate and interesting, the questioner sympathetic and skilled at tactfully drawing his victim out. In the course of discussing each of his many important films (from *The Royal Family of Broadway* in 1930 to *Justine* in 1969) George Cukor provides apt comments on a hundred and one aspects of a Hollywood director's life and work during the great years. He is forthright but unresentful over his setbacks and disappointments, generous in gratitude and praise when these are called for. There are numerous photographs of the director at work, in addition to stills. A most likeable conversation piece.

Adventures with D. W. Griffith: Karl Brown; Secker & Warburg, £4

This is a really splendid book. Karl Brown joined Griffith in his teens as general dog's-body, rose to become assistant to cameraman Billy Bitzer, and parted company when Griffith left Hollywood to return east to Mamaroneck. His account of those notable pioneering days is sharp, shrewd, amusing, moving by turns and exciting throughout – and his style is a joy to read. Scattered through the pages are fascinating technical details of his craft, so lucidly yet expertly written as to be intelligible to the least mechanically-minded film enthusiast. However, it is the making of the great masterpieces, *The Birth of a Nation, Intolerance* and (more briefly) *Broken Blossoms* that form the highlights of the book, and seldom has the creation of a huge and complex work of art been so entertainingly and thrillingly described. See, for instance, his cunning account of various scenes from *The Birth* which seemed to him so flat, foolish and mistaken in the making, and their transformation in his eyes when the whole picture unfolded on the screen.

As a picture of Griffith this book takes its place beside R. M. Henderson's fine biography reviewed last year. It entirely deserves Kevin Brownlow's affectionate introduction – and Mr Brownlow himself has earned our gratitude for persuading its author to write it. Karl Brown went on to become a leading cameraman (*The Covered Wagon*), and a director himself.

The Griffith Actresses: Anthony Slide; Tantivy/Barnes, £3.75

D. W. Griffith has been quite well served during recent months. Last year we had R. M. Henderson's excellent book, this year Karl Brown's *Adventures*, the magnificent Gish sisters album by Lillian Gish (both reviewed in these pages) and now Anthony Slide's disarmingly exuberant accounts of the famous Griffith actresses – Blanche Sweet, Mae Marsh, Lillian and Dorothy Gish, Clarine Seymour, *et al.* Mr Slide's enthusiasm for the silent period is infectious: judge by his "nearly falling out of his seat with excitement" when he glimpsed a Griffith character actress (Kate Bruce) appearing years later during a party scene in the master's last production *The Struggle*. In his brief, enjoyable, well-illustrated sections he is both forthright and informative. He makes a good point that it was foolishly wide of the mark to describe the Griffith heroine as invariably "ethereal": on the contrary, her grim determination to "fight for what she desired" (including the preservation of her virginity) is apparent in almost every film. On one point I pick Mr Slide up: he refers to *Mantrap* (Victor Fleming) as Josephine Crowell's only comedy screen role. On the contrary, this fine character actress was unforgettable as the appalling mother-in-law in one of Harold Lloyd's best comedies, *Hot Water*.

48

THE GRIFFITH ACTRESSES

ANTHONY SLIDE

The MGM Stock Company: James Robert Parish and Ronald L. Bowers; Arlington House, dist. Ian Allan, £4.95

Following *The Fox Girls*, *Paramount Pretties* and *Warner Brothers Presents* from the same House, reviewed last year, comes this massive volume dealing with the Lion of studios. The lives and careers of nearly 150 stars and feature players are presented in the form of a concise, lively profile, a complete filmography and stills from his or her films. The whole – obviously the result of prodigious research – is rounded off with a number of useful appendices and a notably full index. No mere reference book, it can be read straight through its 800 pages with pleasure. Space is allotted to the generally less written-up players, who at last receive their just amount of attention. Paper and binding are exemplary, and the book is a worthy tribute to a unique, if vanished, empire. Note for future editions: on page 315 Louis B. Mayer is reported to have "fortuitously bought up Jean Harlow's contract". It is difficult to imagine the Chief doing any such thing "by chance". Presumably "fortunately" was the word intended, but "fortuitously" appears to have been misused on at least two other occasions. On page 444 Mr Mayer is referred to as "disinterested": again – unlikely. *Un*interested, perhaps?

Sweetheart – The Story of Mary Pickford: Robert Windeler; W. H. Allen, £3.25

An excellent biography – sympathetic yet uncompromising, unassuming yet authoritative, concise yet detailed. Certain aspects of the World's Sweetheart that are revealed – her drinking, screaming four-letter words, inordinate money-grasping, outbursts of pettiness or spite – may shock those filmgoers of the past who wish to retain unsullied memories of the little golden-curled girl, but the final effect of the book is warm, generous and often moving. Among the many illustrations is one of unique interest: a photograph of 1920 showing the actress making up for *Suds*, revealing a wholly unaccustomed – indeed unrecognisable – face, and demonstrating the extent of the miracle she achieved in the conviction of her child impersonations. A word of praise, too, for the charming and appropriate chapter-page decorations.

Mislaid in Hollywood: Joe Hyams; W. H. Allen, £3

The author paints a fairly depressing picture, both of the world of the gossip columnist, and of the world of Hollywood where he worked until – in the final words of his book – he received a rude-awakening. Gossip about the famous, however, has an unholy fascination for most of us, and this is an engrossing pandering to such unedifying curiosity, with its candid camera glimpses of Bogart, Brando, Monroe, Ava Gardner, Cary Grant, *et al.* Its grip slackens somewhat, during the lengthy and intimate account of the author's courtship and winning of Elke Sommer, but tightens up again with a cracking ghost story at the end. Surprisingly, the style of writing is a little slipshod, e.g. 'none of the Kennedys nor even Lawford or Sinatra were included by DiMaggio from the funeral'. Also, an index would have been helpful. On the whole, however, this is an entertaining and perceptive look inside the film capital which, golden age or not, is revealed as a pretty tawdry and tinselly creation – where one's worth was decided by the make of one's car, and where (in Beverly Hills) there was one psychiatrist for every 169 residents.

Cary Grant: Albert Govoni; Robert Hale, £2.50

A sympathetic, revealing, and seemingly authoritative (though "unauthorised") portrait of the man behind the famous screen-star image – a complex, elusive personality some way distant from the light-hearted, debonair actor of *North by Northwest*, *Bringing up Baby*, *The Grass is Greener*, etc. Though various of his films are discussed in their place, this is a private rather than a professional account. Detailed coverage is given of his early life in Bristol, his various marriages, his experiences with LSD, his relationship with his only child – a daughter born when he was in his sixties. The pre-marital euphoria (particularly in the long story of *The Courtship of Dyan*), followed so regularly and inevitably by disillusion and disintegration, make wry reading, and the final effect – despite such hilarious interludes as the press-pursued honeymoon with Dyan Cannon – is oddly sad. Attractively produced and illustrated, with a filmography and synopses, this is a warm-hearted tribute to a man who, in the author's words, "has filled the romantic dreams of untold millions of females" and yet said of his own life "my wives and I were never one".

Mind's Eye: Basil Dean; Hutchinson, £5.50

The first volume of Basil Dean's engrossing autobiography (*Seven Ages*, Hutchinson, 1970) dealt with his early life and career in the theatre up to 1927. The present one starts with the production of his first film – the silent version of *The Constant Nymph*, in writing of which he pays deserved tribute to the "remarkable" star, Mabel Poulton. The book follows in detail his pioneering work at Ealing (the full extent of which is not widely realised); his making of Galsworthy's *Escape*, the first British talking picture to be conceived as such and made with considerable location work: and his launching of Gracie Fields and George Formby on their highly successful popular film careers. The author is rightly proud of his successes, and also refreshingly frank about his failures. A pleasant touch is the reproduction of letters from John Galsworthy and Noël Coward in their handwritten form.

Together with the first volume, this presents an interesting and vivid picture of a dedicated professional at work in the theatre and cinema of the period.

Overture and Beginners, The Story of Dulcie Gray and Michael Denison: Michael Denison; Gollancz, £3.80

Though films occupy only a small part of it, to omit this captivating chronicle would be unforgivable. Both a success story and a tribute to his wife and fellow-artiste, the book traces their lives in detail up to 1948 – when both were established stars – then compresses the following twenty-five years of happy and steadily progressing success into a brief epilogue. Against a single chapter of his own pre-theatrical career, the author devotes eight to that of his wife – justifiably, in view of her adventures during the period. Among films referred to in the book's course are *The Glass Mountain*, *My Brother Jonathan*, *Brighton Rock* and *They Were Sisters*. One point to note: the title of the dominant-mother play – on page 134 – is, of course, *The Silver Cord*, not "Chord"; a slip oddly repeated without query in the generally excellent index.

Mr Denison has the pleasantest and wittiest of styles, and the knack of telling a good story in print. The result is a charming and entertaining autobiography-cum-biography, which even achieves that rarest of delights – the ability to make the reader laugh out loud.

The Fabulous Fondas: James Brough; W. H. Allen, £3

A well-researched, sober and at times moving story of the involved relationships of the famous family. It might be regarded as the definitive example of the generation gap happily bridged – at least to some extent – in later years. The writer has eschewed easy sensationalism and his account is the more absorbing for its evident truthfulness. He is concerned with lives rather than films, but the more important of these (particularly those of the young Fondas, *Barbarella*, *The Trip*, *Easy Rider*) are dealt with in their place. The illustrations, mostly stills, are satisfactorily reproduced. A pity that the blank pages at the end could not have been put to use for a brief index – the book is authoritative enough to deserve one.

Behind the Scenes of Otto Preminger: Willi Frischauer; Michael Joseph, £3.75

Lively, amusing and well-written biography of the formidable dictator–director, based on a personal friendship of over forty years. It is a warts-and-all portrait, and both friends and enemies of the remarkable subject will find plenty to justify their position. All the films are touched on, with numerous hilarious anecdotes of the battles that went on during their making. His methods of work, with all the screaming, raging, bullying and egotism, are frankly presented and the results are assessed fairly and shrewdly – whether successes such as *Laura* and *Anatomy of a Murder*, or failures such as *Skidoo*. Included are a full filmography, a list of stage productions, and a highly amusing end-note by Billy Wilder, who declares he has convincing proof "that Otto Ludwig Preminger is none other than the elusive and dreaded Martin Bormann"! What finally emerges

may not be a wholly lovable personality, but it is certainly a memorable one. Note for future editions: "fortuitous" is twice used (pages 197 and 229) where presumably "fortunate" is intended.

Groucho, Harpo, Chico and sometimes Zeppo: Joe Adamson; W. H. Allen, £3.50

The Marx Brothers are among the more fully covered subjects on the film bookshelf (notably in Allen Eyles' concise yet comprehensive *The Marx Brothers – Their World of Comedy*), but this new volume is welcome on several counts: (1) it contains much new material – even including detailed synopses of discarded versions of *A Day at the Races* and others; (2) it has a generous selection of unfamiliar illustrations; (3) it is hard-hitting in its criticism where justified; (4) it is witty and amusing in its own right. Various sections on each film are prefaced by quotations from the scenario, numerous and very welcome. It is packed with good stories, the accuracy of which it would be churlish to question – and in any case many of them are substantiated in the entertaining notes.

One minor blemish is the absence of a cast-and-credits filmography (though admittedly this is available elsewhere). At times the author's efforts to emulate a Marx Brothers script himself seem a little strained, but on the whole this is a highly enjoyable, often stimulatingly caustic, and spirited evaluation.

Brando: Joe Morella and Edward Z. Epstein; Nelson, £2.75

An "unauthorised biography" that nevertheless presents an interesting, if fairly superficial, account of its subject's life and work. But he is certainly viewed critically, as the full and devastating account of his behaviour during the making of the calamitous *Mutiny on the Bounty* reveals: and the choice of review extracts accompanying the films in the useful reference section presents – so to speak – both sides of the picture. The illustrations are plentiful and excellent.

Brando: Bob Thomas; W. H. Allen, £2.75

Hard on the heels of the Morella/Epstein book above comes this second biography, subtitled "Portrait of the rebel as an artist". Though apparently also, in the strictest sense, unauthorised, it is based on many years of acquaintanceship, and is thus closer to its subject and contains a number of personal interviews. Inevitably covering much the same ground, the books to some extent complement each other. The present one goes more closely into the actual making of the films (being particularly interesting on the recent *The Godfather* and *Last Tango in Paris*); the earlier one scores in the matter of illustrations, which in Mr Thomas's book are confined, with one exception, to stills, one of each film. The present book also, regrettably, lacks an index, though it has a full filmography. Minor discredits include the misuse of "infer" for "imply", "ladened" for "loaded", "Macauley" for "Macaulay". On the whole, though, this is a warm and perceptive study – very likely as detailed a portrait as we shall ever get of its elusive sitter.

Olivier: Ed. by Logan Gourlay; Weidenfeld & Nicolson, £3.25
The editor of this excellent collection of interviews and notes whets our appetites with hints that its subject may one day write his autobiography. Until such a book, or the definitive biography which must surely appear, becomes available, this is a welcome, multi-angled look at the leading actor of our period. The thirty or so contributors, including Sybil Thorndike, John Osborne, William Wyler, Margaret Leighton, Angus McBean, reveal impressions of working with him in various fields. Mr Gourlay draws out his victims with skill, and the contradictory comments are as revealing as the points on which most of them agree. Though mainly concerned with the theatre, his film activities are well represented. Notably absent from the list of boyhood performances are those of his schooldays at St Edward's, Oxford – not, apparently, a particularly happy period.

Lucy: Joe Morella and Edward Z. Epstein; W. H. Allen, £2.75
Chatty and somewhat short on documentation (no index or filmography) but an entertaining and pleasantly readable account of the public and private life of the Queen of the television series, Lucille Ball. The prolific authors present a warm and lively account of a warm and lively personality. One is inclined to feel a twinge of dismay at coming across yet more show-people marriages starting off with fulsome assurances and then following a monotonously predictable collision course. There is a very interesting chapter on the notorious Unamerican Activities committee investigations, with extracts from the records; and there are amusing examples of the wilder flights of "studio biographers".

Irving Berlin: Michael Freedland; W. H. Allen, £3.50
A straightforward, workman-like, and always interesting account of the famous songwriter's life and career – a man who has resolutely refused to authorise a biography or write an autobiography. It follows his incredible progress from penury (he was brought to America at the age of four after seeing his Siberian home burnt to the ground by marauding Cossacks) to one of the best known and most prolific makers of popular music. Films played a less vital part in his life (mainly because he hated the lapse of time between a song's composition and its introduction to the public) but their importance both to his material and creative situation, and to the commercial Hollywood scene, was considerable – e.g. *Top Hat, Holiday Inn, Easter Parade, Alexander's Ragtime Band.* The author's admiration of his subject is obvious, but is not permitted to gloss over the darker shadows of his life

and personality: the result is an authoritative and very readable book.
In fairness, the Verger story (page 95) might have been credited to its author, Somerset Maugham. Note for future editions: Irene Bordoni's name is misspelt on pages 130 and 184 (and in the index), as is that of Philip Hope-Wallace on page 260.

Whatever Happened to Hollywood?: Jesse L. Lasky, Jr.; W. H. Allen, £3.50
Books about the great days of the movie moguls have an unfailing fascination, and this one is among the best. Novelist, poet and screenwriter son of a famous film pioneer, the author recounts his engrossing, hilarious and often moving story with the utmost authority and warmth of spirit, in a style colourful and hypnotic enough to hold any Wedding Guest from the feast. Much of his book is concerned with his work for C. B. De Mille (a decidedly uncompromising portrait) and with the appalling stresses and strains of trying to satisfy that epic taskmaster, but there are many other good stories. With books such as this to perpetuate it, the legend of the golden noon and melancholy sunset of Hollywood is safely preserved for posterity.
It has to be pointed out that an unusual number of misspelt proper-names have slipped by unnoticed, among them: Richard "Arlan", Gene "Austrey", S. N. "Berman", "Frederic" March, "Elisa" Landi, "Clarke" Gable, "Melvin" Douglas, "Philips" Holmes, "Ann" Baxter, General George "McClellen". It was Charles de Roche who gave a "bravura performance" as Pharaoh in the 1923 *Ten Commandments*, not Rod La Rocque; and in the 1956 version De Mille deliberately *misspelt* the Egyptian Princess's name as Nefretiri, giving full reasons in his *Autobiography.*

Storyline: Lenore Coffee; Cassell, £3.25
Lightweight and somewhat scrappily put together, this is nevertheless a warm-hearted and entertaining account of the twenties and early thirties in Hollywood. The author worked as scriptwriter, script doctor and sometimes as general factotum for Harry Garson, De Mille, Goldwyn and Thalberg among others, and her book is full of good (and often unfamiliar) stories about them. Though in general kindly disposed, she has no hesitation in removing a few lids. Her account of what went on during the making of *The King of Kings*, for instance, hilariously dissipates the atmosphere of solemn reverence so carefully built up by contemporary publicity. On another page, her impression of Spencer Tracy is "boorish". One of her early duties was dealing with fan mail, and it will surprise many people to learn of the amount of pernicious filth that it frequently contained. For a professional writer her style is surprisingly clumsy at moments. A few inevitable small errors have crept in ("Edmond" Lowe for "Edmund" – faithfully copied in the index), and the charming frontispiece makes the reader regret the absence of further illustrations. All in all, however, an enjoyable "read".

Light Your Torches and Pull Up Your Tights: Tay Garnett with Fredda Dudley Balling; Arlington House, dist. Idea Books, £5

There is always something a little frustrating in reading an autobiography written "with" or "as told to" a semi-ghost writer. Part of the fascination of an autobiography is its revelation (sometimes subconscious) of the subject's personality. The procedure in the present case is particularly surprising since Tay Garnett is himself a writer who has been responsible for numerous film scripts.

That said, the book is a racy, amusing and at times moving story of a successful commercial (using the word in no derogatory sense) director's life and work in Hollywood. It is full of good stories, private and professional, and spans fifty years of an active career. Anecdotes of stars and other associates abound, together with cliff-hanger accounts of the dangers encountered in making films of action and adventure. Two small points: Mr Garnett rightly describes Loretta Young's sister as gorgeous, but spells her name wrongly – it should be Sally Blane. And the famous silent comedian was Larry Semon, not Seamon.

FILM HISTORY, CRITICISM, ANALYSIS

Memo From David O. Selznick: Selected and edited by Rudy Behlmer; Macmillan, London, £5.95

This massive collection of the notorious paper missiles which, from about 1930 to the early sixties, drove many a Hollywood director almost to the point of suicide or murder is indispensable reading for anyone seriously interested in the American cinema. Selznick was the archetypal "involved" (or as some would say, "interfering") producer, and the book, expertly edited, is an engrossing record. It is only unfortunate that no "in reply to your memo" section could be included. Among the films that were cradled in his all-enveloping arms were *Gone With the Wind* (to which a large section is devoted), *Rebecca, Intermezzo,* the first version of *A Star is Born,* and *Viva Villa!* (one of his favourites). The quality that comes over very strongly from this fine book is his incredible thoroughness: the unceasing anxiety to do justice to a well-known book, the attention to every detail from the burning of Atlanta to the set of Clark Gable's coat collar, the total resolve that the audience should see the best film that it was possible to create. The pages are full of hints and suggestions, some of which could well be borne in mind today. The whole is a monument to the energy, passion, and driving power of one of the most colourful of the often maligned Hollywood tycoons.

Visions of Yesterday: Jeffrey Richards; Routledge & Kegan Paul, £5.50

A large-scale, scholarly and unfailingly engrossing study of the popular cinema in three of its aspects as social history – British imperialism, American populism, and Nazi totalitarianism. Faced with a lengthy book developing a filmic "theme", a reader may well feel a qualm of apprehension, remembering certain previous examples where a writer rides his hobbyhorse roughshod, or distorts his facts to fit the mould of his obsession. Mr Richards, however, writes sanely, clearly, without prejudice and with much entertainment and humour. In his conclusion he states, "I have set out . . . to explore what I have called the Cinema of the Right, three basically conservative movements which have through the medium of film projected their own vision of the perfect society." It is a wholly successful and profitable voyage. This is an important book on two counts – equally valuable for the social historian and the serious filmgoer. It is fully illustrated, and the lengthy filmography contains useful information as to the availability of 16 mm prints.

The Celluloid Weapon: David Manning White & Richard Averson; Beacon Press, £7.45

An interesting, well-informed and lively study of the American feature-film-with-a-message – the "film of social consciousness" – from 1906 to the present day. The subjects discussed extend from war and politics, racial problems, crime and punishment, drug addiction and alcoholism, to social satire (e.g. Billy Wilder) and the optimistic fables of Frank Capra. The authors develop their serious theme with ease and clarity, skilfully combining scholarship and entertainment. Their range is wide, from early Edwin S. Porter and Griffith to the recent "black" cycle and the chilling forecasts of trouble in store.

The book itself, in large format, is most attractively laid out, with well-margined pages and pleasant typography. The numerous stills are a particular feature: a number of them are, unavoidably, old familiar friends, but there is also a refreshingly high proportion of lesser known ones. All are excellently reproduced. This is, in fact, a first-class survey of one particular aspect of the Hollywood product.

The Great Movies: William Bayer; Hamlyn, £4.95

A study with the above title, dealing with sixty films, is obviously based on personal choice, and criticism in that respect is equally obviously irrelevant. What matters is the treatment of the chosen sixty – and this throughout is of the highest quality. The author has an enviable gift of making his every choice (whether an obvious "great" such as *Citizen Kane* or one less generally regarded, such as *The Bad and the Beautiful*) come alive on the printed page. His comments are pithy, persuasive, often original, and hearteningly down to earth. The links between the five films in each of his twelve sections are interestingly demonstrated – particularly Westerns. In individual cases he is especially good on *Shane, Rear Window* (the best short account I have come across), *Kane, The Third Man* and *Blow Up.* Two minor comments: a reference to John Wayne (page 27) may give the impression that *Stagecoach* was his first Western – he had of course appeared in a number previously – and Buster Keaton was slightly more than an "extra" in *Limelight.* But let us not carp: this is a treasure of a book, beautifully produced. The illustrations, particularly those in colour, are stunning.

In cinema history, 60 films deserve to be called THE GREAT

by William Bayer

The Great Movie Serials: Jim Harmon/Donald F. Glut;
Woburn Press, £3.50

An exceedingly full and knowledgeable survey of the cliff-hanger epics – in particular the heydays of the thirties and forties when Republic and Columbia ruled the roost. Close on 400 pages of synopses of Superman, Captain Marvel and the rest might seem a somewhat daunting prospect, but the affection, enthusiasm and welcome humour of the writers (brought up on Saturday matinées) carry the reader almost painlessly through. Script extracts vary the text, and it is doubtful whether a fuller account will ever appear. So keen are the authors to forge ahead that the style, admittedly, is sometimes careless: "incredulous" for "incredible"; "creditable" for "credible"; "most unique"; "inadvertently" for (?) "immediately"; strange phrasings such as "there weren't many viewers back then". Fractured infinitives and misplaced "only's" litter the pages, at times clouding the meaning. Still, this is a racy account and clearly a work of love – a dip into a barrel of happy memories.

Chevalier: Gene Ringgold/De Witt Bodeen; Citadel,
dist. Literary Services, £5.90
The Films of Marlon Brando: Tony Thomas; Citadel,
dist. Literary Services, £5.90

These two volumes are among the very best in this generally excellent series. *Chevalier* in particular is an enchanting tribute to an enchanting personality, beautifully produced and illustrated, detailed in fact and glowing with warmth. To anyone with affectionate memories of this great performer (and who is there who has not?) this definitive account is an essential and treasured possession.
The Films of Marlon Brando is the third book on this star to be included in this survey. Inevitably many of the biographical details and stories are reproduced, but it is the films themselves that receive most attention. It is a most enthusiastic and discerning account, and pleasantly easy to read. Is the author perhaps a little over-scornful of the offbeat *Night of the Following Day*, and over-kind to the impertinent meddling with a masterpiece called *The Nightcomers*? Well, these are personal opinions – and opinions may be permitted to differ. The illustrations are lavish and superbly reproduced, scoring the highest marks.

Rebels: Joe Morella/Edward Z. Epstein; Citadel, dist.
Literary Services, £2.45
The Films of World War II: Joe Morella/Edward Z.
Epstein/John Griggs; Citadel, dist. Literary
Services, £5.90

The first of these excellently illustrated volumes is a paperback issue of the book originally published in 1971, tracing the development of the anti-Establishment hero from John Garfield to Brando (pre-*Godfather*, of course), together with Peter Fonda, Elliott Gould, and with predictions – so far unfulfilled to any extent – concerning Mike Douglas and Joe Namath. The second gives details of some of the best from Hollywood's not wholly inspiring celluloid war efforts.

On balance, the volumes in this most useful and attractive series are probably more satisfying when concentrating on a single star (or a director such as De Mille) but both these issues are well researched and written. The interlocking histories in *Rebels* are neatly dovetailed to develop the authors' theme – though an index might have been useful. The World War II analyses show up the dreadful artificiality of some of even the better films of the period. They are, in fact, (and are described as) "tributes" rather than films, which may be very praiseworthy but does not necessarily make for very memorable cinemagoing. Nice to see, in *Rebels*, a good word for Brando's underrated horror-cum-suspense oddity *The Night of the Following Day*. An unfortunate misprint in the same book has Montgomery Clift "bulging" instead of "bugling" in *From Here to Eternity*.

The Disney Films: Leonard Maltin; Thomas Nelson/
Crown, £4.95

A comprehensive and perceptive critical study. All the full-length features, from *Snow White* to *The Happiest Millionaire*, are treated in detail, with the fullest of credit lists, and the later ones, since Walt Disney's death, are summarised, together with the shorts and television programmes. Both the latter branches are, in addition, fully listed. There is a massive index and a profusion of good black-and-white illustrations. Mr Maltin is an enthusiast without idolatry, and is as unhesitating in his condemnation of the inevitable failures as he is generous in his praise of the many successes. Perhaps he lets the appalling *Alice in Wonderland* and *Sword in the Stone* get off a little too lightly; and not everyone may agree with his raptures over *Mary Poppins*. All in all, however, this is a fine tribute to one of the great names of the fantastical cinema – a man who, at his best and in his own line, may well be described as touched with genius.

The Art of Walt Disney: Christopher Finch; Abrams/
New English Library, £15

Mr Maltin's book (reviewed above) concentrates mainly on the films themselves, from a critical angle. Christopher Finch's enormous volume is concerned with the total Disney image and organisation. The eye-catching cover, with its embossed Mickey Mouse, might give the impression of a splendiferous gift book. This would not do the book anything like justice, for it is in fact a serious, informed and refreshingly well-written study, comprehensive even to including a special section (by Peter Blake), on the architecture and technological implications of Disneyland and Walt Disney world. The films themselves, though fully covered, are considered less from the critical viewpoint than as part of the general development of animation techniques and the widening of their creator's artistic range. The whole book is full of fascinating technical details – the animated productions being given, rightly, far more space than the live-action movies. The multitudinous illustrations (some in two and even four-page folding spreads) are superbly reproduced.

Many of the background paintings for the cartoons, in fact, make worthy pictures in their own right.
For the enthusiast there can be no better expenditure of saved-up book tokens: possess the two volumes together (Maltin and Finch) and you have Disney – as far as is possible between four covers – complete.

The Cinema of Andrzej WAJDA by Bolesław Michałek

The Cinema of Andrzej Wajda: Boleslaw Michalek;
  Tantivy/Barnes, £1.10
A highly recommendable study of the Polish master's
films (fluidly translated by Edward Rothert), from the
famous opening trilogy, *A Generation, Kanal, Ashes
and Diamonds* and its offshoot, *Lotna,* to *The Wedding*
of 1972. It is interesting to learn from the opening
biographical section that, despite the intensely personal
emotion of the great trilogy, Wajda, who was only
eighteen when the war ended, had in fact only a very
"modest experience" of the underground movement.
"I had a posting of no significance and the German
reprisals never came near me." He concludes, "So I
imagine that my war films are a kind of compensation
for the stirring and exciting lives that others led . . ."
A clinching proof of the little book's value is the
appetite it whets for a Wajda film one may have missed
– *The Birch-Wood,* for instance. Historical and
sociological backgrounds are concisely and
adequately drawn in. A minor criticism may be made
that the type used, though crisp and uncramped, is so
small as to be eye-straining. However, this economy
does provide room for a generous selection of stills –
some of them (e.g. at pages 24, 44 and 52) of notable
quality.

Murnau: Lotte H. Eisner; Secker & Warburg, £2.10
The Haunted Screen: Lotte H. Eisner, Secker &
  Warburg, £2.10
The appearance of those two classic studies in the
Cinema Two series, strongly bound paperbacks on
good quality paper, is an event to be doubly welcomed.
The Haunted Screen, among the best studies of German
cinema, traces the influence of Expressionism, in
particular on the films from *Caligari,* through the great
silent period, up to the post-Nazi era. Significant
aspects such as chiaroscuro, studio architecture and
stylised acting are discussed in the work of Pabst, Lang,
Leni, Murnau and other great and lesser figures.
Murnau is an enlarged reprint of the definite work on
this famous director: not for quick reading, and
perhaps giving rather a lot of space to lost or rarely
available films. There are, however, many pages of
absorbing interest, including a detailed account of the
wonderful *Sunrise,* Murnau's first American film and
rightly regarded as his masterpiece. In addition we now
have the full script of *Nosferatu* by Henrik Galeen,
Murnau's own copy with his personal notes – an
invaluable bonus.
Illustrations in both books are excellent, and – in the
case of *The Haunted Screen* – lavish.

Westerns: Philip French; Secker & Warburg, £2.40
  hardback; £1.20 paperback
In the Introduction to this interesting and important
little study, the author quotes Freud's wise qualification
"sometimes a cigar is just a cigar" – a comment to be
borne in mind by all symbol-obsessed writers on the
cinema! Mr French himself has obviously heeded it in
producing this well-balanced and informative
dissertation (a "ruminative monograph" to use his own

words) on the historical, sociological, aesthetic, and
other aspects of the Western genre. Perhaps his
division of the films in relation to four famous
American politicians, Kennedy, Goldwater, Johnson
and Buckley, is a little strained, but not unduly so. The
idea has the attraction of novelty, and indeed he puts up
quite a convincing case for it. He is particularly
interesting on the treatment and significance of
landscape, death and poker games in the Western; but
on all the themes he discusses he has something
illuminating and original to say. This is a meaty little
book, compressing much into little space, and written
in an admirably clear style that is marred only by an
irritatingly reiterative – and at times seemingly
pointless – use of the word "eponymous". Stills are up
to the usual high Cinema One standard.

» Westerns
Philip French

The Western (revised edition): George N. Fenin and
  William K. Everson; Grossman, £7.50
A very welcome reissue of a classic book on its subject,
with additional chapters bringing the history right up
to date, so that the range now extends from *Cripple
Creek Bar-room* (1898) to *The Life and Times of Judge
Roy Bean* (1972). Apart from its authority, scholarship
and readable style, the book is most attractively
produced, with dozens of illustrations nicely
integrated with the text. A "must" – especially for
anyone who does not already possess the 1962 edition.

The Image Makers: Text by Paul Trent, designed by
  Richard Lawton; Octopus Books, £3.95
A resplendent collection of several hundred black and
white and some fifty colour photographs of Hollywood
stars and players from the twenties to the present day.
Though a positive Aladdin's Cave of memories, the
book has more to offer than nostalgia: it presents a
fascinating survey of the ways in which the appearance
of stars and the ways of photographing them have
differed through the decades – and also, just as
interestingly – how they have remained similar. The
reproduction is superb, the turning of each page a
pleasure. It is strange to note how much more
satisfying – more natural and alive – are the black and
white portraits.
At its present price this is an astonishingly inexpensive
treasure house of the "glamour" aspect of the cinema.

Nonfiction Film, A Critical History: Richard Meran
  Barsam; Dutton, £2.45
A first-class study, concise, comprehensive, readable
and informed. The author, Assistant Professor of
English at Richmond College, New York City
University, knows his subject backwards and has the
happy knack of communicating his enthusiasm even to
those whose main interest in the cinema may be the
fictional film. He attempts to define that awkward word
"documentary" and points the distinction between it
and the wider-embracing "non-fiction" film, going on
to discuss both. It deals mainly with the British and
American product (the former coming in for high
praise) but glances also at Russia, France and elsewhere.
The Nazi documentaries are most perceptively treated.
In time it ranges from the earliest days to an excellent
final page on the Rolling Stones at Altamont, *Gimme
Shelter.* Apart from one or two small blemishes of style
("oblivious *to*"; "insightful"), it is difficult to fault this
book. Together with the Lovell/Hillier *Studies in
Documentary* (Cinema One – included in last year's
survey) it makes the best pair of books on the subject
currently available. Highly recommended.

The Animated Film: Ralph Stephenson; Tantivy/
  Barnes, £1.10
A revised and updated reissue of the author's *Animation
in the Cinema* published in 1967. Packed with facts, and
covering the whole spectrum of its subject, from
Britain to Japan, Disney to avant-garde, this is the
most complete and concise guide available. Also
included are technical details from the early days to

computer-animation, set out with admirable clarity. The author's pithy comments raise this attractively produced volume from the dry level of a textbook: it makes, in fact, a most welcome reappearance (even though not everyone will share his high opinion of *Fritz the Cat!*).

A Ribbon of Dreams: Peter Cowie; Tantivy/Barnes, £4.50
Considerably revised and enlarged from the author's 1965 paperback, *The Cinema of Orson Welles*, this is an admirably researched analysis, including, apart from sections on each film, a perceptive chapter on Welles as actor, detailed filmography and lists of his other work, script extracts from *Citizen Kane* and *The Magnificent Ambersons*, and a full bibliography. Pride of space is rightly given to *Kane* – a most penetrating analysis, particularly interesting in the light it sheds on the other characters in the film. Mr Cowie stoutly defends *The Trial*, and is illuminating on the Shakespeare films: the section on *Chimes at Midnight* is interesting as Shakespearean as well as Orsonian analysis.
With its pleasantly apt title (a Wellesian quotation) and its attractive jacket, this is a book for anyone concerned with one of the few true genius figures of the screen.

Ingmar Bergman Directs: John Simon; Davis-Poynter, £3.50
John Simon is among the liveliest and most stimulating of American critics – enjoyable to read even with occasional complete disagreement. This "visual analysis" is a good example of both his perception and his clarity of style – despite his feeding us once or twice with such indigestible mouthfuls as "universalizable" and "distanciation". It consists of long discussions of *The Clown's Evening* (*Sawdust and Tinsel* in Britain, *The Naked Night* in America), *Smiles of a Summer Night*, *Winter Light* and *Persona* – plus an interview with Bergman and a brief essay, the whole accompanied by copious excellently printed frame enlargements. Mr Simon is particularly good on *Winter Light*, arguably one of the director's finest masterpieces: the essay is almost as moving to read as the film is to see. But the whole book, handsomely bound and printed, is a pleasure both to read and to handle.

The Hollywood Professionals, Volume 1: Kingsley Canham; Tantivy/Barnes, £1.10
This new series is concerned with directors whose film titles are probably better known to the general public than their names. The first volume deals with Michael Curtiz, Raoul Walsh and Henry Hathaway. A concise but not skimped commentary is followed in each case by an admirably complete filmography, including a capsule synopsis. Scheduled for future volumes (some of which may well have appeared before this notice) are Henry King, Sam Wood, Lewis Milestones,

Howard Hawks, Edgar Ulmer and Frank Borzage. In all, the series will most usefully cover some of the less built up areas of the film-book landscape.

The Cinema of Luis Buñuel: Freddy Buache; Tantivy/Barnes, £1.05
Despite the author's tendency to give vent to outbursts of spleen against opinions and values with which he happens to disagree, this is the best book at present available on Buñuel's films. From *Un Chien Andalou* to *Tristana*, they are summarised, analysed and (on occasion) idolised with clarity and an infectious enthusiasm, together with a refreshing freedom from foggy metaphysical speculations. The essays on *The Exterminating Angel* and *Belle de Jour* in particular are illuminating studies of two of the director's most complex masterpieces. A special word is due for Peter Graham's easy flowing translation, and all in all the concise volume is good value both as exposition and commentary.

Theories of Film: Andrew Tudor; Secker & Warburg, £2.50 hardback; £1.30 paperback
There is a pleasant story of Beethoven receiving in Heaven a copy of Donald Francis Tovey's entertainingly erudite *Essays in Musical Analysis*, glacing through it, and exclaiming, "My God, did I really mean all that?". The same astonishment may well be felt by some hard-working film director – anxious only to earn an honest million as he wipes the sweat from his brow – on reading the higher reaches of film theorists. Mr Tudor's short work, dealing in the main with Eisenstein, Grierson, Bazin and Kracauer, with important sections on those Terrible Twins *Auteur* and *Genre*, manages to avoid the pitfalls of pretentiousness. He writes with refreshing lucidity and modesty, and in the final analysis puts up a good case for the "necessity" of film theorisation – even if it is in danger of becoming a series of closed-circle discussion far removed from the workaday cinema where the average citizen goes for evening relaxation, and which ultimately depends on his patronage for its very existence. For the serious student, however, this could be an excellent introduction. Illustrations, ranging widely from *Bezhin Meadow* to *Top Hat* to *Drifters* to *The Creature from the Black Lagoon*, are plentiful and well reproduced.

Stargazer: Stephen Koch; Calder & Boyars, £3.95
Mr Koch makes a gallant attempt to elucidate the work of the high-priest of screen *ennui*, Andy Warhol, but, perhaps inevitably, from time to time gets bogged down in his own obscurity – an obscurity not lightened by a style featuring a plethora of fractured infinitives and a misuse of the word "disinterest". Still, all in all, this is the most thorough examination of the films to date – and the author is almost cruelly frank in his estimates. The course of productions is sharply divided by two almost simultaneous events – the success of *The Chelsea Girls* and the attempted murder of Warhol. Mr Koch is scathing in his comments on the films that followed, which are, it seems, mainly the work of Paul Morrissey, but in truth the earlier efforts, more pretentious, come off little better – e.g. eight immovable hours of the Empire State Building, six of a sleeping man's abdomen. The author's most devastating method of exposure is a simple relation of the synopsis of a film – *Harlot*: "The action consists of Montez lasciviously devouring banana after banana while Miss Koshinskie holds a small dog in her lap and stares into the distance, stupefied with boredom. Meanwhile, Tavel, Billy Linich, and the poet Harry Fainlight, out of frame, carry on a more or less inaudible discussion about the great female movie stars" – or *Horse*, of which he has only seen the first reel, consisting of "an inaudible thirty-five minute view of a kid . . . attempting to get a horse to neigh. The horse doesn't." This is a manfully painstaking study of a cinematic offshoot that already seems oddly sterile and jejune.

Music for the Movies: Tony Thomas; Tantivy/Barnes, £4.50
This is a delightful book, combining technical information with biographical sketches and opinions of the leading composers, the whole shot-through with an infectious zest and humour. The measure of the author's skill is that, as well as appealing to those already interested, he is able to arouse an interest which in many filmgoers, may yet be dormant. The long list of composers' scores ranges from Max Steiner to Lalo Schifrin, and numerous films are treated in detail. There are some good (and fresh) stories – it is an unexpected pleasure to find oneself laughing aloud while reading a study of film music! The book is handsomely produced and illustrated, and contains full lists of scores and recordings (the latter extending beyond Hollywood productions).
In this volume the range is limited to composers who worked or work in Hollywood: it is to be hoped that Mr Thomas will now turn his attention to British and European film music and produce a sister book of equal value and entertainment.

Stunt: John Baxter; Macdonald & Jane's, £3.50
This well-illustrated volume is an admirable companion to the Arthur Wise/Derek Ware *Stunting in the Cinema* reviewed in the last issue. Though inevitably covering some of the same ground, Mr Baxter's lively account deals in less detail with technical aspects and more fully with matters such as animals on film, make-up artists and the tricks of "magicians". There are interesting sections on the making of individual films such as *Trader Horn, The Naked Prey* and the 1958 *Ben Hur* (though it is a pity that in the last film the name Messala is misspelt throughout). *Tarzan* is amusingly treated, and it is intriguing to learn that of all animals the chimp is most disliked as co-star. Mention must be made of the scathingly critical "Towards a Bibliography" – all readers should take heed, and intending writers also!

Photoplay Treasury: Crown, dist. Nelson, £4.95
The greatest of fan magazines seems to be an inexhaustible mine for nostalgic digging. Last year we had *The Talkies* (Dover/Constable) – this year the above large and spacious volume. The former has a slight edge on quality of reproduction and includes a few coloured cover pages: the latter the advantage of taking in the silent period from as far back as 1917, and is more conveniently arranged in that the reader does not have to keep turning to the end of the book to follow up the various articles. Both are excellent value. Articles of delicious mushiness continue right through the war years – but there are criticisms too. A survey of the productions for 1917, for instance, remarks on the

poor work of stars as august as Douglas Fairbanks, Mary Garden, Pauline Frederick, and – with extreme daring – Ethel Barrymore herself. Bogart's article defending his anti-Un-American Activities stand and his disavowal of Communism is reproduced, and so are photographs of Liza Minelli as a babe in arms. An enjoyable bedside wallow in the past before turning out the light.

Spellbound in Darkness: George C. Pratt; New York Graphic Society, dist. Idea Books, £4.50
A massive study of the silent cinema in the form of a linking commentary, contemporary articles and reviews, and script extracts. Though dealing in the main with the American film, sections are included on those foreign productions that were screened in the United States. The lengthy extracts from the newspapers, fan magazines and more serious publications of the period are particularly valuable and revealing: tastes and verdicts change, and those at the time of a film's first appearance are at least as valid as those of posterity. Numerous fascinating details are brought to light: such as the fact that comedy sequences featuring Sennett star Chester Conklin were written into Chaney's *Phantom of the Opera* "to relieve tension" – then (mercifully) written out again! The illustrations are so splendid (sixty-six of them) as to make one long for more. A book to be dipped into, perhaps, rather than read solidly through – but unfailingly rewarding to the dipper.

Sixty Years of Hollywood: John Baxter; Tantivy/Barnes, £5.75
A well-illustrated large-format book, surveying the period year by year. Each division starts with an introductory section on the history of production, followed by reviews of one or two of the most interesting, and not always the best-known, films of the year. The author is particularly skilled in threading his (and our) way through the tortuous maze of the amalgamations, separations, uprisings and downfallings of the major and minor companies. His story is full of fascinating details – it may not be widely realised, for instance, that the first film studio in Hollywood was not opened until 1911, and then by two Englishmen. His comments on individual films are stimulating, even if one does not always agree. (Is Samuel Fuller, for instance, *really* a "master"?) Particularly interesting are accounts of the earlier productions, such as the 1927 *King of Kings.*
Two minor points. "John Frankenheimer's contribution . . . can scarcely be *over*estimated," surely, not "*under*estimated" (page 209): and it is perhaps stretching it a bit to describe the archetypal jazz-baby Alice White as a "romantic actress".

50 Years of Movie Posters: John Kobal; Hamlyn, £3.95
A dining-table rather than coffee-table book (17″ × 12″), comprising some hundreds of posters, together with a few music sheets and promotion booklets, from the teens to the fifties. Many reproductions fill a whole page, and at least half are in colour. Not only a feast for nostalgics, but an interesting demonstrations of how much poster styles have changed – and how little. Likenesses were not always striven for with fussy exactness: if the name were to be covered, how many people would recognise the blonde on page 65 as Carole Lombard, rather than, say, Jean Harlow? David Robinson provides an entertaining introduction.

Adventure in the Cinema: Ian Cameron; Studio Vista, £2.95
Romance in the Cinema: John Kobal; Studio Vista, £2.95
The opening volumes of what should be an interesting series. At a first glance the books, doubtless deliberately, have a slightly "film-maggy" appearance but the texts are incisive, intelligent and at times caustic. Both are general surveys, concentrating on the American products with side-glances at other countries. Choice of the plentiful stills is unhackneyed and in general they are well produced, though in some cases their small size makes them rather too cramped for clarity. In *Romance*, Thomas Meighan's name is misspelt twice (and in the index). In the same volume occurs the following grammatical oddity (caption, page 173) – "Every detail in his wonderfully light, airy, deceptively simple films complement each other": a somewhat obscure comment that might be re-worded in future editions. All in all, if the standard keeps up, the series (edited by Sheridan Morley) should make a useful, sturdily bound addition to the film-shelf.

The Golden Age of Sound Comedy: Donald W. McCaffrey; Tantivy/Barnes, £5.75
Taking as his period the thirties and early forties, the author traces such matters as the fading of the great silent comics, the rise of the musical (from the comedy angle), and the flowering of the sophisticated screenplay with an easy and pertinent pen. His comments are often sharp (on Ruby Keeler, Abbott and Costello), and his final list of "bests" – though predictable in some cases (*Nothing Sacred, It's A Gift*) – contains some surprises (*David Harum, Earthworm Tractors*). Nice to see Eddie Cantor's *Roman Scandals* receiving its due. The field is restricted to America, though Ealing is accorded one modest paragraph. Illustrations (stills and interesting advertisements) are generous and reasonably unhackneyed. The glances at some minor and lesser-known examples of commercial cinema are very welcome. Note for future editions: Cyril Ritchard is misspelt Richard on page 187, and, on the same page, Alec Guinness is misspelt Guiness.

56

A Flask of Fields: Ed. Richard J. Anobile; Studio Vista, £2.60
Why a Duck?: Ed. Richard J. Anobile, Studio Vista, £2.50
Who's on First?: Ed. Richard J. Anobile, Studio Vista, £2.50

In these three glossy paperbacks an attempt is made, with the aid of scripts copiously accompanied by frame blow-ups, to preserve on paper highlights from the films of the famous comics W. C. Fields, the Marx Brothers, and Abbott and Costello respectively. Some eight or ten films are treated in each volume. The results of what might have seemed an uncertain experiment are surprisingly successful, and the sequences are vividly recreated on the static printed page.

The appeal of each book will, of course, be strongest to the devotee of its particular subject. Oddly enough it is the Costello book which comes over best. Although often regarded as less successful than the other comedians, their music-hall-type cross-talk scenes are prime examples of nonsense rampant and logic turned upside-down. It is this volume also that comes off best in photographic clarity: but all three are handsome additions to the nostalgic shelf. The degree of eyestrain and back-aches involved in selecting the several hundred frames for each book with such exactitude must have been prodigious.

Film Fantasy Scrapbook: Ray Harryhausen; Tantivy/ Barnes, £6

The author is the recognised master of the animated film which incorporates models with live action, using a process he has christened Dynamation. This entertaining book is the story of his working career, describing the making of such fantasy films as *Mighty Joe Young*, *One Million Years B.C.* and *Jason and the Argonauts*. The latter – deservedly his favourite – contains his most astonishing feat: the battle between three "real" men and seven skeletons. He is modest about his text, and undoubtedly the many illustrations (sketches, stills, frame enlargements) are the main attraction. Nevertheless the writing is full of fascinating details, such as the use of his mother's fur coat to cover a model cave bear (surely a supreme example of parental self-sacrifice); and the creation of an octopus two tentacles short of the usual number due to budget restrictions. The illustrations are charmingly laid out in scrapbook fashion, and include a number from early, little-seen fairy-story films.

A Heritage of Horror: David Pirie; Gordon Fraser, £1.50

An interesting and enthusiastic study of the "English Gothic Cinema" 1946–72, linking it with the early novels of Mrs Radcliffe, M. G. Lewis and Maturin, among others. The theme is interestingly developed and the author's zeal infectious, but some of his claims are a bit high, and this is exaggerated by an earnestly humourless approach. Many of the purely routine rehashings of old themes – vampires, monstrous creativity, lycanthropy, etc. – are raised to pinnacles of significance on which they perch with distinct

uneasiness, commercially successful though they may be. Also, to describe the work of Michael Reeves (who died tragically young) as "of a Keatsian aura" is surely pushing things a bit. Still, there is much to enjoy in this whole-hearted survey. It is pleasant to see the highly entertaining and underrated *Slave Girls* of Michael Carreras receiving its due; and also a good word for Peter Watkins' *Privilege* (as against *A Clockwork Orange*). Henry Frankenstein, incidentally, was the son of a Baron in Hamilton Deane's original production of Peggy Webling's stage version (see page 68). Deane's contribution to the Dracula/Frankenstein saga is too often insufficiently acknowledged.

A Pictorial History of Horror Movies: Denis Gifford; Hamlyn, £1.95

A light-hearted trip through the Halls of Horror, strong on facts and intriguing detail (such as the fact that André de Toth, director of the best-known 3-D horror film *The House of Wax*, was one-eyed and could only see "flat"), less concerned with the deeper implications of the genre's lasting popularity. The author's premise, that for him the horror film must have an element of fantasy, excludes the truly horrific, such as *Psycho* and *Les Diaboliques*, but there are monsters and phantoms here in plenty. Welcome space is given to the lesser-known films, directors and players: such as the old British stalwart Tod Slaughter – with whom I had the memorable pleasure of working years ago! Contrariwise, the author evidently thinks little of Roger Corman, and Dreyer's famous *Vampyr* receives only passing mention. The jokey headings and captions to the illustrations (which are many and excellent) would appear to indicate that he does not regard his subject with any undue seriousness, but his affection for it shines through.

The Thriller: Brian Davis; Studio Vista, 90p

With the limited space available, and a range that extends from Polanski's *Repulsion* to James Bond, from *Les Yeux Sans Visage* to *How to Steal a Diamond . . .*, this cannot be more than a superficial survey – a listing and often inadequate dismissal of titles in a few lines. It may, however, serve as an introduction to fuller reading; and the author does find room for the occasional pertinent observation – such as a reminder that Clouzot's *Le Salaire de la Peur* has more to it than a chilling journey with a load of nitro-glycerine. He also puts in a word for the occasional underrated straightforward thriller, such as the near-horror *The Shuttered Room*, and notes the "bizarre brilliance" of *Peeping Tom*. Stills are plentiful and good.

The House of Horror: Ed. Allen Eyles, Robert Adkinson, Nicholas Fry; Lorrimer, £1.75

This glossy paperback is a history of Hammer Films, famous British horror and fantasy specialists, with interviews, reviews and filmography. In its rather fulsome approach it reads a little like a stylish publicity brochure – though, contrariwise, to read straight through the synopses of horror (Dracula, Frankenstein and the rest) is to experience a sense of desperate straining to give new twists to a series of exhausted

formulae; the rather unhappy descent into uninspired routine of a once imaginative genre. However, as a work of reference it is satisfyingly complete, and there are dozens of well-reproduced illustrations, including a gallery of pin-ups.

Japan – Film Image: Richard N. Tucker; Studio Vista, £2.95

Blessed with the gift of making scholarship easy reading, the author traces the development of Japanese cinema against the background of the country's history and the industry's evolution. Individual films of the leading directors – Kurosawa, Ozu, Ichikawa, Oshima, *et al.* – are discussed and analysed, but the chief value of this well-illustrated (but unfortunately unindexed) book is in its wider aspects, its revelation of the influence of customs, beliefs and character, of the unique Japanese theatre and art, on the work produced for the screen. The book not only increases the understanding of those films we have already seen, but arouses our interest in others that are mentioned in the text but have not yet come our way.

JAPAN:FILM IMAGE
Richard N Tucker

All the Bright Young Men and Women: Josef
Skvorecky; Peter Martin Associates, dist. Tantivy,
£3.50
Originally published (in Canada) in 1971, this is a
"personal history of the Czech cinema" told by a man
who was actively engaged in it, chiefly as a writer.
Modestly described as "not a scholarly work, just a
personal remembrance" it tells the valiant and often
heartbreaking story of the struggle of an art form to
survive against political pressure and bureaucratic
interference – and tells it with an immediacy and a wry
humour that should grip the attention of anyone
interested in the cinema. There are numerous rare and
attractive stills, in the main well enough reproduced;
and the only obstacle to reading the book lies in the
large number of lengthy footnotes set in eye-achingly
small print. This is, however, a small detraction from a
generally absorbing, witty and often highly amusing
chronicle.

Movies in America: William Kuhns; Pflaum/Standard,
dist. Idea Books, £3.25
To justify yet one more survey of Hollywood/American
movie history a book must have something special to
offer. This large-size paperback can, I think, fairly
claim to fulfil that condition. It is written with a
freshness, conciseness and verve which makes it an
admirable introduction to more detailed reading. The
choice of directors to represent trends and periods is,
as it must be, to some extent foreseeable, but each is
admirably summed up in his brief section – and it is
interesting to find Seastrom included with some fine
stills from *The Wind.* The inserted "cameos" are
informative and often amusing, and the illustrations
(many of course familiar, but a good proportion less so),
are excellent. The silent period is particularly well
treated, and there is a perceptive article on Disney.

The Film Business: Ernest Betts; Allen & Unwin,
£5.50
Long one of the least documented fields, British
cinema is at last receiving fuller attention from the
makers of books. Mr Betts has long been a noted critic,
with, in addition, a working knowledge of the industry,
and his book has the weight of authority. It is strong on
the business side, but seems curiously second-hand on
the films themselves. An odd and apparently arbitrary
chopping and changing from past to present tense
makes things at times confusing and irritatingly
difficult to follow, but on the whole he wends his way
deftly through the appalling jungle of British financial
film structure – revealing a pretty sorry picture. On
matters to do with studios, companies, trade unions,
censorship and similar practical matters this is a very
useful and concise record. A few proofing errors (such
as the statement that Tony Richardson directed eleven
films between 1968 and 1969) will doubtless be
attended to in later editions. Note: the cynical Mr
Somerset Maugham would surely be surprised to learn
that he had had any share in *The Man from Toronto!*

What the Censor Saw: John Trevelyan; Michael
Joseph, £4
A survey of the work and development of the British
Board of Film Censors, told with all the polish and
persuasion to be expected from the man who, as
Secretary, steered it with such skill between the cliffs
of opposing criticisms for thirteen years. He defends its
decisions with vigour, and is frank about its errors.
Famous "breakthrough" films mentioned include *The
Moon is Blue, Room at the Top, The Pawnbroker,* and
the Danish *Hugs and Kisses.* The appendices include
the full text of the famous Production Code (USA) of
1956. A "remarkable" document it certainly is, and by
today's standards absurd in parts: but through it runs
a strong belief in the importance of the film, and
concern for its integrity. If the latter had not been quite
so completely despised and cast away it is possible the
cinema today might not be in such a parlous condition.

We're in the Money: Andrew Bergman; Harper, Row,
£1.90
A serious and interesting study of the American
cinema of the thirties from a viewpoint of the
sociological content. Subtitled "Depression America
and Its Films", it sets out to relate the screwball
comedies, gangster movies, anarchistic comedies (such
as the Marx Brothers), musicals and other categories,
to the mores and outlook of the times. Key productions
are perceptively analysed in this respect. It is wrily
amusing to note (page XXII) the success of "Bank
Nights", when lucky-numbered admissions tickets
won prizes, and the eventual suggestion that the films
themselves were not necessary – all that was needed
was the gamble: an idea now come to dreadful
realisation in Bingo.

Hollywood Now: William Fadiman; Thames & Hudson,
£2.50
Unfortunately this arrived just too late for inclusion in
last year's *Film Review,* and events have already
overtaken its first chapter, that on the Industry. The
remaining sections, however, dealing with agents,
directors, stars, writers and producers, are as sharply
relevant as when they were written. Mr Fadiman has a
depressing picture to paint – his account of what
happens to an author's work, for instance, reveals some
appalling situations. Agents in particular appear in a
somewhat murky light, with producers not much
brighter. The future is depicted in far from rosy hues.
Interesting to note that the cassette appears not yet to
have fulfilled the expectations noted at the time of
writing.

The Writer and the Screen: Wolf Rilla; W. H. Allen,
£2.95
Advising and informing without withering into the
aridity of a mere textbook, this compact volume is of as
much interest to the passive film and television viewer
as to the active practitioner. Among many aspects
discussed, the differences between writing novels and
scripts are illuminatingly brought out. The television
section is particularly revealing especially on the
stultifying dreariness of hack writing for the

interminable "series".
The author's own style has its occasional
awkwardness – e.g. the last sentence but one on page
131 with its ambiguous "its": and the use of the word
"logistics" (defined as the military art of quartering
and billeting troops) for the final section of the book
seems somewhat strained. The title of the Steiger/
Poitier film *In the Heat of the Night* is shorn of its
significant first word – an error dutifully reproduced in
the index.
Recommended to all aspirants.

The Motion Picture from Magic Lantern to Sound Film:
Julius Pfragner; Bailey Brothers & Swinfen, £2.25
It was an excellent idea, in a popular history of the
pioneer inventors of the cinema, to have the technical
details and diagrams included in an unusually excellent
and informative index – compiled, it appears, by the
translator, Theodore McClintock. Unfortunately, the
author has seen fit to treat his text in a semi-fictional
manner, not only inventing long conversations,
thoughts and incidents, but even introducing fictional
characters fairly closely concerned in the incidents he
is describing. The result is an unhappy hybrid – a book
that irritates the reader by continually causing him to
exclaim: "But how does he know this is what
happened?" This may be acceptable in a historical
novel, but raises doubtful eyebrows here. The result is
that the index is much the most valuable and
interesting part of the book – which is, in fact, a literary
dog wagged by its tail.

The Complete "Greed": compiled by Herman G.
Weinberg; Dutton, £6
A magnificent collection of 400 large-size stills –
production, film and frame enlargements – together
with a most informative and perceptive introduction,
and fully annotated. A large proportion of the stills are
from the cut sections of this mangled masterpiece, and
the total result is the finest imaginable record of a film
in book form.

Morocco/Shanghai Express: Josef von Sternberg;
Lorrimer, £1.50 paperback; £2.50 hardback
These two Sternberg/Dietrich film-scripts are well up
to the Lorrimer standards, with well-printed stills and
an enthusiastic introduction by Andrew Sarris. The
most intriguing thing about this particular volume is
the realisation it brings of the director's genius in
creating such memorable movies out of (in the first
example at any rate) such trite and foolish material and,
in both examples, breathing life into such flat and
stilted dialogue. Truly a triumph of manner over
matter.

The Bank Dick: W. C. Fields; Lorrimer, £1.25
paperback; £2.50 hardback
Film-script of one of the best of Fields – and
interesting also as an example of how a "vehicle" may
exist only in the personality of its driver. To anyone
reading it without knowledge of the Fields personality
it must appear lugubriously forced and unfunny. As a

memory-jogger of the great comedian at his best, however, it is something to be thankful for, embellished as it is with nostalgic stills.

Two Russian Film Classics: Lorrimer, £1.25 paperback; £2.50 hardback
Pudovkin's *Mother* and Dovzhenko's *Earth* – valuable silent additions to the library of film texts. *Mother* is a straightforward script, *Earth* a sort of post-filming dissertation by the director, completed in 1952. The first is undoubtedly the more vivid as a transference from screen to paper. Good stills.

Masterworks of the German Cinema: Lorrim , £3.50
The new Lorrimer series referred to in last year's book review gets off to an excellent start with this first volume, which contains the film-scripts of *The Golem* (1920 version), *Nosferatu, M* and *The Threepenny Opera.* Format is similar to the existing series of individual scripts, with carefully edited scenario, full credits and cast, and critical note. In addition there is a general introductory essay by Dr Roger Manvell relating the films to their moments in history – both political and cinematic. Future plans include French and British masterpiece volumes, which may well be out before this notice appears. They will be very welcome. Note: the final sequence of *M*, though referred to in Paul Jensen's reprinted analysis, is omitted from the script.

O Lucky Man!: Lindsay Anderson and David Sherwin; Plexus, £1.25
Savages/Shakespeare Wallah: James Ivory; Plexus, £1.50
These first two volumes in a new series of film-scripts are sturdy, well-produced paperbacks to grace any shelf. *O Lucky Man!* in particular, with its decent-sized, crisp stills and frame enlargements, introduction by Lindsay Anderson, and entertaining account of the film's genesis by David Storey in the form of diary extracts, is admirably done. The Ivory book contains introductions to each film by the director and, in the case of *Savages*, a "Motion Picture Treatment" section which is a useful aid to the fuller understanding of a not particularly "easy" film. The *O Lucky Man!* script, incidentally, includes the episodes so regrettably cut when the film was put out on general release.

The War Trilogy: Roberto Rossellini; Lorrimer, £1.95
A valuable addition to the library of notable screen-plays, this stout paperback contains *Rome – Open City, Paisan* and *Germany – Year Zero.* Extreme care has been taken to achieve as great an accuracy as possible, the working scripts being no longer in existence and the available prints generally in poor condition. The text is clearly set out, and so arranged that the detailed and excellent technical data can be followed if required, but need not interfere with a straightforward reading of the scenario. The frame enlargement illustrations are as good as can be expected in the circumstances, and are intelligently chosen.

What?: Gerard Brach and Roman Polanski; Lorrimer, 75p
This is the scenario of Roman Polanski's latest film – a sort of surrealist-neo-Carrollian-Sex-in-Wonderland extravaganza. The script has been written up to make it more readily assimilable than the more technically detailed methods of presentation sometimes turn out to be. Several pages of stills are included, but – surprisingly – no cast or credit lists.

Jesus Christ Superstar: Dir. Norman Jewison; Fountain Press, £1.25
About one hundred large-size stills, mainly in colour, from the film, with relevant quotes from the dialogue, an interesting production note, cast and credits. A handsome, if rather pricey, souvenir book.

REFERENCE

Screen World, 1973: John Willis; Muller, £4.20
This attractive and perennially useful reference book continues into its twenty-fourth year with all its usual features intact – hundreds of stills, portrait photographs of "promising new actors" (interesting and somewhat chastening to glance through back numbers of this section and note how many of the promises have been, and have not been, fulfilled), and of those actors and actresses whom we shall, alas, see no more: very full cast lists, awards, brief biographical details, massive index. A straightforward factual record that is equally useful for study and reminiscence.

The British Film Catalogue: Denis Gifford; David & Charles, £18.50
Gargantuan labour of love, listing casts, main credits and other details (including a one-sentence synopsis) of every British entertainment film from 1874 to 1970. Invaluable – and presumably unbeatable – work of reference for anyone interested in its subject. A complete cross-index helps to make the researcher's task even easier, and the general lay-out – though inevitably somewhat cramped – is, in the circumstances, admirable. One note (No. 13225) – Patrick Hamilton's superb novel was entitled *Twenty Thousand Streets Under the Sky:* the film, incidentally, was such a dire travesty as to have no justifiable claim whatever to be derived from it.

International Film Guide 1974: ed. Peter Cowie; Tantivy/Barnes, £1.50
As indispensable as ever, this "Film Festival in Book Form" again retains all its high standards and low cost. It is mainly, as usual, a survey of world cinema, country by country, together with articles on the five directors of the year (plus full filmographies) – on this occasion John Boorman, István Gaál, John Huston, James Ivory, and, perhaps a little surprisingly, Jean-Luc Godard. Ancillary sections range from book reviews to the Children's Film Foundation, and cover almost every aspect of film-making. There is a full index of films reviewed. The whole is a satisfyingly fat and full volume, crisply printed and illustrated, proudly

indicating the long hours of research and care for accuracy that must have gone to its compilation.

The New York Times Film Reviews 1913–1970, a One Volume Selection: George Amberg; Harper & Row, £6.90
The recent publication of the complete *New York Times* reviews in seven gargantuan volumes (nearly 19,000 films) was a massive boon to researchers and, indeed, to all engaged with, or in love with, the world of the cinema. To bring a portion of this vast collection from libraries and institutions into the home by selecting 400 entries into a single solidly-made book was an excellent idea. To bewail any particular omission (or inclusion) in such circumstances is irrelevant. The choice is catholic enough in any case, by no means confined to the "greats" and, while predominantly American, includes also British and foreign-language productions. If one had to carp, one might have wished for a larger proportion given to the earlier years, reviews of which are so much harder to come by.
From about 1931 full casts are given in addition to credits. The photocopying is in the main admirably clear – the earlier pages understandably coming off worst, but even here they are reasonably legible. In any case this is a book for reference rather than a solid read-through – hence its inclusion in this section, to which it is a meritorious addition.

Chaplin's Films: Uno Asplund; David & Charles, £4.25
This is to my knowledge the most complete reference book on Chaplin films available, and obviously a work of devoted care and research. There are synopses and notes, tables giving the date of the first night of each of the eighty-one films, with full details of length and running times and sections on costumes, types, "cavalcades" and competitors. The illustrated section is not over-generous, but includes a welcome selection of supporting players. The author also goes carefully into the misuse and manipulation of the early shorts. It is odd that so invaluable and badly needed a study should come (via a most readable translation by Paul Britten Austin) from Sweden – where several of Chaplin's films were banned for years as "brutalising" or "tasteless". Note for future editions: Peter Cotes is misspelt Coates on page 20; and Merna Kennedy as Lerna, twice, on page 141.

Movies on Television: Angela and Elkan Allan; Times Newspapers, £1.25
This first British comprehensive guide differs from its American counterparts particularly by including recent films that are not yet available for television (though some may well be by the time this review appears in print) thus keeping itself in advance of "up-to-dateness". It is written in so lively and witty a style that it can be read for pleasure as well as reference: one may disagree violently with some of the more outrageously personal verdicts, but how enjoyable it is to do so! Nearly 400 pages contain about ten films on each, which means a substantial number of titles – even

among the vast number available (some 20,000 say the authors) for showing. Each film is rated by ticks or crosses, and date, stars and directors are given.
One or two small points which will doubtless be corrected in future editions: *Soldier Blue* (apparently dismissed as "infamous") is referred to in Dilys Powell's appreciative Foreword, but I could not find it in the text; Warren Beatty was not in *They Shoot Horses, Don't They?* (illustrations section); *Blow Up* is not accorded any rating at all – doubtless a proof-reading slip.
There is a splendid attack, in the Foreword, on the infamous cutting to fit films into "slots"(!) between the commercials.

The American Movies: Ed. Paul Michael; Garland Books, dist. Idea Books, £5.00
Movie Greats: Ed. Paul Michael; Garland Books, dist. Idea Books, £4.00. The two books sold as a set, £7.50
These two large volumes were originally published in 1969 as one even larger volume, entitled *The American Movies Reference Book – The Sound Era*. The work was severely taken to task by the eagle-eyed American publication *Films in Review*, which devoted several pages to pointing out (*a*) errors of fact and (*b*) inconsistencies of choice. The present issue being, apparently, a straight reprint, all such "errors" and "inconsistencies" are reproduced. However, even a random glance through four or five other reference books, and taking merely half a dozen stars' birthdays, reveals differences throughout. The best advice would seem to be – when reading date data, be sceptical. As regards entry choice – while any encyclopedia must be somewhat arbitrary, it does seem odd, for instance, to include Michael Curtiz in the "Directors" section and omit Preston Sturges; or Henry Koster and omit Sidney Lumet. Credits and cast lists, however, are exceptionally full, and the hundreds of stills well chosen and well reproduced.

Hollywood at War: Ken D. Jones and Arthur F. McClure; Barnes, dist. Thomas Yoseloff, £5.75
Of this book's 320 pages, 293 are given to a filmography of World War II films, listing full cast, director, distributor and release date (1939–45), so that it is properly listed in the reference section despite an introductory essay of eleven large-size pages. The printing of the cast lists is pleasantly generous in size for a filmography and they form a useful record, though fuller technical credits would have been welcome. Basically this is a picture-reference book, and the illustrations are numerous, unhackneyed and well reproduced.

A Handbook of Canadian Film: Eleanor Beattie; Peter Martin Associates, dist. Tantivy, £1.25
A welcome handbook on a national cinema too little known in Britain, containing details of film-makers, writers, professional services, technicians, publications and other items. The extent of the Canadian cinema (French and English) revealed in this book may well

surprise many people: the publication whets the appetite for the films it lists.

The British Film and Television Year Book: Edited by Peter Noble; British and American Film Holdings, £6
Peter Noble's essential hardy annual, not out at the time of writing but due to appear before this edition of *Film Review*, is to be enlarged to include the Common Market in so far as it affects British co-productions. Details of studios, companies, etc., in Sweden, Norway, France, West Germany and elsewhere are to be listed, and some 600 extra biographies, mainly of European artistes, will be added to the main section of the book, together with numerous illustrations. In the same way, the yearly list of films, together with their review dates in the trade publication *CinemaTV*, will be more comprehensive. Overall, the 1974/5 edition is expected to have grown by about 100 pages; and to include a Foreword by Michael Caine.

Late Arrivals

The following titles were received while the *Film Review* was in proof stage, too late for insertion into the classified sections. I have put them together in this additional section, however, rather than hold up their appearance until next year's issue.

Truffaut: Don Allen; Secker & Warburg, £2.50 hardback, £1.30 paperback
In the Introduction to his book (No. 24 in the *Cinema One* series) the author states that "its success . . . depends largely on the extent to which I have succeeded in tempering the warmth of my admiration with the coolness of my critical judgments". It may be fairly said that he has achieved this success, for it is a disarmingly warm-hearted yet clear-sighted appraisal. Mr Allen has the happy knack of making a film which the reader has not seen almost as vivid as the rest, and defends his personal opinions with acumen. He is fairly harsh on *Fahrenheit 451*, particularly interesting on *La Mariée était en Noir*, rightly critical, in a brief note, of the disastrous *Une Belle Fille Comme Moi*, enthusiastic over the enchanting *La Nuit Américaine*. On occasions he sums up neatly in a phrase: on *Tirez sur le Pianiste*, "The essence is elusive; the effect is invigorating" – on Truffaut as a whole, "essentially a director of relationships". Good stills and detailed filmography help to make this a valuable addition to the series.

The Cinema of David Lean: Gerald Pratley; Tantivy/Barnes, £5.00
David Lean is not one of the most prolific directors – fifteen films in some twenty-eight years – but of those fifteen, three are world-famous epics on a vast scale, and among the rest are some of the best novel and play adaptations (Dickens, Coward, Brighouse) to be found in the cinema. Here, each film is provided with an exceptionally full cast and credits list, a note by Lean, and a lengthy comment by the author. In one or two cases there are also interesting technical details, and the whole is rounded off by a gallery of studio portraits of stars and supporting players from the films.
Mr Pratley is an enthusiast: not a word will we hear against his subject, and he sallies forth lance in hand to unseat any carping critic.
Some slips occur in the captions to the earlier stills: e.g. a confusion of wives and actresses in *Blithe Spirit*, and in *The Sound Barrier* (p. 104) Nigel Patrick is misnamed Trevor Howard – who does not appear in the cast list.
We may hope that this excellent study will encourage similar books on other important British directors, hitherto neglected, such as Reed, Asquith, Clayton, Richardson, Frend, Powell, *et al.*

Starring Miss Barbara Stanwyck: Ella Smith; Crown, dist. Nelson. £5.25
A handsome tribute to the career of one of Hollywood's (and later television's) most distinguished stars. I use the word "career" advisedly, for her personal life is barely touched upon. On the other hand, all her films (even the less memorable) are described in detail, with many quotes from those who worked with her – actors, directors, technicians. Miss Stanwyck's generosity and consideration for her fellow-workers, her professionalism and co-operation, are well-known and receive full acknowledgement from her colleagues.
All in all this is both a disarmingly warm-hearted portrait of a most likeable personality, and a valuable addition to the film history of the period, embellished with a profusion of beautifully reproduced stills and publicity portraits. There is a full filmography, together with a good index.

Starring Fred Astaire: Stanley Green and Burt Goldblatt; W. H. Allen, £7.50
Another "handsome tribute", lavishly and well illustrated with stills, frame enlargements and studio portraits. As might be expected, most of the 500 large pages are devoted to the films, but Astaire's early theatrical career is also very adequately covered, and of particular interest (because less easy to trace elsewhere) are the credit, cast and musical number lists of his "live" shows. The films themselves are treated in great detail, full reference sections being followed by accounts which are far more than conventional synopses. Critical comment, dialogue extracts, and much incidental information are included. The section on *The Story of Vernon and Irene Castle*, for instance, contrasts in detail the true story with the film's embellishments and alterations. Elsewhere may be found dozens of such small items as the fact that

Lover was the only Rodgers and Hart number ever sung by Astaire. Appendices include a list of radio and television appearances, a discography, a useful and well set out "Career at a Glance" and a good index. The whole is written with a lively and engaging style. It is difficult, all in all, to avoid that over-used vogue word "definitive" in connection with this excellent study.

Marilyn Monroe: David Robinson and John Kobal; Hamlyn, £2.50
The fascination of Marilyn Monroe seems indestructible; but if yet another book on her life and career is to be justified it must have something special to offer. In this case, without doubt, it is the illustrations – possibly the largest and most comprehensive collection of stills and publicity photographs on the star to be gathered between two covers. The succession of portraits forms a picture history of her life as revealing as the text, as the world-famous face develops from cover-girl to actress; as it matures, saddens, but never loses its magnetism. To emphasise the illustrations, however, is not to belittle the Introduction by David Robinson, skilfully concentrating into some fifteen pages the story of her legendary and ultimately pathetic – rather than tragic – life.

The Films of Dirk Bogarde: Margaret Hinxman and Susan d'Arcy; Literary Services and Production, £4.75
For some time Literary Services and Production have been distributing the generally admirable *The Films of . . .* series published by Citadel of America, several of which have been reviewed in these columns. With the present book they embark on a publishing project of their own, dealing in similar format mainly with British players. They have got off to an excellent start, the authors having compiled a volume equally pleasurable as nostalgia and useful as reference. Brief articles on Bogarde as actor, man and star are followed by cast list, synopsis and reviews for each of his films. Stills, well reproduced, are profuse and intelligently chosen, and there is a fascinating final section on the "changing face" of the actor. An introduction by Joseph Losey, who directed Bogarde in some of his most notable films, is also included. Peter Sellers, Laurence Olivier, the Burtons, Alec Guinness are among those listed for future volumes (with, from further afield, Sophia Loren): if these maintain the standard of the first issue the success of the venture should be assured.

W. C. Fields, by Himself: commentary by Ronald J. Fields; W. H. Allen, £3.95
Compulsive reading for all devotees. The great man's grandson has collected together, in a handsome volume of some 500 pages, a mass of hitherto unpublished material – letters, articles, revue sketches, film scenarios – built around a biographical framework. Some myths and legends have been demolished, but the personality revealed is just as fascinating: a man as

kindly as he was irascible, as generous as he was mean, as lovable as he was prickly, and – judging by some of his letters – surprisingly malleable and unselfish in his professional dealings. Not the least interesting point brought out is the extent to which his material depended on his style. The most hilarious pages, in fact, are those concerned with a real-life court case in which Fields was accused of cruelty to a canary – a wildly absurd episode hardly less grotesque than Beachcomber's Mr Cocklecarrot of beloved memory. The illustrations are many and marvellous. Highly recommended.

The Marx Brothers Scrapbook: Groucho Marx and Richard J. Anobile; W. H. Allen, £3.50
In all probability the majority of people will be attracted to this coffee-table-size volume by the photographs, which are plentiful, rare and fascinating. This is all to the good, for the text itself, mainly a series of interviews with Groucho, is of less interest. The sections on the other brothers and associates, in fact, come off much better. Those with Groucho himself make somewhat sad reading – random reminiscences, tediously foul-mouthed and occasionally surprisingly ungenerous. For reading, as opposed to looking, Joe Adamson's *Groucho, Harpo, Chico and Sometimes Zeppo* (reviewed above and also published, in Great Britain, by W. H. Allen) is infinitely more informative, witty and generally rewarding.

Violence in the Arts: John Fraser; Cambridge University Press, £2.50
There have been instances of so-called studies in cinematic violence that consisted mainly of stills selected apparently for their sensationalism, but with not very much in the way of significant text. Mr Fraser's serious, sometimes provocative and always gripping account neither has nor needs such pictorial props. It is a lively, scholarly and at times deeply disturbing enquiry into the nature, role and function of violence in our society and its reflection in the arts which that society produces. The cinema receives a large part of his attention: his knowledge of the thriller and horror film (and novel) is obviously wide and intimate. Particularly interesting to the filmgoer are his comparisons between *The Godfather* and *A Clockwork Orange*, and his remarks on James Bond, on Franju, on such movies as *Straw Dogs* and *A Man for all Seasons*. Mention should be made of the excellent way in which the many important notes are presented, special headings to each page of the section concerned making references unusually easy to locate in this compellingly readable book.

Bob Hope: Joe Morella, E. Z. Epstein and Eleanor Clark; W. H. Allen, £3.00
The indefatigable Morella/Epstein combination (aided by Eleanor Clark) has come up with another of their popular biographies – as before, lightly written but well researched and tailored to their subject. Wisely, after a brief personal section, each strand of Hope's various activities – radio, television, stage, etc. – is followed

through separately rather than integrated into a straightforward chronological life story. The slowness of Hope's start in each case may come as a surprise to many of his admirers. Cinema takes up about 90 of the 250 pages, and includes a filmography with cast, director and writer. The final section deals interestingly with his many performances to the troops. Stills and photographs are plentiful; and extracts from scripts, together with bad as well as good reviews, are included. A misuse of the word "disinterest" makes odd reading on page 113; and to describe Diana Dors' fall into a Hollywood swimming pool as "infamous" seems a little harsh!

Hollywood and After: Jerzy Toeplitz, trans. Boleslaw Sulik; Allen & Unwin, £4.50
Much the greater (and more interesting) part of this well-researched study deals with the "After", tracing the varying lines of post-Hollywood cinema from the decline of the star/tycoon system and the blockbuster, through the films of youth, protest, violence, sex and underground, towards the unknown but rapidly developing future. The author pulls few punches, demonstrating (in the section on politics) the futility of rebellion without a considered goal, and the sheer silliness and self-indulgence of much of the underground and associated activity. Particularly useful is a lucid summary of the confused scurryings under the looming threat of cassettes and cable television. Though the passage of time will naturally overtake speculations and expectations in these technical fields, an account such as is to be found in this book will retain its value and interest as a contemporary history of a uniquely exciting transitional period.

To Be Continued: Ken Weiss and Ed Goodgold; Crown, dist. Thomas Nelson, £5.25
The sound serials, of fond memory, have been receiving a reasonable coverage of late, but for the devotee there will always be room for so well illustrated and entertainingly written a picture book as the present piece of nostalgia: a book for reference rather than read-through. After an affectionate introduction there follow casts and synopses of a generous selection from 1929 to 1956, together with a final complete list of titles and a good index. The many stills are a major attraction.

This Is Where I Came In: T. E. B. Clarke; Michael Joseph, £3.50
Though the author's work in the cinema occupies only about one-third of his highly entertaining autobiography, it is essential reading for anyone interested in the Ealing of happy memory, or in British films as a whole. Mr Clarke wrote the original screenplays for, among others, *Hue and Cry*, *Passport to Pimlico*, *The Lavender Hill Mob* and *The Titfield Thunderbolt*, and he here delightfully recounts the origins of these classic comedies, together with the adventures and misadventures suffered in their screening. The book is stuffed full of good anecdotes. He describes with generous lack of bitterness the more

recent years, when changes of taste forced him to undertake adaptations of novels and stories rather than work on original ideas; but it is an unhappy reflection on the contemporary cinematic scene that so witty and ingenious a scriptwriter finds himself in such a position. The book deserves an index, but is otherwise thoroughly recommendable.

Six European Directors: Peter Harcourt; Penguin
   Books, 60p
It is to be hoped that no one, in his eagerness to get to a specific director, will skip the Introduction to this Pelican Original, for it is one of the best brief dissertations on the functions and problems of film criticism that I have come across: see (to take just one example) his pages on the three levels of appreciation; *incident, argument* and *imagery.* The six directors, Eisenstein, Renoir, Buñuel, Bergman, Fellini and Godard, are none of them new to discussion and analysis, but are here viewed in the light of their relationship to one another and to their cultural and personal backgrounds, in a style happily free from the pretentious and the turgid. Mr Harcourt is, perhaps, particularly good on Buñuel (thinking highly of *The Diary of a Chambermaid,* less so of *Belle de Jour*), and Fellini (perceptively linked with Berlioz and Cellini). On Godard's catastrophic decline he is regretfully but firmly frank. In all six cases the work of his subjects is illuminated by his fresh, generous but non-idolatrous approach, and even those filmgoers most familiar with the films will surely find their understanding and appreciation heightened by these excellent essays.

The Film Director as Superstar: Joseph Gelmis;
   Pelican, 75p
Underground Film: Parker Tyler; Pelican, 75p
Two useful reprints. In the first the author interviews sixteen directors of what might be called non-traditional class (Warhol, Cassavetes, Coppola, Penn, Jim McBride) on their methods of work and opinions generally. He has a happy aptitude for drawing his subjects out with lively and, one may feel, sometimes unconsciously revealing results. The book originally came out in 1970.
In a new preface to the paperback edition of his often sharply "critical history" of the underground film Parker Tyler defends his approach against attacks in earlier reviews with spirit and some validity – only too often "studies" of "fringes" turn out to be indiscriminate, sometimes rather desperate, paeans. His book is obviously for devotees, but the range of films mentioned is wider than the title might suggest, including, for instance, *The Cabinet of Dr Caligari, L'Immortelle* and Clair's *Entr'acte.* A modest index would have been helpful.

Stardom: Alexander Walker; Penguin, 55p
Another reprint, this time under Penguin's own banner. Mr Walker's enquiry into the history and mystery of the star system from Florence Lawrence to Dustin Hoffman (first published by Michael Joseph in 1970) makes a most welcome appearance in attractive

paperback form. We are taken on a witty (see, for instance, the chapter headings), stimulating, nostalgic journey through one of the most fascinating areas of the fading Hollywood landscape, a journey conducted by a guide who knows his subject and also how to present it in easy, graphic style. Recommended for both the unemotional student and the sentimental old-films-on-TV fan.

Film Design: Ed. T. St John Marner; Tantivy/Barnes,
   in association with London Film School, £1.50
Though primarily a textbook for the student (as which, so far as a layman can judge, it appears admirable) there is a vast amount of information here to interest the ordinary filmgoer. A dozen well-known designers combine their experience and expertise to give information about their work in the studio and on location, including set dressing, model work, special effects, matching, rear and front projection, matte printing and even budgeting, apart from the basic arts of designing and building sets. Complicated processes are made clear even to the ignorant reader by copious illustrations and by diagrams of commendable clarity. Numerous practical examples are taken from well-known films, including the James Bond series, horror films, and titles such as *Fiddler on the Roof, A Clockwork Orange* and *2001, A Space Odyssey.* One small black mark: it is regrettable that, even in a technical work, it should have been thought fit to use such a horrible non-word as "perspectivise"!

Ivan Butler was born in Heswall, Cheshire, educated at St Edward's School, Oxford, and from there went to the Central School of Speech Training and Dramatic Art. He has spent many years in the professional theatre as actor, writer and director. He has had more than twenty plays professionally produced, and also writes for radio, television and on theatrical subjects, in addition to film criticism. He is a member of the Film Section of the Critics' Circle, and is on the Lecture Panel of the British Film Institute. His books on the cinema include: Horror in the Cinema; Religion in the Cinema; The Cinema of Roman Polanski; To Encourage the Art of the Film *(the story of the British Film Institute)*; The Making of Feature Films – a Guide; Cinema in Britain – An Illustrated Survey *and* The War Film. *Mr Butler is married, with one son, and lives in Northwood, Middlesex, England.*

Film, Television and Communication

A Survey by Ralph Stephenson

Art, among other things, is a form of communication. The performer through his art can hold the interest of others, touch their feelings, sway their minds, influence their lives. Much communication is utilitarian, but artistic communication can go beyond the utilitarian, conveying as an end in itself, laughter, excitement, a sense of beauty. In this article we discuss the modern media of film and television as artistic communication of this kind. Two characteristics of artistic communication important for our discussion, are first, that it is generally (despite audience involvement) one-way, from the artist to the audience; and secondly, that the audience is free – free to stay away, free to listen, to view, to walk out, to switch off.

Another characteristic is that artistic communication may be on any scale – it may involve no more than one other person, as in a fireside tale or a bedtime story, or it may include the whole world. Audience size is dependent on the artistic medium, and throughout history the range and power of the media have grown, so that they can reach more people, for a longer time, and with a fuller impact.

For millions of years artistic communication remained slow, uncertain and restricted. The artist could convey his message through statues, wall paintings (and before that, cave paintings), architecture (temples, palaces, pyramids) and the pots, tools and weapons of common use. People would travel hundreds of miles over hundreds of years to contemplate the more splendid of such works of art, and pilgrimages and crusades had a cultural aspect. Books (mainly sacred writings) were laboriously copied by hand and read from: there were not enough copies to go round, and in any case few people could read. In civilisations which – like the Polynesian – did not develop writing, history and legend were embodied in long sagas, committed to memory and passed from generation to generation as part of a priestly tradition. In Asian civilisations, in Greece and Rome, there was dancing, mime, the theatre, puppets. In all these cases the artist's audience was limited by the nature of the medium in which he could embody his work.

Then, in the middle of the fifteenth century, came the invention of printing. This, together with the spread of books (and the new attitudes of scientific curiosity and exploration which grew from them) was to transform the world. After which came the Renaissance, the Reformation, the development of world trade, and the Industrial Revolution. The rate and scale of change accelerated dramatically with each advance, and has gone on accelerating ever since.

As a development of art and communication, the great invention of the nineteenth century was the cinema. Starting as a curiosity, a toy for children, it combined with the new photography to grow into an elaborate art complex – the richest, most difficult art medium yet invented, amalgamating sound, colour, movement and light in an hitherto unknown way.

During the first half of the twentieth century, film, the new artistic medium, was developed and spread by many influences, the bulk of them commercial, with its possibilities and power only half understood. It was the new men in Russia who saw its potential most clearly, who built it up as a social force, and then by bureaucratic controls destroyed its free artistic expression. In the rest of the world the cinema was controlled by big business and became a great entertainment industry, centred for years in America. A mystique was built up of glittering, glamorous people, an artificial empire of fabulous fortunes, fabulous costs, fabulous box-office returns. The coming of sound gradually broke this empire up into national units, but to a large extent the cinema is still in the strait-jacket of this dream of luxury and riches. To some degree it distorts and falsifies the real, artistic, human values which the cinema, like any rich art, is capable of expressing.

Commercial cinema can be the apotheosis of ballyhoo. Costs of feature films and everything associated with them are often beyond reason or sanity. A megalomania more virulent than in other branches of big business seems to attack film functionaries. The machine in some way takes over, and because publicity organisations exist, because large-scale plant and capital are involved, the concept of creative artists working with their own thoughts, ideals and spirit (what in the long run makes art valid and worthwhile) is overlaid by a Frankenstein, robot-like creation, compounded of percentages, deals, rights and cut-backs, controlled by scores of "arrangers" – agents, accountants, salesmen, unionists and promoters. A vicious circle is formed by the fact that costs are enormous, therefore "the product" has to be sold to millions at the highest price, therefore original costs are virtually doubled by enormously expensive, world-wide sales promotion.

The film medium is capable of an infinite variety of forms, from the grandest canvas bringing us the sweep of history or vision of space, to the smallest gem – a ten-minute poem, for example, as is Hattum Hoving's *Sailing*. Yet because of the conditions of the cinema, the medium has remained a theatrical one predominantly favouring works of feature length. There have been novels if you like, but no essays, poetry, articles, discussion, criticism. Short films have flourished in the specialised fields of science and education, but have been largely disregarded as an art form. The treatment of news by the cinema is a disappointing story. It has been different, as we shall see, with television.

As a result perhaps of the big-business aspect of the cinema, it was for a long time not accepted as an art. One can see why. Leading artists of the modern age, having escaped from the patronage of the rich and noble, expected to enjoy respect and leisure and to present their works of art to the public individually and under the best conditions. They were not going to be subservient either to a business machine geared to maximising profits for profiteers, or to technical machines that needed manual skills. There was falsity in these attitudes, too. It is not enough for the artist to follow his spirit and inspiration in a lonely quest for truth. We recognise nowadays that the other face of spirituality and meditation is sociability and loving one's neighbour. The artist has to bring his talents to the group, to work with, to work among. He has to meet with human nature and merging with it may be part of his art. There are group and individual arts and one can be as valuable and important as the other.

Also he has to use the tools of his age. Concrete may be just as interesting a material for the sculptor as alabaster. A blow-torch may serve as well as a chisel. We need artists who are prepared to handle computers as well as paint-brushes. Thus the artist has to come to terms with the group-working and technical apparatus of the cinema.

One feels it is rather a different matter with what one may call the business machine, and here with due regard for management skills, one would like to set the artist free. As material prosperity increases and equipment improves, actual film-making costs can remain steady or even fall. A hundred improvements and advances are available – light-weight cameras, taped sound, faster film, faster lenses, more portable lights, reflectors and what have you. But the conventional costs grow steadily and to present a film *to the public* is a heavier financial undertaking than ever. At the same time, there do not seem to be any easy alternatives. Some form of co-operative? They have sprung up and died away like mushrooms. It is easy to talk about socialism and nationalisation, but they may merely mean substituting bureaucratic for commercial controls. Nevertheless we can take the ideal of *more* opportunities for *more* artists to reach *more* audiences, as a goal to be worked towards – whatever the means.

In the fifties an entirely new phenomenon began to develop – television. Although television uses the same material (film) and although cinema films can be shown on TV and vice versa, nevertheless television should be regarded as an entirely different medium. Its essence was to combine the two existing media of film and sound broadcasting into one. Television was able to create a film "in the air", a film that was everywhere, that only needed a receiver to pick it up. Now it was technically possible, wherever a TV camera could be set up, to take a picture with sound and relay it all over the world in seconds.

A picture? Endless multiple streams of pictures, twenty-four hours a day and five, ten, fifteen – a hundred and fifty channels. All to be had for the price of a TV set and the time to turn a knob. It was a revolution as important as that initiated by the Lumière brothers in 1895. Perhaps, as we have only begun to see the cinema clearly in the perspective of fifty years development, so it will not become clear how TV has affected society until we reach the turn of the century. But we can look at some of the implications, and if we do so, if we try to understand this new monster, perhaps we will have a better chance of guiding its development for the general benefit.

First, we seem to have reached the ultimate in artistic saturation. From being an occasional treat, art has become a continuous accompaniment to life. The development of cassettes may give us still more choice, but even at present one can say

64 that limitation of choice is as likely to be due to human agency (commercial influence, censorship, controls, priorities) as the result of technical limitations.

Television, because of its prolific nature, is more varied and diffuse than the cinema. Less centralised, it is more a local art.

In a way the cinema never did, it encourages the short subject, the topical discussion, the programme on current music or painting. Its news transmissions rival and sometimes outdo the newspapers. But it is still a capitalist art in the sense that the costs of reaching the public are maximal. Certainly there are more competing organisations, more opportunities for individuals to express themselves, than with the cinema. *La carrière ouverte aux talents* is more of a reality. But still – the controls are there. One TV critic complains, "the mechanics of presentation still take priority over the fundamental questions", and "the linkmen, the intermediaries, the interviewers . . . have become more peremptory, impatient, inflexible than their role requires". One keeps seeing the same faces on TV not only as interviewer but as interviewed. A magic circle seems to have formed – people are asked to appear on TV because they are well-known: people are well-known because they appear on TV. When we are supposed to be getting a cross-section of opinion (informed, impartial, liberal, whatever) perhaps we are getting only a series of "what's-my-liners" whose line is to appear on television.

Again, there is the content of programmes. Indignation is worked up about some questions, but are they the right questions, are they *all* the questions? Do we hear enough for instance, about the reasons for the power of big business, which is largely hidden, or the aggressiveness of trade unions which is all too evident?

Then there is the distancing of the performer from the audience. Communication in the modern media has become even more of a one-way business. As the audience grows, the stature of each individual in it is diminished, while the stature of the performer is magnified. At the same time the audience is more casual and less involved. In the old days of theatre there was always the possibility of booing from the gallery. With cinema one could ask for one's money back. But all we can do with TV is switch off. One-way communication has never been regarded as the ideal, and television tries to simulate public participation – by having an invited audience, by telephone questions, by engaging speakers with opposing views. No doubt these attempts are on the right lines – provided they are genuine. Perhaps the most successful of David Frost's programmes was one in which a protest group seized the microphone and tried to "take over" the studio. Of course there are headaches and difficulties in arranging anything impromptu or unscripted and no doubt there is temptation to stage events beforehand. Because the audience is so casual and remote, TV makes surveys to discover what people are watching, but one wonders if these "ratings" are as reliable a guide to preferences as say the cinema box-office, or whether they are as bogus as the political polls. Even if they are accurate, is this the goal? To make the maximum profit? Even apart from its enormous audience, television seems economically better situated than cinema, lying as it does between public utility and private entertainment. It is not tied to a particular film or programme, and can sell a generalised promise of entertainment. Another aspect is that being more localised and diversified than commercial cinema and yet tied down by large broadcasting centres, TV is both freer and less free than film. In social and political influence, it will be very much what controls and interference (or non-interference) allow it to become. Underground film is very much with us, but an underground TV station is unlikely to appear. But then there are video-cassettes.

The distancing of performers in film and television brings a greater degree of glamour. Film-stars are the stock example. D. H. Lawrence in *Film Passion* wrote:

> If all the females who so passionately loved
> the film face of Rudolf Valentino
> had had to take him for one night only, in
> the flesh,
> how they'd have hated him!
>
> Hated him just because he was a man
> and flesh of a man.
> For the luscious filmy imagination loathes
> the male substance
> with deadly loathing.
>
> All the women who adored the shadow of
> the man on the screen
> helped to kill him in the flesh.
> Such adoration pierces the loins and
> perishes the man
> worse then the evil eye.

There was a tendency to praise (or blame) film companies for the creation of stars, but they were able to establish them only because of the nature of modern media. The same phenomenon exists on television. Even on a small screen people are larger and glossier than life, jokes are better, opinions more worthwhile. The impact of TV is the greater in that it comes literally out of the air. A studio is nowhere: its locations everywhere. Its performers have absolute invulnerability. Like gods they could be speaking to us from the heavens – and perhaps one day, with a studio on the moon, they will. TV personalities who turn to politics start with an initial advantage, and for established politicians, TV appearances are of prime importance. Politics seems a sphere in which the widest possible participation under the most ordinary, everyday, extempore (and therefore least glamorous) conditions, should be the ideal of presentation. There is a case for super-saturation and the continuous televising of parliamentary proceedings on their own special channel.

An aspect of glamour is the tendency to "make everything entertainment". "When the whole world becomes a stage, the whole world becomes entertainment", says McLuhan in an interesting half truth. The untidiness and indignity of real life and the intractability of "things", are softened and dissolved on TV. In cooking programmes, small inconvenient kitchens, power-cuts, children, pets, bad-tempered husbands, early or late guests – are non-existent. In extreme cases, like *The Galloping Gourmet*, the whole thing becomes a comedy interlude with little relevance to real-life cooking.

At the same time the pain and tragedy of real life may be dramatised and intensified. Television has brought the world together with an immediacy and vividness that demands sympathy for problems which were once comfortably distant. We can face killing a Chinaman 20,000 miles distant by pressing a button. But can we face seeing him tortured before our eyes? A century ago a great statesman said that America could not endure permanently half-slave and half-free. Today we may ask whether the world can continue half at peace half at war or half-rich and half-poor. Sympathy is an inborn human trait, and the pain of watching the atrocities of Vietnam or the misery and starvation of the still-remaining famine areas, is a new social factor in world politics. Goodwill towards men is not new, but television is capable of giving it an expanded, global significance.

Both film and TV are unique for exposition or explanation with their combination of words and images, expert comment, charts, moving diagrams, live examples. In this field TV has been more active than cinema. It is difficult to see how understanding and knowledge can fail to grow as a result of programmes on economics, politics, sociology, natural history, anthropology, painting, architecture and a host of other subjects. TV coverage of the last election made it plain that total votes did not correspond with seats in Parliament and raised the question of electoral reform. An article or newspaper report would not have had the same dramatic impact.

Television has enlarged our breadth of interests while at the same time competing with their pursuit. It may introduce us to chess, fishing or rugby football, but an endless stream of ready-made entertainment may reduce active participation in sports, pastimes and hobbies. Allied to this "not-doing-but-watching" aspect of television is what has been called "the self-reflecting nature of the media". The programme itself may become the subject of concern instead of what the programme is about. For instance what matters in sex (as in life) is what people do and feel. The effect of some discussions is to shift the emphasis from freedom of action to freedom to talk about the subject.

Our monster then shows us many faces, some good, some bad and some potentially either. What is desirable for the best development, the best art? First there should be the widest possible access to the means of expression. Ideally we should *all* be able to appear on the box if we have something to say and can give it utterance. The more stations, the more programmes, the more performers, the better. A development that could enrich television is the marketing of video-cassettes. In this field the maximum of competition from all over the world should be encouraged; the manufacture and sale prevented from falling into the hands of a few. One would wish it as varied and lively as book publishing or the present market in discs, and perhaps there should be cassettes in public libraries. Then programmes should be subject to the minimum of controls – bureaucratic, sectional, racial, political. The British system of a balance between public corporation and commercial enterprise (with control of advertising) seems a reasonable one. To ensure competition, stations and channels should be expanded to the limit the traffic will bear. Educational and charitable foundations should be prompted to enter the field, local interests encouraged.

As a balance to this proliferation and a guide to the reeling viewer, a strong, vigorous,

66   independent body of critics is of the greatest
importance. All human activity thrives, or
should thrive, on criticism, and the arts are
no exception. The bigger and more pervasive
the media, the more important the function
of the critic. The condition of liberty is
eternal vigilance, and honest personal
opinion (which with much viewing becomes
informed opinion) is our most important
guarantee of liberty, quality and eternity in
the arts.

Self-criticism is difficult and the value of the
different media as critics of one another
should be recognised. We all depend on
press coverage and criticism of movies and
TV. Occasional TV programmes on the press
are for their part welcome. Television has
done something to bring historical aspects of
the cinema into perspective. A recent TV
programme commented fairly if critically on
the "Oscars" of the British Film Academy
(to use its old title). For a similar treatment
of TV's own awards one would have to look
to the daily or weekly press.

Finally an informed and critical viewing
public is the best safeguard of all. No doubt
it is best to plan one's viewing, and casual
switching on is unlikely to give the same
enjoyment. But even with the latter there
will be the occasional unexpected programme
to absorb and delight us. Like any art or
entertainment the more one brings to
television the more one is likely to take away.
The cultivation of a critical approach, in-
depth analysis and discussion about viewing
– all are good. In the end we will get the
television we deserve.

NO STAMP OF APPROVAL

by Oswell Blakeston

There have been postage-stamps in England to commemorate artists, athletes, scientists and even politicians; but a stamp expert was most indignant when I enquired if there had ever been any stamps in this country to commemorate our film-stars. "Nothing like that," he snapped energetically.

Why not? Surely our stars are among our public heroes? Perhaps some of them would look a little out of place on dignified stamps of Her Majesty's Government; but what could be more decorous, and rewarding for all film and theatre lovers, than, say, an issue devoted to Sir Laurence Olivier? Why should authority behave as if the cinema was still a rather dubious backstairs entertainment? British film-lovers should boil with frustration; and I started to ask around to find out how stars have fared in other countries.

Well, Monaco has frequently honoured Grace Kelly with her portrait on a stamp. Yet perhaps that isn't as encouraging as it might be were the lady not a Princess as well as a star. In the Argentine, too, they've paid tribute on stamps to Eva Peron. Again I think this only just counts as the lady was married to the President as well as being a film actress.

And this – this tiny this – was as far as I could get with the stamp collectors I know. However, our National Postal Museum came up with the information that there have been stamps on Will Rogers and Walt Disney in the States. A leading stamp magazine obliged with the dates: Will Rogers, issued on the 4th of November, 1948; and Walt

68 Disney, on the 11th of September, 1968. But otherwise all museums and magazines could suggest was that I paid a fee and joined a stamp club which specialises in thematic collection. But I'd already made so many enquiries by this time – yes, I didn't forget our separate Museum of Postal History – I couldn't believe club members would be able to tell me anything more about stamps and the cinema, although they probably could give me sheets of information about stamps and turnips. (Ha! yes, I know the French did one of those, the French, as gourmets, really appreciating the turnip.) So it's disgraceful neglect, isn't it? How dare authority deem footballers worthy of stamps and think film-stars are infra bloody dig? I got worked up about this; and then the thought came to me – has the cinema got an official patron saint? I mean, irrespective of one's feelings about religion, it's another slight if the cinema hasn't got a saint. There seem to be saints for everything else, for people who've lost their purses or their way or who are dying at sea. It's recognition of the cinema that's our pride; and the answer Pride gets is that officially there's no saint to spare for the cinema.

An important religious newspaper suggested to me that one might care to think of St Genesius as a friend of strolling players; and that St Gabriel might conceivably be claimed as a champion for TV workers dealing with communications; but films had absolutely been cold-shouldered by the cardinals who deal with such matters in the Sacred Congregation of Rites.

Then I heard of a religious community which supports a pious cult of St John Bosco as the patron saint of the cinema. I went to see the father superior of the order, and he told me about St John Bosco.

He was the son of a poor Italian farmer. He became a priest, and then sought out sinners in the underworld. On such dangerous missions he was protected by a fierce and terrifying dog which appeared mysteriously at opportune moments.

I'm afraid I didn't take very kindly to the story. Did the Holy Father think the cinema was part of the underworld? or that the son of an Italian farmer, born in Piedmont in 1813, was the most suitable candidate to feel well disposed to modern film luminaries? "Ah," he said, "you see John Bosco himself wrote plays to further reform in the educational system; and he also made good use of the magic lantern for instructing young members of his flock. So there you are."

But I wasn't. I regret I found educational playlets and a magic lantern in Sunday School rather dim; and I hope a savage dog doesn't nip me in the night for saying so now. I feel, however, impelled to pass on the story because it emphasises another snub for the cinema, another proof that still many people in high places don't take the cinema seriously.

It's hard for us to believe, and hard for us to bear, isn't it. So what's wrong?

My friend, C. H. B. Williamson, who's worked since 1928 for the most weighty film trade paper in this country, thinks prejudice lingers because methods of film promotion have not kept up with progress. Today we have marvellously sophisticated and intelligent films, but propagandists continue to advertise them with the old clichés which belong to untalented barkers at third-rate circuses.

"Stupendous!" "The Film Of The Year!" "Magnificent!" the propagandists trumpet about any mediocre production, and they make the whole film world seem juvenile. You can't devalue words in this way and keep the respect of people who hold standards. It's the promotion men who are keeping the cinema image that of the raree show in certain influential eyes. They are blocking the accolade of stamps and saints; and they'll need a pretty good patron saint of their own to save them from the damnation to which those, who believe that the art of the film should be honoured, would cheerfully assign them.

FILM CRITICISM

Alexander Walker, the film "Critic of the Year" for 1973–4 talks to **John Mountjoy** about his job and his ideas.

Alexander Walker of the London *Evening Standard* recently "knighted" Critic of the Year by the I.P.C., the giant publishing corporation, says he enjoys current pictures more than he used to in say, 1960, because they are now much more interesting. In those years, pictures were primarily concerned with entertaining patrons. Only a few recognised the real-life existence of a society with problems. Nowadays, every other one says something about a sick world. To the point when, he says, he sometimes shouts "Show me a picture to review. Not a social phenomenon."

Nevertheless, although he foresees a decreasing number of picture houses, he insists that film-making and film-makers will not only survive but increase. The pattern of today's life is centred, and centred securely, round and in the home. Partly because of the violent society in which we live: partly, inflation! Some moviegoers now have no option; they *must* stay at home.

In any case, family fun is no longer in the local cinema. It stays put in the front parlour. Which doesn't mean that the big cities will lose all their "grand" Gaumonts or Odeons. The first-run houses will stay. But to recapture their lost audiences the big screen producers will have to work with or for Television, the Cinema's successor. They will assuredly never return to the cinemas although, through TV, they might return to Cinema.

70 "What are your Walker standards, your yardsticks from which you like or dislike a film?"

"The first standard is to be read no matter what conclusions I've come to. If readers don't read it, then I haven't written it. Criticism is partly communication – a true fact often forgotten. It is also a matter of technique. A critic must hold his reader's attention. No matter how brilliant his insight, if he bores readers then he, like the flop film producer, has also lost his public. In other words, he needn't have bothered.

"I have never been able to say specifically what I look for in films because I see each film as a particular problem case on its own, that is to say, how can I recreate the pleasure or antipathy I have ciné-experienced when I write my column in a different setting? William Wordsworth said that poetry is emotion recollected in tranquillity. I hope that film criticism is emotion recollected in tranquillity. It isn't always that in my office."

Does he read the synopsis story before the film begins? If it is a subject-plot he dislikes, doesn't that prejudice him?

Walker laughed. "Never, never. I look only to see the showing time. I never read the book or play from which it is adapted. I foresee that one of my possible epitaphs might be 'How long does it last?' the first and only question I ask when I attend the press show."

Our Mr Walker has a W. C. Fields sense of humour!

And on many occasions (*Mahler* is an example) he seems in his reviews merciless, heartless, humourless. He tears the celluloid to shreds.

With what justification? He thought; then,

"A very, very bad film. Such *are* made – to the industry's disadvantage. Over-publicised, over-sold. Possibly too high a value and price put on it by its maker or its distributor. There is always a certain reaction to the conditions and climate in which a film is projected. Principally, it is the ingredient in the film which is either obnoxious or distasteful or working against the film by, say, the egotistical desire of the director."

Which makes his choice of the best actor of the year doubly interesting – Marlon Brando in *The Last Tango in Paris*.

And why? His reasons show the Walker mind in large-screen Technicolor:

"He gives a performance of wonderful physicality. But not only that. It is the performance of an actor who is able to integrate some of the roles he has played in films into his particular "Tango" part. If you recall the soliloquies he engages in with Maria Schneider you realise that he is not talking about the imaginary childhood of an imaginary character but he is recapitulating roles he's already acted. He plucks from his painful Hollywood experience the kind of autobiography he encapsulates into his particular part. He is truly remarkable.

"Claire Bloom is my female choice – for her sheer precision of technique in *A Doll's House*."

Alexander Walker's fourth book, *Hollywood, England* now published, argues that the British Film Industry did its best work whenever it had not only American backing but also American know-how and enthusiasm. This and his previous three books prove how seriously he takes the film medium to which he is professionally committed in Radio and TV as well as in the Press.

RELEASES OF THE YEAR IN PICTURES

(You will find more detailed information about the films illustrated in a later section of this volume—The Year's Releases in detail)

One of the most beautifully wrought thriller films of the year was Fred Zinnemann's smooth, unhurried, but always tremendously tense and atmospheric adaptation of the Frederick Forsyth best-selling book *The Day of the Jackal*, the story of a brilliantly planned, coldly ruthless attempt on the life of General de Gaulle in the early 1960s. In the key role of the hired professional assassin, Edward Fox gave an outstanding performance. (A CIC release.)

In another world altogether, that of the arrogantly but amusingly incredible, was the new James Bond opus from Harry Saltzman and Albert R. Broccoli, *Live and Let Die*, in which a new 007 was introduced in the person of ex-"Saint" Roger Moore. He is called upon in this United Artists release to smash a Black Power organisation out to get world domination through dope! (Inset: though less gimmicky than some of the Bond movies, there were some amusing espionage "aids", including this man-carrying delta-wing kite.)

Michael Winner's UA film *Scorpio* was an international espionage thriller in which Burt Lancaster (right), as a suspected American agent condemned to be liquidated by his bosses, is offered asylum by his Russian opposite number Paul Scofield (left) as he is pursued by his selected assassin, ex-workmate and pal Alain Delon (above).

For Universal's *Charley Varrick* Walter Matthau switched from his usual line of comedy to adding only slight and occasional comic touches to his dramatic role of a part-time crook who, after a disastrous bank raid, finds himself well and truly in the criminal big-time with a vast Mafia bank-roll on his hands and the knowledge that, a marked man, he now has only his wits to save him from a most unpleasant end! All the thrills were beautifully controlled by old-timer Don Siegel. With Matthau, his young companion in crime, newcomer Andy Robinson.

Updated and otherwise somewhat controversially changed (and likely to affront at least some of novelist Raymond Chandler's more devoted fans) UA's *The Long Goodbye* was based on one of his famous "private eye" Philip Marlowe detective cases, with Elliott Gould presenting an odd portrait of Marlowe, making him a kind of male slut!

74

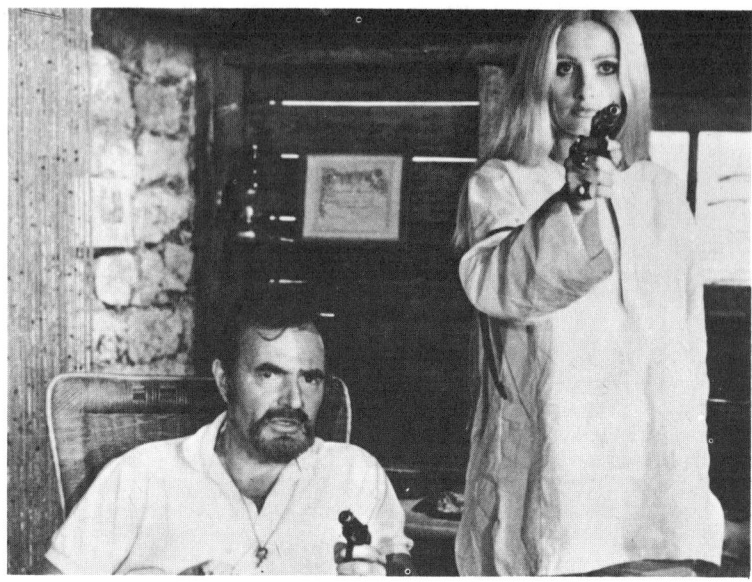

Paul Newman looking a little shocked as he is made to realise that the female (Dominique Sanda) is still deadlier than the male: in the pay-off scene in Warners' rather confusing though slick and finely (John Huston) directed espionage thriller *The Mackintosh Man*.

Another deadly female (Jill Ireland) in the MGM–EMI release *Cold Sweat*, a complicated and not always too easy to follow crime thriller set against French Riviera backgrounds. James Mason, the other gunholder in this scene, played one of the parcel of crooks double-crossing each other as they attempt to get a fortune-making cargo of drugs ashore from their ship.

None of the so-called *Friends of Eddie Coyle* do much to save him when the chips are down. He is put on the death list of his gangster bosses because he becomes suspected of leaking vital information to the cops in order to escape an illegal liquor rap. A grey, sad-looking Robert Mitchum played Eddie, the ageing, worried racketeer fringe man in this Peter Yates-directed, CIC-released crime thriller.

Cop James Booth feels he is on to something in Scotia–Barber's routine whodunit *Penny Gold*, in which the background to all the evil was the rare stamp business. Mr Booth's quizzical companion is Nicky Henson.

Robert Duvall commandeers a bus to pursue the crook's getaway car in a hectic and funny chase through New York, one of the best sequences in CIC's *Badge 373*, a violent, exciting crime thriller based on some of the true facts of the life of tough, ruthless cop Eddie Egan and his fight against the dope-runners.

A note of real mystery sustained MGM's *Slither* – until the final routine explanation! The story concerned a search for an embezzled fortune hidden somewhere along the Californian coastline, a search carried out by a quartet who are always shadowed by two mysterious black vans . . .! Involved in this particular struggle: Sally Kellerman, James Caan and Louise Lasser.

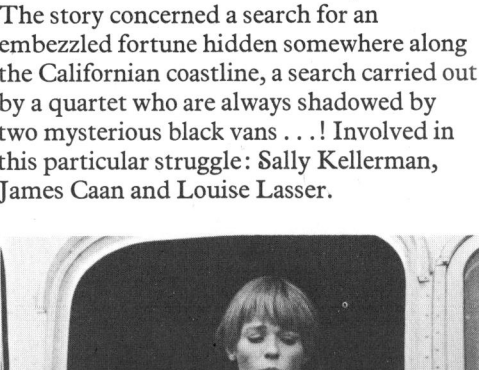

A crime thriller of a much lighter mould, the appeal of which was aimed largely at junior moviegoers, was Disney's *Diamonds on Wheels*, in which a big diamond robbery becomes mixed up with a car rally when the crooks think their loot has been hidden in one of the competing cars.

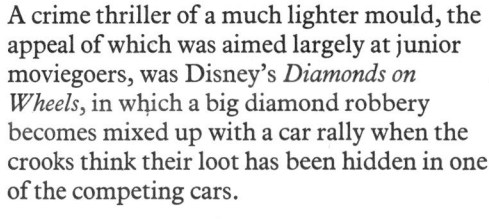

76

A neat but, alas, not outstandingly successful switch was attempted in Warners' *Cleopatra Jones*, in which Negress Tamara Dobson (shown dealing effectively with crook Bill McKinney) played a sort of black, female James Bond, out to smash a dope ring (led, by the way, by a white villainess).

In the small flood of black-slanted films from American producers, now realising the potential of the coloured market, Fox's *Trouble Man* was a straightforward, violent gangster piece in which the fact that bad or good characters were nearly all black was purely incidental and played no vital part in the routine story. Mr T was played by Robert Hooks, shown killing the crime boss in his lavish penthouse flat.

Line-up of suspects sampling James Coburn's (top of table) champagne include James Mason (almost hidden, left), Joan Hackett, Richard Benjamin, Raquel Welch and Ian McShane – all thought by their host as being possibly implicated in the killing of his wife, in the Columbia–Warner whodunit, *The Last of Sheila*. Set considerably on and around a yacht along the French Riviera coast, the film offered a complicated, but on balance, fairly presented murder mystery for the moviegoers to solve.

Back to the Mafia and gang warfare – *circa* 1967 – in Fox's *Honour Thy Father*, one of the many similar, fairly minor thrillers which followed in the fortune-making footsteps of *The Godfather*. This one, made in New York, had Raf Vallone (centre) as one of the stars.

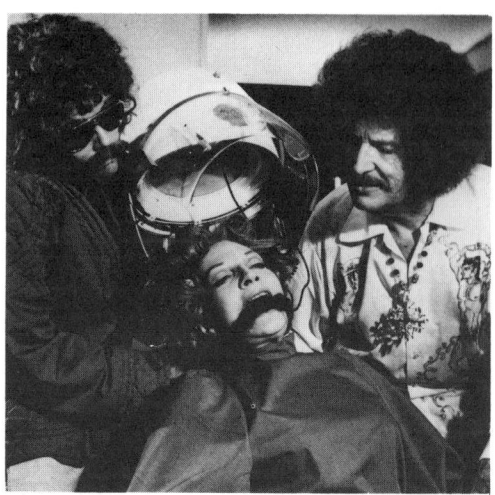

A little difficult, maybe, to recognise
Diana Rigg in the wig, dark glasses
and moustache; nor easy, possibly, to
recognise Vincent Price (playing her father)
with that fizzy thatch; easier though to
recognise their gagged victim, Coral Browne,
in the often gory thriller – with lighter
moments – about a mad actor's revenge on
his critics in UA's *Theatre of Blood*.

Julie Christie and Donald Sutherland played
the wife and husband who become the centre
of some very mysterious happenings in
Venice which follow the tragic death of their
small daughter in an English stream in
Nicolas Roeg's stylish (but some might say
a little confusing) production of the Daphne
du Maurier story *Don't Look Now*, released
by British Lion. A brilliant ingredient in the
spooky events was the director's superb
capture of the feel and the atmosphere of the
wintry Venice backgrounds.

Polished horror was the keynote of Fox-
Rank's *The Legend of Hell House*, an account
of an investigation carried out by a physicist
and a team of mediums into the strange and
eerie happenings at the big Belasco Mansion,
happenings which understandably cause the
horror expressed here by investigators Roddy
McDowall and Gayle Hunnicutt.

A very practical explanation was finally offered for the mysterious apparitions that occur in Avco–Embassy's thriller *Night Watch* which, after building up considerable tension, ended with a twist offering a really big surprise. Elizabeth Taylor (left) gave a big performance as the wronged wife of the cad (the late Laurence Harvey) who is planning to go off with her best friend (Billie Whitelaw) centre.

Great stuff for spine-shudder addicts, Cinerama's *Vault of Horror* was a follow-up to *Tales from the Crypt*, with which it shared the format of a collection of characters being cooped up together and telling their separate stories of nightmares . . . or real experiences . . . or what? One of the best of the five episodes was that shared by sister Anna and brother Daniel Massey, called "Midnight Mass" and concerning his ruthless effort to steal her inheritance.

Fifth in the "Ape" films, Fox's *The Battle for the Planet of the Apes* gave an impression that the series was beginning to get a little tired! Anyway, this latest chapter in the simian saga was concerned with the efforts of the revolting (!) apes to get down to some sort of peaceful co-existence with their former human bosses.

Fun-fantasy was the keynote for Disney's *The World's Greatest Athlete*, a family comedy about a young Tarzan-type, found in the African wilds who, brought back to America by a college coach, wins every sporting event on the board with ridiculous ease. Tim Conway played the phenomenon.

80

Intrigued, star Jon Finch takes a look at some of the scientific marvels of the future in EMI's often amusing (if not *always* intentionally so) fascinatingly visual but otherwise dubious farrago about the creation of a new computerised Messiah in *The Final Programme.*

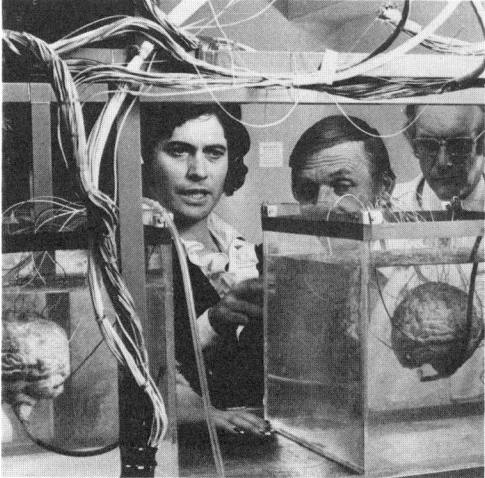

A thriller fantasy of unusual kind was MGM–EMI's rather gloomy look into the future, *Soylent Green,* set in a period when an over-populated, excessively polluted world turns to scientific cannibalism when all other food has run out! Shown is the way that the authorities salutorily sort out demonstrators in 2022! (Inset: star Charlton Heston with the late Edward G. Robinson, who made his last screen appearance in this movie.)

First-rate cinematic hokum was provided by Fox–Rank's release *The Neptune Factor – An Undersea Odyssey* which, though generally undervalued by the critics, was a well-produced, conventional thriller which did keep up for long periods a feeling of tension as it told its story about the efforts to rescue the crew of a small submarine which has been the victim of an underseas earthquake (thus foretelling a news story of some months later). Those involved in the rescue operation included Ernest Borgnine, Yvette Mimieux (an unlikely but certainly lovely underseas exploration expert) and Ben Gazzara.

In the cinema it certainly never rains but it pours and it was a little ironical that two films of Ibsen's classic drama *A Doll's House* should be made and released more or less simultaneously! In Joseph Losey's version, shown here, there were some fine performances, including one from Trevor Howard (centre) as the old Doctor; but some strange casting, such as Jane Fonda in the star role of Nora, weakened the film's impact. Also shown, David Warner and Delphine Seyrig (right).

82

All sugar and spice was MGM's *The Great Waltz*, a musical based on the lives of some of the famous Strauss family. Beautifully sung and played, the script failed to keep up to the top standard of the film's visual assets. Horst Bucholz played Johann Strauss junior, Mary Costa was the lovely singer playing opera star Jenny Treffz.

Peter O'Toole as the tilter of windmills and James Coco as his chubby follower in UA's *Man of La Mancha*, based on the stage musical which in turn was based on the classic story of that brave, mad old knight Don Quixote. But even O'Toole's delicious performance couldn't bring great success to the film.

An Oscar nomination for her first film role was the achievement of the ex-Supremes (pop group) member Diana Ross in CIC's musical story of Billie Holiday, *Lady Sings the Blues*, which followed Billie's triumphant success as a singer and her tragic defeat and death by drugs.

A quiet picnic for Peter Finch and Liv Ullmann in Columbia's re-make as a musical of James Hilton's classic *Lost Horizon* (originally made by Frank Capra with Ronald Colman in 1937), with Peter as Conway, the discoverer of a lost Utopian world hidden in the high Andes.

The remarkable story of *Jesus Christ, Superstar* was that it began life as a L.P. disc, was made into a fantastically successful stage musical (on both sides of the Atlantic) and was then made by Universal into a stunningly beautiful film. Based on the last days of Christ, it was simplified, vulgarised and remarkably entertaining: moving too, in the final phrase. Ted Neeley played Christ.

If ever a film lived up to its title it was Melvin Frank's *A Touch of Class*, a polished, sophisticated comedy about the romance of a typical American male on the make – in London – and the cool English divorcée he finds easy to seduce and then, too easy to fall deeply in love with! It was superbly acted by the two stars, Glenda Jackson and George Segal.

John Braine's *Room at the Top* anti-hero Joe Lampton returned in Hammer's adaptation of the TV series *Man at the Top* with Kenneth Haigh as the ever-pushing, ruthlessly ambitious Joe – here going a-hunting in the company of Nanette Newman.

The human triangle in the Hemdale production of the Graham Greene novel *England Made Me* – German tycoon Peter Finch, mistress–secretary Hildegarde Neil, and her idle young brother Michael York. And they play out the relationship to its bitter end against a background of a Germany which in 1935 was rapidly becoming more and more Nazified. (Inset: Michael Horden, left, as the seedy but dedicated journalist, emerged with the acting honours.)

Novelist Robert Bolt certainly did no penny-pinching in his first directing–producing assignment for MGM-EMI, *Lady Caroline Lamb*, in which his wife Sarah Miles starred in the title role, giving a rather strange performance as the wilful, silly wife of the future P.M. Lord Melbourne. (Inset: the scene where Lady Caroline, who tops her follies by an outrageous affair with the poet Lord Byron, played by Richard Chamberlain, plays his black slave at a fancy dress ball.)

One of the most delightful non-Disney cartoon features ever was the Scotia–Barber release (last Christmas) *Charlotte's Web*, a classic children's tale about the runt pig saved from death – in fact taken to fame and fortune – by the kindly advice of spider Charlotte.

86

Though *Millhouse* sounded like the name of a racehorse, it was in fact the title of a cruelly revealing documentary assembled by Emile de Antonio from extracts from various speeches given by President Nixon over the years.

Second feature film cartoon from the *Fritz the Cat* team, *Heavy Traffic* (released by Black Ink Films) was, like its predecessor, rude, vulgar and raucous – and extremely inventive as it told a story about an Italian gangster father, a Jewish momma and their naïve son.

Though on the thin side, MGM–EMI's comedy *Every Little Crook and Nanny* had its moments, enough one would have considered to get it a wider showing than it had! Amusing Lynn Redgrave played the British girl whose business is ruined by a Mafia boss (Victor Mature) and decides to get even with him by taking up the position of Nanny to his son and then carrying through a wild kidnap plot.

A sequel to the financially successful first Steptoe film was almost inevitable and it duly arrived from MGM–EMI as *Steptoe and Son Ride Again,* with Wilfrid Brambell and Harry H. Corbett carrying on their famous love–hate television feud as they buy a dud greyhound and end up with a horse and a half!

One sometimes wonders what would happen to the cinema if it were not for television and the theatre, from which so much material is taken for the routine movies. Among this year's many play adaptations was Columbia's film of the long-running stage comedy-farce *No Sex Please, We're British,* which was about some bank employees who become innocently involved with bulk pornography! One of the main farceurs was little Ronnie Corbett with (inset) Arthur Lowe and Beryl Reid in amusing support.

Probably intended as the first of a series, Hemdale's *Tiffany Jones* was heavy on glamour, a little light on fun, as it related Miss Jones's (Anouska Hempel, right) adventures when she's caught up in various farcical foreign political machinations, during which she constantly strips, or is stripped, down to the bare facts. Zirdanian ambassador looking a little, understandably, confused, is Eric Pohlmann.

Not in fact a scene from another "Carry On" comedy – but Sally Geeson spoiling Sid James's nap in the Rank release of *Bless This House*, a Peter Rogers film based on the popular television series with the same title.

A comedy on a less than comic theme: Fox's *The War Between Men and Women*, based on the writings of American humorist James Thurber; the story of a newspaper cartoonist who is going blind and, when he reluctantly marries his mistress, finds the problems of a ready-made family added to those of increasing difficulties in seeing. Jack Lemmon was quite magnificent in the role, with grand support from Barbara Harris as the wife.

Jack Lemmon gave another delightful performance in Billy Wilder's comedy *Avanti!*, playing an American businessman who, when he goes to Italy to sort out the affairs of his late father, finds all sorts of surprises, including Juliet Mills, playing the daughter of his father's also deceased mistress who stops at nothing in order to get her way and have the dead couple buried together in the land where they loved!

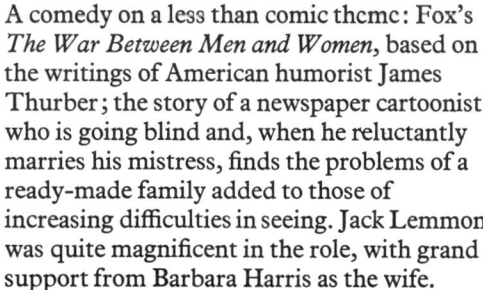

Even if Warners' *Class of '44* lacked some of the impact of *Summer of '42* it had many compensations as it continued the story of the three school-friends through University, early love affairs and the effects of the war to final maturity. A warm portrait of young America of that period, it offered a valid contribution to screen Americana. The friends, as before, were played by Gary Grimes (centre) Jerry Houser and Oliver Conant.

Fox's *The Other* (from the novel by Thomas Tryon) was based on the old theme of two identical twins, one good and the other . . . well, in this case little short of a public menace (here he is – Martin Udvarnoky – enjoying himself by scaring poor Portia Nelson out of her wits); and all very menacingly set against a background of a Connecticut small town during the summer of '35.

A little difficult to classify, Columbia's *Love and Pain and the Whole Damn Thing* can perhaps be best described as a tragi-comedy which though it contained some genuine comedy was at times almost painfully sad as it related the story of two inhibited, afflicted people – Maggie Smith (seen here with a "wolf" who is preparing to pick her up) and Timothy Bottoms – who meet on a foreign holiday tour and fall awkwardly in love. These two did their considerable best to lift the film on to a level it would otherwise never have been likely to reach.

90 This year we've had several Australian productions on view (the most yet) and though some of them were interesting none of them were ever likely to set the cinematic bush on fire! Fox–Rank's *Nickel Queen*, filmed on location in Perth and the adjacent mining territory, was worth noting as bringing Googie Withers back to the screen, playing the title-role, that of a saloon owner who becomes the innocent centre of a large-scale "con" plot. Direction was by Miss Withers' husband, John McCallum.

Another minor movie from "down under" was LMG's *Stork*, a somewhat dated piece about a young drop-out whose favourite pleasures are drinking beer, eating prawns and sounding-off on the subject of Revolution. The part was played by Bruce Spence. The chick is Madeline Orr.

Columbia's *The Adventures of Barry McKenzie* was based on the strip-cartoon Aussie character who comes to this country and is soon being fleeced and fooled by "the Pommy bastards!" It was all very coarse, occasionally revolting and only mildly funny. Barry Crocker played Barry.

For her performance as the bitter slut in Fox's oddly titled *The Effect of Gamma Rays on Man-in-the-Moon Marigolds*, Joanne Woodward won the 1973 Cannes Film Festival female acting award. Directed by her husband Paul Newman, she played the middle-aged widowed mother of two teenage daughters, one as bright as a penny whose experiments give the film its title (played brilliantly by Nell Potts) and the other less bright and very much the product of her disturbed home life. A highly individual effort, this again was a case of a superior film deserving of far greater exposure than it had.

Still with the Australian output, MGM–EMI's *Sunstruck* had a certain amount of charm, some good laughs, and British comedy star, Harry Secombe, playing a Welsh emigrant teacher in Australia's back-of-beyond who, after taming his pupils, knocks them into such musical shape that they win the big town choral prize. And Harry wins the homespun beauty Maggie Fitzgibbon.

Another of the year's most original, and highly critically acclaimed films was Lindsay Anderson's Warner release *O Lucky Man!* in which various facets of modern life were pilloried; such as police corruption, crooked politics, big-bent-business and, of course, finally man's general inhumanity to fellow man. And the movie highlighted a truly gifted performance by Malcolm McDowell, making a kind of inverted Pilgrim's Progress!

92

Rich in suggestions, with many themes taken up briefly and then abandoned, Stanley Kramer's *Oklahoma Crude* for Columbia was presented as "a love story with a difference", a claim in terms of life true, in terms of cinema false! Faye Dunaway played the determined woman owner of an oil well fighting the Organisation who are determined to take her over by fair means or foul, but finally failing to do so through the help she gets from a rough casual worker who becomes her employee and then her lover – George C. Scott. John Mills (centre) played her father.

Warner's *The Scarecrow* was a sad story of two men, both misfits in society, who team up as they dream of success but get side-tracked and smashed both by their temperaments and their loyalty to each other. Gene Hackman turned in a brilliant performance as the fiery ex-convict, with Al Pacino as his ex-seaman pal.

The spectacular Mississippi countryside, lovingly photographed in all its rich colours, was the background for UA's engaging adaptation of Mark Twain's classic story of boyhood, *Tom Sawyer*, in which Johnny Whitaker gave a very winning performance in the title-role. With him (left) watching the riverboat make its call at the local "landing", Mark's great pal Huckleberry Finn – played by Jeff East.

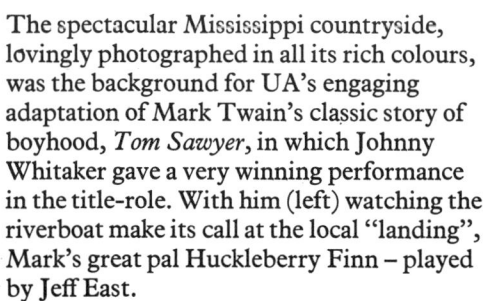

A quieter, romantic river interlude in UA's *White Lightning*, shared by Burt Reynolds and Jennifer Billingsley. Reynolds played the bootlegger whose aim in life is to revenge his brother, deliberately drowned in a mangrove swamp by the crooked sheriff. The violence was in this film's case lightened by the touches of humour injected into the story.

Jack Lemmon shares a bed with Patricia Smith in Paramount's *Save the Tiger*. He played a wealthy but restless American businessman who breaks the law in order to save his firm from going "broke", but is always aware that his action is partly motivated by his picture of himself as an old-time American hero-type.

Right out of the ordinary, always intriguing if not in the final analysis quite successful, was Columbia's *The King of Marvin Gardens*, a loosely constructed, otherwise untidy but magnificently atmosphered story of two brothers (Jack Nicholson, left, and Bruce Dern); one a failed and bitter writer, the other a gangster-employed small-time con man, and the two women whose presence leads to the sudden eruption of violence. All seen against a vividly pictured, wintry, windy Atlantic City.

94 Fox's *Emperor of the North*, though set against and giving some sort of idea of the Great American Depression of the thirties, was in fact the simple story of the – finally deadly – confrontation of two strong characters, the train guard (Ernest Borgnine) who boasts that no tramps ride his train and stay alive and the expert "bum" (Lee Marvin) whose boast is that there is no train he cannot "ride". And, suitably enough, the brutal, bloody climax of this rivalry takes place on a moving train.

A straightforward adaptation of the Neil Simon stage comedy, Paramount's *Last of the Red Hot Lovers* presented Alan Arkin as a man in his fifties who suddenly gets the sex itch and makes three funnily abortive efforts to seduce females lured to his mother's flat while she's away. In this episode it is Renée Taylor who is the sex object!

With a South African background, Scotia–Barber's *The Winners* was the story of a ruthlessly ambitious man who determines that all his sons shall excel in sporting and other activities, and the drama concerned the family's eventual rebellion.

Joseph Strick's *Janice* – from Contemporary – was a sordid but highly effective end even memorable story of a little trollop (Regina Baff) who is picked up by a couple of young truck driver-owners (Robert Drivas and Barry Bostwick) and lures them into crime and, finally, is instrumental in causing the death of one of them. An interesting addition to Americana.

Another look at the Great American Dream was in Fox's *The Last American Hero*, the story of a toughly independent young Stock Car driver (Jeff Bridges, posing with Valerie Perrine after winning a race) who refuses all financially attractive offers to join the Big Boys and is determined to fight his own way to the top of the business. And some pretty exciting drives he has, too!

Sad and sentimental and with undertones of *Love Story*, Sidney Poitier's Cinerama release *A Warm December* (which he directed and himself starred in), was the story of a hopeless love affair between Doctor Poitier, on holiday in London, and the Ambassador's daughter he meets (Esther Anderson) who, it is revealed, apart from her obligations to her country, is suffering from a fatal disease!

Big John was back, walking tall again in Warner's *Cahill*, familiar but good enough a Western to be consistently entertaining as Wayne played the fearless, honest Marshal so busy with bringing the lawbreakers to justice that he neglects his sons, so much indeed that behind his back they are lured into a plan to rob a bank!

96 Universal's *Showdown* was a minor but adequate Western rich in star value – Rock Hudson, Dean Martin and Susan Clark – telling a story about the reluctant confrontation of a Sheriff and his old pal, now turned outlaw train robber.

Richard Crenna as *The Man Called Noon* in the Scotia–Barber film of that title, the story of a man without a memory trying to track down his past, a quest in which he is, often violently, assisted by a rather mysterious character played by Stephen Boyd (left).

Gregory Peck, freed after a seven-year jail sentence for bank robbery and now living only to have revenge on the ex-partner who betrayed him, does his best to keep cool as bar girl Susan Tyrrell is abused by the three hoodlums – Robert F. Lyons, John Chandler and Pepe Serna – hired to track him in Universal's *Shoot Out*.

Sam Peckinpah's *Pat Garrett and Billy the Kid* for MGM retold once again on the screen the story of that infamous outlaw, presenting it as a mixture of fact and legend, but finally leaning heavily on the legend as it softened the portrait. Visually good, verbally less so: with Kris Kristofferson as the Kid (left), James Coburn as the lawman (right).

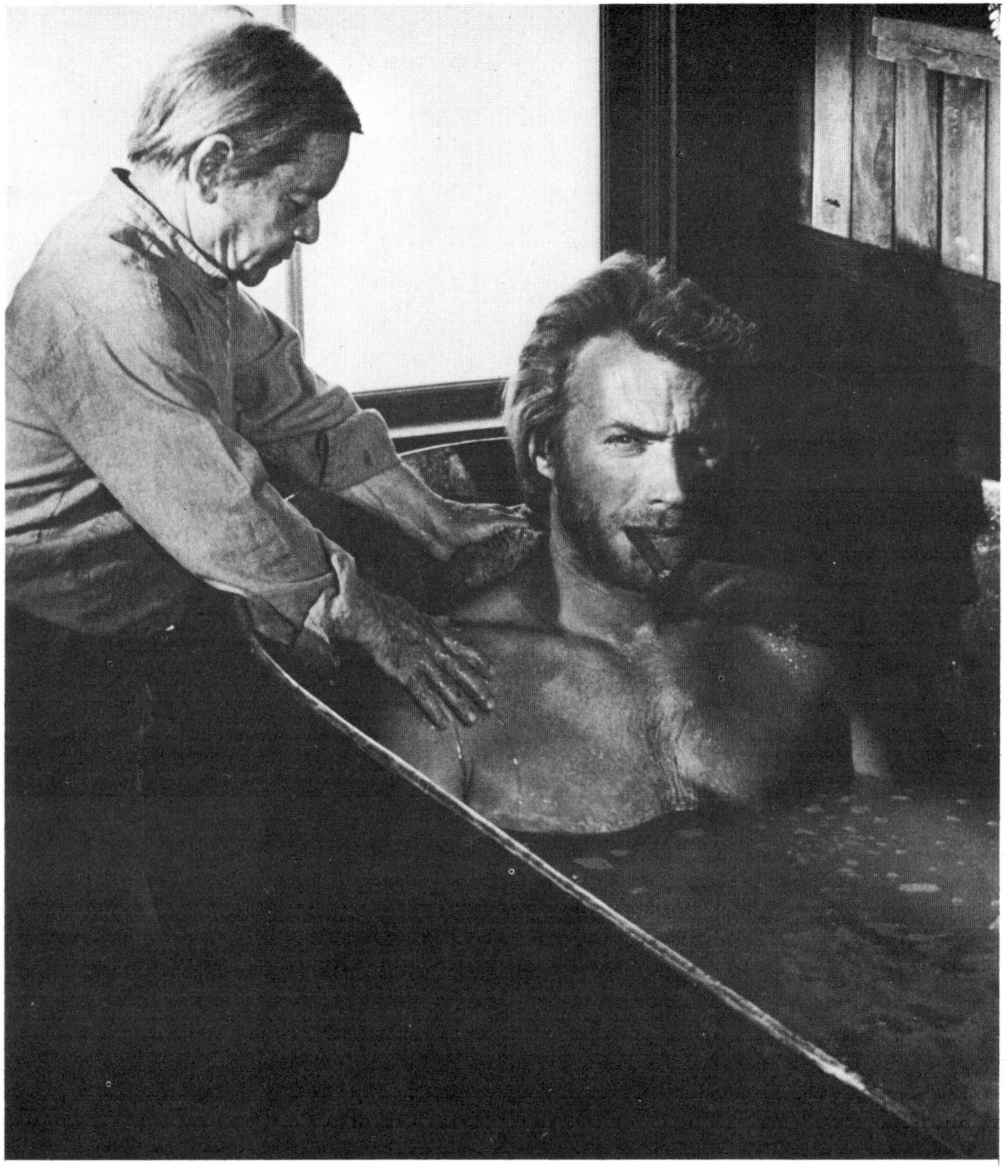

Cliff Robertson's Columbia film *J. W. Coop* –
for which as well as starring he wrote the
screenplay, both directed and produced,
and otherwise achieved a long-held
ambition – was highly acclaimed in some
critical quarters and it certainly had depth
and originality as it told the story of a rodeo
rider who after a ten-year enforced absence
from the circuit (because of a jail sentence)
determines to get back into the big-time.

Clint Eastwood was back in his "Man With
No Name" kind of role (now directing
himself though) in Universal's *High Plains
Drifter*, a sadistically inclined tale in which a
whip is used as a killing weapon against the
villains.

98

In the same league was *Mistress Pamela*, which was based on the old Samuel Richardson novel about Miss P's efforts to avoid being bedded until the marriage knot is well and truly tied.

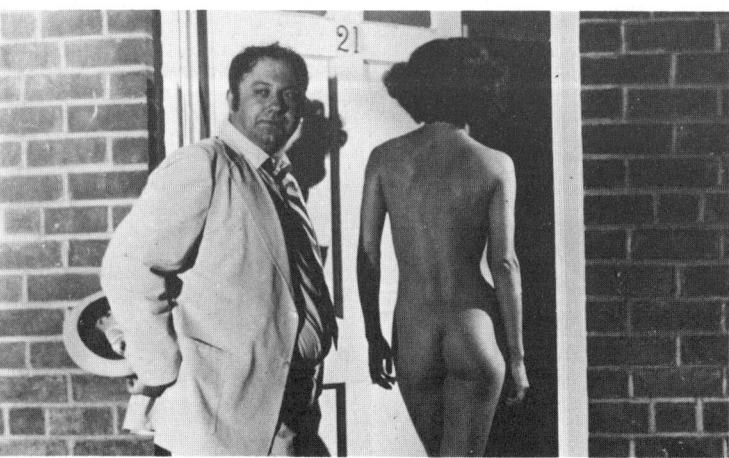

Though less of the first feature films continue to concentrate on sexual explicitness, the stream of smaller sex films continue unabated – and largely unabridged! Typical was New Realm's *Secrets of a Door to Door Salesman*, the secrets, as you might guess, being wholly sexual.

As outrageous – if not more so – than any of the sex films released in the period under review was Eagle's *Super Dick*, the story of a fat little "private eye" whose investigations are more sexual than criminal and whose adventures include a number of (closely observed) seductions to the accompaniment of some particularly coarse language. Allen Garfield played the title role.

A Film About Jimi Hendrix from Warners
was in fact just that; an insight for his fans
into the man and his music.

Also strictly for pop fans was Columbia's
Wattstax, the film record of a black concert
given in the summer of '72 as part of the
annual Watts Festival in California.

A mixed critical reception was accorded the
Italian-made adaptation of the old John
Ford classic play *'Tis Pity She's a Whore* in
which Fabio Testi and Charlotte Rampling
played the brother and sister whose
incestuous passion leads to such unpleasant
ends for both of them. Nearly all the
enthusiastic reviewers commented
considerably on the film's visual beauties –
and horrors.

UA's English-speaking, Italian-made Western *Man of the East* was a comedy about an English milord who goes Way Out West and is changed by the life – and the assistance of three of his father's old pals – from a tenderfoot to a toughie who beats the villain at his own rough games and walks off with the girl. Terence Hill was the youngster: Riccardo Pizzuti his villainous opponent.

Santee, from Columbia, was about another of those tough Western heroes who are never quite able to hide a heart of gold: Glenn Ford played a bounty hunter who adopts the son (Michael Burns) of one of his victims and eventually wins the lad over to the extent of his helping his new "dad" to wipe out the gang who had killed Santee's own son.

James Mason and Robert Preston, teachers both, if of different calibre, in Paramount's *Child's Play*, a screen adaptation of the David Merrick Broadway play about a school faced with a mysterious outbreak of violence.

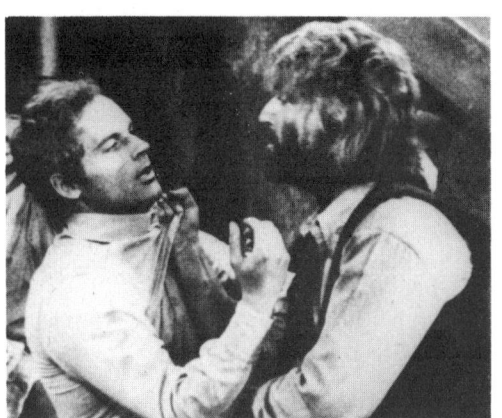

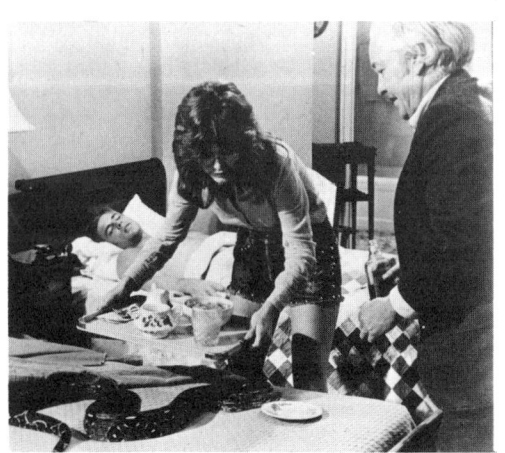

Hardly the sort of thing you'd expect to find on the counterpane! However, the reptiles turn up in the strangest places and in the oddest forms in Universal's *Sssnake*, a creepy little piece about an ophiologist whose experiments are aimed at turning human beings into snakes! Those sharing the horrors included Dirk Benedict, Heather Menzies and Strother Martin.

Marlon Brando and new star Maria Schneider in Bernardo Bertolucci's controversial, censor-tilting UA film *Last Tango in Paris*, which, though taking sex to the extremes, was all rather sad in the relation of a purely animal affair which ends in disaster and death. Some critics found the film brilliant and Brando's performance great; others (like this one) found the film far less artistically or otherwise exciting and Brando's performance an uneven mixture of good and bad.

Well, Fox–Rank's Western *Blindman* did manage to inject a note of novelty into the proceedings by making the gun-toting hero totally blind! This, however, doesn't stop him from tracking down and effectually removing the villains who have stolen fifty lovely ladies that he has been assigned to escort to San Diego. And even if he doesn't see much of his charges, we, the audience that is, saw *plenty* of them!

Right out of the Western rut was CIC's *Bad Company*, a story about some American Civil War draft dodgers robbing and killing (and being killed) as they struggle Westwards. A hard edge of reality was lightened by some nice touches of humour. Cast included Jeff Bridges.

102

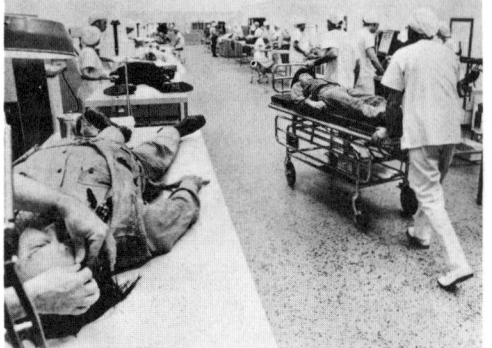

You might say that MGM's *Westworld* was a very different kind of Western indeed; certainly there was a very large ingredient of science-fiction in the story about a luxury holiday resort where the robots (including mean gunman Yul Brynner), which are there for the convenience of the guests, suddenly begin to rebel and start shooting back! (Top: the robots get their nightly repairs after being shot up and otherwise abused by the happy holidaymakers.)

Sadly underrated (and under-shown), Martin Ritt's *Sounder* for Fox was a small classic of a film; a charmingly simple, unpretentious and consistently credible picture of a devoted American Negro family in the Deep South during the Great Depression. Paul Winfield as the father and Cicely Tyson as the mother both gave beautifully sincere and moving performances.

The two rough families whose feud over a meadow which lies between their respective properties gave tough motivation to MGM's *The Lolly-Madonna War*. Family leaders, and feuders-in-chief, were played by Rod Steiger (top, r) and Robert Ryan (bottom, l).

What can one usefully say about another "series" success, "On the Buses", now reaching with *Holiday on the Buses*, its third feature, with Reg Varney (right) and all the other television series favourites.

Anglo–EMI's *Take Me High* was a rather cheery little British musical in which Cliff Richard played a successful Birmingham banker (Merchant league) who finds love, a sensational new dish (The Brumberger) and an eccentric millionaire (Hugh Griffith, right) in that city.

The twenty-fifth of the famous British "Carry On" comedies, Peter Rogers' *Carry on Girls* took the mickey out of the Beauty Queen business and involved most of the usual team of comics, including Sid James, shown struggling to untangle battling Barbara Windsor and Margaret Nolan.

Joan Sims (right) and the original stage play's author Ray Cooney were among those involved in LMG's farce-film *Not Now Darling*, which included plenty of those misunderstandings, embarrassments and confusions which are the life-blood of this kind of entertainment.

Not up to the top Boulting Brothers' comedy standards, *Soft Beds, Hard Battles,* set in and around a plush Paris brothel during the last war, appeared mainly designed to give Peter Sellers a chance to present a gallery of highly diverse characterisations, from a Japanese Prince and a doddery old French General to Hitler himself, and with all this he, and the film, only achieved a very mild level of fun.

Cybill Shepherd tries hard to convince dubious parents Eddie Albert and Audra Lindley what a wonderful fellow her wooer Charles Grodin (right, with first wife, Jeannie Berlin) is, in Neil Simon's funny comedy, for Fox–Rank, *The Heartbreak Kid.*

With the Bond image wearing a bit thin round the edges the moviemakers have, in some cases with a certain amount of desperation one feels, been turning to a female variation on the theme with a number of movies highlighting rough and tough feminine 007 types. One such was Miracle's *Big Zapper*, starring Linda Marlowe as a gal whose physical charms give little clue to her highly professional use of feet and fists and, when needed, gun!

Fox's *Gordon's War*, a brutally efficient film about a (black) Vietnam veteran who forms his own private army to cleanse Harlem of the dope-pushers, was only one of a number which at their heart had a disturbing philosophy that Authority, being unable or unwilling to cope with social problems, the private citizen was compelled to take the law into his own hands to bring any justice to the solving of them. The "Army" in this war were played by David Downing, Paul Winfield, Tony E. King and Carl Lee.

Godfrey Cambridge and Raymond St Jacques played the two coloured Harlem detectives whose task it is to find out who is behind an outbreak of murders – *circa* 1932. And it was all presented in slyly satirical vein in Columbia–Warner's *Come Back Charleston Blue*.

Another in the considerable batch of black films to be released this year was Universal's *That Man Bolt*. Bolt, played by Fred Williamson, has the job of getting a million dollars from Hong Kong to Mexico City, and achieving this in spite of every plot the criminal opposition can throw at him to stop him reaching his destination.

106

Paul Newman and Robert Redford were the co-stars in the Oscar-awarded CIC release *The Sting*, a delightfully witty and amusing story of double-dealing and intricate plotting in Chicago in the gangster era of 1936.

Remember "Dirty Harry" – the detective played by Clint Eastwood who gave that tough crime thriller its title? Well, he returned as dour and tough as ever in a follow-up movie, Warner's *Magnum Force*, in which he becomes caught up in a series of brutal murders of San Francisco's vice-ring executives by – as we know – motor-cycle cops. And all very blood-splattered and efficient it was, too.

The success of *The Godfather* sired a whole string of Mafia-motivated movies of which, if not the greatest, Hal Wallis's Universal crime thriller *The Don is Dead* had much, including great expertise, to recommend it. It was the usual story about a split between the "families"; and in this case the bloody war between them engineered by the power-hungry type planning to scramble to the top over the dead bodies. Anthony Quinn played the Don, the leader who allows passion to rule his head and falls accordingly.

Swopping his usual Western wilds scene for the city streets in Warner's *McQ*, John Wayne borrowed just a little from Mr Eastwood as he played the rough, tough cop who takes the investigation of his pal's murder into his own hands rather than leave it to too slow departmental routine!

MGM's *Walking Tall* gave another glimpse, and a frightening one, of graft and corruption in America through the story, based on facts, of an ex-pro wrestler Sheriff who comes into headlong conflict with the gamblers, grafters and whoremongers who have taken over his town. Nearly killed by them, he recovers to fight back, and by using their own violent weapons eventually drive them out. With Joe Don Baker (here nursing his murdered wife) giving a good performance as the honest man fighting the – corrupt – System.

Shoot first and ask the questions later is the motto of dedicated but over-rough New York 'tec Charles Bronson in Michael Winner's Columbia release *The Stone Killer*; and that way of working makes it hard for him to get permission from his dubious supervisor to play his hunch and investigate what he thinks is the first signs of an outbreak of major gang warfare. He proves right, too, but not in time to stay the bloodbath.

108

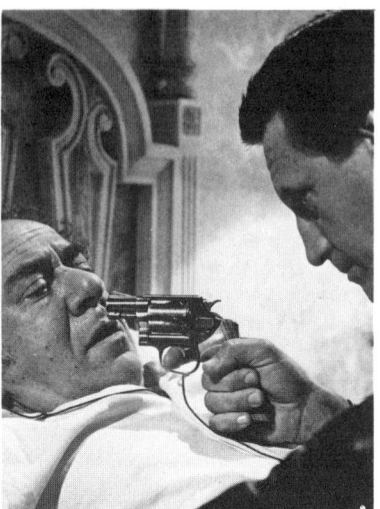

In a year in which cop films proliferated, Fox's *The Seven-Ups* was as professionally slick as the best of them, telling a story about a rather unconventional team of New York detectives (Victor Arnold, Jerry Leon, Ken Kercheval and Roy Scheider) whose special job it is to bring the big boys to book, big enough to bring them not less than a seven-year sentence when they are caught. In the film the team become caught up in a complicated inter-gang war which they only break up at the cost of the life of one of the team. (Right: Unconventional cop Scheider tries an unconventional way of obtaining evidence.)

It's good in the sort of welter of violence which rages across the scene too often these days to come across a nice, cosy, honestly sentimental film like Julian Wintle's *The Belstone Fox*, made for Fox. Based on the David Rook novel, the film was about the strange, deep friendship between a fox and a hound brought up together and the drama and death to which it leads. Bill Travers played the understanding woodsman, Heather Wright the daughter of the huntsman, Eric Porter (right) who suffers for his tolerance. And the marvellously trained fox gave the outstanding performance!

One of the most movingly acted, psychologically credible and thoroughly convincing – indeed, in many ways outstanding – films of the year was the distressingly narrowly shown Columbia film *Summer Wishes, Winter Dreams*, a story of a middle-aged American couple (Joanne Woodward and Martin Balsam) who have to take stock of themselves when the death of the wife's mother suddenly shakes them out of their routine lives.

A quite superb recapture of the mood, the technique and the content of those old screen favourites of the thirties and forties was in Columbia's *The Way We Were*, a sentimental (a real "Woman's Weepie") story of an ill-fated romance between a young left-wing causes agitator and the conventional college athlete, which survives several storms only to inevitably founder in the end. A nice performance by Robert Redford and one of the best straight ones of her career by Barbra Streisand.

Liv Ullmann and Gene Kelly, both better than their roles in Columbia's overly sentimental *40 Carats*, a highly unrealistic story of the love affair between a forty-year-old divorcée (Miss Ullmann) and the eighteen-year-old American boy she meets on a beach in Greece!

There was a great deal of talent in Fox–Rank's *Sleuth* and it showed it every frame of the way! Adapted by Anthony Shaffer from his big stage success, directed by the very civilised and subtle Joseph L. Mankiewicz, it was superbly performed by Laurence Olivier and Michael Caine – the entire cast! A long, cruel duel of wits, changing mood and pace with brilliant timing, it gripped and thrilled for every one of its 138 polished minutes.

More detection in British Lion's *The Wicker Man*, in which a young mainland Scots cop arrives on a close and unwelcoming island community to investigate the mystery of a missing child, and soon finds himself surrounded by an atmosphere of paganism and ignorance. Edward Woodward played the, increasingly horrified, investigator and the script was written by *Sleuth* writer Anthony Shaffer.

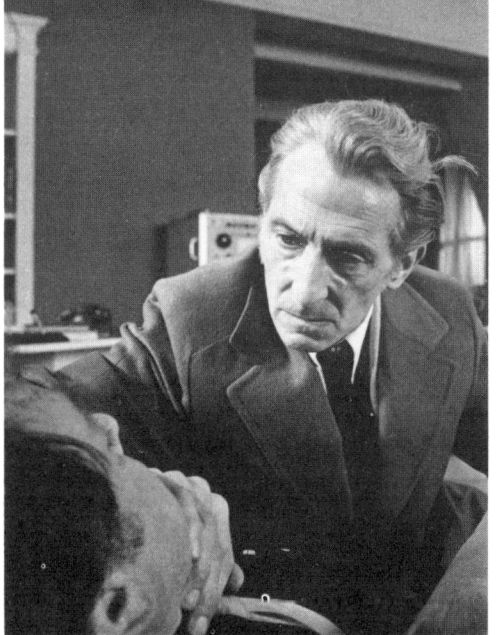

A rather odd, but surprisingly successful, blend of documentary, science-fiction and espionage thriller, Avco–Embassy's *The Day of the Dolphin* managed in spite of its sudden and quite astonishing switches, to maintain a good level of entertainment as it told a story about a dedicated scientist (George C. Scott, shown with fellow scientist Trish Van Devere) whose increasingly successful efforts to verbally communicate with his dolphin pets are interrupted by some spies, who abduct them for the nastiest possible reasons.

Some might think that the basis of Scotia–Barber's *Executive Action*, a highly fictional and theoretical account of the possible truth behind the assassination of the late President Kennedy, has considerable dangers. Burt Lancaster and Robert Ryan played leaders of a group of Texas tycoons who, the film suggested, because of their dislike of the Kennedy policies and their implication, had the President murdered.

The familiar thriller team of Christopher Lee and Peter Cushing were at it again in Hammer–Warner's *The Satanic Rights of Dracula*, in which the bad old baron's efforts to plague the world away is thwarted by his old enemy.

112

Understandably alarmed, Gayle Hunnicutt, the nerve-racked wife with the horrible hubbie in the Hemdale thriller *Voices*, in which, after a night of terror, the twosome find the morning brings even more disturbing events.

Here he is, the rat's best friend (in the person of little Lee Harcourt Montgomery), in the Cinerama follow-up *Ben* to their previous rodent thriller success *Willard*. Leader rat Ben, having survived the holocaust in the finale of the first film, decides to take revenge on the citizens in this sequel.

Richie Havens, as Othello, serenades Season Hubley, as Desdemona, in Cinerama's *Catch My Soul*, a contemporary musical "interpretation" of the Shakespeare play.

Warner's *Enter the Dragon* was the last film to star Bruce Lee, the martial and unarmed combat expert, prior to his death. He played a secret agent sent to a mysterious fortress island to smash the owner's plans for conquest, a task carried out with amusing nonchalance.

By giving the screen adaptation of the stage rock musical success *Godspell* a new dimension, taking it out into the streets, the parks and even on to the roofs of New York, the Columbia film was excitingly visual as well as vocally attractive. And the cast of ten young and talented youngsters added much to this modern variation on the Bible story of St Matthew.

114 Heat and hard labour mark Warner's *Adam's Woman*, the story of a young American seaman deported from Liverpool to the Australian penal colony (for a crime of which he is innocent) and there winning a much interrupted way to freedom and honour!

The ogre in different guise – Hitler greets the small daughter of one of his lieutenants with a smile in *Swastika*, a VPS documentary about the rise and fall of Hitler's Germany.

Candy Clarke and Charlie Martin Smith share a borrowed car in CIC's *American Graffiti*, a nostalgic glance back at the way the young set spend one evening and night in a small Northern Californian town in 1962, at the end of which some go and some stay, none of them knowing anything about the war that was to take its toll of them. A brilliant, almost casually convincing creation of a time, a place and a people.

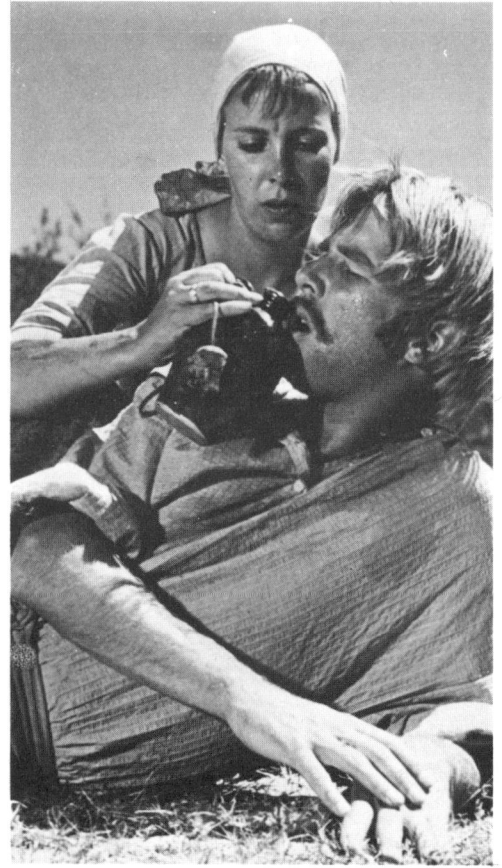

Richard Jaeckel and Sheree North, pawns of a crime syndicate in MGM's thriller *The Outfit*, in which (left) Robert Duvall and Joe Don Baker are also involved.

Robert Shaw as the chauffeur in Columbia's beautifully restrained, consistently captivating screen adaptation of the L. P. Hartley story, *The Hireling*, about a young widowed milady (Sarah Miles, left) and her changing relationship with her driver. Shaw was magnificent and Miss Miles made this her best screen performance yet.

116

Back to Hammer for their Avco–Embassy release *Frankenstein and the Monster From Hell* came director Terence Fisher, one of their most successful Gothic-style horror-creators of the past, to guide Peter Cushing in his sixth essay at the role of the nasty old Baron, who on this occasion uses an insane asylum as a cover for his monster-creating hobby and is uncovered by a young and sane inmate (and disciple) Shane Briant.

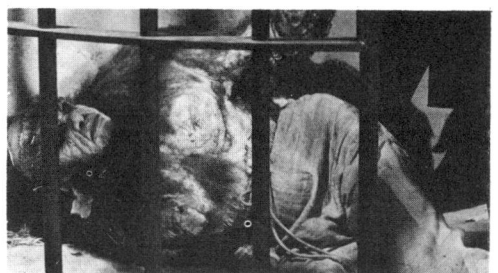

Scotia-Barber's *The Affair* had over-sentimentalised echoes of *Love Story* all along this tale of a poor little cripple girl (Natalie Wood) bowled over by a handsome young lawyer (Robert Wagner) and left with only her brother to offer her comfort when the affair comes to an end.

Rather unusual was Conrad Rooks' (he wrote the screenplay, produced and directed) film based on the Herman Hesse Nobel Prize-winning novel *Siddhartha*, the story of a young Brahmin seeking a meaning to life in India some twenty-five centuries ago. This Columbia release had a full measure of charm, a gentle philosophical undercurrent and a nice array of performances by an Indian cast, including Shashi Kapoor as the seeker after truth. The film was made entirely in India.

Peter Cushing up to more horrors in British Lion's *The Beast Must Die*, as guest at a strange house-party hosted by a big-game hunter who tells the assembled company he is now after the biggest game of all – a werewolf; and adds to that the suggestion that his quarry may well be anyone of them! As the Beast appears the horrified company include – apart from Mr Cushing, left – Calvin Lockhart, Tom Chadbon, Michael Gambon and Ciaran Madden.

More shudders in British Lion's *Blood Sisters*, an eerie tale about the survivor of Siamese twin sisters who, although looking quite a dish, turns out to be a really nasty piece of work. She was played by Margot Kidder and it was the right name for the part!

A slight variation on the horror theme in Miracle's wryly titled *House of Whipcord*, the story of a strange nightmare jail in which floggings, solitary confinement and death by hanging are the order of the horrible day and our heroine totters from one incredulous experience to another before the final corpse-littered escape. It was all played straight and effectively in its cruel, sadistic way.

A breath of fresh, Utah, mountain air was brought by Disney's animal life feature, *Run, Cougar, Run*, a stunningly photographed story of a cougar family and its varying relationship with Man in the high Red Mesa country.

Though made primarily – one assumes – for children, *Swallows and Amazons* was a film to be enjoyed by everyone: a quite charming account of a largely uneventful holiday spent in the Lake District by four children (Simon West, Sophie Neville, Zanna Hamilton, Stephen Grendon); they picnic, sail and come into friendly opposition with another couple of kids they call The Amazons (the names being taken from those of their respective sailing craft).

Careless scientist Jim Dale with his dog Digby, the animal he feeds with an experimental formula in error in Fox's *Digby the Biggest Dog in the World*, and so starts the creature growing to such an extent that the Army is finally sent to hunt it down and put it down! It was all mildly amusing.

Lots of fun and fantasy, too, in Disney's *Herbie Rides Again*, which carried on the story of the magic Volkswagen car which made its bow in *The Love Bug* a few years ago. Helen Hayes, centre, played the old lady fighting the developers to whose aid the car, its owner (Ken Berry) and his girl-friend (Stephanie Powers), literally spring into action.

To that master of cinematic magic Ray Harryhausen must go a lot of the credit for the fun and games in Columbia's clever and amusing fantasy *The Golden Voyage of Sinbad*, for it was the maestro's amazing "effects" – such as a ship's figurehead coming to fighting life – which were the highspots of this film of the magic rivalry between hero Sinbad (John Phillip Law) and the nasty magician (Tom Baker) who seeks to destroy him. Caroline Munro is the frightened onlooker.

UA's *Cops and Robbers* was a subtle title for it referred to two cops who, while still with the police force, become big-time robbers when, after a successful small-time, experimental, and spontaneous shop hold-up, they plan, and nearly succeed in bringing off a ten-million-dollar robbery! The Robber cops were played by Cliff Gorman and Joe Bologna.

Peter Sellers' best performance on the screen for some years was in Scotia–Barber's *The Optimists of Nine Elms*, in which he played with touching reality an old, ex-Music Hall star, now living in a derelict factory with his dog, who is wooed and finally won over to friendship by a couple of cheeky cockney kids, played winningly by Dona Mullane and John Chaffey.

In contrast to *Cops and Robbers*, Paramount's *Serpico* was the story of an obstinately honest New York cop (played by Al Pacino) whose refusal to join in the corruption which is rife among his fellows leads, at least indirectly, to his being gunned down and nearly murdered – and from this, a belated and hardly wholehearted investigation into graft in the Force. And the film was claimed to be based on a true story.

120

Basically a "chase" story, Fox's *Lady Ice* was all about an investigation carried out by a Private Eye (Donald Sutherland) hired by an Insurance Company to smash the increasingly successful activities of a group of jewel thieves. Lady in the scene is Jennifer O'Neill.

What could only be described as a most successful cinematic hybrid, United Artists' *Billy Two Hats* was a strongly thematic Western – about Isolation and its effects – which was written in Scotland (Billy in fact is a Scottish old-timer, played by Gregory Peck), planned in London, made in Israel, and concerned the deep friendship between Billy and a young half-breed (Desi Arnaz Junior).

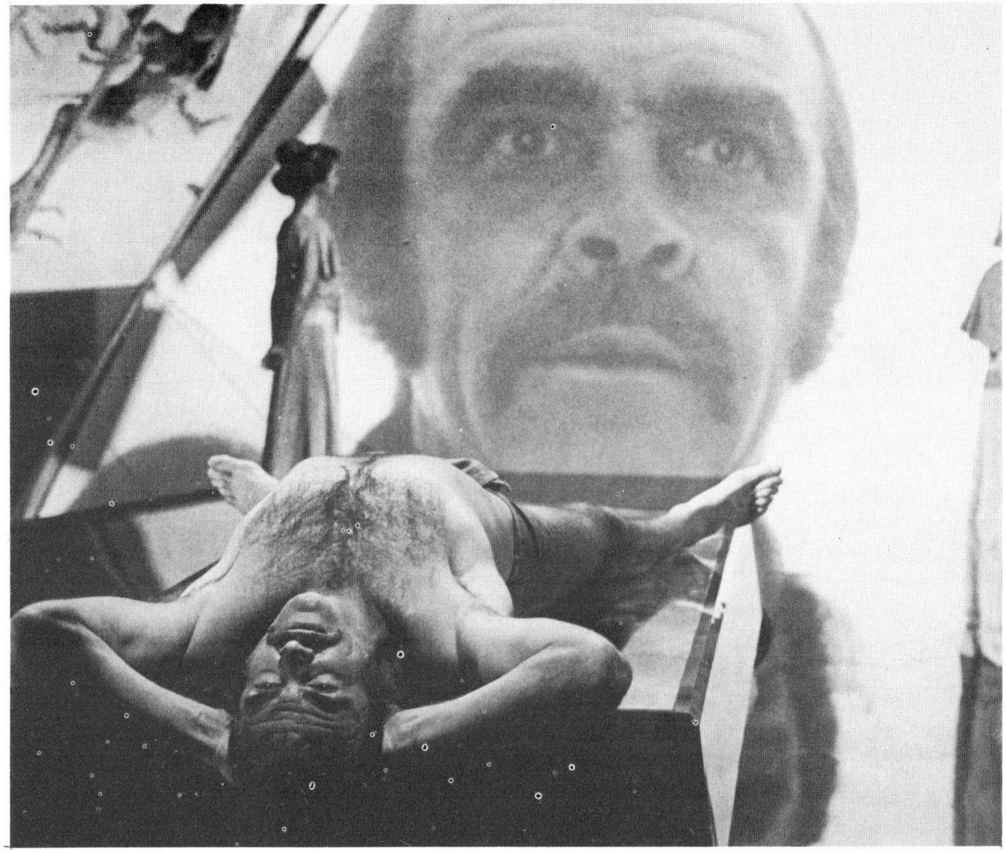

A more serious, somewhat high faluting, look into the future was undertaken by Fox's *Zardoz*, in which Sean Connery, a leader of The Exterminators, turns against the Society which employs him and the "God" he is supposed to serve to bring chaos, before himself starting – with pretty Charlotte Rampling's aid – a brand new line of human endeavour. And the effects were certainly remarkable.

One of his most carefully tidied and story-strong films yet, UA's Woody Allen production (he co-wrote and directed it) *Sleeper* was a variation on the Rip Van Winkle theme, with Woody Allen as the frozen "stiff" revived two hundred years hence into a world where, in spite of all the technical and scientific advances, there are still "underground" struggles against a totalitarian regime. Funniest sequence was where the awakened sleeper disguises himself as a servant robot and as such nearly meets with disaster.

122

For her performance in Paramount's *Paper Moon*, Tatum O'Neal deservedly won an Oscar; it was a remarkably assured and wonderfully timed comedy performance opposite her real daddy Ryan O'Neal, who also gave an outstanding performance as a personable young con man selling bibles to the bereaved, picked up and eventually ruled by the small daughter of one of his ex-girl friends. And the background was a very effectively recreated American Midwest of the 1930s.

Portrait of a frightened lady – Mama the Turk, played by Patricia Hayes – in the Hemdale thriller *Blue Movie Blackmail*.

Rip Torn with new (Elayne Heilveil, left) and old (Ahna Capri, right) girl-friends in the Fox–Rank film *Payday*.

Dennis Hopper (centre) flanked by the two Redskins (Jay Verela and José Torvay) who, when all his efforts to turn from baddie into goodie in the town of Dime Box have failed dismally, help him to get back to his old job of bank-roll stealing in Fox's mildly amusing and rather unusual Western *Kid Blue*.

123

Sheriff Richard Harris leads the way in Columbia–Warner's Western *The Deadly Trackers*, based on the Samuel Fuller story *Riata*, in which a sheriff whose wife and son have been killed by bank-robbers grimly tracks them down even when they flee across the border into Mexico.

Randy Quaid, Otis Young and Jack Nicholson as escort and prisoner in Columbia's salty comedy about a couple of American tars who, along the way to the jail, decide to let their prisoner have a final fling, in *The Last Detail*.

Harvey Keitel and Amy Robinson, who find love among the dirt in Warner's *Mean Streets* –.a moving and convincing story of life in the Little Italy district of New York.

San Francisco detectives Walter Matthau and Bruce Dern question Mari Gallo in the course of their *Investigation of a Murder* (an apparently needlessly brutal one, the relentless killing of the driver and a bus-load of passengers), the Fox thriller which invited the audience to solve the case for themselves as the action progressed.

First-class production quality, a very starry cast, and a good performance (within context) by Jack Palance – as the antique dealer with an idol in his basement who rocks off his trolley and starts to bring it human sacrifices – could never quite hide the wild improbabilities of the story in EMI's *Craze*.

124 George Segal and Susan Anspach in Columbia–Warner's *Blume in Love*, a rather slow, meandering story of a couple's courtship, marriage, divorce and rather odd post-marital relationship which was always somewhat uncomfortably convincing. It was also something of a more than usual one-man band piece, being written, directed and produced by Paul Mazursky.

Edward Woodward (right), playing the title-role of *Callan*, the TV-born hero, takes a drink with his intended victim, Carl Mohner, and his girlfriend, Catherine Schell, in this scene from the EMI film which, slick, brutal and entertaining, presented a picture of British Secret Service methods which left a queasy feeling in the stomach.

THE CONTINENTAL FILM

One of the most outstanding films from any country to be presented in 1973 was François Truffaut's classic, definitive film about moviemaking and moviemakers, *La Nuit Américaine – Day for Night*, in which, playing the harassed, insomniac director himself (with star, Jacqueline Bissett, left) he followed the production of a film from optimistic beginning, through misfortune, to final disaster and salvage. The film included a wonderful performance by Valentina Cortese (above, right).

Another of the best French films of the period was Claude Sautet's subtle and quietly amusing comedy *César et Rosalie*, a story about an independently-minded divorcée and the two very contrasting men in her life; tough businessman Yves Montand and artist Sami Frey, between whom she finds it impossible to choose, because in fact she really needs both!

126 In his *Les Noces Rouges – Blood Wedding*, Claude Chabrol told, as brilliantly as ever, a story of violent passion in a small, quiet Loire Valley town, where the sexual greed for each other of Michel Piccoli and Stéphane Audran leads to bloody murder, and then retribution, brought about, ironically enough, by the daughter's devotion to her mother.

In contrast to his gently amusing *La Nuit Américaine* François Truffaut's *Une Belle Fille Comme Moi – A Gorgeous Bird Like Me*, was a black-tinged satire: the wryly amusing biography of a sexually attractive girl who, at the age of nine, after putting her irritating father out of the way, climbs her way towards the top by attracting and then removing useful men from her path when their usefulness has served her purpose! And playing the ruthless Camille Bliss was Bernadette Lafont (with Claude Brasseur and Philippe Léotard).

Up to top French standards, Philippe de Broca's *Louise* was the moving love story of middle-aged, lonely teacher Jeanne Moreau and the feckless, charming and childish young man – Julian Negulesco – she picks up, takes home into her bed and her heart, knowing all the time that she cannot control the situation for it is an utterly impossible one with only one possible ending.

Anicée Alvina (right) in *Le Rempart des Béguines* played the pretty little teenager who falls in love with her father's mistress and is shocked when she is told that the woman is about to become her stepmother!

One of the year's most delightful comedies from any origin was the Swiss film *L'Invitation – The Invitation*, which, directed by Claude Goretta with great subtlety, charm and deep understanding of human nature, told the simple story of a party given in a garden one hot summer's day, when drink tears away inhibitions and true characters are revealed. Lovely performances from a universally faultless cast.

Pier Paolo Pasolini's *The Canterbury Tales* was his own, personal, Italian view of some of Chaucer's rude Pilgrim's stories, made ruder – and nuder – (as in this scene from "The Cook's Tale") by Pasolini, who himself (inset) played a part in the goings-on!

128 The Pasolini picture was soon followed by a number of other Italian films taking their material from the same Chaucerian source (it was suggested by the titles – a suggestion, by the way, in some cases open to argument!). One such: *The Other Canterbury Tales.*

More rough – Italian – medieval fun and explicit frolics occurred in *Get Thee to a Nunnery,* in which the lusting lads and lovely ladies are driven by a plague to take shelter in an unusual sort of Florentine monastery.

Tuo Vizio E Una Stanza Chousa E Solo Lo Ne La Chiave, boldly translated into *Excite Me* for British moviegoers, was an initially fascinating but eventually less than successful Italian effort to bring the horrors of Edgar Allan Poe's story *The Black Cat* to the screen, with Edwige Fenech as the star.

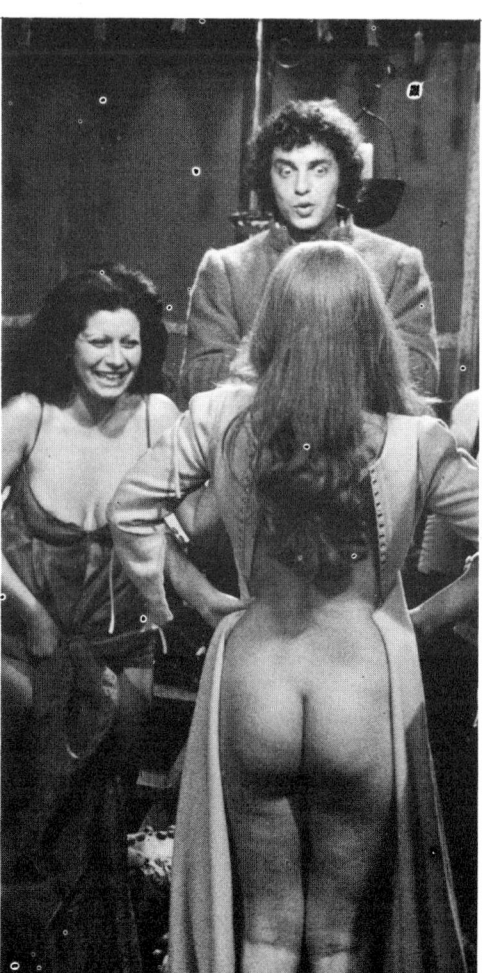

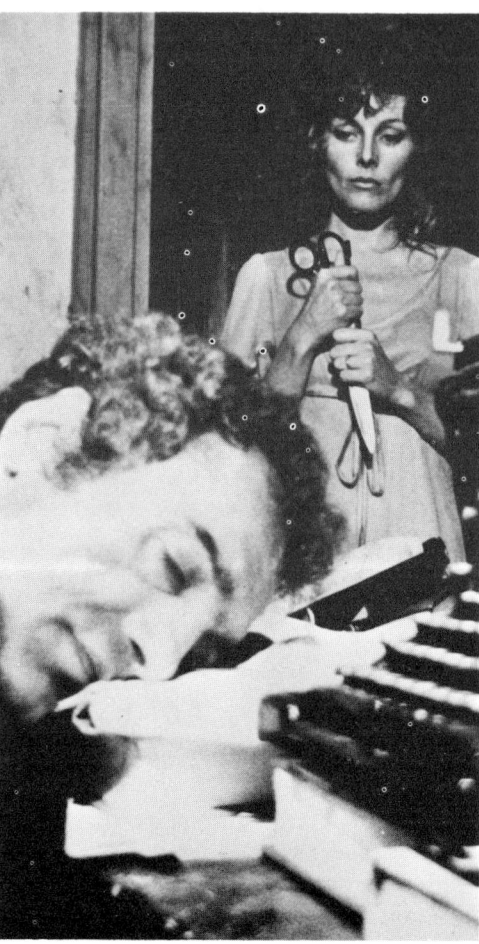

Irina Kupchenko as Liza and Leonid
Kulagin as Fyodor Lavretsky in Andrei
Mikhalkov-Konchalovsky's lovingly
atmosphered adaptation of the Turgenev
story *A Nest of Gentlefolk*, a highly literary
telling of this tale about a young nobleman
searching for a better milieu than that in
which he has been living, the decadent
French society of the period.

One of the quite considerable number of
Run-Run Shaw, made-in-Hong Kong movies
generally released in Great Britain in 1973,
*The Intimate Confessions of a Chinese
Courtesan* was about a girl sold into the
business who never gives up her intention of
having her revenge on the woman responsible
for her moral degradation.

Some of the other films from Hong Kong
released in the period, many of them from
the Shaw Brothers' studios, all of them
melodramas with plenty of bloody unarmed
and sometimes armed combat, some of them
starring the very popular Bruce Lee (who
died suddenly during the year, see "In
Memoriam" section) were: *Fist of Fury*
(starring Bruce Lee) (*right*); *The New
One-armed Swordsman* (starring Li Ching)
(*below*); *The Killer* (*bottom*); and *The Big Boss*
(another to star Bruce Lee) (*bottom right*).

There were some fine performances, notably that of Gunnel Lindblom as the wife (seen with Aino Taube as her mother), in Alf Sjöberg's screen adaptation, which he directed, of the grim Strindberg play *The Father*, the sombre story of a wife deliberately driving her husband mad but also suggesting something of the fascinating love–hate relationship between the sexes, as seen by the Scandinavian dramatist.

Jan Troell's *The Emigrants* was the first of a two-part epic film – the most lavish and large-scale movie ever to be produced in the Swedish studios – about a Swedish family who, knocked down by constant adversity, decide to emigrate to the New World and begin again there: this film finishing when they have reached their goal and decide to build their home. Leisurely, wonderfully photographed, and with some fine performances including those from the two main characters, played by Liv Ullmann and Max von Sydow.

An unexpected cinematic treasure was Daryush Mehrjui's *The Cow*, an Iranian film which with love and humour related the story of a beloved cow, the pride and joy of a whole village, and its sad demise.

From South America came Alexandro Jodorowsky's somewhat pretentious but visually effective puzzler *El Topo – The Mole* which, owing something to Buñuel, Fellini and the so-called "Spaghetti Westerns" also had an authentic atmosphere of its own as it told a confusing story of violent and bloody incidents set largely in a desert, all suggesting there was more depth in the piece than there probably was! Not content with directing and writing the film, Jodorowsky also played the leading role.

Though visually magnificent, Franco Zeffirelli's *Brother Sun, Sister Moon*, the story of St Francis of Assisi, was less satisfactory in both script and performances; with Graham Faulkner playing the young monk.

Yves Montand as the kidnapped American who is revealed as a right-wing agent in a South American state in Costa-Gavras's dedicated political thriller, *State of Siege*. (Costa-Gavras is probably best-known for his previous political thriller *Z*).

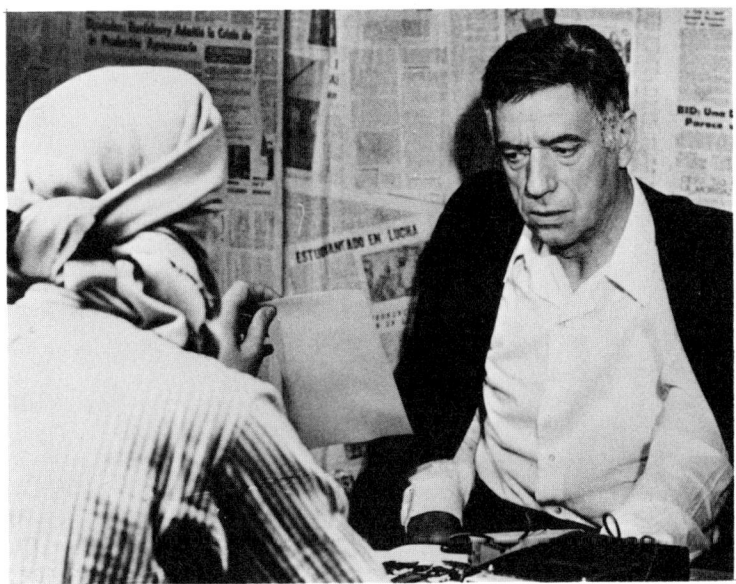

132

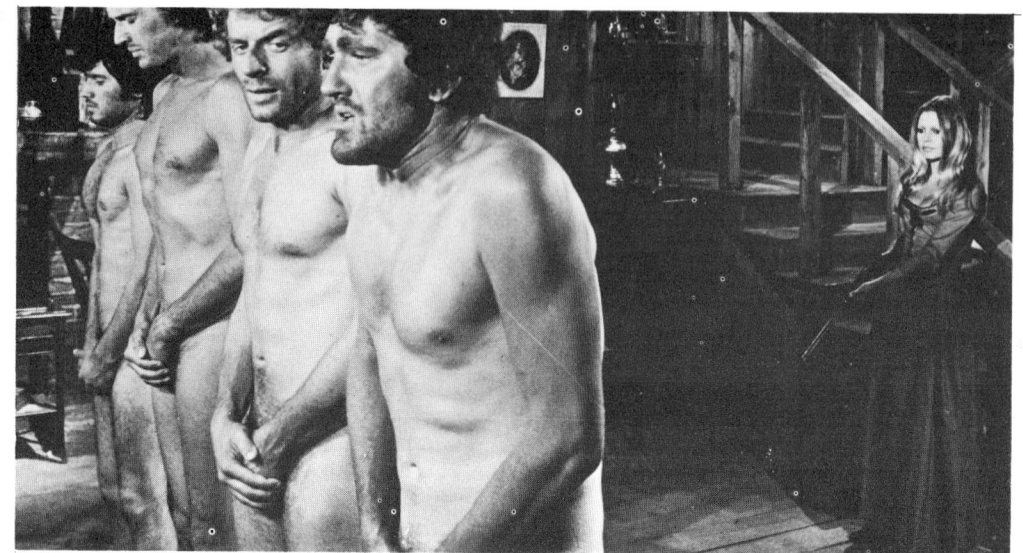

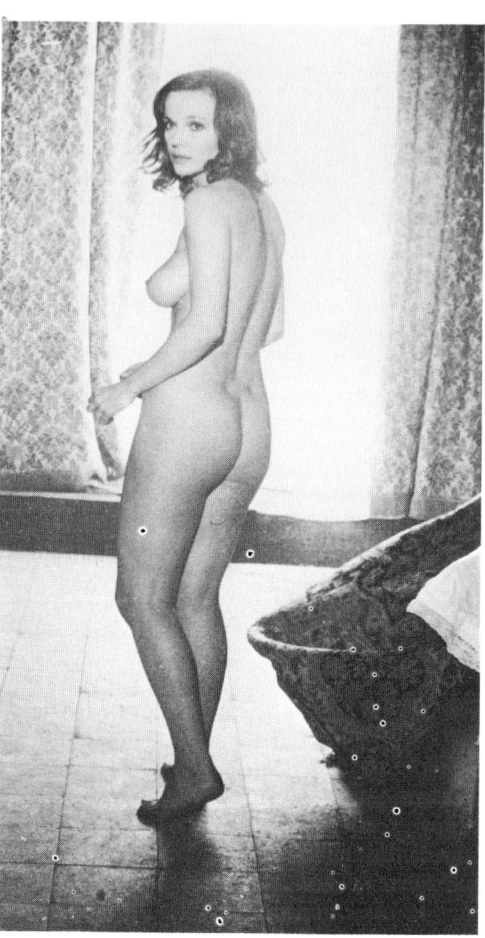

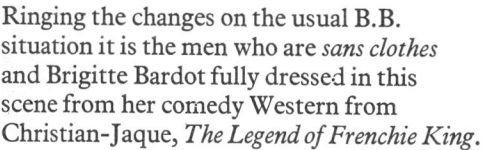

Ringing the changes on the usual B.B. situation it is the men who are *sans clothes* and Brigitte Bardot fully dressed in this scene from her comedy Western from Christian-Jaque, *The Legend of Frenchie King*.

Having turned to urban problems and people, Satyajit Ray brings to them the same artistry, sympathy and understanding that he did when he was concerned with the provincial scene, and his *Company Limited* (released by Contemporary) was an absorbing account of the way a young Anglicised Calcutta executive sacrifices some of his integrity in his ambitious climb to a director's chair. A wonderfully balanced film, with some extremely good performances including those of Barun Chanda as the young man and Sharmila Tagore as his lovely sister-in-law.

The Warner release *Malizia* was an amusing story, set against Sicilian backgrounds, about a fourteen-year-old boy's erotic interest in his new and pretty young stepmother (Laura Antonelli, with new husband, Turi Ferrov) which leads her, in a gesture of kindness, to sexually initiate the lad on the wedding eve!

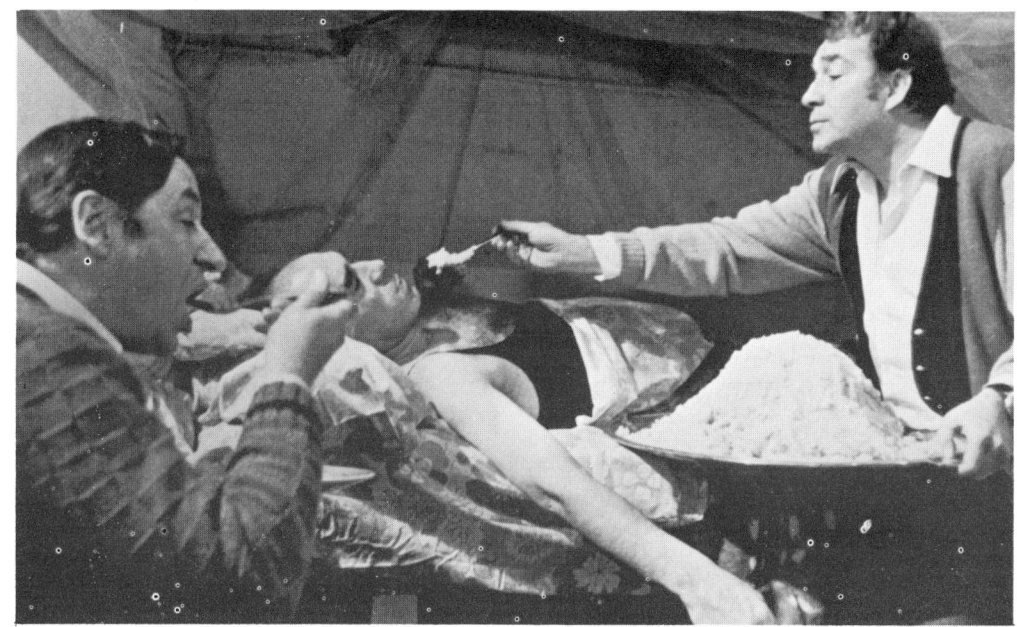

A rough roll in the hay in *Tales of Erotica*, a four-part Italian sex film set in the year 1550 and telling the stories of four females trying to steer the course of justice away from themselves by using their ultimate charms.

Certainly not a pretty film, Marco Ferreri's *La Grande Bouffe – Blow-Out* met with a very mixed reception. Extremely well made and with some sort of vague symbolic message hidden within it about the way our Society is going, it was on the surface a bleakly bawdy comedy about four professional friends who incarcerate themselves within a Paris house and deliberately set out to eat their way to death – a journey to be enlivened by sex! The comedy was supplied by such touches as the explosion of an overworked toilet. Many found it all somewhat repellent, while others thought it just funny. In this typical scene are three of the four friends, played by Philippe Noiret, Ugo Tognazzi and Michel Piccoli, who is also shown right (fourth was Marcello Mastroianni).

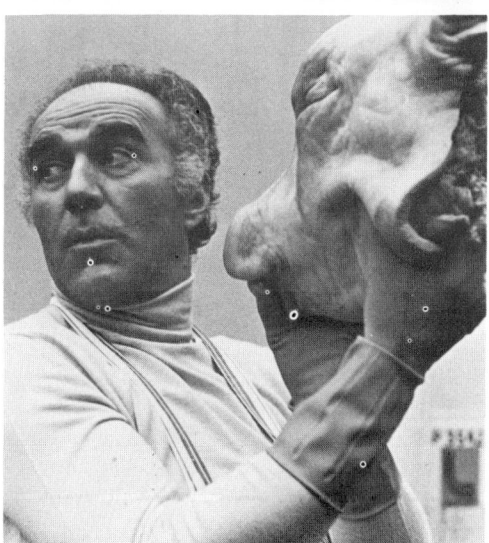

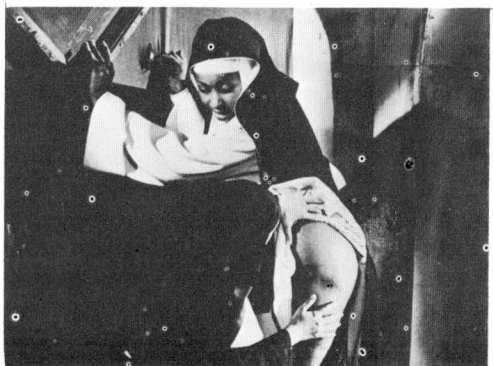

Italy, more than any country, continues to produce a steady flow of portmanteau pictures, a number of filmlets woven into a loosely strung whole: such as Cinecenta's *Aretino's Blue Stories*, a package of erotic sketches played against a background of medieval Italy.

134

Ex-playboy boss, Jean-Paul Belmondo, explains that he means Business, after having taken over his murdered dad's conglomerate empire in EMI's release *The Inheritor*, a slick, shallow and not too well English-dubbed French production.

A lot of the confusion which may appear in the story of MGM-EMI's English-dubbed *The Serpent* is cleared up if you care to see it as a parallel to the famous Philby spy case. Yul Brynner played the Russian KGB defector who as a proof of his change of heart releases to the West a list of important and high-placed Soviet spies in Europe. (Inset: American FBI chief Henry Fonda and French detective Philippe Noiret suspiciously examine the defector).

Contemporary's *Boesman and Lena* emerged as one of the most sincere and moving importations of the year, a fine adaptation of the Athol Fugard stage play which, though primarily concerned with the effects of apartheid, put forward the plight of the dispossessed in any country: beautifully acted by Yvonne Bryceland and Athol Fugard.

Amanda's import *Flesh on Fire* was from Greece, a peasant melodrama about a wife who runs off with a gypsy and is duly killed by the outraged hubbie; and all the passion was unexpectedly punctuated by some gay singing and dancing sequences!

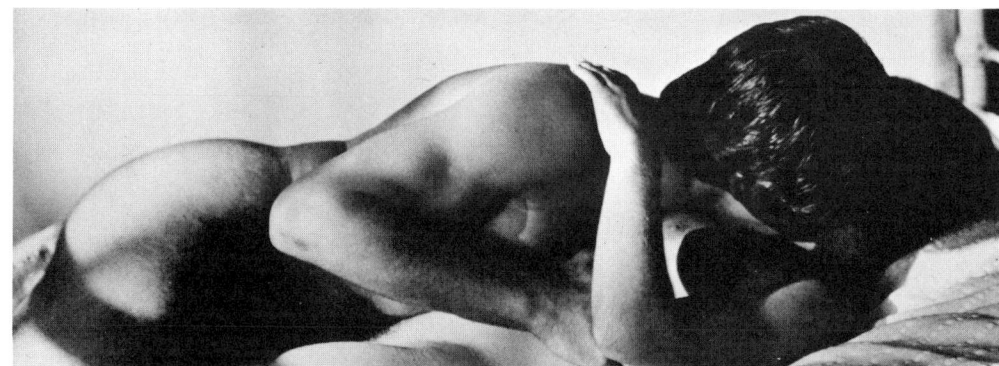

After a long time in the no-certificate wilderness Miracle's *Quiet Days in Clichy* won an X in 1974. In fact this Danish screen adaptation of the Henry Miller book was a rather dreary sandwich of explicit sexual encounters interleaved with night tours of Paris.

After all the violent Cops and Robbers films from America it was an extra pleasure to welcome the gentle and simple Israeli comedy, Monarch's *The Policeman*, the story of a warm-hearted cop who is about to be compulsorily retired because of his apparent ineptness, when he is saved by the local crooks, who in a return kindness stage a crime and arrest especially for his benefit! Itzko Rachaminov played the cop and the film introduced a quite sensational new glamour personality in Nitza Shaul.

Angela Mao, the martial arts expert in Cathay's Hong Kong production *Hap-Ki-Do*, a story of a feud between a newly established school of instruction and the horrid Black Bears Society.

Almost deserving to be included in my 'The Neglected Ones?' feature (which, by the way, has been dropped from this particular volume), *Fellini's Roma* had far less showing than it should have had, for it was in many ways a wonderful and certainly an outstanding movie. A highly personal impression of the Italian capital city, without linking story, just a collection of reminiscent scenes, Fellini's great artistry added them up to a unforgettable cinematic experience. One sequence was a reconstruction of a silent movie, with Angela de Leo; another quite outstanding one was the fashion parade of religious vestments.

Reminiscent? Well it's a scene from Nando Cicero's Border Film release entitled *The Last Italian Tango!* It was all about a young man who, leaving his brothel-keeping wife, falls in with and then falls in love with a prostitute. When he finds out her trade he is so disgusted he makes off . . . with the damaged damsel in hot pursuit.

Sydne Rome shows Hugh Griffith that girls are still girls – and the old man, overcome by the visual proof of the fact, happily succumbs in Roman Polanski's quite crazy sex comedy *What?*, set in a villa on the Rivièra. Newcomer Miss Rome (below), who never wears more and often quite a lot less than a pajama top throughout the movie, made a very good impression, showing something of the earlier Marilyn Monroe personality.

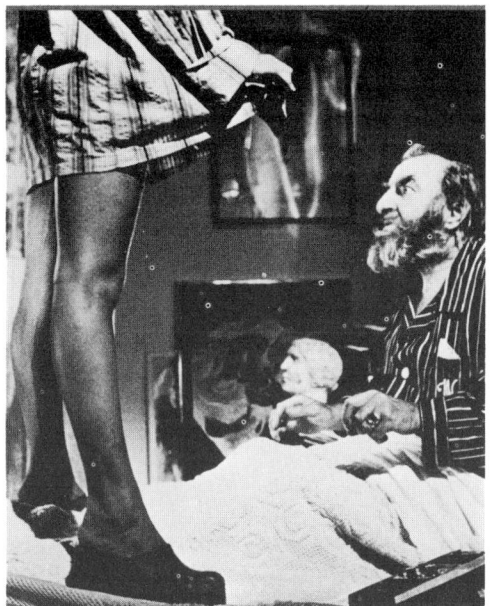

With *Lacombe Lucien* – a Fox–Rank release – Louis Malle made a new departure in turning to a story about a bovine peasant lad (Pierre Blaise) who during the last years of the war in Europe tries ineffectually to join the Resistance and then drifts into the ranks of the French fringe of the Gestapo, and there finds expression for his callous egotism, and love with a Jewish girl (Aurore Clement – seen with her father, played by Holger Lowenadler, who gave the outstanding performance of the film).

Target's *Hellfighters of the East* was the story of four Korean War veterans who find life in "peacetime" Seoul more dangerous and exciting than at any time during the war.

And still the Kung Fu thrillers poured into the stream of releases. Cathay's *Way of the Dragon* – which the late, ubiquitous Bruce Lee directed as well as starred in – was the story of a young man who comes to Rome to help out his Chinese restaurateur relative when the latter is threatened by gangsters.

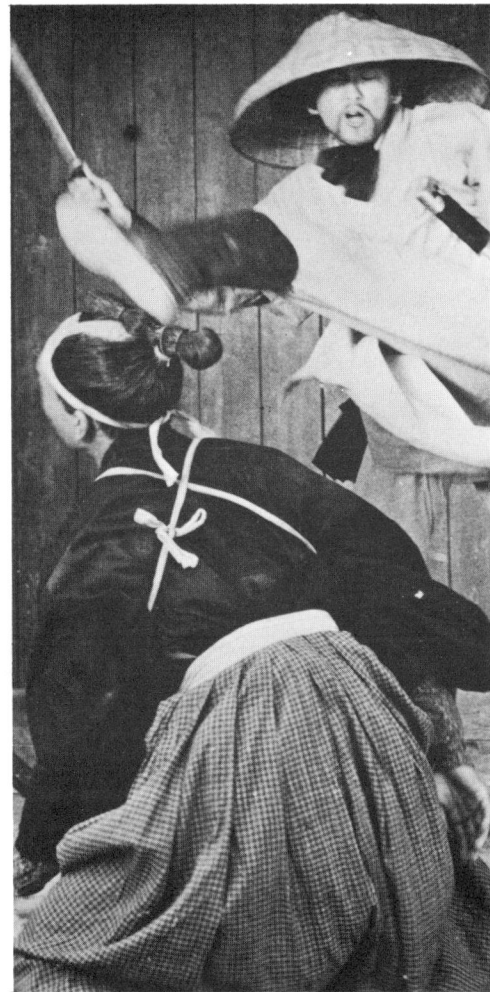

Cathay's *Beach of the War Gods* was again concerned with the Chinese struggle against the Japanese, this time set in a period four centuries ago and ending with the inevitable confrontation of the champions.

Target International's *Les Intrus – Menace –* was never quite as exciting a crime thriller as it might, indeed, should have been. It was the story of a French surgeon who is asked a million-dollar ransom if his small child is not to be killed by the two thugs who take over his house. Charles Aznavour played the doctor rather stolidly and Marie Christine Barrault played the wife.

The chase nears its end as fugitive Lino Ventura, high in the Austrian Alps, realises that once more the Russian agents are on his track and that time is running out for him, for as a defector who has exposed to the British a Soviet spy ring he can expect no mercy. Variety's *The Silent One* was French, dubbed into English, long, often slow, and beautifully photographed.

Jean-Louis Trintignant as the professional killer who, when he's done his lethal job in Los Angeles for his client in *The Outside Man*, finds that he in his turn has become the target of a group of killers who are determined that he shall never again reach France.

Claude Chabrol's *Nada*, from Connoisseur, marked a new departure for this director; the political thriller. And quite brilliant an example of the genre it was, too, about a small anarchist group of misfits and failures who, quite ineptly, kidnap the American Ambassador in Paris and are then surrounded in their hide-out and slaughtered by the authorities, who in their way are quite as ruthless and careless about human lives as their opponents. Shown, some of the gang in their last stand, Didier Kaminka, Mariangela Melato and Fabio Testi.

Some of the ingredients which lifted the Fox French (English-dubbed) comedy *The Tall Blond Man with the One Black Shoe* well above the average were the delightful zaniness of the story (about Secret Service agents more intent on scoring over each other than the enemy), the performance of Danny Kaye-ish hero Pierre Richard, and the reappearance of delicious Mireille Darc – as the ultimate weapon to break down male resistance! Here Mademoiselle Darc is successfully doing her "breaking" job on poor Pierre.

Vilgot Sjoman's (the Swedish director who will always be recalled for his, at that time, way-out sex film, *I Am Curious, Yellow*) Eagle release *Till Sex Do Us Part* was a comedy about a wife who won't let her husband have intercourse with her because she has an obsession that when he does she'll die! It's only towards the end of the film that she decides that it may be worth taking the chance! Leads were played by Solveig Ternström and Börje Ahlstedt.

One of the best French films of the year, in many ways a quite considerable classic, was Gala's Thomas Pascal comedy *Spring Into Summer*, which drew a wonderfully live and delicately true portrait of family life in a small provincial French town, more particularly of their teenage daughter Annie (played beautifully by Annie Cole) who in the warm weeks of summer loses her innocence quite deliberately and never lets it become more than a passing incident. Extremely amusing, quite captivating, and one of the films emanating from any country to be recalled with a warm sense of pleasure.

Jean-Paul Belmondo as the harassed author and Jacqueline Bisset as his pretty neighbour who, to his disgust, falls in love with the hero he has created rather than with him in the French, English-dubbed Columbia–Warner release *How to Destroy the Reputation of the Greatest Secret Agent*.

Leila Schenna as Rima, the teenage girl who represents something of the dilemma of all the young people living in primitive communities, in the Franco-Algerian film *Ramparts of Clay*, released by Contemporary Films in this country. It is set in a remote village in Southern Tunisia, where the girl, confronting despair, accepts the futility and necessity of her daily visit to the well.

WORLD ROUND-UP

by Peter Armitage

The cinema flags or spurts forward but it never stands still. Statistics on box-office returns and numbers of films in production give some idea of the state of business revealing crisis in some places, prosperity in others.

It is much more difficult to draw conclusions about trends on the screen and very easy to embark on flippant speculations about what comes next after The Mafia, corrupt and disillusioned cops, Kung Fu, Gatsby. . . . Noting that nostalgia, in some form, is evident in many other places than the English-speaking cinema, it can be portentously suggested that obsession with the past is dominant everywhere. At worst this kind of "analysis" is positively misleading, and at best it is highly superficial for it never reveals much.

The truth is that the still rich and abundant variety of world cinema defies quick and easy diagnosis. One can do no better than sample survey the new films and those in the pipeline. There are indications that great things are beginning to happen in Africa, Canada, Australia, and many other places, but the countries in this survey are deliberately limited to those whose films have already made a significant impression on us.

FRANCE

French cinema is still booming. All the best-known names are fully employed, with the exception of Truffaut, who is pausing to think how best to exploit the new freedom he should have as a result of the great international success of *La Nuit Américaine – Day for Night*. The older generation carries on through Buñuel's *Les Fantômes de la Liberté*, Carné's *La Merveilleuse Visit* based on H. G. Wells, and Bresson has at last completed his long-cherished *Lancelot du Lac*.

Other old hands are on familiar ground: Cayatte making *The Tiger and the Elephant* with Jean Gabin and Sophia Loren; Franju, who once made *Eyes Without a Face*, has made *L'homme sans Visage* about a faceless man who tries to steal the treasure of the Knights Templar; Allio has made *Rude Journée pour la Reine* with Simone Signoret; and Robbe-Grillet's *Glissements Progressifs du Plaisir* had the usual trappings of bondage and voyeurism and he moved on to *Le Jeu avec le Feu* with Philippe Noiret, Jean-Louis Trintignant and Anicée Alvina.

Sequels in the pipeline are Robert's *Return of the Big Blond*, Deray's *Borsalino and Co.* with Alain Delon, and this category might also include *Le Magnifique* which reunites de Broca and Belmondo, the team that made *That Man from Rio*. Belmondo also stars in *Stavisky*, Resnais's first film for five years. More prolific directors like Chabrol turn new films out in rapid fire and after *Nada*, he turned to *Soul Sick* with one of his favourite writers, Paul Gégauff, in front of the cameras, and is also working on *Goddy*, to be filmed in England with Richard Burton as the Dean of a public school. The eclectic Louis Malle's latest film, *Lacombe Lucien*, is about a young boy during the Occupation who joins the Gestapo when he is turned down by the Resistance.

Many other films deserve mention: Delville's *Le Mouton Enragé*; Bertuccelli's *Le Desert des Tartares* with Jacques Perrin, Henry Fonda, Oliver Reed, James Fox and Laurence Olivier; Sautet's *Vincent, François, Paul et les Autres* with Montand, Serge Reggiani; Ferreri's *Custer* with Noiret, who is also in Tavernier's prize-winning *The Watchmaker of St Paul*; Lautner's *Crimes* with Delon and Mireille Darc; Bertrand Blier's *The Waltzers* with Miou-Miou and Gerard Depardieu; Arabal's *J'irai comme un cheval fou*.

After two straight Occupation dramas, Jean Yanne scored a great popular success with *The Chinese in Paris*, a comic fantasy of Paris occupied by the Chinese, whose diplomatic protests only heightened public interest in the film.

The sure-fire box-office stars are very careful about their appearances and often find their way into co-productions: Catherine Deneuve went to Spain for Buñuel's *The Girl with the Red Boots* and then Italy for Bolognini's *The Murri Affair*, and Alain Delon, after *Creezy*, directed by Pierre Granière-Deferre, also went to Italy for a new version of *Zorro*. A growing number of the hard-worked top actors are not content to stay in front of the cameras and in addition to established actor-directors like Jean Yanne and Jean-Claude Brialy, whose latest is *Un Amour de Pluie* with Romy Schneider, the ranks are being joined by actresses like Anna Karina (with *Vivre Ensemble*) and probably

142

Scene from M. Audiard's *Comment Réussir Dans La Vie Quand On Est Con et Pleurnichard*.

Annie Girardot and Marlène Jobert flank French comedian Pierre Richard (who made such a big impression in *The Tall Blond Man with the One Black Shoe*) in Forlani's *Juliette et Juliette*.

Brigitte Bardot in Mag Bodard's *L'Histoire Très Bonne et Très Joyeuse de Colinct Trousse-Chemise*.

Jean Gabin in *L'Affaire Dominici*.

Catherine Deneuve in Jacques Demy's *L'Evènèment le Plus Important Depuis que L'Homme A Marché Sur La Lune*.

Jean-Paul Belmondo in Alain Resnais's *Stavisky*.

Jacqueline Bisset – in chains – in *Le Magnifique*.

Jeanne Moreau who has written a script, *The Actresses*, and wants to direct.

The future prospects seem bright with some highly promising projects like Lelouch's *Lifetime*, a history of the twentieth century in pictures and songs, and the French–Soviet co-production of *Anna Karenina* to be directed by Jacques Demy with Maya Plisetskaya in the title-role, music by Michel Legrand and Pierre Cardin costumes.

ITALY

Box-office takings were up about a quarter last year, a new state-owned circuit was started and, not surprisingly, the studios are now highly active with some of the veterans making comebacks after very serious illnesses.

When Visconti returned in a wheelchair to direct Burt Lancaster, as a professor in love with a girl young enough to be his grand-daughter, in *Conversation Piece*, the set was visited by a host of celebrities to mark the event. De Sica recovered enough to appear in front of the cameras as well as to direct Sophia Loren and Richard Burton in *The Voyage*. Other great directors who do not deliver a new work each year have completed their latest films. Antonioni's latest was *The Reporter* with Jack Nicholson and Maria Schneider, Patroni-Griffi's was *The Driver's Seat* with Elizabeth Taylor and, in *Amarcord*, Fellini again taxed the patience of those who regard his every effort as another slice of self-indulgent autobiography and delighted those who will never tire of endless variations on his familiar fantasies. Pasolini completed his *Thousand and One Nights* and also helped write Sergio Citti's

collection of sketches set in Papal Rome, *Bawdy Tales*, which stars Citti's brother, Franco, and Ninetto Davoli, both favourite actors of Pasolini. Even Zeffirelli, who has turned his back on the cinema more than once, is being lined up to direct George C. Scott and Peter O'Toole in *Dante's Inferno* with music by Shostakovitch, choreography by Moiseyev and art direction by Danilo Donati.

Women directors are also going strong. Lina Wertmuller followed up her *Film of Love and Anarchy* with *Everything's in Place, Nothing's in Order*, which sounds as if it could be a sequel. Liliana Cavani continued to be highly controversial with *Milarepa*, a spiritual voyage touching upon the virtues of non-violence and mystical faith, with actors playing dual roles in past and present, and *The Night Porter*, played by Dirk Bogarde, who twelve years earlier had been a storm-trooper, now having a sado-masochistic love affair with a concentration camp victim.

Lizzani's *Last Days of Mussolini* with Rod Steiger, Henry Fonda, Lisa Gastoni and Franco Nero is the most publicised of a group of films looking back to the war and beyond which also includes Maselli's *Mission in Fascist Italy* with Gianmaria Volonte, Annie Girardot and Renato Salvatori. Nationalism is also evident in another group which includes Zampa's *Italian Go Home* and Loy's *I Go, Fix America and Return*. Many more films have interesting features: for example, Brusati's *Bread and Chocolate* with Nino Manfredi, Sordi's *While There's War There's Hope* starring himself, Taviannis' *Allonsenfans* with Mastroianni, Bolognini's *Libera My Love* with Cardinale

144 and Rondi's *The Stake* with Harriet Andersson.

WEST GERMANY

Currently only about one in five of West German films in production is intended for the large rather than the small screen. The prospects stir little hope and, as elsewhere, the film workers' unions are pressing for more state support. What does get made is a very mixed bag. The most fashionable name internationally, Rainer Werner Fassbinder's last work was a version of Fontane's *Effie Briest*, though he was also the producer of Lommel's *The Tenderness of Wolves*, the story of a child murderer of the twenties who was portrayed by Peter Lorre over forty years ago in Fritz Lang's *M*. Fassbinder made a brief appearance in this film and Lommel reciprocated in *Effie Briest*.
Not many films have stars with world-wide fame but among those that do there is Schaaf's *Dreamtown* with Per Oscarsson, Reitz's *Journey to Vienna* with Elke Sommer, Lilienthal's *Icaros* with Lionel Stander and Schenk's new version of Schnitzler's *La Ronde* with Helmut Berger, Maria Schneider, Sydne Rome and Senta Berger.
The other films capable of being exported are those with a strong sex component like *Over Night*, the tour of a promiscuous heroine directed by actress Karin Thome, Marischka's *The Miner's Wife* in which Anne Graf strays from the marital straight and narrow, and Fleischmann's *Dorothea's Revenge* about a sixteen-year-old who is rather similar in nature to Terry Southern's *Candy*. Among the more experimental, low-budget films is Herbst's *The Fantastic*

Kurt Raab in Ulli Lommel's West German film *The Tenderness of Wolves*.

World of Matthew Madson, a tale of astronauts on an unnamed planet.

HOLLAND AND BELGIUM

While activities may languish in the major film-producing countries, two or three good features can make a golden summer in small countries like Holland and Belgium. These countries have long been highly regarded for excellent shorts and documentaries and two of the famous documentarists, Bert Haanstra and Henri Stork, have scored some success with their features, *Ape and Super Ape* and *Fêtes of Belgium*. Fiction films have also made some mark and Paul Verhoeven's *Turkish Delight* has been followed up by Frans Weisz's *The Frame-up* and *Lady on the Fence*, Pim de la Parra's *Frank and Eva*, *Living Apart Together* and Benoit Lamy's *Home, Sweet Home*. Perhaps the most respected of the Belgian directors is André Delvaux, who has followed his *Rendezvous at Bray* and *The Man Who Had His Hair Cut Short* with *Belle* which stars Jean-Luc Bideau and Daniele Delorme.

SWITZERLAND

Swiss cinema surfaced again on the international scene after many years of obscurity with Alain Tanner's *The Salamander*, Michel Soutter's *The Surveyor* and Claude Goretta's *The Invitation*. Given some government support, the revival does not seem to be in imminent danger of petering out.
Goretta went on to make *The Wedding Day* and Tanner has followed up with *Return from Africa*, *Charles Dead or Alive* and *Middle of the Road* with Philippe Leotard. Soutter's achievement impressed Jean-Louis Trintignant enough for him to join Marie Dubois in his next film, *The Escapade*.
In addition to French co-productions, film-making in Switzerland has had a strong attraction for Germans like Maximilian Schell, whose *The Pedestrian* had a remarkable cast including Peggy Ashcroft,

Jean-Luc Bideau and Daniele Delorme in André Delvaux's Belgian film *Belle*.

Josee Destoop and François Marthouret in Alain Tanner's – Swiss – production *Return From Africa*, about a young couple's abortive trip to that country.

Scene from Jan Troell's *The New Land*, following the story of the Swedish family we saw leave their native land and start a pioneer life in America in *The Emigrants*.

Elizabeth Bergner, Lil Dagover, Françoise Rosay and Peter Hall among many others. The story concerns a leading industrialist whose muckraked war crimes as a Nazi officer eventually catch up on him.

SWEDEN

The final stages of the reform of the Swedish film industry have now been reached but most of the current production is along familiar lines. The sex films include Wickman's progress of a nymphomaniac, *Anita*, Ahlberg's sequel to *Fanny Hill*, *Around the World with Fanny Hill*, and *Bed of Lust*, described as "Sweden's first wholly pornographic feature in colour with actors from the pornography business". The director of *Thriller – A Cruel Story* hides behind the pseudonym Alex Fridolinski and the film is the first to be totally banned by the Swedish censor. It is about a girl rendered mute by the trauma of childhood rape who grows up to be a narcotics addict exploited in an exclusive bordello. There are also documentaries with self-explanatory titles like *Report from the Swedish Sex Jungle*.

Some well-known directors have produced characteristic work: Kjell Grede, *A Simple Melody*; Jorn Donner, *Baksmalla*; Jan Halldoff, *Stone Face* and *Wedding party – Swedish Style*. Vilgot Sjoman may at last be living down his scandal success of the *Curious* films with *A Handful of Love*, starring Ingrid Thulin and set in the context of the 1909 general strike. It sounds like the sort of film that Bo Widerberg might have made but he too may have moved on with *Stubby*, a comedy about a six-year-old boy

146 who gets into the Swedish national football team.

So far as the cinema is concerned, Ingmar Bergman is lying fallow, making a TV series of six *Scenes from Marriage* with Liv Ullmann, but germinating film scripts like *The Magic Flute* and projects like *The Merry Widow*, which with Barbra Streisand sounds as intriguing as Erich von Stroheim's classic made in the mid-twenties.

SPAIN

Reports suggest that the Spanish cinema is not in great shape as it no longer attracts the same volume of US and international production which sustained its well-being for so many years. None the less it still provides a suitable locale for Kung Fu westerns like *Blood Money* with Lee Van Cleef, and Orson Welles remains faithful with *The Other Side of the Wind* which stars John Huston, Rich Little, Mercedes McCambridge, Lilli Palmer, Edmond O'Brien, Paul Stewart, Susan Strasberg, Peter Bogdanovich and Cameron Mitchell. With Luis Berlanga working in Paris, the leading domestic director, Carlos Saura, has broken new ground in his treatment of the Spanish Civil War with *La Prima Angelica* possibly indicating some relaxation of political censorship. Victor Erice made an auspicious début with *The Spirit of the Bee-hive*, the story of a young girl obsessed with the presence of an imaginary Frankenstein. Jaime de Arminan's *My Dearest Senorita*, a comedy involving a sex change, has been highly successful and won an Oscar nomination.

A scene from the Spanish film, *My Dearest Senorita*, directed by Jaime de Arminan.

USSR

There have been some interesting new developments in Soviet film-making, particularly in the extension of co-production beyond the usual East European partnerships and in the release of a number of films which apparently show some deviation from orthodox political attitudes. No doubt the major part of production is along familiar lines, especially the mainstream historical epics like Ozerov's *Communists* and Bondarchuk's *They Fought for Their Motherland*, and the faithful treatments of reputable literary works, Ptouchko's *Ruslan and Ludmila*, Alov and Naumov's *Till Eulenspiegel*, Heifitz's return to Chekov,

Bad Good Man, and Samsonov's *Much Ado About Nothing*.

Some of the co-productions are "regular" like Balatov's version of Dostoevsky's *The Gambler*, Kuliyev's *Wuthering Sea* and Golub's *Remember Your Mother*, all made with the Czechs, and to a lesser extent, Ryzanov's *Extraordinary Adventures of the Italians in Russia* made with Dino de Laurentiis. What is new is the Japanese co-production, *Moscow My Love*, and even more so the agreement to make films with the US including a planned version of Maeterlinck's *The Bluebeard*, possibly directed by George Cukor.

At a time when a director like Paradjanov, best known abroad for *Shadows of Our Forgotten Ancestors*, is arrested after the release of his latest film *Sayat Nova*, and what sounds like a hard line propaganda documentary is being made on Solzhenitsyn, there has been a string of modest, personal and sometimes, experimental films such as Shepitko's *You and I*, Absulada's *Molba*, Ioseliani's *Singing Blackbird*, Zhalakyavichus's *That Sweet Word – Liberty* and Shengelaya's *Pirosmani* which was given the British Film Institute Award for 1973. The biggest stir has been created by Shukshin's *The Red Snowball Tree*. The story sounds like the Soviet variant of that old chestnut about the hardened criminal who, on release, decides to go straight and opts for the simple life with the farmer's daughter, only for his old gang to catch up with him producing tragic consequences. The excitement has been caused by the fatalistic overtones, the religious symbols and the non-conformist absence of reference to the party or anything uplifting.

EASTERN EUROPE

For the past two decades, first the Poles, then the Czechs and later the Hungarians were in the forefront of world cinema. Currently nobody seems to be pre-eminent or making the running. This impression may owe a lot to the fact that a new Jancso film is overdue and Wajda, at least temporarily, has returned to the theatre. In all these countries there is still much looking back to the war and to earlier revolutionary events. Heroes are most often factory directors or workers suddenly presented with, or spontaneously becoming aware of, a crisis of conscience which makes them realise the selfishness of their ways. Some of the films likely to show on the international scene are:
Hungary – Karoly Makk's *Cat's Game*, Peter Bacso's *The Last Chance*, Istvan Szabo's *25 Fireman Street* with the Polish actress Lucyna Winniczka, Andras Kovacs's *Fallow Land*, Marta Meszaros's *Riddance*, Zoltan Varkonyi's *Innocent Assassins*;
Poland – Zanussi's *Illumination*, Zebrowski's *Salvation*, Has's *The Sandglass*, Lomnicki's *Awards and Distinctions*, Nasfeter's *Butterflies*, and *Mazepa* directed by the popular actor Gustaw Holoubek;
Czechoslovakia – Brynych's *What Colour is Love?* Balik's *Lovers in the Year One* and *Miss Golem*, Podskalsky's *A Night at Karlstein*, Uher's *Valley*, Kachyna's *Legend* and Vavra's *Days of Betrayal*; Rumania – *The Power and the Truth*, *With Clean Hands*.

JAPAN

The decline in cinema-going has struck the film industry in Japan rather later than in most other countries and only now is it beginning to bite deep. The annual production of feature films is still around the 400 mark but further contraction seems inevitable. Even at this relatively healthy level of production, many of the most famous film-makers have not made new films for some years and the most active directors seem to be those who have wives who are leading actresses like Shinoda (Shima Iwashita), Oshima (Akiko Koyama) and Yoshida (Mariko Okada). Shinoda's latest films are *Himoko* and *The Petrified Forest*, Oshima's is *Dear Summer Sister* and Yoshida's is *Coup d'Etat*, about a political revolutionary in the militaristic Japan of the thirties.

Some of these films are rather difficult for foreign audiences to fully appreciate and this is probably true of the top box-office attraction domestically, *The Human Revolution*. Directed by Masuda from a popular book by Ikeda, this film is likely to impress the few Western critics who see it but as a dramatisation of Buddhist beliefs its commercial success is likely to be confined to Asia.

Among the films which may find their way into art houses are Narushima's *Time Within Memory* in which a man in his forties, haunted by his relationship with his mother and her mysterious death, searches for his youth; Higashi's satirical fantasy, *Satori*, about a strange omniscient being with magic powers, a young working girl and a young man who only wants to sleep; and Kon Ichikawa's *The Wanderers*, a somewhat comic period piece about a band of petty thieves, farmers' sons but social outcasts with their own code of conduct and frequently behaving like cut-price samurai.

A scene from Shengelaya's *Pirosmani*, the Russian film given the BFI's 1973 Award.

Scene from Risto Jarva's Finnish film *One Man's War*.

A Scene from Krzystof Zanussi's Polish film
Illumination

A scene from Otakar Vavra's
Czechoslovakian film *Days of Betrayal*.

Katia Paskaleva in Bulgaria's *The Goat Horn*,
directed by Jan Zahradnik.

A scene from Kon Ichikawa's comic period
piece *The Wanderers*.

AWARDS AND FESTIVALS

The 1973 "Oscars", those coveted awards given out each year by the American Academy of Motion Picture Arts and Sciences, contrary to most years did manage to spring some sort of surprise by *not* handing out to the generally "tipped" *Exorcist* more than two awards: those for "Best Screenplay based on material from another medium" (William Peter Blatty) and "Best Sound" (Robert Knudson and Chris Newman).

Best Film
THE STING (CIC)

Best Actor
JACK LEMMON in *Save the Tiger* (CIC)

Best Actress
GLENDA JACKSON in *A Touch of Class* (Avco–Embassy)

Best Supporting Actor
JOHN HOUSEMAN in *The Paper Chase* (Fox–Rank)

Best Supporting Actress
TATUM O'NEAL in *Paper Moon* (CIC)

Best Art Direction
THE STING (Henry Bumstead–CIC)

Best Cinematography
CRIES AND WHISPERS (Sven Nykvist–Gala)

Best Costume Design
THE STING (Edith Head–CIC)

Best Direction
THE STING (George Roy Hill–CIC)

Best Documentary
Feature: *THE GREAT AMERICAN COWBOY*.
Short: *PRINCETON, A SEARCH FOR ANSWERS*

Best Film Editing
THE STING (William Reynolds–CIC)

Best Foreign Language Film
DAY FOR NIGHT (Col-War)

Best Original Dramatic Score
THE WAY WE WERE (Marvin Hamlisch–Col-War)

Best Score Adaptation
THE STING (Marvin Hamlisch–CIC)

Best Song
THE WAY WE WERE (Music: Marvin Hamlisch; Lyrics: Alan and Marilyn Bergman–Col-War)

Best Short
Animated: *FRANK FILM*.
Live Action: *THE BOLERO*

Best Screenplay based on material not previously published
THE STING (David S. Ward–CIC)

Best Screenplay based on material from another medium
THE EXORCIST (William Peter Blatty)

Those English (female) equivalents to the "Oscars", the "Stellas", the annual awards given out by the British Society of Film and Television Arts – presented this year at the Royal Albert Hall at the beginning of March by Princess Anne – went considerably to European films and film-makers. This was the line-up:

Best Film
DAY FOR NIGHT

Best Director
FRANÇOIS TRUFFAUT for *Day For Night*

Best Actress
STEPHANE AUDRAN in *The Discreet Charm of the Bourgeoisie* and *Just Before Nightfall*

Best Supporting Actress
VALENTINE CORTESE in *Day For Night*

Best Actor
WALTER MATTHAU in *Pete 'N' Tillie* and *Charley Varrick*

Best Supporting Actor
ARTHUR LOWE in *O Lucky Man!*

Most Promising Newcomer
PETER EGAN in *The Hireling*

150 **United Nations Award**
STATE OF SIEGE (Director: Costa-Gavras)

John Grierson Award for Best Short Film
CARING FOR HISTORY

Best Specialised Film
A MAN'S WORLD

Best Animated Film
TCHOU TCHOU

Robert Flaherty Award for best feature length documentary
GRIERSON

Best Screenplay
LUIS BUÑUEL and JEAN-CLAUDE CARRIERE for *The Discreet Charm of the Bourgeoisie*

Best Cinematography
ANTHONY RICHMOND for *Don't Look Now*

Best Art Direction
NATASHA KROLL for *The Hireling*

Best Costume Design
PHYLLIS DALTON for *The Hireling*

Best Film Editing
RALPH KEMPLEN for *The Day of the Jackal*

Best Sound Track
LES WIGGINS, GORDON K. McCALLUM and KEITH GRANT for *Jesus Christ Superstar*

Anthony Asquith Memorial Award
ALAN PRICE (for the music of *O Lucky Man!*)

Every year the American cinema trade paper *The Motion Picture Herald* takes a poll among all American cinemas to find out which stars bring the most money into their box-offices. This year (1973, that is) the order of popularity was as follows:

1: Clint Eastwood; 2: Ryan O'Neal; 3: Steve McQueen; 4: Burt Reynolds; 5: Robert Redford; 6: Barbra Streisand; 7: Paul Newman; 8: John Wayne; 9: Charles Bronson; 10: Marlon Brando; 11: Gene Hackman; 12: Liza Minelli.

A similar sort of merit list compiled in Great Britain, but of films not stars, made interesting reading:

1: *Live and Let Die*; 2: *The Godfather*; 3: *A Clockwork Orange*; 4: *Snow White* (re-issue); 5: *The Poseidon Adventure*; 6: *Last Tango in Paris*; 7: *Cabaret*; 8: *The Day of the Jackal*; 9: *Lady Caroline Lamb*; 10: *That'll Be the Day*; 11: *Lady Sings the Blues*; 12: *Lost Horizon*.

Now some of the prizes handed out at the various film Festivals around the world.

Moscow July 1973
Some fifty awards of various kinds were handed out at the end of this fourteen-day Festival, the main prizes going to:

OKLAHOMA CRUDE (America), *THAT SWEET WORD LIBERTY* (USSR) and *LOVE* (Bulgaria), splitting the "Best Film" prize three ways
Best Children's Film: *PINOCCHIO*, with Gina Lollobrigida (Italy)
Popular Science Award: *THE SUN IS RED* (Denmark) and *UNDERCURRENTS* (GB)
Anti-Fascist Award: *SUTJESKA* (Yugoslavia)
Anti-Imperialist Award: *THOSE YEARS* (Mexico)
Political Film Award: *MATTEOTI ASSASSINATION* (Italy)

Leipzig December 1973
Special Prize: *EL TIGRE SALTO Y MATO* (Cuba)
Golden Doves: *ROMENSKA JA MADONNA* (USSR); *TAY HO – THE VILLAGE IN THE 4th ZONE* (East Germany) and *POWESTJ OF PERWOJ WESNE* (USSR)
Silver Doves: *VROMOLKY STRMOV* (Czechoslovakia); *LOWCA* (Poland); *RUNAN CAYAN* (Peru); *EL ORO ES TRISTE* (Columbia) and *ON THE NILE* (Egypt)
Additional Prizes: *WEIL ER EIN PALASTINENSER* 1st (West Germany) and *OPERATION – THE LAST PATROL* (USA)
Special Mentions: *LIEBER MOHR* (East Germany); *HERBST IN EINER GENOSSENCHAFT* (Mongolian People's Republic); *EPOKA I LUDZIE* –

COPERNICUS (Poland); *THE OLD ONE* (Hungary); *DER AUFSCHREI DIESES VOLKES – VOLIVIEN* (Argentina); *100 YEARS OF SCHOOLBOOKS IN JAPAN* (Japan) and *HERTA LINNEROVA* (Czechoslovakia).

Valentina Cortese (who, incidentally, won the Stella for the "Best Supporting Performance") with Jean-Pierre Aumont in François Truffaut's *Day for Night – La Nuit Américaine*, which won the British Society of Film and Television Arts Award, the Stella, for the best film of 1973.

Awards and Festivals

Cork June 1973

Feature Awards

Music: *CHILD'S PLAY* (USA) and
CRYSTAL BALL (Poland)
Art Direction: *UNCLE VANYA* (USSR)
and *THE ADVENTURES OF BARRY
McKENZIE* (Australia)
Editing: *THE STUFF THAT DREAMS
ARE MADE OF* (FRG) and *THE SILENT
MAN* (France)
Screen Writing: *CHILD'S PLAY* (USA)
and *THE EFFECT OF GAMMA RAYS
ON MAN-IN-THE-MOON
MARIGOLDS*
Photography: *CHILD'S PLAY* (USA)
and *JOURNEY* (Canada)

Shorts

General Interest/Documentaries: *THE
WATER CYCLE* (New Zealand) and
WINGS AND THINGS (UK)
Animation: *LA LINEA NUMERO 5* (Italy)
and *ILUZJA* (Poland)
Films on Art: *LA MORT DU JEUNE
POETE* (France) and *HOW PAINTINGS
ARE CREATED* (Australia)
Short Story Fiction Films: *MIMI* (USA)
and *UN PIRD BOYS* (Belgium)

San Sebastian October 1973

Golden Shell First Prize: *EL ESPIRITU
DE LA COLMENA* (*The Spirit of the
Beehive*) – Director: Victor Erice (Spanish)
Silver Shells: *PAPER MOON* – Director:
Peter Bogdanovich (USA); *A TOUCH OF
CLASS* – Director: Melvin Frank (GB) and
THE WEDDING – Director: Andrzej
Wajda (Poland)
Best Male Performance: LINO VENTURA
for *La Bonne Annee* (France) and
GIANCARLO GIANNINI for *Sono Stato

Lo* (Italy)
Best Female Performance: GLENDA
JACKSON for *A Touch of Class* (GB) and
FRANÇOISE FABIAN for *La Bonne
Année* (France)
Best Short: *OCISTNA LAZEN*
Special Mention to DAVID WOLPER,
producer of *Visions of Eight*
Critics Circle Award: *PAPER MOON*

Berlin July 1973

First Prize – Golden Bear: Satyajit Ray's
DISTANT THUNDER (India)
Special Jury Prize – Silver Bear: André
Cayatte's *WHERE THERE'S SMOKE
THERE'S FIRE* (France)
Runners-up – Silver Bears: Leopoldo Torre
Nilsson's *THE REVOLUTION OF THE
SEVEN MADMEN* (Argentina); Yves
Robert's *THE TALL BLOND MAN WITH
ONE BLACK SHOE* (France); Norbert
Kueckelmann's *THE EXPERTS* (West
Germany); Arnaldo Jabor's *ALL NUDITY
WILL BE PUNISHED* (Brazil) and David
Hemmings' *THE 14* (GB)
Short Subject Awards
First Prize – Golden Bear: Robin Lehman's
COLTER'S HELL (GB)
Second Prize – Silver Bears: Aleksander
Ilic's *THE OWL* (Yugoslavia) and Pedrag
Golubovic's *JOSEF SCHULZ* (Yugoslavia)
Catholic (OCIC) and Protestant Awards:
*WHERE THERE'S SMOKE THERE'S
FIRE* (France). Also *THE RETURN
FROM AFRICA* (Switzerland); *SHOTS IN
THE FACTORY* (Finland) and *JOSEF
SCHULZ* (Yugoslavia)
International Critics FIPRESCI Prize:
Claude Chabrol's *LES NOCES ROUGES*
(France) and *LO STAGIONALE* (Italy)

Cannes 1974

Grand Prix – Francis Ford Coppola's *THE
CONVERSATION* (CIC)
Best Screenplay – Steven Spielberg's
SUGARLAND EXPRESS (CIC)
Best Actor – Jack Nicholson in *THE LAST
DETAIL*
Best Actress – Marie Jose Nat in *VIOLONS
DU BAL* (France)
Special Jury Prize – *IL FIORE DELLE
MILLE E UNA NOTTE*, directed by
Pier Paolo Pasolini (Italy)
Jury Prize – Carlos Saura Fov *LA PRIMA
ANGELICA* (Spain)
Grand Prix – Shorts – *OSTROV* (USSR)
Jury Prize – Shorts – *LA FAIM* (Canada)
International Film Critics Award –
LANCELOT DU LAC (Robert Bresson –
France) and *ANGST ESSEN SEELE AUF*
(Fassbinder – Germany)
Grand Prix de la Commission Supérièure
Technique du Cinéma Français – *MAHLER*
The jury paid special tribute to Charles
Boyer for his role as Baron Raoul in
STAVISKY

Tehran March 1974

Grand Prize: *LUCKY LUCIANO* –
directed by Francesco Rosi (Italy)

FILM FUTURE

In this next section of *Film Review*, as every year, we break out of the plan of covering just the twelve months between the first day of July of one year and the last day of June the next (in this case 1973–4) and look into the future, unencumbered by having to worry about dates. Some of the films in the next few pages, you'll be seeing on your screens almost as soon as the book is published, others may not be released for many months and, indeed, some may even be more than a year away (it does happen, though not often).

In any case this is just a skimming of the cream – we hope! – and for each film illustrated there are many more in the pipeline in various stages of planning or production. If there are gaps then it is only because the right kind of material or information was not obtainable.

But I would at this late point like to once again reiterate my sincere gratitude for the film companies and their press and publicity representatives who year by year serve me – yes, and you! – so well and conscientiously. I would mention names but it would be rather unfair in that so often it is those behind the scenes to whom I am as much indebted as those whom I know. Anyway, the general assistance given me in preparing this book is immense and very greatly appreciated: as I have said here and elsewhere on many occasions, without that cheerful and willing help there would have never been the thirty annual *Film Review* volumes which now stand on my shelves (one volume covered two years you may recall).

Michael Caine in UA's *The Wilby Conspiracy*, an adventure drama based on the Peter Driscoll novel and filmed entirely in Kenya. Michael's co-stars will be Sidney Poitier and Nicol Williamson and the cast includes screen newcomers Prunella Gee and Persis Khambatta – a recent "Miss India".

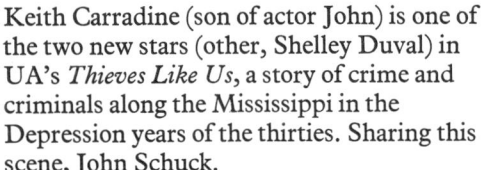

Keith Carradine (son of actor John) is one of the two new stars (other, Shelley Duval) in UA's *Thieves Like Us*, a story of crime and criminals along the Mississippi in the Depression years of the thirties. Sharing this scene, John Schuck.

More crime and criminals in UA's *The Bank Shot*, with George C. Scott as the master criminal who escapes from jail in order to pull off a very strange bank raid indeed.

Ian Bannen and Sophia Loren in a romantic moment from UA's drama *The Voyage*.

Bruno Zannin and Magali Noel in the new Fellini film, from UA, *Amarcord*, further reminiscences of Fellini's own past life.

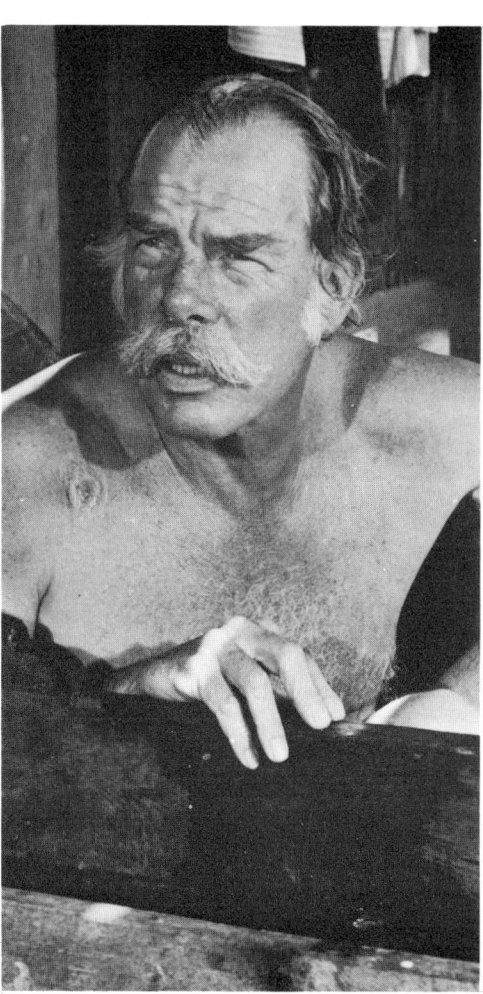

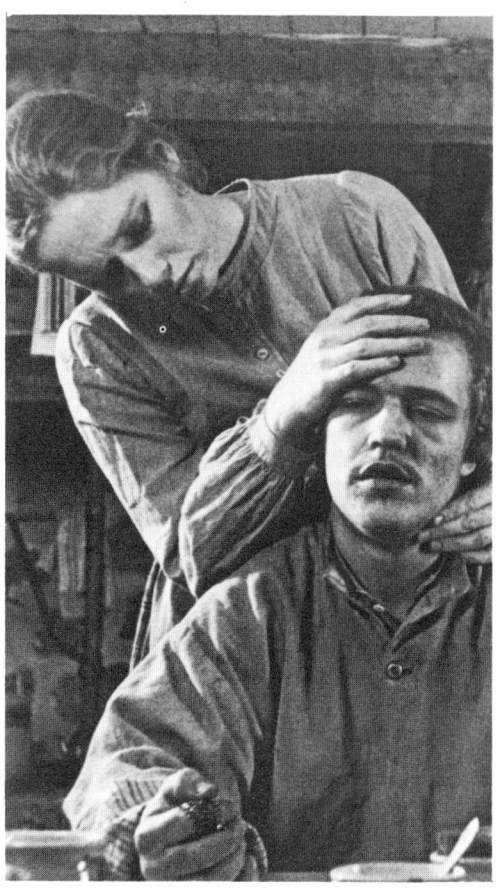

Clint Eastwood in somewhat unfamiliar garb in UA's *Thunderbolt and Lightfoot*, a story of a bank-robber whose preoccupation is to escape from the fellow members of his gang as much as from the cops.

Yet another film about a bank-robber is UA's *The Spikes Gang*, the story of the unfortunate effect that the much-wanted Harry – played by Lee Marvin – has on the lives of three boys who come into contact with him.

The second part of the most epic-scale film ever to emerge from the Swedish studios (the first part was *The Emigrants*), Jan Troell's *The New Land* (released by Warner Bros) continues the story of the Swedish family who make their home in America (Minnesota) and struggle against all the pioneering difficulties. Shown: Liv Ullmann and Eddie Axberg.

Jack Lemmon and Anne Bancroft in Warner's Melvin Frank production of the Neil Simon play *The Prisoner of Second Avenue*.

Gene Hackman and Melanie Griffith in *The Dark Tower*, a Warner Bros whodunit "with such a twist ending that the final scene was deleted from all scripts so that the identity of the murderer remained a secret even to the cast"!

Liv Ullmann as ex-Queen Christina of Sweden in Warner's *The Abdication*, the story of her confrontation with the Vatican in 1655, an adaptation of the Ruth Wolff stage play with the same title.

Lucille Ball (right) who – all the American reports suggest – gives such a tremendous performance in the title-role of the film adaptation of the famous stage musical *Mame*, brought to the screen by Warner Bros.

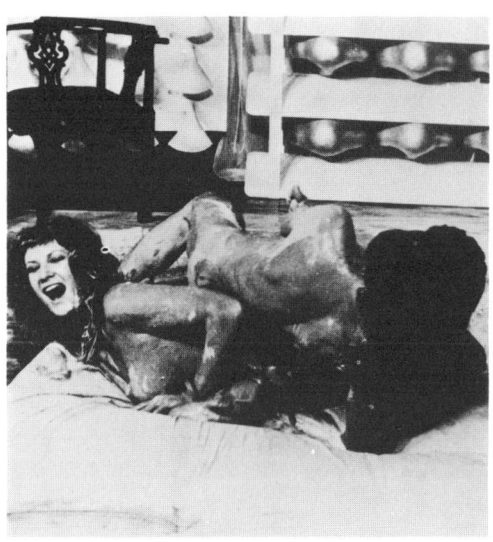

Some lively all-in wrestling from Warner's Australian production *Alvin Purple*, the story of a young man (Graeme Blundell), whom women find quite irresistible.

Due for a summer release, Warner's *Blazing Saddles*, is a Mel Brooks comedy-satire about Westerns starring Gene Wilder, Slim Pickens, etc.

160

Scott Wilson, Mia Farrow and Robert Redford, the last in the title-role in the Jack Clayton-directed film – the third – of the F. Scott Fitzgerald novel *The Great Gatsby*, released by CIC.

Frank Finlay and Richard Chamberlain as two of Dumas's *Three Musketeers* in the Fox comedy film of that title which is due for a late August general release.

Max von Sydow as the Priest struggling
against the Devil in William Peter Blatty's
film of his own novel *The Exorcist*, directed
by William Friedkin.

Charles Bronson as the melon farmer driven
into murder by the action of a crooked labour
organiser in the Mirisch–Fleischer film
Mr Majestyk, due for general release on
July 21, 1974.

162

Sergei Bondarchuk in Andrei Mikhalkov-
Konchalovsky's new Russian film of the
famous stage play by Anton Chekov,
Uncle Vanya, due for release from
Contemporary some time in 1974.

Risto Taulo in the 1970 Finnish film
Here, Beneath the North Star, which
Contemporary Films will be releasing later
in 1974.

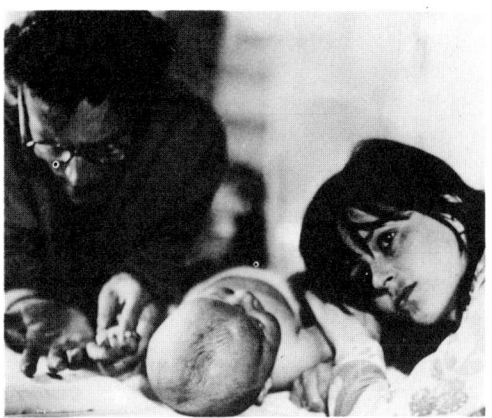

Stanislav Latello and Malgorata Pritulak in Contemporary's Polish importation, *Illumination*.

The crowd gathers around Goldie Hawn in the Richard Zanuck production for CIC, *The Sugarland Express,* which was premièred in London in June (1974) and is due for general release later in the year.

Bank-robbing maestro Lee Marvin with his
three apprentices – Gary Grimes, Ron
Howard and Charlie Martin Smith – in the
Mirisch–Fleischer, UA release (July 21,
1974) *The Spikes Gang*, a Western with an
old-time moral that crime doesn't pay – as
it certainly doesn't for any of this quartet!

Elizabeth Taylor and Helmut Berger in the
Scotia–Barber release *Ash Wednesday*, the
first film to deal with the controversial
subject of rejuvenation surgery, something
which Miss Taylor undergoes in order to
attempt to recapture her erring husband.

Omar Sharif and Julie Andrews, co-stars
of the Scotia–Barber release *The Tamarind
Seed*, the story of a romance that develops
between a divorced young woman assistant
at the British Foreign Office, handling
secret information, and the handsome
Russian spy from Paris, a romance which
alerts and alarms the Secret Services of both
governments.

Burt Reynolds takes liberties with Anitra Ford's face in Robert Aldrich's Paramount production *The Longest Yard* which, incidentally, was written by Tracy Keenan Wynn.

Jon Voight and Mary Tamm in Columbia's *The Odessa File*, the Frederick Forsyth story of a young reporter's investigation of the organisation he finds protecting and helping former members of the German SS.

Saving gas again? The two in the
bathtub are Michael Sarrazin and, quite
incorrectly dressed for the occasion, Barbra
Streisand in the Columbia comedy *For Pete's
Sake*, which takes the mickey out of crime.

Goldie Hawn as *The Girl From Petrovka* in the Universal film of that title based on the book by George Feifer and co-starring Hal Holbrook, Anthony Hopkins and Gregoire Aslan.

Bill Dee Williams as the coloured crime-fighting cop whose big reputation leads to him being sent to Mexico to help the local Chief of Police there break up the rackets which are permeating his corps in Columbia's *The Take*.

Pilot Robert Redford takes a swing in Universal's *The Great Waldo Pepper*, which was written, directed and produced by George Roy Hill.

Violence in a cold climate, in Phillip
Kaufman's Paramount film *The White Dawn*,
co-starring Warren Oates and Timothy
Bottoms.

Jack Nicholson gets a pistol pointed at his head in Roman Polanski's Paramount picture *Chinatown*, in which his co-stars are Faye Dunaway and John Huston.

Universal's Mark Robson film *Earthquake* should be something of an experience, for it has been made in a new "Sensurround" process, which is claimed to involve the audience as never before, and as the story is about a giant earth tremor which strikes Los Angeles that should be quite something! Main players involved include Charlton Heston, Ava Gardner, George Kennedy, Richard Roundtree and many others.

That great French mime Marcel Marceau makes his (American) film début in Paramount's thriller *Shanks*, and makes it a double début – as you may or may not observe in this scene. The film was both directed and produced by William Castle.

172

Barry Brown, Cybill Shepherd and Julio del Prete in the Peter Bogdanovich production, which he also directed, for Paramount, *Daisy Miller*, based on a Henry James novel.

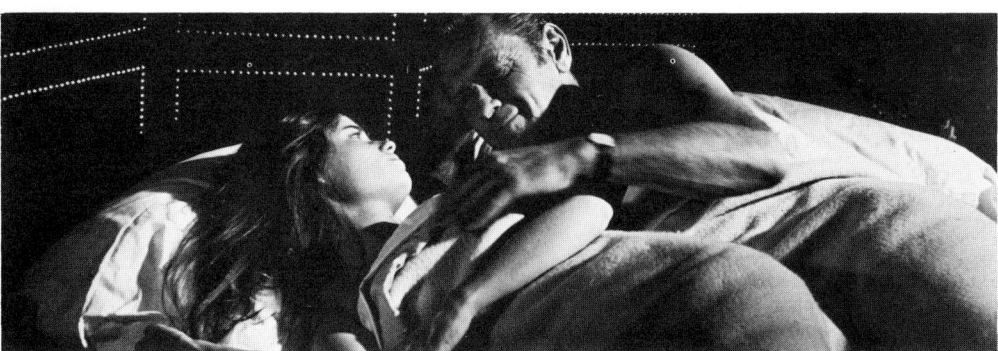

William Holden in bed with Kay Lenz in CIC's *Breezy*, which was directed by Clint Eastwood, his first film in which he hasn't appeared in the cast.

Another in the proliferating Cops and Robbers cycle will be MGM's *The Super Cops*, based on a true story about two New York policemen, with Ron Liebman as star (co-cop star is David Selby).

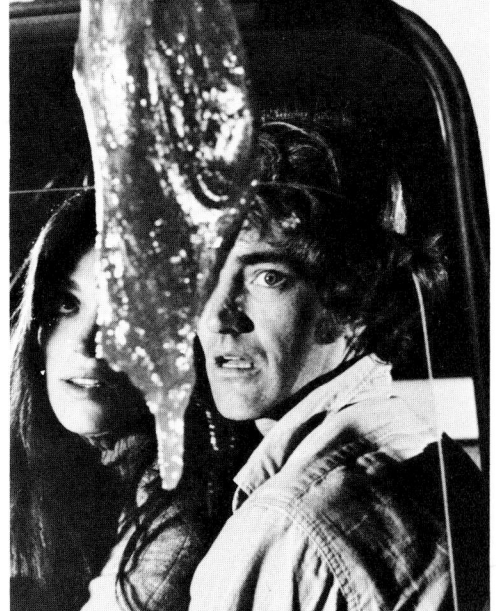

They're looking at it, Gwynne Gilford and Robert Walker, and obviously wonder what they should do next in the Fox thriller *Beware The Blob!*

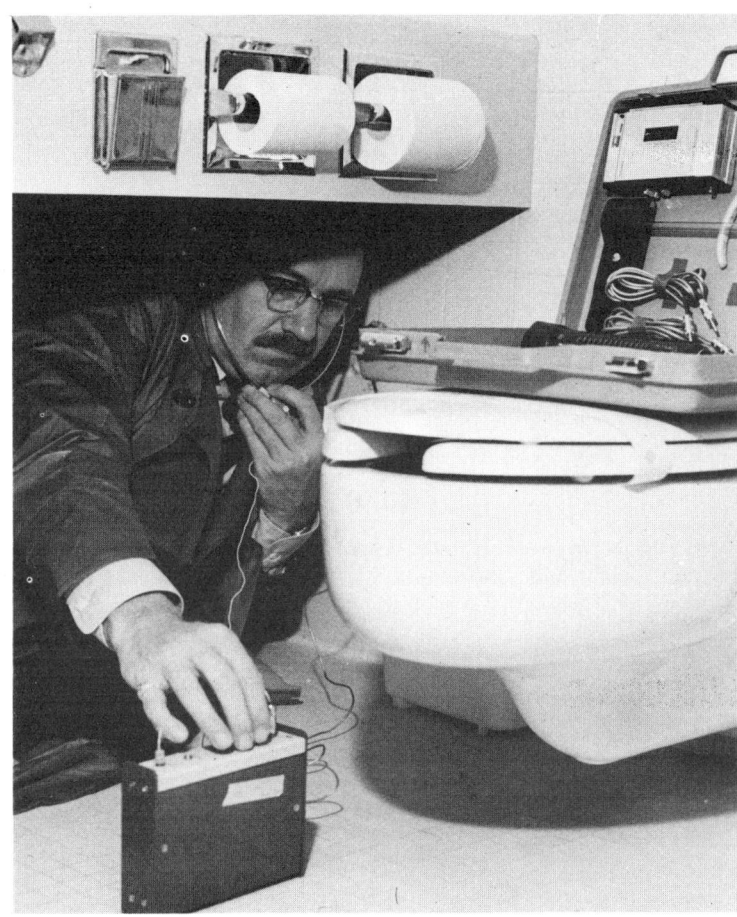

Marsha Mason and James Caan in the Fox film *Cinderella Liberty*, the story of a sailor who finds a family, adopts it, loves it, and finally shoulders its responsibilities.

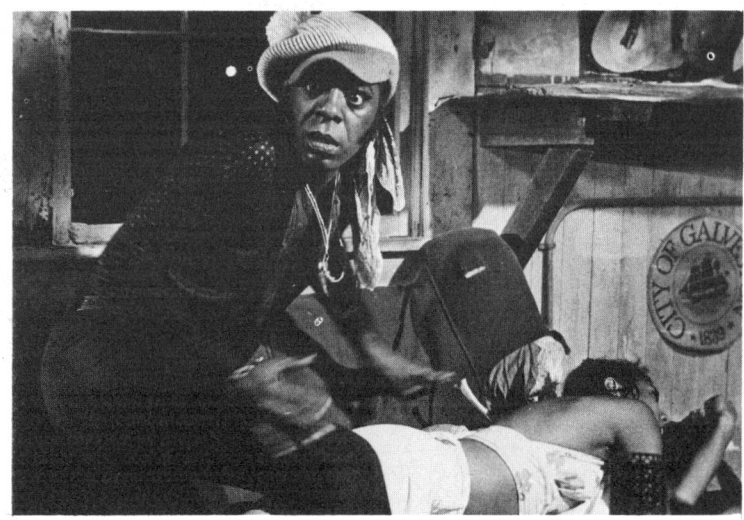

Almost certain to emerge as one of the most outstanding movies of the 1974–5 period will be the Francis Ford Coppola film – he wrote, directed and produced – for Paramount, *The Conversation*, the theme of which is the highly topical one of bugging and buggers: Gene Hackman playing the expert whose job leads to a traumatic experience.

Murder most foul . . . Lincoln Kilpatrick (playing "Billy Most") kills Angela Gibbs (as Francine) in the Fox–Rank release *Together Brothers*.

174

The old gang, including Peter Butterworth, Barbara Windsor and Sid James, all take part in the next "Carry On" episode that we shall see, *Carry on Dick*, made as usual by the Rogers–Thomas combination for Rank–Fox release.

Diahann Carroll breaks up a fight between youngsters Eric Jones and Socorro Stephens in the Fox film *Claudine*.

Jon Voight plays a young teacher who brings sympathy and new ideas to his job of teaching backward coloured pupils in a small island community – and runs into trouble because of his methods in *Class*.

You can, if you like, take it as significant that during the making of the new Steve Krantz feature cartoon for Fox, *The Nine Lives of Fritz the Cat*, two of the assistants in the animation department staged their own small strike on the grounds that the film was too anti-Nixonish inclined!

Franco Nero, playing the title-role in the Rank release *The Monk*, the story of a good man, Father Superior in a Middle Ages Monastery, brought to perdition by the lures of a woman.

Fox's *11 Harrowhouse* is an adaptation of the book by Gerald A. Browne about a plot to steal some twelve billion dollars' worth of diamonds! A glittering cast includes James Mason, Candice Bergen, Trevor Howard and John Gielgud, and a great deal of the film was shot on location in London.

Timothy Bottoms, Graham Beckel, Regina Baff and James Naughton in the Fox–Rank release *The Paper Chase*, which uses a novel background of – American – law school and follows the careers of several of the students as they pursue both their studies and their private lives.

Some unfamiliar names head the cast of the Cinerama film *The Irish Whisky Rebellion* which includes two newcomers in Stephen Joyce and Harry Regan.

Room-mates in more than one sense –
Laurie Walters and Don Johnson in the
Cinerama (Fox–Rank release) film of the
R. H. Rimmer best-seller *The Harrad
Experiment*, a reference to a college where
open "sexual communion" is encouraged!

Among the Disney feature films to be
revived in 1974 (and '75) will be *Song of the
South*, a delightful cartoon not seen on the
screens these many years. Others in the
revival list include *Peter Pan* and *That Darn
Cat*.

Susan George, playing half the title-role in
the Rank–Fox release *Dirty Mary, Crazy
Larry* (co-star is Peter Fonda), which is
about two car-crazy youngsters who extort
the money to buy a racing car and are then
forced to flee across country in it with the
cops in hot pursuit.

New, however, is the Disney film of the Ian Cameron thriller, *The Island at the Top of the World*, about four Polar explorers who discover a lost land among the snows. Cast includes David Hartman and Donald Sinden.

New, too, is Disney's *Superdad*, with Bob Crane and Kathleen Cody as the happy couple in a story about the "Generation Gap" – seen from a comedy angle.

Due for a Royal Première in London on August 8, 1974, Fox–Rank's *Caravan to Vaccares*, starring Charlotte Rampling and David Birney, is based on one of the Alistair MacLean thrillers, with Miss Rampling an English photographer and Mr Birney an impecunious young American who picks her up.

That very funny all-animal cartoon version of *Robin Hood* was originally planned as the Disney Christmas release but it has now been brought forward to the summer.

James Garner and a camel share the leading roles with young Clay O'Brien in Disney's *One Little Indian*, the story of a U.S. deserter trying at the same time to get his young Indian friend to his mother on the Reservation and to avoid the pursuing U.S. Cavalry.

Burt Reynolds comforts Sarah Miles in MGM's *The Man Who Loved Cat Dancing*, a story of the American West in the pioneer days of the late 1800s, based on the Marilyn Durham best-seller.

If you recall, and with pleasure, Lewis Gilbert's *Friends*, you'll be interested in his sequel, *Paul and Michelle*, for Paramount, which takes up the story of the young lovers some three years after the point at which the previous film left them. And the couple are again played by Sean Bury and Anicée Alvina.

Maria Schneider, the young girl who co-starred with Brando in *Last Tango* will soon be seen on the screen again, this time with Jack Nicholson in Michelangelo Antonioni's *The Passenger*, for MGM.

Michael Caine on the run in the Don Siegel film *The Black Windmill*, based on the Clive Egleton book *Seven Days to a Killing*, for Universal.

Burt Lancaster breaks out of a tight corner in Universal's *The Midnight Man*, an adaptation of the David Anthony story *The Midnight Lady and the Mourning Man* which Lancaster also co-scripted (with Roland Kibbee).

Kirk Douglas not only stars in Paramount's *Scalawag*, but also makes his début as a film director on this Western story about a wooden-legged bandit on a treasure-hunt.

RELEASES OF THE YEAR IN DETAIL

You will find the various abbreviations of words in these pages quite simple to follow: Dir for Director, Pro for Producer and Mins. for Minutes (length of the film) etc. In some cases the complicated credits, especially with co-productions, have presented problems; so, too, have the various tie-ups between producing and releasing companies. The, comparatively, recent amalgamations that have occurred, such as MGM and EMI, 20th Century-Fox (Fox) and Rank have made it difficult in many cases to know what to include and what to omit and may have finally resulted in some ambiguities, but in every case an honest effort has been made to sort out the confusion and to give the credits as fully as convenient. Incidentally, because the release dates for some of the films released between the middle and end of June 1973 were only fixed very late, after we had gone to press with last year's annual, it was therefore impossible to include them in last year's *Review* and they have been included here. The films in question are: *Jennifer on My Mind, Showdown, Shootout, Nickel Queen,* and *Confessions of a Police Captain.*

1973-74

Adam's Woman
The story of a young American seaman sent to the Australian penal colony for a misdemeanour (of which in fact he is innocent) who rebels and fights against his fate and eventually wins a chequered way to freedom. Cast: *Beau Bridges, Jane Merrow, John Mills, James Booth, Andrew Keir, Tracy Reed, Peter O'Shaughnessy, John Warwick, Harry Lawrence, Katy Wild, Mark McManus, Harold Hopkins, Doreen Warburton, Clarissa Kaye, Peter Collingwood, Tim Eliot, Stewart Ginn, Tom Oliver, Helen Morse, Margaret Christensen, Judith Fisher, Alexandra Hynes, Ken Goodlet, Alexander Hay.* Dir: Philip Leacock. Pro: Louis F. Edelman. Screenplay: Richard Fielder. (Columbia–Warner.) Rel: March 3. Colour. 115 Mins. Cert. AA.

The Adulteress
French, English-dubbed, story of the wedding of a young Frenchman, son of a diplomat, and a pretty Swedish girl, and the events that led up to it. Cast: *Patrice Pascal, Catherine Cazan, Lause Montoussemy, Michelle Pescello, Pierre Forget.* Dir: Christian Lara. Pro: Maggie Gillet. (Orion–Cinecenta.) Rel: Floating. Colour. 69 Mins. Cert. X.

Adultery
One of the Oswalt Kolle, German, sex discussion films – vividly illustrated of course. This one is about marital infidelity. Cast: *Heidrun Kussin, Kathrin Kretschmer, Marianne Lebeau, Bert Hochschwarzer, Dieter Kaiser, Gerd-Joachim Danzmayr.* Dir: Alexis Neve. Pro & Screenplay: Oswalt Kolle. (Arca–Winston–Target International.) Rel: Floating. Colour. 75 Mins. Cert. X.

The Adventures of Barry McKenzie
Private Eye strip-cartoon Aussie character Barry comes to Britain and is soon being fleeced and cheated by the Pommy bastards! Mildly amusing, coarse and at least once revolting! Cast: *Barry Crocker, Barry Humphries, Peter Cook, Spike Milligan, Dick Bentley, Dennis Price, Julie Covington, Avice Landon, Joan Bakewell, Paul Bertram.* Dir: Bruce Beresford. Pro: Phillip Adams. Screenplay: Barry Humphries & Bruce Beresford. (Longford–Columbia–Warner.) Rel: Dec. 1. Colour. 113 Mins. Cert. X.

The Affair
Overly sentimental little piece along *Love Story* lines about a cripple girl who falls in love with a handsome lawyer but finally turns to her ever-loving brother for comfort and stability when the affair becomes too intense and finally smashes up. Cast: *Natalie Wood, Robert Wagner, Bruce Davison, Jamie Smith Jackson, Pat Harrington, Kent Smith, Paul Ryan, Frances Reid, Mark Roberts, Anna Aries.* Dir: Gilbert Cates. Pro: Aaron Spelling & Leonard Goldberg. Screenplay: Barbara Turner. (ITC–Spelling/Goldberg–Scotia–Barber.) Rel: May 19. Colour. 92 Mins. Cert. A.

American Graffiti
Another piece of nostalgic Americana: a very convincing portrait of a time (1962), and a place (a small town in Northern California) and of some of the young people who live, love, play and (in one case) finally leave there. Meandering, warm, amusing with some delightful performances from a wholly starless cast. Cast: *Richard Dreyfuss, Ronny Howard, Paul Le Mat, Charlie Martin Smith, Cindy Williams, Candy Clark, Mackenzie Phillips, Wolfman Jack, Bo Hopkins.* Dir: George Lucas. Pro: Francis Ford Coppola. Screenplay: George Lucas, Gloria Katz & Willard Huyck. (Lucas–Coppola–Universal–CIC.) Rel: Mar. 31. Colour. 110 Mins. Cert. AA.

Andrei Rublev
Extremely long, slow and consistently sombre Russian film which in separated episodes is loosely concerned with the adventures of three artist-monks on their way to paint icons in Moscow in 1400. Lots of spectacle on the grand scale, some surprising nudity and a little sadism among all the barbarism and blood. Cast: *Anatoly Solonitsyn, Ivan Lapikov, Nikolai Grinko, Nickolai Sergeyev, Irma Raush, Nickolai Burlyayev, Rolan Bykov.* Dir: Andrei Tarkovsky. Screenplay: Andrei Mikhalov-Konchalovsky & Andrei Tarkovsky. (Mosfilm–Columbia–Warner.) 146 Mins. Cert. AA. Rel: Floating; first shown at the Bloombury Cinema Sept., 1973.

Angels As Hard As They Come
The "Angels" here are the Hell's variety and the unedifying story is about gang rivalry, drugs and murder. Cast: *Scott Glenn, Charles Dierkop, Gilda Texter, James Iglehart, Gary Littlejohn, Gary Busey, Janet Wood, Don Carerra, Brendan Kelly, Larry Tucker, Cheri Latimer, Marc Seaton, John Taylor, Dennis Art, Niva Davis, Hal Marshall, Steve Slauson.* Dir: Joe Viola. Pro: Jonathan Demme. Screenplay: J. Demme & J. Viola. (New World–New Realm.) Rel: Floating. Colour. 87 Mins. Cert. X.

Ape and Super-Ape
Another brilliant feature-length documentary from Holland's foremost moviemaker: with the thesis that man can learn a great deal from the animal kingdom and ideas drawn from the new science of ethology. Bert Haanstra shows the tenderness and importance of maternal care and, contrastingly, the callous manner in which the animal treats his live food. Wonderfully photographed in magnificent colour; with some humour, and a few touches of horror! Dir & Pro: Bert Haanstra, with the co-operation of Anton Koolhaas, Rolf Orthel & Rob Halkhoff. (Haanstra/Unicorn–Gala.) Rel: Floating; first shown at the Gala Royal, Nov., 1973. Colour. 103 Mins. Cert. AA.

Aretino's Blue Stories
Another medieval Italian erotic excursion: the stories of an amorous mamma and her three nubile daughters, all married and unfaithful and all pretty clever at disguising their infidelity. Cast: *Luciano De Ambrosis, Fiorella Masselli, Marisa Traversi, Geraldine Stewart, Giorgio Favretto, Franca Gonella, Giuliana Giuliani, Diego Della Valle, Enrico Miotti.* Dir: Enrico Bomba. Pro: Sergio Simonetti. Screenplay: Odoardo Fiory & Enrico Bomba. (Vascello Films–Cinecenta.) Rel: Floating. Colour. 91 Mins. Cert. X.

Assassin
Another story of an ordered assassination and the strange parallel between killer and victim as together they reach the end of the same black road. Cast: *Edward Judd, Frank Windsor, Ian Hendry, Ray Brooks, John Hart Dyke, Mike Shannon, Verna Harvey, Mike Pratt, Frank Duncan.* Dir: Peter Crane. Pro: David M. Jackson. Screenplay: Michael Sloan. (Crane/Sloan–Pemini.) Rel: Dec. 1. Colour. 83 Mins. Cert. X.

L'Attentat – Plot
French political espionage thriller, based controversially on the known facts of the kidnapping in France of left-wing Moroccan politician Ben Barka and his presumed murder (aided and abetted – the film suggests – by the high ranks of the French police and the various Secret Services!). Interesting in these implications but also highly acceptable as a thriller without knowledge of them. Sedately but well directed, finely acted by a starry cast: *Jean-Louis Trintignant, Michel Piccoli, Jean Seberg, Gian-Maria Volonté, Michel Bouquet, Bruno Cremer, Daniel Ivernel, Philippe Noiret, François Périer, Roy Scheider.* Dir: Yves Boisset. Pro: Yvon Guezel. Screenplay: Ben Barzman, Basilio Franchina & Jorge Semprun. (Transinter/Terza/Corona–Curzon.) Rel: Floating; first shown at the Curzon, June, 1973. 124 Mins. Cert. A.

Avanti!
Billy Wilder comedy with black edges about a high-powered American businessman who goes to Italy to arrange for his father's car-crash-killed body to be buried back in the States but once there comes upon some startling facts about his dad (and then himself) as he learns that killed with him was his long-standing mistress, whose daughter wants the bodies of the lovers to remain romantically together in Italy and is prepared to go to some lengths to see that this does indeed happen. Cast: *Jack Lemmon, Juliet Mills, Clive Revill, Edward Andrews, Gianfranco Barra, Franco Angrisano, Pippo Franco, Franco Acampora, Giselda Castrini, Raffaele Mottola, Lino Coletta, Harry Ray, Guidarino Guidi, Giacomo Rizzo, Antonino Faa'di Bruno, Yanti Sommer, Janet Agren, Maria Rosa Sclauzero, Melu'valente, Aldo Rendine.* Dir, Pro &

184 Screenplay (the last in collaboration with I. A. L. Diamond): Billy Wilder; based on the play by Samuel Taylor. (Mirisch/Phalanx/Jalem–UA.) Rel: July 1. Colour. 144 Mins. Cert. A.

Back Alley Princess
About the adventures of a couple of good-hearted young acrobats who pick pockets in a good cause and continue their Robin Hood careers by rushing to the rescue of their benefactor's gangster-snatched daughter. Cast includes: *Shang Kuan, Ling Feng, Samuel Hui, Angela Mao.* Dir: Lo Wei. Pro: Raymond Chow. (Golden Harvest–Cathay Films.) Rel: June 16. Colour. Cert. X.

Bad Company
Original and quite outstanding Western set in Ohio in 1863 and following the trail of a group of young draft dodgers of the period as they rob, fight (sometimes die) and struggle westward. An unusual story with the advantage of a beautifully photographed background, many touches of humour and a hard edge of conviction. Cast: *Jeff Bridges, Barry Brown, Jim Davis, David Huddleston, John Savage, Jerry Houser, Damon Cofer, Joshua Hill Lewis, Geoffrey Lewis, Raymond Guth, Edward Lauter, John Quade, Jean Allison, Ned Wertimer, Charles Tyner, Ted Gehring, Claudia Bryar, John Boyd, Monika Henreid, Tod Martin.* Dir: Robert Benton. Pro: Stanley R. Jaffe. Screenplay: David Newman & Robert Benton. (Jaffilms–Paramount–CIC.) Rel: Floating. Colour. 92 Mins. Cert. X.

Badge 373
Tough, expert, thrilling and violent crime melo "inspired by the exploits of Eddie Egan" (the real-life New York cop who was involved with *The French Connection* case). About a New York 'tec who's suspended from the Force when a suspect he's chasing falls off the roof to his death (did he fall or was he pushed?) but, dedicated and unswerving, carries on his own rough line of investigation when his ex-partner is murdered and eventually achieves his grim purpose by cornering and killing the Puerto Rican crime boss responsible for the crime. Cast: *Robert Duvall, Verna Bloom, Henry Darrow, Eddie Egan, Felipe Luciano, Tina Christiani, Marina Durell, Chico Martinez, Jose Duval, Louis Cosentino, Luis Avalos, Nubia Olivero, Sam Schacht, Edward F. Carey, "Big" Lee, Duane Morris, John Marriott, Joel Veiga, Mark Tendler, Robert Weil, Rose Ann Scamardella, Pete Hamill, Larry Appelbaum, John McCurry, Bob Farley, Tracy Walter, John Scanlon, Jimmy Archer, Ric Mancini, Mike O'Dowd, Robert Miano, Pompie Pomposello, Hector Troy, Miguel Alejandro, Harry Collazo, Damian Colon.* Dir & Pro: Howard W. Koch. Screenplay: Pete Hamill. (Koch–Paramount–CIC.) Rel: Aug. 12. Colour. 104 Mins. Cert. X.

Battle for the Planet of the Apes
Yet another chapter in the popular Simian saga: how, after an atomic holocaust sparked off by the educated Apes' revolt against their less intelligent human bosses, the survivors try to get down to peaceful co-existence – achieved only after a struggle against some human mutants who have also survived. Cast: *Roddy McDowall, Claude Atkins, Natalie Trundy, Severn Darden, Lew Ayres, Paul Williams, Austin Stoker, Noah Keen, Richard Eastham, Frances Nuyen, Paul Stevens, Heather Lowe, Bobby Porter, Michael Stearns, Cal Wilson, Pat Cardi, John Landis, Andy Knight, John Huston.* Dir: J. Lee Thompson. Pro: Arthur P. Jacobs. Screenplay: J. W. Corrington & J. H. Corrington; from a story by Paul Dehn. (APJAC–Fox–Rank.) Rel: Aug. 5. Colour. 86 Mins. Cert. A.

Beach of the War Gods
Another action piece from Hong Kong, all about the brave villagers of Lee, who stand barring the way to Hangchow, besieged by the pirates from Japan in the latter part of the Ming Dynasty. Cast: *Wang Yu, Lung Fei, Tien Yeh.* Dir: Wang Yu. Pro: Raymond Chow. (Golden Harvest–Cathay.) Rel: Floating. Colour. 82 Mins. Cert. AA.

The Beast Must Die
About a big-game hunter who after assembling the usual crowd of cinematic types in his hunting lodge announces to them that he is now about to pursue, catch and kill the biggest quarry in his life, a werewolf; and then explains that all around the table are possibles for the position! Cast: *Calvin Lockhart, Peter Cushing, Charles Gray, Anton Diffring, Marlene Clark, Ciaran Madden, Tom Chadbon, Michael Gambon.* Dir: Paul Annett. Pro: Max J. Rosenberg & Milton Subotsky. Screenplay: Michael Winder. (Amicus–British Lion.) Rel: May 19. Colour. 92 Mins. Cert. X.

Bed-Partners
German sex film about a sixteen-year-old cutie who answers an advert and becomes the sexual playmate of a "swinging" couple. Cast: *Marion Forster, Astrid Boner, Harry Kalenberg, Ellen Umlauf.* Dir & Screenplay: Kurt Nachmann. Pro: Heinz Pollak. (Lisa/Divina–Mark Associates.) Rel: Floating; first shown at the Classic, Charing Cross Road, Jan., 1974. Colour. 79 Mins. Cert. X.

Bella Antonia Prima Monica e Poi Dimonia – Naughty Nun
More Italian medieval sexy high jinks, largely centred around a painter who likes to more than paint his model! And it's all rather painful! Cast: *Edwige Fenech, Piero Focaccia, Riccardo Garrone, Dada Gallotti, Elio Crovetto, Luciana Turina, Renato Cecilia, Romano Malaspina, Umberto D'Orsi, Tiberio Murgia, Josanne Tanzilli, Sandro Dori, Carla Mancini, Gianni Pulone, Malisa Longo, Lucretia Loue.* Dir: Mariano Laurenti. Pro: Gianfranco Couyoumdjian. Screenplay: Carlo Veo; based on a book by Pietro Aretino. (Flora/National/Lea–Border.) Rel: Floating; first shown at the Jacey, Trafalgar Square, June, 1973. Colour. 82 Mins. Cert. X.

Bella di Giorno Moglie di Notte – Wife By Night
Sex film from Italy about a wealthy, neglected wife who turns to the Call Girl business for kicks, then disgusted, reveals all to hubbie, who admits to her horror he knew about it all along . . . so, furious, she ups and shoots him! Cast: *Eva Czemerys, Nina Castelnuovo, Anna Miserocchi, Umberto Raho, Pietro Torrisi, Ennio Biasucci, Lee Banner, Enzo Liberti, Fernando Cerulli, Renato Pinciroli, Carla Mancini, Franco Marletta, Terence Long, Gianluca Boccardi.* Dir: Nello Rossati. Pro: Tiziano Longo. Screenplay: Franco Daniels & Nello Rossati. (Peg–Miracle.) Rel: Floating; first shown at the Classic, Charing Cross Road, Aug., 1973. Colour. 79 Mins. Cert. X.

Une Belle Fille Comme Moi – A Gorgeous Bird Like Me
François Truffaut turns to black-edged satirical comedy with a fictional biography of a sexually fascinating girl who after removing her irritating father at the age of nine, thereafter makes her way to the top by using her allure to trap the men she needs in the climb and then disposes of them as best she can. Not vintage Truffaut but still a nice compact example of a kind of humour rather too rare on the screen. Cast: *Bernadette Lafont, Claude Brasseur, Charles Denner, Guy Marchand, André Dussollier, Philippe Léotard, Anne Kreis, Gilberte Géniat, Danièle Girard, Michel Delahaye.* Dir: François Truffaut. Adaptation & Screenplay: Jean-Loup Dabadie & Truffaut; based on the Henry Farrel novel *Such a Gorgeous Kid Like Me.* (Les Films du Carosse/Columbia–Gala.) Rel: Floating; first shown at Berkeley One, June, 1973. Colour. 98 Mins. Cert. X.

The Belstone Fox
A good, old-fashioned, honestly sentimental, essentially British film – based on the David Rook novel *The Ballad of the Belstone Fox* – about the deep friendship that develops between a fox-hound puppy and a fox cub which persists, embarrassingly for the huntsman, when they grow up and are forced to take opposite sides of the hunting fence, a situation which leads, virtually directly, to the death of the huntsman. With the humans never deeply etched, it is the wonderfully trained animals who take most of the performing honours, though *Eric Porter* (huntsman), *Rachel Roberts* (wife), *Bill Travers* (woodsman), *Jeremy Kemp* (master), *Dennis Waterman* (huntsman's assistant) and *Heather Wright* (daughter) all give pleasant performances. Dir: James Hill. Pro: Sally Shuter. Screenplay: James Hill. (Julian Wintle–Fox–Rank.) Rel: Jan. 6. Colour. 103 Mins. Cert. A.

Ben
A follow-up to that rodent-riddled box-office bonanza *Willard*, beginning where that film ended, the holocaust of which Ben, ratty leader of the rodent army, is the only survivor. Now his human friend is a weak little lad who, when the population rise against the rats (after their stores have been plundered by the creatures) and grimly exterminate them, swears to revenge his pal . . . a forward-looking glance to a follow-up that will surely come! Cast: *Lee Harcourt*

Montgomery, Joseph Campanella, Arthur O'Connell, Rosemary Murphy, Meredith Baxter, Kaz Garas, Paul Carr, Richard Van Vleet, Kenneth Tobey, James Luisi, Lee Paul, Norman Alden, Scott Garrett, Arlen Stuart, Richard Drasin. Dir: Phil Karlson. Pro: Charles A. Pratt. Screenplay: G. A. Ralston. (BCP–Cinerama.) Rel: Floating. Colour. 94 Mins. Cert. X.

The Best of Benny Hill
Titularly explanatory, with *Benny* going through his routine of TV comedy successes. Rest of cast: *Connie Georges, Anne Irving, David Prowse, Michael S. Martin, Michael Moore, Jan Butlin, Jackie Wright, Verne Morgan, Valeria N. St John, Eira Heath, André Melly, Leslie Goldie, Jenny Lee Wright, Bob Todd, Bettine Le Beau, Henry McGee, Charmaine Seal, Nicholas Parsons, Patricia Hayes, Sue Bond, David Hamilton, Nicole Shelby, Arthur Hewlett, Ted Taylor, Geraldine Burnett, Carol Mills, Ziena Merton.* Dir & Pro: John Robins. Script: Benny Hill. (Euston–EMI.) Rel: May 26. Colour. 87 Mins. Cert. A.

The Betty Boop Follies
A collection of Max and Dave Fleischers' Betty Boop cartoon shorts, the big, mini-skirted, Boop-a-doop-dooping animated star of the thirties; updated with "electronic colour". And quite a revelation for anyone not familiar with the period. (National Telefilm Associates.) Rel: Floating. Colour. 93 Mins. Cert. U.

The Big Boss
Yet another in the 1973 flood of Hong Kong-made thrillers, this one about a boss who is also a crook and who is brought low, very low, by unarmed combat specialist *Bruce Lee.* Rest of cast: *Maria Yi Yi, James Tien.* Dir: Lo Wei. Pro: Raymond Chow. (Cathay–Golden Harvest Films.) Rel: Floating; first shown at the Carlton, Nov., 1973. Colour. 98 Mins. Cert. X.

The Big Bounce
Ryan O'Neal as the handsome young ex-G.I. who comes under the evil influence of ruthless little *Leigh Taylor-Young,* who involves him in a deliberate auto smash, eggs him into a fight and then tries to murder him when he won't for her sake take to crime! Rest of cast: *James Daly, Robert Webber, Lee Grant, Cindy Eilbacher, Noam Pitlik, Kevin O'Neal, Van Heflin.* Dir: Alex March. Pro: William Dozier. Screenplay: Robert Dozier; from the novel by Elmore Leonard. (Greenway–Warner.) Rel: Floating. Colour. 102 Mins. Cert. X.

Big Zapper
A sort of pop version of a female 007, with *Linda Marlowe* as the gal with guns, arms, legs and other natural (38") attributes and accessories who can use them all with deadly effect in beating the villains at their own violent game. Rest of cast: *Gary Hope, Jack May, Sean Hewitt, Richard Monette.* Dir & Pro: Lindsay Shonteff. Screenplay: Hugh Brody. (Miracle.) Rel: Floating. Colour. 90 Mins. Cert. X.

Billy Two Hats
A written-in-Scotland, planned-in-London, made-in-Israel Western! And a pretty good example, too. All about isolation and its effects, in a story of the strong friendship between Scottish old-timer *Gregory Peck* and young half-breed lad, *Desi Arnaz, Jr.* Rest of cast: *Jack Warden, Sian Barbara Allen, David Huddleston, John Pearce, Dawn Littlesky, Vincent St Cyr, Zev Berlinsky, Henry Medicine Hat, Antony Scott.* Dir: Ted Kotcheff. Pro: Norman Jewison & Patrick Palmer. Screenplay: Alan Sharp. (Algonguin–UA.) Rel: May 5. Colour. 99 Mins. Cert. AA.

Birds of Prey
Cops and robbers thriller with the difference that the fighting and chasing is almost entirely done in helicopters. Cast: *David Janssen, Ralph Meeker, Elayne Heilveil, Harry Klekas, Sam Dawson, Don Wilbanks, Gavin James.* Dir: William Graham. Pro: Alan A. Armer. Screenplay: Robert Boris & Rupert Hitzig. Created by Richard Gimbel. (Tomorrow Entertainment–British Lion.) Rel: Oct. 14. Colour. 75 Mins. Cert. U.

The Birth of a Legend
Documentary about the rise and rise of that famous silent screen duo *Mary Pickford* and *Douglas Fairbanks,* with some significant extracts from their feature films and some startling newsreel cuts. Dir & Pro: Matty Kemp. Narrated by Leslie Gargan. (Pickford–Gala.) Rel: Floating. 26 Mins. Cert. U.

The Bitches – see Les Chiennes

Black Decameron – Il Decamerone Nero
The obvious colour switch! Five little filmlets all based on erotic stories of the Renaissance period: (a) *The Beautiful Queen,* with *Beryl Cunningham, Jacqueline Scott, Serigne N'Dyaye Gonzales.* (b) *The Cure of the Crazy Woman,* with *Fatou Diame, Dauda M'Baye, Mamadou Diop.* (c) *The Punished Lovers,* with *Youssapha Ba, Josy McGregory, Omar Seck, Badou Kasse.* (d) *The Prostitute's Revenge,* with *Line Senghor, Samba, Page Seidou, Medun Foge.* (e) *What I Haven't Done: Simoa's Endless Search,* with *Djbril Diop, Lucien Lemoine, Issa Niane, Isabelle Djallo, Youma, Birtha Gassama.* Dir: Piero Vivarelli. Pro: Alfredo Bini. Screenplay: Vivarelli, Ottario Alessi. Based on the book by Leo Frobenius. (Finarco–Eagle.) Rel: Floating. Colour. 93 Mins. Cert. X.

Black Belt Jones
Black Kung Fu and whatever, with *Jim Kelly* the coloured expert of the title who comes up against a nasty gang of hoodlums persuaded by a Mafia man to gain possession of the deeds of some property he wants. Rest of cast: *Gloria Hendry, Malik Carter, Scatman Crothers, Alan Weeks, Eric Laneuville, André Phillipe, Vincent Barbi, Nate Esformes, Mel Novak, Eddie Smith, Alex Brown, Clarence Barnes, Earl Brown, Esther Sutherland, Sid Kaiser, Doug Sides.* Dir: Robert Clouse. Pro: Fred Weintraub & Paul Heller.

Screenplay: Oscar Williams. Rel: May 19. Colour. 83 Mins. Cert. X.

Blacula
The chiller-diller that got away from Hammer! In fact American International made this tongue-in-cheek black variation on the old blood-sucker theme, with *William Marshall* the unfortunate fellow who in 1815 asks the Count to sign an anti-slavery petition and in reply gets bitten by a furious Dracula for his pains. Sealed in a coffin stored in a New York warehouse, Blacula at last wakes up now, all these years later, and immediately starts to search for his staple food and fun . . . Rest of cast: *Vonetta McGee, Denise Nicholas, Thalmus Rasulala, Gordon Pinsent, Charles Macaulay, Emily Yancy, Lance Taylor, Sr., Ted Harris, Rick Metzler, Jitu Cumbuka, Logan Field, Ketty Lester, Elisha Cook, Eric Brotherson.* Dir: William Crain. Pro: Joseph T. Naar. Screenplay: Joan Torres & Raymond Koenig. (American International–Columbia–Warner.) Rel: Floating. Colour. 93 Mins. Cert. X.

Bless This House
Broad British farce based on the TV series of the same name and largely concerned with a suburban household full of types and their, equally typed, neighbours. Cast: *Sidney James, Diana Coupland, Terry Scott, June Whitfield, Peter Butterworth, Sally Geeson, Robin Askwith, Carol Hawkins, Janet Brown, George A. Cooper, Patsy Rowlands, Bill Maynard, Wendy Richard, Marianne Stone, Julian Orchard, Tommy Godfrey, Ed Devereaux, Johnny Briggs, Frank Thornton, Norman Mitchell, Patricia Franklin, Brian Osborne, Marjie Lawrence, Lindsay Marsh, Michael Nightingale, Myrtle Reed, Molly Weir, Maggie Wright, Margaret Lacey, Michael Howe, Georgina Moon, David Rowlands, Billy Cornelius.* Dir: Gerald Thomas. Pro: Peter Rogers. Screenplay: Dave Freeman. (Peter Rogers–Fox–Rank.) Rel: July 22. Colour. 89 Mins. Cert. U.

Blindman
The Western with a difference: the fast-riding, straight-shooting hero is . . . Blind! This is the story of his tracking down and retrieving fifty lovely lassies he is supposed to be escorting to San Diego but who are stolen from him! Cast: *Tony Anthony, Ringo Starr, Agneta Eckemyr, Lloyd Batista, Magda Konopka, Raf Baldassare . . .* plus fifty beautiful women! Dir: Ferdinando Baldi. Pro: Tony Anthony & Saul Swimmer. Screenplay: Vincenzo Cerami, Piero Anchisi & Tony Anthony. (Abkco–Fox–Rank.) Rel: Jan. 20. Colour. 96 Mins. Cert. X.

Blood and Sand
Revival of the 1922 silent movie starring *Rudolph Valentino,* as the matador who rises to the top, becomes over-confident, is gored, recovers and then, afraid, enters the ring again to be finally killed. Rest of cast: *Lila Lee, Nita Naldi, George Field, Walter Long, Rose Rosanova, Leo White, Charles Belcher, Jack Winn.*

186 Dir: Fred Niblo. Screenplay: June Mathis; based on the novel by Vincente Blasco Ibañez. (Famous Players–Lasky–Vaughan Films.) Rel: Floating. 80 Mins. Cert. U.

Blood Sisters

Some nasty business caused by the surviving sister of a separated Siamese twin combination, who turns out to be the evil half of the team and though looking like her good twin is a real little devil! Cast: *Margot Kidder, Jennifer Salt, Charles Durning, Bill Finley, Lisle Wilson, Barnard Hughes, Mary Davenport, Dolph Sweet.* Dir: Brian de Palma. Pro: Edward R. Pressman. Screenplay: Brian de Palma & Louisa Rose. (Pressman Williams–British Lion.) Rel: May 19. Colour. 92 Mins. Cert. X.

Blue Movie Blackmail

The case of the brilliant detective assigned to investigate the drug traffic between the Middle East and America who finds the difference in the rewards between being on the right and wrong side of the legal fence too tempting and becomes a double-crossing drug-runner. Cast: *Ivan Rassimov, Patricia Hayes, Luciano Catenacci, Glacomo Rossi Stuart, Leon Vitali, Stephanie Beacham, Red Carter, Verna Harvey, Cec Linder, Ben Carra.* Dir: Massimo Dallamano. Pro: Ross MacKenzie & Leonardo Pescarolo. Screenplay: M. Dallamano & Sandy MacRae. (Clodio/Italian International/Monymusk–Hemdale.) Rel: Floating. Colour. 97 Mins. Cert. X.

Blume in Love

Long, slow, meandering but uncomfortably convincing story of a marriage, through courtship to divorce and eventual state of balance when, after the ex-husband has raped his ex-wife and she is pregnant, she sees some sort of future relationship for them if not within the marital state. Cast: *George Segal, Susan Anspach, Kris Kristofferson, Marsha Mason, Shelley Winters, Donald F. Muhich, Paul Mazursky, Erin O'Reilly, Annazette Chase, Shelley Morrison, Mary Jackson, Ed Peck, Jo Morrow, Gigi Ballista, Ian Linhart, Mario Demo, Erika Von Kessler, Dennis Kort, Judy Ann Elder, Carol Worthington.* Dir, Pro & Screenplay: Paul Mazursky. (Columbia –Warner.) Rel: Floating. Colour. 116 Mins. Cert. X.

Boesman and Lena

Extremely moving South African story of human relationships among the dispossessed of the world, seen against a background of Apartheid: a penetrating and enthralling story of two human derelicts, an adaptation of the brilliant play by Athol Fugard. Cast: *Yvonne Bryceland, Sandy Tube, Percy Sieff, Robert Penacchi, Athol Fugard, Val Donald, Frank Zietsman, Bert Coppin.* Dir: Ross Devenish. Pro: Johan Wicht. Screenplay: Athol Fugard, from his own stage play. (Bluewater–Contemporary.) Rel: Floating; first shown at the Paris Pullman, Feb., 1974. Colour. 102 Mins. Cert. A.

Bonnie's Kids

Only vague reminders of Bonnie and Clyde remain in this story of the two daughters whose unedifying careers encompass murder, mayhem and sexual casualness. Unlike their mother, though, they survive right to the end of the movie and beyond. Cast: *Tiffany Bolling, Robin Mattson, Leo Gordon, Steve Sandor, Scott Brady, Lenore Stevens, Alex Rocco, Timothy Brown, Max Showalter, James Lydon, Nicholas Cortland, Luanne Roberts, Glen Stensel, John Baer, Larry Blake, James Dunn.* Dir: Arthur Marks. Pro: Charles Stroud. Screenplay: Arthur Marks. (Tommy Productions–Variety.) Rel: Floating. Colour. 105 Mins. Cert. X.

Boy Who Cried Werewolf

The lad's dad is bitten and in turn starts to bite, but nobody will believe the boy when he tries to tell them about it! Routine vampire horrors. Cast: *Kerwin Mathews, Elaine Devry, Scott Sealey, Robert J. Wilke, Susan Foster, Jack Lucas, Bob Homel, George Gaynes, Loretta Temple, Dave Cass, Herold Goodwin, Tim Haldeman, John Logan, Eric Gordon, Paul Baxley.* Dir: Nathan H. Juran. Pro: Aaron Rosenberg. Screenplay: Bob Homel. (RKF–Universal–CIC.) Rel: Nov. 25. Colour. 93 Mins. Cert. X.

Brother Sun, Sister Moon

Franco Zeffirelli's magnificent visual qualities of his story of the earlier years of St Francis of Assisi are poorly served by a far less magnificent script and some colourless performances: though *Alec Guinness*'s portrait of Pope Innocent III brings a closing note of moving sincerity to the piece. Rest of cast: *Graham Faulkner, Judi Bowker, Leigh Lawson, Kenneth Cranham Michael Feast, Nicholas Willatt, Valentina Cortese, Lee Montague, John Sharp, Adolfo Celi, Francesco Guerrieri.* Dir: Franco Zeffirelli. Pro: Luciano Perugia. Screenplay: Suso Cecchi D'Amico, Lina Wertmüller & Franco Zeffirelli. (Euro/Vic–Paramount–CIC.) Rel: Floating. Colour. 122 Mins. Cert. U.

Busting

Elliott Gould and *Robert Blake* as two honest but brutal New York cops struggling to keep their own integrity and to bring down the grafters in their own ranks but doing it in such a violent and brutal way that one wonders if the ends justify the means – well, almost! Rest of cast: *Allen Garfield, Antonio Fargas, Michael Lerner, Sid Haig, Ivor Francis, William Sylvester, Logan Ramsey, Richard X. Slattery, Margo Winkler, John Lawrence, Cornelia Sharp, Erin O'Reilly, Danny Goldman, Nick St Nicholas, Ibycus, Howard Platt, Jack Knight, Mimi Doyle, Jessica Rains, Carl Eller, John Furlong, Kai Hernandez, Napoleon Whiting, Andy Stone, Dominique Pinassi, Ron Cummins, Elaine Partnow, Karen Anders, Dee Carroll.* Dir & Screenplay: Peter Hyams. Pro: Irwin Winkler & Robert Chartoff. (Chartoff–Irwin–UA.) Rel: June 9. 93 Mins. Cert. X.

Cahill

Familiar but well-made John Wayne Western with *Big John* riding tall as the fearless, indefatigable marshal whose neglect of his own sons leads them into a spot of bank robbing trouble. Some nice humorous moments from *Neville Brand* as the Indian Chief guide. Rest of cast: *George Kennedy, Gary Grimes, Clay O'Brien, Marie Windsor, Morgan Paull, Dan Vadis, Royal Dano, Scott Walker, Denver Pyle, Jackie Coogan, Rayford Barnes, Dan Kemp, Harry Carey, Jr., Walter Barnes, Paul Fix, Pepper Martin, Vance Davis, Ken Wolger, Hank Worden, James Nusser, Murray Macleod, Hunter Von Leer.* Dir: Andrew V. McLaglen. Pro: Michael A. Wayne. Screenplay: Harry Julian Fink & Rita M. Fink, based on a story by Barney Slater. (Warner.) Rel: Nov. 11. Colour. 102 Mins. Cert. AA.

Callan

Slick, fast but once again over-brutal story of British Secret Service Agent Callan, put "on ice" for some years because of a suspected developing conscience, recalled by MI5 or whatever to kill a charming German arms and ammunition smuggler with the idea of at the same time removing the menace and the suspect agent by laying a trail for the murder to his door, a plan he just about outwits to stay alive – though marked by his double-crossing, dirty and devious boss (the film is splendid anti-recruiting propaganda for the Service) for later attention! Cast: *Edward Woodward, Eric Porter, Carl Mohner, Catherine Schell, Peter Egan, Russell Hunter, Kenneth Griffith, Veronica Lang, Michael da Costa, Dave Prowse, Don Henderson, Joe Dunlop, Anne Blake, Nadim Sawalha.* Dir: Don Sharp. Pro: Derek Horne. Screenplay: James Mitchell. (EMI.) Rel: June 23. Colour. 106 Mins. Cert. A.

The Call of the Wild

The story of a dog in the Yukon in the Gold Rush days, the master he loves and whose life he saves, and the call of the wolf which leads him to become a legend. Cast: *Charlton Heston, Michèle Mercier, Raimund Harmstorf, George Eastman, Maria Rohm, Juan Luis Galiardo, Sancho Gracia, Freidhelm Lehmann, Horst Heuck, Rik Battaglia, Alf Malland, Alfredo Mayo, Jody Hanson, Sverre Wilberg, Olav Pedersen, Per Amvik, Torbjorn Halvorsen, Hans Stormoen, Kare Siem, Dan Rosse, Roy Bjornstad, Ola B. Johannessen, Per Tofte, Antonio Mayans, Jennifer Roberts.* Dir: Ken Annakin. Pro: Harry Alan Towers. Screenplay: Peter Welbeck, Wyn Wells & Peter Yeldham; based on the story by Jack London. (Massfilms/CCC/Izaro/Oceania/UPF/ Towers of London–MGM–EMI.) Rel: Aug. 5. Colour. 105 Mins. Cert. U.

La Campana del Inferno – The Bell of Hell

Italian murder mystery thriller about the macabre revenge of Aunt Martha and her nephew who, newly out of a mental asylum, has failed to kill her and her three daughters! Cast: *Renaud Verley, Viveca Lindfors, Alfredo Mayo, Maribel Martin, Nuria Gimeno, Christine Betzner.* Dir & Pro: Claudio Guerin Hill. Screenplay: Santiago

Moncada. (Hesperia–Films la Boétie–Border Films.) Rel: Floating. Colour. 96 Mins. Cert. X.

Cancel My Reservation
Bob Hope as the TV star who comes to his Phoenix ranch to find a little peace but finds instead a girl in his bed, the sheriff's suspicion that he's a murderer, and some dead bodies before the wise words of a 110-year-old Indian Chief solve everything! Rest of cast: *Eva Marie Saint, Ralph Bellamy, Forrest Tucker, Anne Archer, Keenan Wynn, Henry Darrow, Doodles Weaver, Betty Carr, Herb Vigran, Pat Morita, Gordon Oliver, Buster Shaefer, Chief Dan George.* Dir: Paul Bogart. Pro: Gordon Oliver. Screenplay: Arthur Marx & Robert Fisher; based on the Louis L'Amour novel *The Broken Gun.* (Naho–MGM–EMI.) Rel: Aug. 26. Colour. 87 Mins. Cert. U.

The Canterbury Tales
Pier Paolo Pasolini's highly individual idea of the Chaucer Pilgrims' stories, with himself as the writer: a rude, rough and generally unfunny collection of filmlets, with strange accents, lots of full frontal nudity (both sexes), lush backgrounds and some strained performances. Cast: "Prologue": *Pier Paolo Pasolini, Laura Betti, J. P. Van Dyne, Derek Deadman, George Bethell Datch.* "The Merchant's Tale": *Hugh Griffith, Josephine Chaplin, Oscar Fochetti, Giuseppe Arrigo, Elizabetta Genovese.* "The Friar's Tale": *Franco Citti, Daniel Buckler, Tony Moore.* "The Cook's Tale": *Ninetto Davoli.* "The Miller's Tale": *Michael Balfour, Jenny Runacre, Dan Thomas, Peter Cain, Martin Philips.* "The Wife of Bath's Tale": *Laura Betti, Reg Stuart, Tom Baker, Judy Stewart-Murray.* "The Steward's Tale": *Eamann Howell, Patrick Duffett, Albert King, Eileen King, Heather Johnson.* "The Pardoner's Tale": *Robin Asquith, Martin Whelar, John McLaren, Edward Monteith, Alan Webb.* "The Summoner's Tale": *John Francis Lane, Hugh McKenzie Bailey, Settimio Castagna.* Dir & Screenplay: Pier Paolo Pasolini, based on the Geoffrey Chaucer stories. Pro: Alberto Grimaldi (PEA/Artistes Associés–UA.) Rel: Floating. Colour. 109 Mins. Cert. X.

Captain Kronos – Vampire Hunter
Rather jolly bloodsucker hokum with our hero a professional smeller-out of vampires, here tracking down a series of suspicious events to the local great Lady D. and it is her and her resurrected hubbie that he has to confront and defeat before being free to go on along the road to seek more vampires . . . ! Cast: *Horst Janson, John Carson, John Cater, Shane Briant, Caroline Munro, Ian Hendry, Wanda Ventham, Lois Daine, William Hobbs, Terence Sewards, Trevor Lawrence, Perry Soblosky, Susanna East, Stafford Gordon, Brian Tully, Joanna Ross, Elizabeth Dear, Lisa Vollings, Caroline Villiers, Neil Seiler, Paul Greenwood, Olga Anthony, Robert James, Peter Davidson, Penny Price, John Hollis, Jacqui Cook, Gigi Gurpinar, Steve James, B. H. Barry, Barry Smith, Ian McKay, Roger Williams.* Dir: Brian Clemens. Pro: Albert Fennell & Brian Clemens. Screenplay: Brian Clemens. (Hammer–Bruton.) Rel: Floating. Colour. 91 Mins. Cert. AA.

Carry On Girls
The twenty-fifth of the C.O. comedies and much like all the others in the sense that it is very British, often blue, and a great giggle for all those cinemagoers who have made every one of that quarter century of movies a real fortune-taker at the B.O. Cast: *Sidney James, Joan Sims, Kenneth Connor, Barbara Windsor, Bernard Bresslaw, June Whitfield, Peter Butterworth, Jack Douglas, Patsy Rowlands, Joan Hickson, David Lodge, Valerie Leon, Margaret Nolan, Sally Geeson, Angela Grant, Wendy Richard, Arnold Ridley, Robin Askwith, Patricia Franklin, Jimmy Logan, Brian Osborne, Bill Pertwee, Marianne Stone, Brenda Cowling, Zena Clifton, Mavise Fyson, Laraine Humphreys, Pauline Peart, Caroline Whitaker, Barbara Wise, Carol Wyler.* Dir: Gerald Thomas. Pro: Peter Rogers. Screenplay: Talbot Rothwell. (Peter Rogers–Fox–Rank.) Rel: Jan. 13. Colour. 88 Mins. Cert. A.

Cat and Mouse
Suspense thriller with *Kirk Douglas* as the jealous madman determined to kill his wife – and letting her know about it in advance! Rest of cast: *Jean Seberg, John Vernon, Sam Wanamaker, James Bradford, Bessie Love, Beth Porter, Suzanne Lloyd, Mavis Villiers, Elliott Sullivan, Bob Sherman, James Berwick, Valerie Colgan, Margo Alexis, Stewart Chandler, Robert Henderson, Louis Negin, Jennifer Watts, Tony Sibbald, Don Fellows, Francis Napier, Roy Stephens, Elsa Pickthorne.* Dir: David Petrie. Pro: Aida Young. Screenplay: John Peacock. (Assoc. London Films–EMI.) Rel: June 2. Colour. 90 Mins. Cert. AA.

Catch My Soul
Rock musical version of Shakespeare's *Othello,* set against a background of an American hippy community and with some of Shakespeare's lines mixed in with some very modern additions! And with a collection of highly variable musical numbers. Cast: *Richie Havens, Lance LeGault, Season Hubley, Tony Joe White, Susan Tyrrell, Bonnie Bramlett, Delaney Bramlett and his band, Allene Lubin, The Family Lotus.* Dir: Patrick McGoohan. Pro: Richard Rosenbloom & Jack Good. Screenplay: Jack Good, based on his own stage musical. (Metromedia–Fox–Rank.) Rel: Floating. Colour. 95 Mins. Cert. A.

César and Rosalie
Gently memorable French film which with understanding and subtlety tells the story of the independent-minded young divorcée and the two contrasting men in her life; the rough, strong, rich scrap-iron merchant and the quiet artist. And the way that, once intertwined, they cannot unscramble their lives or part with each other for anything more than a limited period. Superbly acted, brilliantly directed. Cast: *Yves Montand, Romy Schneider, Sami Frey, Umberto Orsini, Eva Marie Meincke, Bernard Le Coq,* Gisella Hahn, Isabelle Hupper, Henri-Jacques Huet, Pippo Merisi, Carlo Nell, Hervé Sand.* Dir & co-Screenplay (with Jean-Loup Dabadie): Claude Sautet. (Fildebroc–UPF–Mega–Paramount/Orion–Gala.) Rel: Floating; first shown at ABC 1, July, 1973. Colour. 105 Mins. Cert. AA.

Charley Varrick
Walter Matthau rings the changes by playing a crop-duster who does a few small bank robberies as a sideline but eventually comes unstuck by not only being caught in the act but finding his loot includes three-quarters-of-a-million dollars of Mafia hot money and is thereafter always fighting a battle of wits against the pursuing cops and crooks. It all adds up to a tightly assembled thriller with a few lighter, Matthau, touches to relieve the violence. Rest of cast: *Joe Don Baker, Felicia Farr, Andy Robinson, John Vernon, Sheree North, Norman Fell, Benson Fong, Woodrow Parfrey, William Schallert, Jacqueline Scott, Marjorie Bennett, Rudy Diaz, Colby Chester, Charlie Briggs, Priscilla Garcia, Scott Hale, Charles Matthau, Hope Summers, Monica Lewis, Jim Nolan, Tom Tully, Albert Popwell, Kathleen O'Malley, Christina Hart, Craig Baxley, Virginia Wing, Donald Siegel.* Dir & Pro: Don Siegel. Screenplay: Howard Rodman & Dean Riesner; based on the novel *The Looters* by John Reese. (Universal–CIC.) Rel: Oct. 28. Colour. 111 Mins. Cert. X.

Charlotte's Web
Totally delightful feature cartoon based on the children's classic fairy-tale about the runt pig saved from death by a little girl and raised to fame and fortune through the kindness of Charlotte the spider. Charming and quite, quite captivating. Cast of voices: *Debbie Reynolds, Henry Gibson, Paul Lynde, Agnes Moorehead, Pamelyn Ferdin, Martha Scott, Herb Vigran, Dave Madden, John Stephenson, Bob Holt, Don Messick.* Dir: Charles A. Nichols & Iwao Takamoto. Pro: Joseph Barbera & William Hanna. Screenplay: Earl Hamner, Jr.; based on the novel by E. B. White, (Hanna/Barbera/Sagitarius–Scotia Barber.) Rel: Dec. 23. Colour. 96 Mins. Cert. U.

Les Chiennes – The Bitches
French sex drama about a young man who answers an advert for a "Male Companion" and finds himself increasingly embroiled in a mini-harem, sensual pleasures, jealous scenes and, finally, murder. Cast: *Janine Reynaud, Michel Lemoine, Françoise Dammien, Marie-Hélène Règne, Nathalie Zeiger, Latana Decaux, Virginie Vignon, Jean Berger.* Dir: Michel Lemoine. Pro: Bernard Launois. Screenplay: Michel Lemoine, from the novel by Jean Breton. (Art du Siècle–Cinecenta.) Rel: Floating; first shown at Centa Cinema, Aug., 1973. Colour. 75 Mins. Cert. X.

Child's Play
Screen adaptation of the stage play by Robert Marasco about the eruption of violence in an American Catholic Boys' School. Cast: *James Mason, Robert Preston, Beau*

188 Bridges, Ronald Weyand, Charles White, David Rounds, Kate Harrington, Jamie Alexander, Brian Chapin, Bryant Fraser, Mark Hall Haefeli, Tom Leopold, Julius Lo Iacono, Christopher Mann, Paul O'Keefe, Robert D. Randall, Robbie Reed, Paul Alessi, Anthony Barletta, Kevin Coupe, Christopher Hoag, Stephen McLaughlin. Dir: Sidney Lumet. Pro: David Merrick. Screenplay: Leon Prochnik; based on the play by Robert Marasco. (Paramount–CIC.) Rel: Dec. 1. Colour. 100 Mins. Cert. X.

The Chinese Connection
Another in the sudden flood of Run-Run Shaw, made-in-Hong Kong Kung-Fu melodramas: this one all about boxing and allied rackets. Cast: *David Chiang, Ti Lung, Li Ching, Liu Lan-Ying, Ku Feng, Chen Hsing, Ching Miao, Yang Chih Ching, Canony Chaeh, Wang Chung, Tang Ti, Hu Wei.* Dir: Chang Cheh. Pro: Runme Shaw. Screenplay: I Kuang. (Shaw–MGM–EMI.) Rel: Sept. 23. Colour. 86 Mins. Cert. X.

Chinese Vengeance
A Shaw Family (Hong Kong) production in which in the closing years of the Ching Dynasty in China a man convicted of the murder of a Provincial Governor and his assistant pleads guilty and then relates his reasons for the killings. Cast: *David Chiang, Ti Lung, Chen Kuan-tai, Ching Li, Tien Ching, Li Hsiu-hsien, Fan Mei Sheng, Cheng Lei, Wang Ching-Ho, Yeng Tse-lin, Wang Kunag Yu, Liu Kang, Cheng Kang Yeh, Tang Yen-tsan.* Dir: Chang Cheh. Pro: Run Run Shaw. Screenplay: I Kunag, Chang Cheh. (MGM–EMI.) Rel: June 9. 85 Mins. Cert. X.

Ciao! Manhattan
Feature documentary about the life, and death, of Edie Sedgwick, the socialite who became Warhol's first "super-star", drifted into drugs and died at the age of twenty-eight. Cast: *Edie Sedgwick, Wesley Hayes, Isabel Jewell, Geoff Briggs, Paul America, Viva, Pat Hartley, Roger Vadim, Christian Marquand, Allen Ginsberg.* Dir & Screenplay: John Palmer & David Weisman. (Black Ink Films.) Part colour; part black and white. Rel: Floating. 90 Mins. Cert. X.

Cisco Pike
1972 American film about a group-leader pop-star of the sixties who, retired from the business, is driven back into dope-pushing by a bent Los Angeles cop. Cast: *Kris Kristofferson, Karen Black, Gene Hackman, Harry Dean Stanton, Viva, Joy Bang, Roscoe Lee Browne, Chuy Franco, Severn Darden, Herb Weil, Antonio Fargas, Douglas Sahm, Don Sturdy, Alan Arbus, Frank Hotchkiss, Hugh Romney, James Oliver, Nawana Davis, Timothy Near, Lorna Thayer, William Traylor.* Dir: Bill L. Norton. Pro: Gerald Ayres. Screenplay: Bill L. Norton. (Acrobat–Columbia–Warner.) Rel: Floating, from May, 1973. Colour. 101 Mins. Cert. X.

Class of '44
A film which follows the three school pals of *Summer of '42* (quickly reduced to two as one enlists in the U.S. Marines) as they graduate, go to University, love, lose and generally grow up towards maturity. Warmly observed, charming, and very – naturally – American. Cast: *Gary Grimes, Jerry Houser, Oliver Conant, William Atherton, Sam Bottoms, Deborah Winters, Joe Ponazecki, Murray Westgate, Marion Waldman, Mary Long, Marcia Diamond, Jeffrey Cohen, Susan Marcus, Lamar Criss, Michael A. Hoey, Dan McDonald, Jan Campbell.* Dir & Pro: Paul Bogart. Screenplay: Herman Raucher. (Columbia–Warner.) Rel: Sept. 23. Colour. 95 Mins. Cert. AA.

Cleopatra Jones
The first of what is probably intended as a series of black-slanted Bond-type movies with *Tamara Dobson* as a sort of black feminine equivalent to 007 smashing the dope ring, led by Momma *Shelley Winters*, which has engineered the closure of her rehabilitation centre: and doing it with some Bond-like gadgets and her wizardry at Karate! Rest of cast: *Bernie Casey, Brenda Sykes, Antonio Fargas, Bill McKinney, Dan Frazer, Stafford Morgan, Mike Warren, Albert Popwell, Caro Kenyatta, Esther Rolle, Paul Koslo, Joseph A. Ternatore, Hedley Mattingly, George Reynolds, Angela Gibbs, John Garwood, Theodore Wilson, Christopher Joy, John Aldreman, Keith Hamilton.* Dir: Jack Starrett. Pro: William Tennant & Max Julien. Screenplay: Max Julien & Sheldon Keller. (Columbia–Warner.) Rel: Jan. 13. Colour. 89 Mins. Cert. X.

Climax – see Ich-das Abenteuer heute eine Frau zu sein

Cold Sweat
Somewhat complicated crime thriller set against backgrounds of the French Riviera and concerning devious crossings and double-crossing by the crooks as they try to get a drug shipment into the country. Cast: *Charles Bronson, Liv Ullmann, James Mason, Jill Ireland, Michel Constantin, Jean Topart, Yannick Delulle, Luigi Pistilli.* Dir: Terence Young. Pro: Robert Dorfman. Screenplay: Shimon Wincelberg & Albert Simonin; based on a novel by Richard Matheson. (Corona/Fair–MGM–EMI.) Rel: July 1. Colour. 94 Mins. Cert. AA.

Come Back Charleston Blue
Sly little black comedy along drily satirical lines about a couple of Harlem 'tecs who are assigned the task of finding who's responsible for an outburst of murders somehow connected with black gangster C.B., who was killed by Dutch Schultz way back in 1932! Cast: *Godfrey Cambridge, Raymond St Jacques, Peter De Anda, Jonelle Allen, Maxwell Glanville, Minnie Gentry, Dick Sabol, Leonardo Cimino, Percy Rodrigues, Toney Brealond, Tim Pelt, Darryl Knibb, Marcia McBroom, Adam Wade, Joseph Ray, Theodore Wilson, Dorothi Fox.* Dir: Mark Warren. Pro: Samuel Goldwyn, Jr. Screenplay: Bontche Schweig & Peggy Elliott, based on the Chester Himes novel, *The Heat's On.* (Formosa–Columbia–Warner.) Rel: Floating. Colour. 100 Mins. Cert. X.

Company Limited
The second of Satyajit Ray's films to deal with Indian urban problems; a deep and absorbing, gently satirical but steadily sympathetic study of a young sales executive in a British-owned Calcutta electrical manufacturers and his efforts to gain a coveted seat on the board, at one time seriously threatened by the discovery of some bad workmanship and only saved by resort to some nasty engineering of political unrest. Beautifully balanced, timed and acted. Cast: *Barun Chanda, Parmita Choudhury, Sharmila Tagore, H. Chattopadhyaya, Haradhan Banerjee, Indira Roy, Promode Ganguly.* Dir, Screenplay & Music: Satyajit Ray. Pro: Bharat S. Rana. (Rana–Contemporary.) Rel: Floating; first shown at the Academy, Feb., 1974. 112 Mins. Cert. U.

Confessions of a Police Captain – see Confessione di un Commissario di Polizia al Procuratore della Repubblica

Confessione di un Commissario di Polizia al Procuratore della Repubblica – Confessions of a Police Captain
About a dedicated Italian inspector of police who, unable to get the hated villain to justice by fair means, tries it by foul, and when that misfires kills the man and then offers himself up for judgement. A mixture of crime thriller and political corruption exposure which falls rather sadly between the two stools. Cast: *Martin Balsam, Franco Nero, Marilù Tolo, Claudio Gora, Arturo Dominici, Michele Gammino, Luciano Lorcas, Giancarlo Prete, Adolfo Lastretti, Calisto Calisti, Wanda Wismara, Giancarlo Badessi.* Dir: Damiano Damiani. Pro: Bruno Turchetto & Mario Montanari. Screenplay: Damiano Damiani & Salvatore Laurani. (Euro International/Explorer–Avco Embassy.) Rel: June, 1973. Colour. 105 Mins. Cert. X.

The Con Men
Comedy about a mine inherited by an illiterate family and the subsequent efforts of everyone from bandits to sheriff to get the deeds away from them! Cast: *Jack Palance, Timothy Brent, Lionel Stander, F. Romana Coluzzi, Renzo Palmer, Maria Vico Villardo.* Dir: Enzo G. Castellari. Pro: Franco Palaggi & Virgilio De Blasi. Screenplay: Castellari, Gianni Simonelli, Tito Carpi & J. Maesso. (F. P. Cinematografica & Canaria-Fox–Rank.) Rel: Floating. Colour. 91 Mins. Cert. A.

Cops and Robbers
In fact the title is quite subtle, for it means cops who are *also* robbers, bent cops in fact! It all starts when a cop holds up a chemist's shop and with the till takings safely in his pocket finds it so easy he tells his pal, who gets grandiose ideas about stealing $10,000,000 – and very nearly gets away with it, subsequently becoming encouraged to try and double-cross the Mafia. Beneath a superficially exciting and smooth story of crime are all sorts of psychological suggestions about the possible breakdown of society because of general greed and contempt of the moral precepts on which it

works. Cast: *Cliff Gorman, Joe Bologna, Dick Ward, Shepperd Strudwick, Ellen Holly, John Ryan, Nino Ruggeri, Gayle Gorman, Lucy Martin, Lee Steel, Jacob Weiner, Frances Foster, Arthur Pierce, Martin Cove, Jim Ferguson, Walter Gorney, Frank Gio, Jeff Ossuno, Joseph Spinell, George Harris II.* Dir: Aram Avakian. Pro: Elliott Kastner. Screenplay: Donald E. Westlake. (Kastner–UA.) Rel: April 28. Colour. 89 Mins. Cert. AA.

The Corpse Grinders
Rather delightful horror-thriller parody about a firm of cat's-meat manufacturers who quite accidentally discover that when a human body goes into the hopper their sales graph leaps, and take advantage of the discovery with the help of the local gravedigger! Only when the cats start trying to get their favourite diet direct from the living source does the inevitable investigation start . . .! Cast: *Sean Kenney, Monika Kelly, Sanford Mitchell, J. Byron Foster, Warren Ball, Ann Noble, Vince Barbi, Harry Lovejoy, Earl Burnam, Zena Foster, Ray Dannis, Drucilla Hoy, Curt Matson, Charles "Foxy" Fox, Stephen Lester, William Kirschner, George Bowden, Don Ellis, Mike Garrison, Andy Collings, Mary Ellen Burke.* Dir & Pro: Ted V. Mikels. Screenplay: Arch Hall & Joseph L. Cranston (C.G. Productions–Anthony Balch.) Rel: July 1. Colour. 72 Mins. Cert. X.

The Cow
An Iranian film – and a very good one, too – which details, with insight, humour and love, the life in a small Iranian village whose preoccupations are with each other, the threatening bandits on the skyline and the demise of the wonderful cow which for so long has been not only the owner's, but the whole village's pride and joy. Cast: *Ezat Entezami, Ali Nasirian, Jamshid Mashayekhi, Shojazedeh, Jafar Vali, Ramezanifar.* Dir & Pro: Daryush Mehrjui. Screenplay: Daryush Mehrjui & Golam Hossein Saedi, based on the latter's story. (Caspian Studios–Connoisseur.) Rel: Floating; first shown at Academy Two, June, 1937, 101 Mins. Cert. A.

Craze
Grand Guignolish British thriller about a professional antiques dealer and amateur black magic dabbler who begins to topple off his trolley and bring human sacrifices to the nasty little idol in the basement. After the fourth victim the cops move in and the idol gets its fifth victim – its worshipper! All highly unlikely, but smoothly, and gorily directed and with a very high-class cast: *Jack Palance, Diana Dors, Julie Ege, Edith Evans, Hugh Griffith, Trevor Howard, Michael Jayston, Suzy Kendall, Martin Potter, Percy Herbert, David Warbeck, Kathleen Byron, Venecia Day, Marianne Stone, Dean Harris.* Dir: Freddie Francis. Pro: Herman Cohen. Screenplay: Aben Kandel & Herman Cohen: based on the Henry Seymour novel *Infernal Idol.* (Harbor–EMI.) Rel: June 2. Colour. 96 Mins. Cert. X.

Daddy Darling
The old problem of the teenager suddenly faced by her beloved father with a new "mother" and the way in which she reacts to the situation. Cast: *Helle Louise, Gio Petre, Lise Henningsen, Søren Stromberg, Lisa Thomson, Tove Maes, Kyo Feze, Inger Gleerup.* Dir & Screenplay: Joseph W. Sarno. Pro: Kenn Collins. (Target International.) Rel: Floating; first shown at Classic, Charing Cross Road, February 1974. Colour. 95 Mins. Cert. X.

The Day of the Dolphin
A rather unconventional, but by and large very successful, blend of documentary, science-fiction, highly unusual love story and espionage thriller about a dedicated scientist with a great *rapport* with the dolphin he has hand-reared and who he is teaching a sort of basic English when the spies abduct the creature and try to use it for their explosive ends! Wonderful dolphin footage – these intelligent mammals emerge as the stars, along with *George C. Scott,* who gives his usual, convincing portrait of the scientist. Rest of cast: *Trish van Devere, Paul Sorvino, Fritz Weaver, Jon Korkes, Edward Herrmann, Leslie Charleson, John David Carson, Victoria Racimo, John Dehner, Severn Darden, William Roerick, Elizabeth Wilson, Julie Follansbee, Florence Stanley, Brooke Hayward, Pat Englund, Willie Meyers, Phyllis Davis.* Dir: Mike Nichols. Pro: Robert E. Relyea. Screenplay: Buck Henry, based on the novel by Robert Merle. (Joseph E. Levine–Avco Embassy.) Rel: Feb. 10. Colour. 120 Mins. Cert. U.

The Day of the Jackal
Fred Zinnemann's leisurely-paced, yet consistently taut and beautifully wrought screen adaptation of the Frederick Forsyth thriller about a meticulously planned but finally unsuccessful attempt on the life of General Charles de Gaulle in the early 1960s. With a fine, neatly underplayed performance by *Edward Fox* as the young professional English killer (whose code name gives the story its title) hired by the OAS as a last attempt – following several abortive ones – to kill the man they considered had betrayed France by giving independence to Algeria. Rest of cast: *Terence Alexander, Bernard Archard, Michel Auclair, Alan Badel, Tony Britton, Denis Carey, Adrien Cayla-Legrand, Cyril Cusack, Maurice Denham, Vernon Dobtcheff, Jacques Francois, Olga Georges-Picot, Raymond Gerome, Barrie Ingham, Derek Jacobi, Michel Lonsdale, Jean Martin, Ronald Pickup, Eric Porter, Anton Rodgers, Delphine Seyrig, Donald Sinden, Jean Sorel, David Swift, Timothy West.* Dir: Fred Zinnemann. Pro: John Woolf. Screenplay: Kenneth Ross. (Warwick–Universal–CIC.) Rel: Oct. 21. Colour. 142 Mins. Cert. A.

The Deadly Trackers
Grim, bloody and doom-laden Western about an American sheriff who, when his wife and child are killed by bank robbers trapped in his town, sets out to

track down and kill the quartet even though it entails his illegal crossing of the border into Mexico. Cast: *Richard Harris, Rod Taylor, Al Lettieri, Neville Brand, William Smith, Paul Benjamin, Pedro Armendariz, Jr., Kelly Jean Peters, Sean Marshall, Read Morgan, Joan Swift, William Bryant, Ray Moyer, Armando Acosta, Federico Gonzalez, John Kennedy.* Dir: Barry Shear. Pro: Fouad Said. Based on the Samuel Fuller story *Riata.* (Columbia–Warner.) Rel: May 19. Colour. 104 Mins. Cert. X.

Deaf and Mute Heroine
The rather sad romance of a deaf and mute expert swordswoman who rescues her lover from the gamblers who are holding him but finds him dead at the end of the climactic battle. Cast: *Helen Ma, Tong Tick, Wong Shilley, Lee Ying, Tang Ching.* Other credits not given. (Golden Harvest–Cathay Films.) Rel: June 16. Colour. 86 Mins. Cert. X.

Deaf Smith and Johnny Ears
European-made Western (also known as *Los Amigos*) about two friends of Sam Houston who are handed the task, in 1834, of aborting the threat of a dictatorship in the State of Texas: with *Anthony Quinn* and *Franco Nero* as the couple. Rest of cast: *Pamela Tiffin, Ira Furstenberg, Franco Graziosi, Adolfo Lastretti, Renato Romano, Francesca Benedetti, Franca Sciutto, Tom Felleghy, Cristina Airoldi, Renzo Moneta, Romano Puppo, Enrico Casadei, Luciano Rossi, Lorenzo Fineschi, Mario Carra, Antonio Faa Di Bruno, Giorgio Dolfin, Margherita Trentini, Fulvio Grimaldi, Paolo Pierani.* Dir: Paolo Cavara. Pro: Joseph Janni & Luciano Perugia. Screenplay: Harry Essex, Oscar Saul, Paolo Cavara, Lucia Drudi & Augusto Finocchi. (Compagnia/Idea–MGM–EMI.) Rel: July 22. Colour. 92 Mins. Cert. AA.

Death Kick
The usual mixture of the martial arts and a slim story about good and bad men and eventual triumph of good over evil. Cast: *Chen Ping, Ku Feng, Wang Hsieh, Lin Wei-tu, Han Shao-hsiung, Chan Shen, Yuan Man-tzu, Hunag Kan, Shih Lu-chieh.* Dir: Ho Meng-hua. Pro: Run Run Shaw. (Shaw Bros.– EMI.) Rel: June 9. Colour. 85 Mins. Cert. X.

Diamonds on Wheels
Disney film, of special appeal to junior, which against a background of an exciting motor-car rally tells a story of a diamond robbery, which becomes intricately bound up with the rally when the crooks believe that their loot – stolen from them by one of their own gang – is hidden in one of the rally cars! Cast: *Patrick Allen, George Sewell, Richard Wattis, Allan Cuthbertson, Derek Newark, Peter Firth, Spencer Banks, Cynthia Lund, Andrew McCulloch, Christopher Malcolm, Barry Jackson, Dudley Sutton, George Innes, George Woodbridge, Patrick McAlliney, Royston Tickner, Maggie Hanley, Robin Langford, Candace Glendenning, Mark Edwards, James McManus, Ambrosine Phillpotts,*

Arthur Hewlett, Tom Bowman. Dir: Jerome Courtland. Pro: Ron Miller. Screenplay: William Robert Yates; based on the novel *Nightmare Rally* by Pierre Castex. (Disney.) Rel: Aug. 19. Colour. 85 Mins. Cert. U.

Diary of a Nymphomaniac
Jacqueline Laurent as the wife who believes her hubbie when he tells her that the murder charge - of a prostitute – for which he has been accused was not his work, and sets out to investigate for herself the circumstances of the murdered girl. Cast: *Mona Proust, Anne Libert, Doris Thomas, Howard Vernon*. Dir: Clifford Brown. Pro: Robert de Nesle. Screenplay: Jesus Franco Manera. (Comptoir Français–New Realm.) Rel: Floating. Colour. 76 Mins. Cert. X.

Digby, The Biggest Dog in the World
Mildly funny fantasy-comedy about an accident-prone young scientist who accidentally gives a newly-invented "growth" drug to his dog, which soon becomes the size of an elephant and is hunted by the Army with the idea of putting him down . . . Cast: *Jim Dale, Spike Milligan, Angela Douglas, John Bluthal, Norman Rossington, Milo O'Shea, Richard Beaumont, Dinsdale Landen, Garfield Morgan, Victor Spinetti, Harry Towb, Kenneth J. Warren, Bob Todd, Margaret Stuart, Molly Urquart, Victor Maddern, Frank Thornton, Sandra Caron, Edward Underdown, Ben Aris, Sheila Steafel, Clovissa Newcombe, Rob Stewart, Maxine Casson, Henry McGee*. Dir: Joseph McGrath. Pro: Walter Shenson. Screenplay: Michael Pertwee, from a story by Charles Isaacs, based on a book by Ted Key. (City Investing Co.-Walter Shenson Films-Fox-Rank.) Rel: April 21. Colour. 88 Mins. Cert. U.

A Doll's House
Joseph Losey's film of the Ibsen play classic, with a number of cast weaknesses and an odd throwaway of the piece's main theme. *Jane Fonda* miscast as Nora, *David Warner* struggling gamely with a role too old for him to bring real conviction to it, but *Trevor Howard* as the old doctor and *Edward Fox* as the villain both impressive. Rest of cast: *Delphine Seyrig, Anna Wing, Pierre Oudrey, Frode Lien, Tone Floor, Morten Floor, Ingrid Natrud, Freda Krogh, Ellen Holm, Dagfinn Hertzberg*. Dir & Pro: Joseph Losey. Screenplay: David Mercer. (World Film Services/Films la Boétie–British Lion.) Rel: Floating. Colour. 106 Mins. Cert. A.

The Doll Squad
A feminine switch of the Bond theme: a small group of individually talented, lovely young ladies working as the team of the title, are officially asked to investigate the plans of a master criminal who from his island lair plans to subjugate the world with his new variation of the bubonic plague germ! And how those dollies put paid to all that! Cast: *Michael Ansara, Francine York, Anthony Eisley, John Carter, Rafael Campos, William Bagdad, Lillian Garrett, Lisa Todd, Gustave Unger,*

Bertil Unger, Curt Matson, Herb Robbins, Dru Landers, Jean London, Leigh Christian, Sherri Vernon, Bret Zeller, Carol Terry, Tura Satana, Judy McConnell*. Dir & Pro: Ted V. Mikels. Screenplay: Jack Richesin, Pam Eddy & Ted V. Mikels. (Mikels-Nation Wide Film Distributors.) Rel: Floating. Colour. 101 Mins. Cert. X.

The Don is Dead
Polished, well-made, violent gangster film about the split and subsequent bloody warfare between the different "families" of the Mafia, engineered by one back-seat planner who aims to take over the whole outfit. Cast: *Anthony Quinn, Frederic Forrest, Robert Forster, Al Lettieri, Angel Tompkins, Charles Cioffi, Jo Anne Meredith, J. Duke Rosso*. Dir: Richard Fleischer. Pro: Hal B. Wallis. Screenplay: Marvin H. Albert, based on his novel. (Hal Wallis–Universal–CIC.) Rel: Mar. 10. Colour. 117 Mins. Cert. X.

Don Quixote
Film of the stage ballet produced in Australia, choreographed, directed and danced by *Rudolf Nureyev* (with *Robert Helpmann* co-directing). Rest of cast: *Ray Powell, Francis Croese, Lucette Aldous, Colin Peasley, Marilyn Rowe, Kelvin Coe, Gailene Stock, Carolyn Rappel, Ronald Bekker, John Meehan, Rex McNeill, Rodney Smith, Joseph Janusaitis, Frederick Werner, Alan Alder, Paul Saliba, Susan Dains, Julie da Costa, Leigh Rowles, Marilyn Rowe, Patricia Cox, Janet Vernon, Gary Norman, Dancers of the Australian Ballet*. Dir: R. Nureyev & R. Helpmann. Pro: John Hargreaves. (Walter Reade Org.–International Arts Inc.) Rel: Floating; first shown at the Bloomsbury Cinema, Jan., 1974. Colour. 111 Mins. Cert. U.

Don't Look Now
Adaptation of the Daphne du Maurier story about the strange sequel in a wintry Venice – where the husband has a job restoring a church (the atmosphere beautifully caught) – to the tragic death in England of his small daughter. A chilly mystery never fully, or at least clearly revealed, but always fascinating. Cast: *Julie Christie, Donald Sutherland, Hilary Mason, Clelia Matania, Massimo Serato, Renato Scarpa, Gioorgio Trestini, Leopoldo Trieste, David Tree, Ann Rye, Nicholas Salter, Sharon Williams, Bruno Cattaneo, Adelina Poerio*. Dir: Nicolas Roeg. Pro: Peter Katz. Screenplay: Allan Scott & Chris Bryant; based on a story by Daphne du Maurier. (British Lion) Rel: Nov. 18. Colour. 110 Mins. Cert. X.

The Double Headed Eagle
Compilation film from feature, documentary, newsreel, and other sources, covering the history of the rise of the Third Reich. Dir: Lutz Becker. Pro: Sanford Lieberson & David Puttnam. Screenplay: Lutz Becker & Philippe Mora. (VPS Films.) Rel: Floating. Colour. 93 Mins. Cert. U.

Eagle in a Cage
The eagle is Napoleon and this concerns his enforced stay on Elba after his defeat and capture by his enemies. Cast: *John Gielgud, Ralph Richardson, Billie Whitelaw, Kenneth Haigh (as Napoleon), Moses Gunn, Ferdy Mayne, Lee Montague, Georgina Hale, Michael Williams, Hugh Armstrong, Athol Coats*. Dir: Fielder Cook. Pro & Screenplay: Millard Lampell. (National General–Group W/Ramona–Cinerama.) Rel: Floating. Colour. 102 Mins. Cert. A.

The Effect of Gamma Rays on Man-in-the-Moon Marigolds
Joanne Woodward won the 1973 Cannes Festival acting prize for her performance in this, husband Paul Newman's film based on the off-beat play by Paul Zindel: the story of a bitter, repressed, sluttenly middle-aged widow and her two teenage daughters, one as bright as a penny and coolly impervious to her mother's bad influence, the other neurotic and suffering from fits and very much a product of the tension at home. And it's the cool one's experiment with "exposed" seeds of the marigold, more especially her success, that brings about the terrible, spiritual, climax. Rest of the cast: *Nell Potts* (a beautifully restrained performance as the bright daughter), *Roberta Wallach, Judith Lowry, Richard Venture, Carolyn Coates, Will Hare, Estelle Omeis, Jess Osuna, David Spielberg, Ellen Dano, Lynn Rogers, Roger Serbagi, John Lehne, Michael Kearney, Dee Victor*. Dir & Pro: Paul Newman. Screenplay: Alvin Sargent; based on the Paul Zindel play. (Newman–Foreman–Fox–Rank.) Rel: Floating. Colour. 101 Mins. Cert. AA.

Electra Glide in Blue
A sort of Western, set in Arizona, transcribed into terms of cops and motor-bikes: the story of a cop who wants to become a detective but when he does is so disillusioned that he opts to return to the throbbing, two-wheel beat! Cast: *Robert Blake, Billy (Green) Bush, Mitchell Ryan, Jeannine Riley, Elisha Cook, Royal Dano, David J. Wolinski, Peter Cetera, Terry Kath, Lee Loughnane, Walter Parazaider, Joe Samsil, Jason Clark, Michael Butler, Susan Forristal, Lucy Angle Guercio, Melissa Green, Jim Gilmore, Bob Zemko, J. N. Roberts, Rock Walker, Alan Gibbs, Scott Dockstader, Mickey Alzola, Ron Rondell, Madura*. Dir & Pro: James William Guercio. Screenplay: Robert Boris. (Guercio/Rupert Hitzig–UA.) Rel: March 10. Colour. 113 Mins. Cert. X.

El Topo – The Mole
Extraordinary Alexandro Jodorowsky film from South America which, a collection of visual pyrotechnics, contains references to Fellini, Buñuel and "The Man With No Name" Westerns, but emerges as very much a violent and bloody work of film art on its own account. With a story which defies orderly or even possible condensation: a string of appropriately unrelated incidents, many set in the desert, which could have much or little significance, in the sense you can read into the film almost anything you like, so

intricate and ambiguous is it. Cast: *Alexandro Jodorowsky, Brontis Jodorowsky, Mara Lorenzio, David Silva, Paula Romo, Hector Martinez (El Borrado), Juan Jose Gurrola, Victor Fosado, Agustin Isunza, Jacqueline Luis, Jose Antonio Alcaraz, Felipe Diazgarza, Robert John, Julien de Meriche.* Dir & Screenplay: Alexandro Jodorowsky. Pro: Roberto Viskin. (Panic-Abkco.) Rel: Floating; first shown at the Curzon, Oct., 1973. Colour. 120 Mins. Cert. X.

The Emigrants
The first part of a long, lavish and epic-scale story of a Swedish family who, hit time and time again by adversity, decide to emigrate to America and get as far as Minnesota, where by the side of a lake they stop and start to build their new home in the new world. Very leisurely paced; superbly visual. Cast: *Max von Sydow, Liv Ullmann, Eddie Axberg, Svenolof Bern, Alina Alfredsson, Allan Edwall, Monica Zetterlund, Pierre Lindstedt, Hans Alfredson, Ulla Smidje, Eva-Lena Zetterlund, Gustaf Färingborg, Ake Fridell, Agneta Prytz, Halvar Bjork, Arnold Alfredsson, Bror Englund, Tom C. Fouts, Peter Hoimark, Erik Johansson, Staffan Liljander, Goran Lundin, Ditte, Lasse and Pelle Martinsson, Yvonne Oppstedt, Linn Ullmann, Annika Nyhammar.* Dir (photographed & edited): Jan Troell. Pro: Bengt Forslund. Screenplay: Jan Troell & B. Forslund; based on four novels by Vilhelm Moberg. (Svensk Filmindustri-Columbia-Warner.) Rel: Floating. Colour. 150 Mins. Cert. AA.

Emperor of the North
(Originally called *Emperor of the North Pole* in America.) A story of America in the midst of the thirties depression, the unemployed who took to the railroad to move about the country searching for work, providing a major problem for the railways: in particular the confrontation and feud which develops between a train captain (*Ernest Borgnine*) who boasts that no tramp rides his train and stays alive and the super-bum (*Lee Marvin*) who boasts there's no train that he can't ride! Rough, exciting and full of marvellous steam-train footage. Rest of cast: *Keith Carradine, Charles Tyner, Malcolm Atterbury, Simon Oakland, Harry Caesar, Hal Baylor, Matt Clark, Elisha Cook, Joe Di Reda, Liam Dunn, Diane Dye, Robert Foulk, James Goodwin, Ray Guth, Sid Haigh, Karl Lukas, Edward McNally, John Steadman, Vic Tayback, Dave Willock.* Dir: Robert Aldrich. Pro: Kenneth Hyman. Screenplay: Christopher Knopf. (Inter-Hemisphere-Fox-Rank.) Rel: Sept. 30. Colour. 119 Mins. Cert. AA.

England Made Me
Screen version of the Graham Greene novel – his fourth, written in 1935 – set in the increasingly Nazified Germany of the thirties and explaining the murder by a ruthless tycoon (planning to move his business secretly to America) of his English mistress's idle but dangerous young brother. Cast: *Peter Finch, Michael York, Hildegard Neil, Michael Hordern, Jos Ackland, Tessa Wyatt, Michael Sheard, Bill Baskiville,*

Demeter Bitenc, Mira Nikolic, Vladimir Bacic, Maja Papandopulo, Vladan Zivkovic, Cvetka Cupar. Dir: Peter Duffell. Pro: Jack Levin. Screenplay: Desmond Cory & Peter Duffell; based on the Graham Greene novel. (Atlantic-Hemdale.) Rel: June 24 & July 1, 1973. Colour. 100 Mins. Cert. AA.

Enter the Dragon
Another made-in-Hong Kong movie, a sort of Eastern 007 adventure with the late *Bruce Lee* (this was his last film; he died soon after it was completed at the age of thirty-two) recruited as an agent to take part in a Festival of the martial arts on a mysterious island ruled over by a sinister figure who makes his fabulous wealth from dope. So violent, so incredible, such hokum, it works out as grand filmic fun. Rest of cast: *John Saxon, Ahna Capri, Bob Wall, Shih Kien, Angela Mao Ying, Betty Chung, Geoffrey Weeks, Yang Sze, Peter Archer, Jim Kelly.* Dir: Robert Clouse. Pro: Fred Weintraub & Paul Heller. Screenplay: Michael Allin. (Warner/Concord-Columbia-Warner.) Rel: Jan. 13. Colour. 98 Mins. Cert. X.

The Erotic Adventures of Zorro
A very strange, and highly unexceptional, American-German-French co-production set in the city of Los Angeles, circa 1820, and attempting to "send-up" the famous character made famous on the screen by the late Douglas Fairbanks. Cast: *Douglas Frey, Robyn Whitting, Penny Boran, Jude Farese, John Alderman, Lynn Harris, Michelle Simon, Bruce Gibson, Sebastian Gregory, Mike Peratta, Ernie Dominy, Becky Perlman, Kathy Hilton, Allen Bloomfield, Gerard Broulard, Cory Brandon, David Villa, Fermin Castillo de Muro, Jesus Valdez, David Friedman, Robert W. Cresse.* Dir: Robert Freeman. Pro: David Friedman & William Allen Castleman. Screenplay: Mona Lott, Joy Boxe & David F. Friedman. (Entertainment Ventures/Atlas/Alpha-France-Grand National.) Rel: Floating. Colour. 84 Mins. Cert. X.

Everybody's At It
(Known in the U.S. as *The Female Response*.) Sacked woman's lib journalist Marjorie Hirsch sets out to prove herself by setting up a sex seminary – and the stories revealed are the evidence! Cast: *Raina Barrett, Jacque Lynn Colton, Michaela Hope, Jennifer Welles, Gena Wheeler, Roz Kelly, Lawrie Driscoll, Edmund Donnelly, Todd Everett, Richard Wilkins, Phyllis MacBride, Suzy Mann, Curtis Carlson, Herb Streicher, Anthony Scott Craig, Richard Lipton.* Dir: Tim Kincaid. Pro: Richard Lipton. Screenplay: Tim Kincaid & David Newburge. (Filmpeople/American International-New Realm.) Rel: Floating. Colour. 70 Mins. Cert. X.

Every Little Crook and Nanny
Pretty thin but not unamusing comedy about a British girl, running a Music and Dance School in America, whose premises are commandeered by a big-time Mafia gangster and, swept into the job of Nannying the man's son when he goes a-holidaying in Europe, plans a wild

scheme to organise the kid's abduction so she can restart her school with the ransom money! Cast: *Lynn Redgrave, Victor Mature, Paul Sand, Maggie Blye, Austin Pendleton, John Astin, Dom DeLuise, Louise Sorel, Phillip Graves, Lou Cutell, Leopoldo Trieste, Pat Morita, Phil Foster, Pat Harrington, Severn Darden, Katharine Victory, Mina Kolb, Bebe Louie, Lee Kafafian, Sally Marr.* Dir: Cy Howard. Pro: Leonard J. Ackerman. Screenplay: Cy Howard, Jonathan Axelrod & Robert Klane. (MGM-EMI.) Rel: Floating. Colour. 92 Mins. Cert. A.

Evil Fingers – see Giornata Nera per l'Ariete

Excite Me – see Il Tuo Vizio E una Stanza Chiusa e Solo Io ne ho la Chiave

Executive Action
A fictional, theoretical account of what might have been the true story behind the assassination of President Kennedy, with all the dangerous implications involved! A somewhat uneasy mixture of newsreel fact with imaginative fiction, suggesting that the murder was planned and carried through by a group of influential Texas businessmen scared of Kennedy's liberal policies. Cast: *Burt Lancaster, Robert Ryan, Will Geer, Gilbert Green, John Anderson, Paul Carr, Colby Chester, Ed Lauter, Walter Brooke, John Brascia, Richard Bull, Sidney Clute, Deanna Darrin, Lee Delano, Lloyd Gough, Richard Hurst, Robert Karnes, James MacColl, Joaquin Martinez, Dick Miller, Oscar Oncidi, Tom Peters, Paul Sorenson, Hunter Von Leer, Sandy Ward, William Watson.* Dir: David Miller. Pro: Dan Bessie & Gary Horowitz. Screenplay: Dalton Trumbo. (Edward Lewis-National General-Scotia-Barber.) Rel: Feb. 24. Colour. 91 Mins. Cert. A.

False Witness
Neat little thriller about a man who, knowing he has a fatal brain tumour, offers to solve a previously unsolved kidnapping case and does it by laying a trail of clues leading to himself, reckoning to pass the reward on to his widow. But the plot gets out of hand when after being convicted he is successfully operated upon! Cast: *George Kennedy, Anne Jackson, Eli Wallach, Steve Ihnat, William Marshall, Joe Maross, Dana Elcar, Walter Brooke, Anita O'Day, Joan Tompkins, Robert Sampson, Leonard Stone, Stewart Moss, Charlene Holt, Robert Donner, Pamela Murphy, Abigail Shelton, Douglas Henderson, Robert Patten, Richard McMurray.* Dir: Richard A. Colla. Pro: Robert Enders & Everett Freeman. Screenplay: John T. Kelly; from a story by R. Enders. (Freeman/Enders-MGM-EMI.) Rel: Floating. Colour. 88 Mins. Cert. A.

The Father
A generally successful Swedish screen adaptation of the grim Strindberg play which in telling its sombre story of a wife who deliberately drives her husband into

madness is also concerned with a careful examination of the complicated love–hate relationship between the sexes: that and man's lasting psychological sense of loss of the warmth and simplicity of his womb-life. Cast: *Georg Rydeberg, Gunnel Lindblom, Lena Nyman, Jan-Olaf Strandberg, Tord Stål, Sif Ruud, Axel Düberg, Aino Taube, Helena Brodin, Yvonne Lundeqvist, Bo Hollsten, Olle Björling, Einy Eriksson, Lickå Sjöman.* Dir & Screenplay: Alf Sjöberg. Pro: Sigurd Jorgensen. (Svenska Filminstitutet & Sveriges Radio–Gala.) Rel: Floating; first shown at the Berkeley, Nov., 1973. Colour. 100 Mins. Cert. X.

Fellini's Roma
An acutely personal impression of Rome by Fellini, who, ignoring any pretence of a story, gathers together a series of incidents from his memory and imagination and transmutes them by his sheer artistry into cinematic gold, including gem-like sequences such as the reconstruction of the Music Hall of the thirties, the brothels and a magnificent satirical fashion show of religious garb. Cast: *Peter Gonzales, Fiona Florence, Britta Barnes, Pia de Doses, Marne Maitland, Renato Giovanneli, Elisa Mainardi, Stefano Mayore, Galliano Sbarra, Anna Magnani, Gore Vidal.* Dir, Pro & Written (the last with Bernardino Zapponi): Féderico Fellini. (Italo Francese Ultra–UA.) Rel: Floating. Colour. 118 Mins. Cert. X.

Les Félines – The Cats
French film about a neglectful husband, a glamorous wife, the man's mistress and the girl the wife brings in to break up the liaison . . . but it ends rather oddly with the wife and the girl beginning to like each other a lot . . .! Cast: *Janine Reynaud, Nathalie Zeiger, Jacques Insermini, Pauline Larrieu, Georges Géret, Nadia Vasil, Stan Rol.* Dir: Daniel Daert. Pro: René Lévy. (Reda–Cinecenta.) Rel: Floating; first shown at the Cinecenta, Nov., 1973. Colour. 90 Mins. Cert. X.

The Female Bunch
Minor American feature about a gang of Women's Lib ladies hiding out in the desert, financed by a little drug trafficking. But they're finally driven into violence and murder when they are found out by a Man! Cast: *Russ Tamblyn, Jenifer Bishop, Jeffrey Land, Lon Chaney, Jr., Alisha Lee, Mike Weirdles.* Dir: Al Adamson. Pro: R. Nussbaum. Screenplay: Jale Lockwood & Brent Nimrod. (Dalia–Grand National.) Rel: Floating; first shown at Oscar, Oct., 1973. Colour. 75 Mins. Cert. X.

A Film About Jimi Hendrix
Feature documentary about the pop-singer; the man and his work. A Joe Boyd, John Head, Gary Weis production. (Columbia–Warner.) Rel: July 29. Colour. 102 Mins. Cert. X.

The Final Programme
Visually fascinating and highly imaginative but otherwise less attractive science-fiction mish-mash about a computerised Messiah created at the end of our Civilisation to lead the survivors into a dubious new one! Often funny, even if perhaps not always

intentionally so! Cast: *Jon Finch, Jenny Runacre, Sterling Hayden, Harry Andrews, Hugh Griffith, Julie Ege, Patrick Magee, Graham Crowden, George Coulouris, Basil Henson, Derrick O'Connor, Gilles Millinaire, Ronald Lacey, Sandy Ratcliffe, Mary MacLeod, Sarah Douglas, Dolores Del Mar, Sandra Dickinson.* Dir, Written & Designed: Robert Fuest; based on the novel by Michael Moorcock. Pro: John Goldstone & Sandy Lieberson. (Goodtimes Enterprises/Gladiole–MGM–EMI.) Rel: Oct. 7. Colour. 89 Mins. Cert. X.

Fist of Fury
Roistering made-in-Hong Kong adventure drama set in 1908 Shanghai and relating the duel between the School of Chinese Martial Arts and the rival Japanese Arts Association, with lots of authentic Kung-Fu unarmed combat. And it was all a smash hit in the Orient. Cast: *Bruce Lee, Miao Ker Hsiu, Tien Foong.* Dir & Screenplay: Lo Wei. Pro: Raymond Chow. (Golden Harvest–Cathay Films.) Rel: Nov. 4. Colour. 106 Mins. Cert. X.

The Fists of Vengeance
More action from Hong Kong: the story of the defeat of the Japanese Samurai by the brave young Chinese Government officer with the help of The People during the Japanese Occupation of China. Cast (includes): *Kung Bun, Tong Chi, Shoji Harada, Loh Bik Wan, Lou Peng, Chao Gin.* Dir: Chan Hong Man. Screenplay: Haw Chan. (Avco-Embassy.) Rel: May 12. Colour. 77 Mins. Cert. X.

The Five Crazy Boys
French comedy about a quintet of Normans who decide to team up and form a pop-group, called Les Charlots – and the series of comic disasters to which this leads them. Cast: *Les Charlots, Jacques Dufilho, Marion Game, Jacques Siller, the Martin Circus and The Triangle.* Dir & Screenplay: Claude Zidi. Pro: Michel Ardan. (Belles Rives–Fox–Rank.) Rel: Floating. Colour. 84 Mins. Cert. U.

Flesh on Fire
Greek film; peasant melodrama about the wife who runs off with a gypsy and is then killed by the husband, with interpolated sequences of music and dancing. Cast: *Lakis Komninos, Helen Erimou, Dim Bislanis, Aina Maouer, Iordanis Marinos.* Dir: George Papakostas. Pro: Takis Vlassis. Screenplay: Petros Makedon. (Faros–Amanda.) Rel: Floating. Colour. 97 Mins. Cert. X.

The 14
Film based on a headline-hitting true story about the efforts of a family of fourteen children to stay together as a family when their mother and father die and the sympathetic authorities after letting them go it alone for a while decide that they need more adult care. Cast: *Jack Wild, June Brown, Liz Edmiston, John Bailey, Cheryl Hall, Anna Wing, Diana Beevers, Alun Armstrong, Keith Buckley, Tony Calvin, Frank Gentry, Paul Daly, Christian Kelly, Peter Newby, Richard Heyward, Terry Ives, Christopher Leonard, Sean Hyde,*

Alfons Kaminsky, Wayne Brooks, Mark Hughes, Wayne Dyer. Dir: David Hemmings. Pro: Robert Mintz & Frank Avianca. Screenplay: Roland Starke. (Avianca Productions–MGM–EMI.) Rel: Nov. 23. Colour. 106 Mins. Cert. A.

40 Carats
Highly unrealistic, confected and overly sentimental story of the love-affair between a forty-year-old divorcée and an eighteen-year-old boy whom she meets on the beach in Greece, sleeps with and, defying all reason, weds! Cast: *Liv Ullmann, Edward Albert, Gene Kelly, Binnie Barnes, Deborah Raffin, Billy Green Bush, Nancy Walker, Don Porter, Rosemary Murphy, Natalie Schafer, Sam Chew, Jr., Claudia Jennings, Brooke Palance.* Dir: Milton Katselas. Pro: M. J. Frankovich. Screenplay: Leonard Gershe, based on a stage play by Barillet & Gredy adapted by Jay Allen. (Frankovich–Columbia–Warner.) Rel: Floating. Colour. 109 Mins. Cert. A.

Frankenstein and the Monster from Hell
Director Terence Fisher comes back to Hammer, after several years, to take up the horror banner and in the first part of this thriller stamps his Gothic sense of the macabre upon it, but then lets the script get away from him! All about a Frankenstein disciple who is committed to an insane asylum and there finds that the director of the place is the bad old Baron himself, using his position to carry on his monster-creating experiments in the basement! – and with *Peter Cushing* in the Baron role for the sixth time. Rest of cast: *Shane Briant, Madeline Smith, John Stretton, Bernard Lee, Clifford Mollison, Dave Prowse, Patrick Troughton, Charles Lloyd Pack, Janet Hargreaves, Philip Voss, Sheila D'Union, Christopher Cunningham, Winifred Sabine, Lucy Griffiths, Norman Mitchell, Norman Atkyns, Michael Ward, Mischa de la Motte, Elsie Wagstaff, Sydney Bromley, Victor Woolf, Tony Harris, Jerold Wells.* Dir: Terence Fisher. Pro: Roy Skeggs. Screenplay: John Elder. (Hammer–Avco-Embassy.) Rel: May 12. Colour. 99 Mins. Cert. X.

The Friends of Eddie Coyle
Sad, melancholy Peter Yates film about the fringes of the world of American crime in which ageing, worried "messenger boy" *Robert Mitchum* moves, wheeling and dealing in an effort to carry out his job and at the same time give his friendly cop enough information to get him off the hook which a charge of transporting illegal liquor is likely to put him in jail for a several-year stretch! The whole sordid story suggests that there is, in fact, precious little honour among thieves. Rest of cast: *Peter Boyle, Richard Jordan, Steven Keats, Alex Rocco, Joe Santos, Mitchell Ryan, Peter Maclean, Kevin O'Morrison, Marvin Lichterman, Carolyn Pickman, James Tolkan, Margaret Ladd, Matthew Cowles, Helena Carroll, Jane House, Michael McCleery, Alan Koss, Dennis McMullen, Judith Ogden Cabot, Jan Egleson, Jack Kehoe, Robert Anthony, Gus Johnson, Ted Maynard, Sheldon Feldner.* Dir: Peter Yates. Pro & Screenplay: Paul Monash; based on the book by George V.

Higgins. (Paramount–CIC.) Rel: Nov. 18. Colour. 103 Mins. Cert. X.

Fury
Love and revenge in eighteenth-century Russia, with *Oliver Reed* the brutal landowner lusting for his adopted daughter, whose brother – knowing that landowner Palizyn killed their parents and burnt their home – returns to stir up the restless peasants and persuade them into open revolt. All very melodramatic and with a script that is no great literary watermark. Rest of cast: *Claudia Cardinale, John McEnery, Raymond Lovelock, Carol André, Zora Velcova.* Dir: Antonio Calenda. Pro: Marcello Danon & Harry Saltzman. Screenplay: Edward Bond, Antonio Calenda & Ugo Pirro; based on the novel *Vadim* by Mikhail Lermontov. (Da.Ma.–Lowndes–Fox–Rank.) Rel: Floating. Colour. 112 Mins. Cert. AA.

The Gamblers
A comedy about gamblers gambled against and con men conned as they all struggle to make their illicit pot of gold. Cast: *Suzy Kendall, Don Gordon, Pierre Olaf, Kenneth Griffith, Stuart Margolin, Richard Woo, Massimo Serato, Faith Domergue, Relia Bashich, Tony Chinn.* Dir & Screenplay: Ron Winston. Pro: Sidney Glazier. Based on the Nikolai Gogol play. (UM–Fox–Rank.) Rel: Floating. Colour. 92 Mins. Cert. U.

Garringo
1969 Spanish–Italian Western which with plenty of bloodshed and violence relates the story of a young man who tries to revenge himself on the officers of the American Cavalry who tried, convicted and killed his father on a charge of treason. The film's title is the name of the officer detailed to the elimination of this gun-happy, note-writing and, finally, thieving young thorn in the U.S. Army's side. Cast: *Anthony Steffen, Peter Lee Lawrence, Solvi Stubing, Jose Bodalo, Raf Baldassarre, Luis Marin, Barta Barry, Lorenzo Robledo, Guillermo Mendez, Rossana Rovere, Maria Monterrey, Antonio Molino Rojo, Luis Induni, Frank Brana.* Dir: Rafael Romero Marchent. Screenplay: Giovanni Scolaro, Romero Marchent & Arpad de Riso. (Tritone Profilms/Cinematograficas–Golden Era.) Rel: Floating, from July, 1973. Colour. 91 Mins. Cert. X.

Gawain and The Green Knight
Arthurian legend about knights and chivalry and magic and great adventure, based on a medieval poem and aimed at the young audience. Cast: *Murray Head, Ciaran Madden, Nigel Green, Anthony Sharp, Robert Hardy, David Leland, Murray Melvin, Tony Steedman, Ronald Lacey, Willoughby Goddard, George Merritt, Peter Forbes-Robertson, Pauline Letts, Richard Hurndall, Peter Copley, Geoffrey Bayldon, Jerold Wells, Michael Crane, Jack Woolgar, Sue Ellis Jones.* Dir: Stephen Weeks. Pro: Philip Breen. Screenplay: Philip Breen & Stephen Weeks. (Sancrest–UA.) Rel: Aug. 12. Colour. 93 Mins. Cert. U.

Get Thee to a Nunnery
Rude fun in medieval Florence and thereabouts when the plague drives the lusting lads and luscious ladies into a rather odd sort of monastery. Cast: *Sergio Leonardi, Nazzareno Natale, Krista Nell, Antonia Santilli, Elio Marconato, Patrizia Auditori, Luciano Timoncini, Enrico Lazzareschi, Gabriella Giorgielli, Loredana Mongardini, Andrea Bosich, Maecelle Ginnette, Franco Mazzieri.* Dir: Mario Sequi. Screenplay: Alfredo Tucci & Mario Sequi. (Capitolina–Gala.) Rel: Floating; first shown at Berkeley One, Oct., 1973. Colour. 91 Mins. Cert. X.

Giornata Nera per l'Ariete – Evil Fingers
Thin, contrived little Italian whodunit with lots of murders and even a greater prodigality of red herrings! Cast: *Franco Nero, Pamela Tiffin, Maurizio Bonuglia, Edmund Purdom, Wolfgang Preiss, Ira Furstenberg, Renato Romano, Rossella Falk, Silvia Monti, Guido Alberti, Lucio Baroli, Agostina Belli, Corrado Gaipa, Andrea Scotti, Irio Fantini.* Dir: Luigi Bazzoni. Pro: Manolo Bolognini. Screenplay: Mario di Nardo, Mario Fenelli & Luigi Bazzoni; based on the story by D. M. Devine, *The Fifth Cord.* (Dario/BRC–Target.) Rel: Dec. 1. Colour. 80 Mins. Cert. X.

Gli Altri Racconti Canterbury – The Other Canterbury Tales
Not letting Pasolini have it all his own way, fellow countryman Mino Guerrini comes up with a further collection of six of the Chaucer tales (more than once removed) to be tied up as a saucy sexy package! Cast: *Leonora Vivaldi, Mirella Rossi, Alida Rossano, Enza Sbordone, Antonia Di Leo, Francesco D'Adda, Giafranco Quadrimi, Giacoma De Michelis, Amelin Sassaroli, Giuseppe Volpe, Vincenzo Maggio, Rolando Prosperi, Francesco Angelucci, Gianni Ottaviani, Teodro Carra, Samuel Montealegre, Mariama Camara, Fortunato Cecilia, Assunta Costanzo, Roberto Borelli, Joceline Munchenbach.* Dir: Mino Guerrini. (Transeuropa/Italian International–E. J. Fancey.) Rel: Floating; first shown at the Jacey Tatler, June, 1973. Colour. 92 Mins. Cert. X.

Godspell
Gay, fast-paced film of the stage rock musical, taken out into the streets, parks and on to the roofs of New York to give it a new and excitingly visual background. And this basically rather threadbare modern variation on the Gospel According to St Matthew is played out by a group of ten vital and talented youngsters. Cast: *Victor Garber, David Haskell, Jerry Sroka, Lynne Thigpen, Katie Hanley, Robin Lamont, Gilmer McCormick, Joanne Jonas, Merrell Jackson, Jeffrey Mylett.* Dir: David Greene. Pro: Edgar Lansbury. Screenplay: David Greene & John-Michael Tebelak; based on the latter's stage play conception and direction (with music and lyrics by Stephen Schwartz). (Lansbury/Duncan/Beruh–Columbia–Warner.) Rel: Feb. 17. Colour. 101 Mins. Cert. U.

The Golden Voyage of Sinbad
Arabian Nights fairy-tale, with Captain Sinbad

searching for the missing section of a magic amulet and having to ward off the spells cast by his evil magician rival, who activates the Captain's ship figurehead into murderous life and later does the same thing with a six-armed, cutlass-carrying god! And lots of fun from Harryhausen's clever effects in Dynamation. Cast: *John Phillip Law, Caroline Munro, Tom Baker, Douglas Wilmer, Martin Shaw, Gregorie Aslan, Kurt Christian, Takis Emmanuel, John D. Garfield, Aldo Sambrell.* Dir: Gordon Hessler. Pro: Charles H. Schneer & Ray Harryhausen. Screenplay: Brian Clemens, from the story by Clemens and Harryhausen. (Morningside–Columbia–Warner.) Rel: April 7. Colour. 105 Mins. Cert. U.

Gordon's War
Brutally efficient, violent, "black" film about a Vietnam veteran U.S. Army Negro Captain who coming home to find his wife has just died from drug addiction proceeds to recruit a trio of his old buddies and wage a violent, bloody, full-scale war against Harlem's drug-pushers. Cast: *Paul Winfield, Carl Lee, David Downing, Tony King, Gilbert Lewis, Carl Gordon, Nathan C. Heard, Grace Jones, Jackie Page, Charles Bergansky, Adam Wade, Hansford Rowe, Warren Taurien, Ralph Wilcox, David Connell, Richelle LeNoir, Michael Galloway.* Dir: Ossie Davis. Pro: Robert L. Schaffel. Screenplay: Howard Friedlander & Ed Spielman. (Palomar–Fox–Rank.) Rel: Jan. 20. Colour. 90 Mins. Cert. X.

A Gorgeous Bird Like Me – see Une Belle Fille Comme Moi

La Grande Bouffe – Blow-Out
Controversial Italian film which tells a story about four friends (a lawyer, a chef, an airline pilot and a television star) who decide for some unexplained reasons to commit suicide by eating themselves to death, which they proceed to do in a Paris house with the help of some prostitutes (who soon become sick and frightened and leave) and a weighty schoolmarm whose sexual and other appetites prove large enough to outlast them all. Some of the incidents are coarse, crude and otherwise objectionable (typical joke, an exploding, overloaded toilet!) but the critics gave it their first prize, all the same, at the Cannes Festival! Cast: *Marcello Mastroianni, Ugo Tognazzi, Michel Piccoli, Philippe Noiret, Andrea Ferreol.* Dir: Marco Ferreri. Pro: Jean-Pierre Rassan. Screenplay: Marco Ferreri and Rafael Ascona. (Mara/Capitolina/Films 66–Gala.) Rel: Floating; first shown at the Curzon, Dec., 1973. Colour. 133 Mins. Cert. X.

The Great Northfield Minnesota Raid
Ambiguous Western which throws a few pails of whitewash over such infamous bandits as the Younger and the James Brothers by at times suggesting they were hard done by and more sinned against than sinning! Presented in a sort of semi-documentary style with melodramatic inserts. Cast: *Cliff Robertson, Robert Duvall, Luke Askew, R. G. Armstrong, Dana Elcar, Donald Moffat, John Pearce, Matt Clark, Wayne*

Sutherlin, Robert H. Harris, Jack Manning, Elisha Cook, Jr., Royal Dano, Mary-Robin Redd, Bill Callaway Arthur Petersen, Craig Curtis, Barry Brown, Nellie Burt, Liam Dunn, Madeleine Taylor Holmes, Herbert Nelson, Erik Holland, Anne Barton, Marjorie Durant, Inger Stratton, Valda J. Hansen. Dir: Philip Kaufman. Pro: Bruce Graham. Screenplay: Philip Kaufman. (Universal–Rank.) Rel: Oct. 26. Colour. 90 Mins. Cert. X.

The Great Waltz
Lushly sugar-coated, superbly visual, beautifully sung and played, less happily scripted story of the Strausses, papa and son Johann, and the latter's often stormy marriage. Cast: *Horst Bucholz, Mary Costa, Rossano Brazzi, Nigel Patrick, Yvonne Mitchell, James Faulkner, Vicki Woolf, Susan Robinson, George Howe, Lauri Lupino Lane, Michael Tellering, William Parker, Ingrid Wayland, Lorna Nathan, Hermione Farthingale, Elizabeth Muthsam, Franz Aigner, Helmut Janatsch, Marty Allen, Dominique Weber, Guido Wieland, Paola Loew, Prince Johannes Schonburg-Hartenstein.* Dir, Pro & Screenplay: Andrew L. Stone. (Stone/MGM–EMI.) Rel: July 1. Colour. 134 Mins. Cert. U.

Hammer
Another look at the crooked, gangster-controlled American fight business, with *Fred Williamson* as the boxer who won't lie down to order. Rest of cast: *William Smith, Stack Pierce, Jamal Moore, John Quade, Charles Lampkin, Mel Stewart, Elizabeth Harding, Vonetta McGee, Bernie Hamilton, Juan de Carlos, D'Urville Martin, Pierre Lott, George Wilber, Johnny Silver, Nawana Davis, Leon Isaac, Phillip Jackson, Al Richardson, Tracy Ann King, Gene Le Bell, Jimmy Lennon.* Dir: Bruce Clark. Pro: Al Adamson. Screenplay: Charles Johnson. (Essaness/Schwartz–UA.) Rel: July 1, 1973. Colour. 89 Mins. Cert. X.

Hap-Ki-Do
Feud between a newly established martial arts school and the nasty Black Bears Society which ends in a well-administered lesson to the latter by the youngsters. Cast: *Angela Mao, Carter Wong, Pai Ying.* Dir: Huang Feng. Pro: Raymond Chow. Screenplay: Ho Jen. (Golden Harvest–Cathay.) Rel: Floating. Colour. 90 Mins. Cert. X.

Happiness in Twenty Years
Documentary about the Twenty Flowering Years in which Czechoslovakia spread her independent wings before the Soviets stepped in and brutally clipped them. Commentary spoken by *Orson Welles.* Dir, Pro & Written: Albert Knobler. (Antegor–VPS.) Rel: Floating; first shown at Academy Three, Sept., 1973. 90 Mins. Cert. U.

Harry in Your Pocket
The art and the trade of professional pocket-picking, with *James Coburn,* the expert, assisted by old-timer *Walter Pidgeon,* teaching youngsters *Trish Van Devere* and *Michael Sarrazin* how to do the job! And when he gets a crush on the girl the movie swings towards the

old triangle theme. Rest of cast: *Michael C. Gwynne, Tony Giorgio, Michael Stearns, Sue Mullen, Duane Bennet, Stanley Bolt, Barry Grimshaw.* Dir & Pro: Bruce Geller. Screenplay: James Buchanan & Ron Austin. (Cinema Video–UA.) Rel: Nov. 11. Colour. 103 Mins. Cert. AA.

Hausfrauen – Report III – Give 'Em an Inch
German-made package of erotic adventures. Cast includes *Angelika Baumgart, Gernot Möhner, Alexander Allerson.* Dir: Eberhard Schröder. Screenplay: W. P. Zibaso. (TV 13–New Realm.) Rel: Floating; first shown at the Classic Moulin, Oct., 1973. Colour. 78 Mins. Cert. X.

The Heartbreak Kid
Quite amusing comedy about a brash young salesman who, having married in haste, meets a more apparently exciting girl on the second day of his honeymoon and by the third has cast off his bride and set off in stern pursuit of the new quarry which, when he wins her, turns out to have at least some of the qualities which put him off his first wife! Cast: *Charles Grodin, Cybill Shepherd, Jeannie Berlin, Eddie Albert, Audra Lindley, William Prince, Augusta Dabney, Mitchell Jason, Art Metrano, Marilyn Putnam, Jack Hausman, Erik Lee Preminger, Tim Browne, Jean Scoppa, Greg Pecque, Doris Roberts.* Dir: Elaine May. Pro: Edgar J. Scherick. Screenplay: Neil Simon, based on a Bruce Jay Friedman story. (Palomar–Fox–Rank.) Rel: June 23. Colour. 106 Mins. Cert. AA.

Heavy Traffic
Second cartoon feature from the team which made *Fritz the Cat*: Underground Comic orientated, inventive, rude and raucous. All – vaguely – about an Italian gangster father, a Jewish Momma and their drawing-mad, innocent son. Dir & Screenplay: Ralph Bakshi. Pro: Steve Krantz. (Film Creations/Krantz–Black Ink.) Rel: Floating. Colour. 75 Mins. Cert. X.

Hellé
Turgid little French film set in the High Savoy mountain country and concerning a pretty little deaf mute who has become the local whore but reveals potentialities for speech and real affection when a returning student refuses to accept that she is either stupid or immoral. Cast: *Jean-Claude Bouillon, Didier Haudepin, Muria Mauban, Bruno Pradal, Gwen Welles, Maria Schneider, Robert Hossein, Georges Poujouly, Dora Doll, Monique Mélinand, Dorothée Blanck, Paul Gégauff, Dyane Vernon, Michel Dacquin, Rudy Lenoir, Pascal Cousin, Max Montavon, Jean Rupert, Isabelle Missud, Christian Toma.* Dir: Roger Vadim. Pro: Michel Zemer. Screenplay: Jean Mailland & Monique Lange. (Filmsonor/Marceau/Paradox–LMG.) Rel: Floating; first shown at the Classic, Windmill, Oct. 1973. Colour. 95 Mins. Cert. X.

Hellfighters of the East
Four fighting "experts" from the Korean war find existence in peace-time Seoul more exciting, bloodier and more dangerous than war-time, as they tangle with

a drug-running gang and are forced into confrontation with them in a battle which brings heroes' deaths! Cast: *David Chiang, Ti Lung, Lily Li, Ching Li, Wang Chung, Chen Kuan-Tai, Yasuaki Kurata, André Marquis.* Dir: Chang Cheh. Pro: Runme Shaw. Screenplay: I. Kuang & Chang Cheh. (Shaw Bros.–Target International.) Rel: Floating. Colour. 102 Mins. Cert. X.

Herbie Rides Again
Disney's amusing sequel to *The Love Bug*, with the little Volkswagen whose adventures include a run up the cables of the Golden Gate Bridge (when pursued by the minions of the villain). The car springs to the defence of an old lady who won't give in to millionaire property developers. Cast: *Helen Hayes, Ken Berry, Stefanie Powers, John McIntire, Keenan Wynn, Huntz Hall, Ivor Barry, Dan Tobin, Vito Scotti, Raymond Bailey, Liam Dunn, Elaine Devry, Chuck McCann, Richard X. Slattery, Hank Jones, Rod McCary.* Dir: Robert Stevenson. Pro: Bill Walsh. Screenplay: Bill Walsh, based on a story by Gordon Buford. (Disney.) Rel: April 14. Colour. 88 Mins. Cert. U.

Hero Bunker
War story set in Greece, taking place mostly in a bunker where some young men, caught by the war, hide out, to sally forth in rescuing the girl who has helped them and, captured by the enemy, is about to be executed. Cast: *John Miller, Maria Xenia, Fernando Bislani,* etc. Dir: George Andrews. (Cathay Films.) Rel: Floating. Colour. 95 Mins. Cert. A.

The Heroes
Italian–French–Spanish comic-strip-type World War II melodrama in which the various characters involved are all struggling to get their hands on a two-million-dollar gold fortune hidden in an ambulance, driven by a lovely Greek prostitute who is determined to hang on to the money herself! Cast: *Rod Steiger, Rosanna Schiaffino, Rod Taylor, Claude Brasseur, Terry-Thomas, Gianni Garko, Aldo Giuffrè, Paolo Giusti, Nino Segurini, Angel Aranda, Miguel Bosè, Antonio Pica.* Dir: Duccio Tessari. Pro: Alfredo Bini. Screenplay: Luciano Vencenzoni & Rene Havard. (Gerico–Finarco/Corona–Transinter/Atlantida–Paladin.) Rel: Floating. Colour. 100 Mins. Cert. AA.

High Plains Drifter
Clint Eastwood back (but now under his own direction) with his Man With No Name mantle in another somewhat sadistic Western adventure in which whippings to death are a salient feature of the brutal action. Rest of cast: *Verna Bloom, Mariana Hill, Mitchell Ryan, Jack Ging, Stefan Gierasch, Ted Hartley, Billy Curtis, Geoffrey Lewis, Scott Walker, Walter Barnes, Paul Brinegar, Richard Bull, Robert Donner, John Hillerman, Anthony James, William O'Connell, John Quade, Jane Aull, Dan Vadis, Reid Cruickshanks, James Gosa, Jack Kosslyn, Russ McCubbin, Belle Mitchell, John Mitchum, Carl C. Pitti, Chuck Waters, Buddy Van Horn.* Dir: Clint Eastwood. Pro: Robert Daley. Screenplay: Ernest Tidyman. (Malpaso–

Universal–CIC.) Rel: Sept. 2. Colour. 102 Mins. Cert. X.

The Hireling
Leisurely paced, restrained and artistic adaptation of the L. P. Hartley story of the twenties and the relationship that develops between a young widowed Milady after a breakdown and the hire-car chauffeur who restores her morale and then falls desperately in love with her, a love which, conscious of the gulf of class, she finally and firmly rejects. Fine camerawork, and a great sense of the period: superb performance by *Robert Shaw* as the ex-Sergeant Major whose self-discipline covers a tendency to violence, and an only slightly less impressive one by *Sarah Miles* as the widow. Rest of cast: *Peter Egan, Elizabeth Sellars, Caroline Mortimer, Patricia Lawrence, Petra Markham, Ian Hogg, Christine Hargreaves.* Dir: Alan Bridges. Pro: Ben Arbeid. Screenplay: Wolf Mankowitz. (World Film Services–Columbia–Warner.) Rel: Sept. 30. Colour. 108 Mins. Cert. A.

Holiday on the Buses
Another in the line of broad, British "bus" comedies based on the popular television series. Cast: *Reg Varney, Doris Hare, Michael Robbins, Anna Karen, Bob Grant, Stephen Lewis, Kate Williams, Hal Dyer, Arthur Mullard, Queenie Watts, Sandra Bryant, Eunice Black, Gigi Gatti, Franco Derosa, Henry McGee, Maureen Sweeney, Wilfrid Brambell.* Dir: Bryan Izzard. Pro & Screenplay: Ronald Chesney & Ronald Wolfe. (Hammer–Anglo–EMI.) Rel: Dec. 26. Colour. 85 Mins. Cert. A.

Honour Thy Father
The story behind the large-scale Mafia gang war which erupted in America in 1967, with lots of killings and general mayhem. Cast: *Joseph Bologna, Brenda Vaccarc, Raf Vallone, Richard S. Castellano, Joe De Santis, Marc Lawrence, Louis Zorich, Felice Orlandi, Robert Burr, Carmine Caridi, Anthony Charnota, Leonardo Cimino, Sam Coppola, Nick Discenza, Gilbert Green, Antonia Rey, James J. Sloyan.* Dir: Paul Wendkos. Pro: Harold D. Cohen. Screenplay: Lewis John Carlino; based on the Gay Talese book. (Halcyon–Metromedia–Fox–Rank.) Rel: Dec. 15. Colour. 92 Mins. Cert. AA.

Hot, Hard and Mean
South American film about two escaped girl convicts and their chase by the cops, guerrillas and gangsters, ending in the battle which sets one free while the other is killed. Cast: *Pam Grier, Margaret Markov, Sid Haig, Lynn Borden, Zaldy Zshornack, Laurie Burton, Eddie Garcia, Alona Alegre, Dindo Fernando, Vic Diaz, Wendy Green, Lotis M. Key, Alfonso Carvajal, Bruno Punzalah, Ricardo Herrero, Jess Ramos.* Dir: Eddie Romero. Pro: John Ashley & Eddie Romero. Screenplay: H. R. Christian. (New Realm.) Rel: Floating. Colour. 83 Mins. Cert. X.

House of Whipcord
Fantasy about a model girl in London who is lured into a private prison where the wardress tortures, whips and even hangs the inmates that rouse her ire! Cast: *Barbara Markham, Patrick Barr, Ray Brooks, Ann Michelle, Penny Irving, Sheila Keith, Dorothy Gordon, Robert Tayman, Ivor Salter, Judy Robinson, Karen David, Jane Hayward, Celia Quicke, Celia Imrie, Ron Smerczak, David McGillivray, Barry Martin, Tony Simpson.* Dir & Pro: Pete Walker. Screenplay: David McGillivray. (Heritage/Pete Walker–Miracle.) Rel: Floating. Colour. 102 Mins. Cert. X.

How To Destroy the Reputation of the Greatest Secret Agent
French-made, English-speaking comedy with *Jean-Paul Belmondo* as the adventure story-writer whose hero has a much grander time than his harassed creator and who, when the lovely girl opposite falls in love with the created rather than the creator, does his best to kill off his brain-child. Rest of cast: *Jacqueline Bisset, Vittorio Caprioli, Monique Tarbes, Raymond Gerome, Hans Mayer, Jean Lefebvre, André Weber, Rodrigo Puebla, Bruno Gargin, René Barrera, Etienne Assena, Raoul Guilad, Hubert Deschamps, Jean-Pierre Rambal, Thalie Fruges, Bernard Musson, Jack Berard, Jouis Havarre, Gaetan Noel, Charly Koubesserian.* Dir: Philippe de Broca. Pro: Alexandre Mouchkine & Georges Danciger. Screenplay: Francis Veber. (Columbia–Warner.) Rel: Floating. Colour. 92 Mins. Cert. A.

Ich, das Abenteuer heute eine Frau zu sein – Climax
German film about a young wife who tries hard to make her marriage a success though her husband is unable to sexually satisfy her. After various efforts to assuage her hunger she turns finally to the doctor whose efforts to educate her sexually include taking her as a mistress! Cast: *Renate Carol, Frank Glaubrecht, Ingo Baero, Joey Flueger, Bert Hochschwarzer, Marianne Lebeau.* Dir: Roswitha vom Bruck. Pro: Werner M. Lenz. Screenplay: Denise de Boer & Roswitha vom Bruck. (Arca Winston–SF.) Rel: Dec. 1. Colour. 77 Mins. Cert. X.

I Escaped from Devil's Island
A black variation on this suddenly popular filmic theme with *Jim Brown* as the Negro killer-convict actually getting away from the infamous French penal colony but not getting away with it in the end. Rest of cast: *Christopher George, Rick Ely, Richard Rust, James Luisi, Bob Harris, Robert Phillips, Jan Merlin, Paul Richards, Gabriella Rios.* Dir: William Witney. Pro: Roger Corman & Gene Corman. Screenplay: Richard L. Adams. (Corman–UA.) Rel: June 9. 87 Mins. Cert. X.

The Inheritor – L'Héritier
French-made, apparently indifferently dubbed (into English) story about a playboy who comes back from America to take over his dad's vast and varied European empire (everything from steel-mills to newspapers) and astonishes everyone with the left-wing-slanted enthusiasm – and efficiency – with which he does it. Scares some, too, when having established that his father's plane crash was no accident, starts the wheels working so that he can get even with the business enemies who had hoped that the killing would put them into a takeover position. Slick, shallow and well produced. Cast: *Jean-Paul Belmondo, Càrla Gravina, Jean Rochefort, Charles Denner, Maureen Kerwin, Michel Beaune, Jean Martin, Maurice Garrel, Pierre Grasset, François Chaumette, Anna Orso, Marcel Cuvelier, Fosco Giachetti.* Dir: Philippe Labro. Pro: Jacques E. Strauss. Screenplay: P. Labro, Jacques Lanzmann. (President/Cinetel/Euro International–EMI.) Rel: March 24. Colour. 112 Mins. Cert. A.

Intimate Confessions of a Chinese Courtesan
She's abducted and sold into the business after family misfortunes but never gives up her intention of taking revenge on the woman responsible for her situation. Made in Hong Kong. Cast: *Lily Ho, Yueh Hua, Betty Tung Lin, Wan Chung-shan, Fan Mei Shan, Ku Wen Tsung, Chan Shen, Fang Mien, Chen Hao, Li Hao.* Dir: Chu Yuan. Pro: Runme Shaw. Screenplay: Chiu Kang-chien. (Shaw–MGM–EMI.) Rel: Oct. 7. Colour. 83 Mins. Cert. X.

Intimidades de Una Prostituta – Sex is the Name of the Game
Argentine film about final regeneration of a Buenos Aires prostitute who takes to the game in order to exist and is saved by the love of an understanding millionaire! Cast: *Isabel Sarli, Sabina Olmos, Armando Bo, Jorge Barreiro, Riccardo Passano, Fidel Pintos, Guillermo Bataglia, Horatio Bruno, Reynando Mompel, Raul Del Valle, Alfredo Hens, Olanka Wolk, Nestor Mancini.* Dir: Armando Bo. Pro: Juan Pitrau. Screenplay: Dalmiro Saenz & Armando Bo. (SIFA–Columbia–Warner.) Rel: Floating; first shown at the Jacey Tatler, Oct., 1973. Colour. 93 Mins. Cert. X.

The Intimate Desires of Women
Another lesson about sexual compatibility and the like from Germany: marriage, happiness or disaster? Mr Gottlieb has the answer. Cast: *Frank Nossack, Ingrid Back, Rainer Brandt, Ruth Eder, Harald Dietl, Hans Krull, Günther Stoll, Eva Christian.* Dir: F. J. Gottlieb. Pro: Horst Wendlandt. Screenplay: Franz Seitz, from the book by Dr Theodore H. Van de Velde. (Rialto–Gemini Films.) Rel: Floating. Colour. 68 Mins. Cert. X.

Les Intrus – Menace
French-made, English-dubbed thriller about a cool, suave thug who arrives at the home of a famous surgeon and tells him that he will kill his child unless he gets a million-franc ransom, and how the doctor eventually outwits him to kill two crooks and face up to the problem of whether he is guilty of murder. Rather awkwardly dubbed and with *Charles Aznavour* giving a much too dead-pan, stolid performance as the medico, taking the thrills out of the thriller! Rest of cast:

196 *Raymond Pellegrin, Marie Christine Barrault, Katia Aznavour, Albert Minski.* Dir: Sergio Gobbi. Pro: Roger Williame. Screenplay: Sergio Gobbi & Charles Aznavour. (Paris–Cannes–Target International.) Rel: Floating; first shown at the Classic, Victoria, April, 1974. Colour. 90 Mins. Cert. AA.

Investigation of a Murder
Detectives *Walter Matthau* and *Bruce Dern* as the San Francisco detectives leading a squad assigned the bringing to justice of a killer who jumps on a bus, massacres the driver and his eight passengers and then jumps off again. Rest of cast: *Lou Gossett, Albert Paulsen, Anthony Zerbe, Val Avery, Cathy Lee Crosby, Mario Gallo, Joanna Cassidy, Shirley Ballard, William Hansen, Jonas Wolfe, Paul Koslo, Louis Guss, Lee McCain, David Moody, Ivan Bookman, Clifton James, Gregg Sierra, Warren Finnerty, Matt Clark, Joseph Bernard, Melvina Smedley, Leigh French, James Klavin, Anthony Costello, John Francis, John Frederick Vick, Wayne Grace, Cheryl Christiansen, James Christy, David Belrose, Dawn Frame, Ellen Nance, Lavelle Robey, Hobart Nills Nelson, Capt. Gus Bruneman, The San Francisco Strutters.* Dir & Pro: Stuart Rosenberg. Screenplay: Thomas Rickman, based on the novel by Per Wahoo and Maj Sjowall. (Fox–Rank.) Rel: June 23. Colour. 112 Mins. Cert. X.

L'Invitation – The Invitation
Delightful French-speaking Swiss film which with subtlety, imagination and a shrewd understanding of human nature examines a group of people at a staff party, given on a hot afternoon in a sunny garden, who, as the hired barman dispenses potent drinks, gradually reveal their true characters. Beautifully acted and directed. Cast: *Michel Robin, Jean-Luc Bideau, François Simon, Pierre Collet, Jean Champion, Corinne Coderey, Rosine Rochette, Jacques Rispal, Neige Dolski, Cécile Vassort.* Dir: Claude Goretta. Pro: Yves Gasser. Screenplay: Claude Goretta & Michel Viala. (Group 5/Citel/Planfilm–Connoisseur). Rel: Floating; first shown at the Academy, Oct., 1973. Colour. 100 Mins. Cert. AA.

The Invitation – see L'Invitation

J. W. Coop
A real one-man effort with *Cliff Robertson* (who nursed the project for several years before launching it) directing himself as star and producing his own screenplay about a cowboy rodeo rider who comes out of jail after a ten-year stretch determined to climb back to circuit stardom and does in fact achieve it, but at a cost. Rest of cast: *Geraldine Page, Cristina Ferrare, R. G. Armstrong, R. L. Armstrong, John Crawford, Wade Crosby, Marjorie Durant Dye, Paul Harper, Son Hooker, Richard Kennedy, Bruce Kirby, Larry Mahan, Mary Robin Redd, Dennis Reiners, John Ashby, Kathy Beaudine, Robert Christensen, Larry Clayman, Velma Cooper, Sandy Dempsey, Myrtis Dightman, Quail Dobbs, Judy Farrell, Frank Hobbs, Billy Hogue, Charles W. Knapp, Jay MacIntosh, Jim Madland, Bill Martinelli,*

Clyde "Cisco" Maye, Gus Peters, Beverly Powers, Sharron Ray, Claude Stroud, Wayne Taylor, Augie Vallejo. Dir, Pro & Written: Cliff Robertson. (Robertson & Associates–Columbia.) Rel: Floating; first shown at Screen on the Green, Islington, Aug., 1973. Colour. 112 Mins. Cert. AA.

Janice
The sad and sordid story of a little trollop who is picked up by a couple of truck drivers and the way in which she brings them to crime and to the death of one of them. All very well done. Cast: *Robert Drivas, Regina Baff, Barry Bostwick, David Bauer.* Dir & Pro: Joseph Strick. Screenplay: Judith Rascoe, from an original story by Joseph Strick. (Laser–Contemporary.) Rel: Floating; first shown at the Bloomsbury Cinema, Dec., 1973. Colour. 84 Mins. Cert. X.

Jennifer on my Mind
About some pretty useless, rich American dope addicts, a story which starts in Venice and ends there, one dead body later! Cast: *Michael Brandon, Tippy Walker, Lou Gilbert, Steve Vinovich, Peter Bonerz, Renee Taylor, Chuck McCann, Bruce Kornbluth, Barry Bostwick, Jeff Conaway, Joseph George, Nick Lapadula, Jack Hollander, Mike McClanathan, Allan Nicholls, Ralph J. Pinto, Lieb Lansky, Robert De Niro, Victor Rendina, Erich Segal.* Dir: Noel Black. Pro: Bernard Schwartz. Screenplay: Erich Segal, based on the Roger L. Simon novel *Heir*. (J. M. Schenck–UA.) Rel: Floating. Colour. 90 Mins. Cert. X.

Jesse and Lester
The story of two brothers who inherit their uncle's land and immediately fall out as to what they should do with it (one wants a church, the other a brothel) and how eventually they each get their way, at least for a while! Cast: *Richard Harrison, Donal O'Brien, Anna Zinneman, George Wong, Gino Maturano.* Dir: James London. Pro: Richard Harrison & Fernando Piazza. Screenplay: Renzo Genta, based on a story by Richard Harrison. (H. P. International–Cathay Films.) Rel: Floating. Colour. 97 Mins. Cert. X.

Jesus Christ Superstar
The remarkable musical – rock opera so-called – which began life as a long-playing record, the success of which persuaded the people concerned to make it into a stage musical, the transatlantic success of which in turn made the film inevitable. It's the last days in the life of Jesus, often jazzed-up, verbally simplified, sometimes vulgarised but consistently stunningly photographed against marvellous Holy Land backgrounds and, if only finally, moving. Certainly a most unusual and interesting and, yes, highly entertaining movie. Cast: *Ted Neeley* (Jesus), *Carl Anderson* (Judas), *Yvonne Elliman* (Mary Magdalene), *Barry Dennen* (Pilate), *Bob Bingham, Larry T. Marshall, Joshua Mostel, Kurt Yaghjian, Philip Toubus, Pi Douglass, Jonathan Wynne, Richard Molinare, Jeffrey Hyslop, Robert LuPone, Thommie Walsh, David Devir, Richard Orbach, Shooki Wagner, Darcel Wynne, Sally Neal, Vera Biloshisky, Wendy Maltby, Baayork Lee,*

Susan Allanson, Ellen Hoffman, Judith Daby, Marcia McBroom, Leeyan Granger, Kathryn Wright, Denise Pence, Wyetta Turner, Tamar Zafria, Riki Oren, Lea Kestin, Adaya Pilo, Zvulun Cohen, Meir Israel, Itzhak Sidranski, David Rejwan, Amity Razi, Avi Ben-Haim, Haim Bashi, David Duack, Steve Boockvor, Peter Luria, David Barkan, Danny Basevitch, Cliff Michaelevski, Tom Guest, Stephen Denenberg, Didi Liekov, Doron Gaash, Noam Cohen, Zvi Lehat, Moshe Uziel. Dir & Pro: Norman Jewison. Pro: N. Jewison & Robert Stigwood. Screenplay: Melvyn Bragg & Norman Jewison, based on the original book by Tim Rice. (Jewison–Universal–CIC.) Rel: Oct. 21. Colour. 107 Mins. Cert. A.

Kid Blue
Mildly amusing comedy Western with possibly deeper intentions as it tells a story about a failed train robber trying to go straight in the town of Dime Box, where everyone appears to be nasty, hypocritical or just plain stupid, eventually turning the unprepossessing "hero" back to a life of crime. Cast: *Dennis Hopper, Warren Oates, Peter Boyle, Ben Johnson, Lee Purcell, Janice Rule, Ralph Waite, Clifton James, Jose Torvay, Mary Jackson, Jay Varela, Claude Ennis Starrett, Jr., Warren Finnerty, Owen Orr, Richard Rust, Howard Hessman, M. Emmet Walsh, Henry Smith, Bobby Hall, Melvin Stewart, Eddy Donno.* Dir: James Frawley. Pro: Marvin Schwartz. Screenplay: Edwin Shrake. (Schwartz–Fox–Rank.) Rel: Floating. Colour. 100 Mins. Cert. A.

The Killer
Another of the Run-Run Shaw, made-in-Hong Kong all-action melos. This time our formidable fighting hero becomes entangled with the dreaded Black Hand Gang which he and his brother, interrupted in fraternal fighting, join together to effectively wipe out! Cast: *Chin Han, Wang Ping, Tsung Hua, Ching Miao, Yang Chih Ching, Chiang Nan, Cheng Lei, Li Hao, Chi Lien-kuei, Wang Kuang Yu, Hsia Hui, Ku Feng.* Dir: Chu Yuen. Pro: Run-Run Shaw. Screenplay: Kuo Chia. (Shaw–Columbia–Warner.) Rel: Sept. 9. Colour. 93 Mins. Cert X.

King of Kung Fu
Hong Kong melodrama about the way a couple of brave girls take on the might of the evil Chiu and his terrorist son and with the help of a government agent battle their way to victory. Cast: *Alex Lung, Steve Yu, Yukio Someno, Christine Hui, Han Kuo Chia, Yu Lung, Soon Nam, Chiu Ming, Yuen Hwa.* Dir: Chiang Yee Ziong. Pro: Jimmy L. Pascual. (Emperor–Golden Era.) Rel: Floating. Colour. 90 Mins. Cert. X.

The King of Marvin Gardens
Strongly atmosphered, fascinating, untidy and uneven film about two brothers, the failed, bitter writer who has become a (seemingly) boring late, late-night radio chatterer and the con man, working for a Negro racketeer in Atlantic City, who cons himself most of all. The never fully explained relationship between the latter and the two women in his camp leads to the

suddenly violent, tragic climax. It all adds up to something which is, at the least, "different"! Cast: *Jack Nicholson, Bruce Dern, Ellen Burstyn, Julia Anne Robinson, Benjamin "Scatman" Crothers, Charles Lavine, Arnold Williams, John Ryan, Sully Boyar, Josh Mostel, William Pabst, Gary Goodrow, Imogene Bliss, Ann Thomas, Tom Overton, Maxwell "Sonny" Goldberg, Van Kirksey, Tony King, Jerry Fujikawa, Conrad Yama, Scott Howard, Henry Foehl, Frank Hatchett, Wyetta Turner.* Dir & Pro: Bob Rafelson. Screenplay: Jacob Brackman. (BBS–Columbia–Warner.) Rel: Floating. Colour. 104 Mins. Cert. X.

King, Queen, Knave
The odd, German, story of a young man, the elder woman who falls in love with him, and the inventor of a fabric uncannily akin to human skin . . . and how this plays a big part in the tragedy which follows. Cast: *David Niven, John Moulder Brown, Gina Lollobrigida, Mario Adorf, Carl Fox-Duering, Barbara Valentin, Sonia Hofmann, Erica Beer, Christine Schuberth, Felicitas Peters, Christopher Sandford, Elma Karlowa, Mogens von Gadow.* Dir: Jerzy Skolimowski. Pro: Lutz Hengst. Screenplay: David Shaw & David Seltzer based on the novel by Vladimir Nabokov. Rel: Floating; first shown at the Classic, Victoria, Nov., 1973. Colour. 92 Mins. Cert. X.

Kung Fu – The Headcrusher
Hong Kong action melo about a couple of undercover drug department operatives who go to jail in order to infiltrate and break up a notorious drug gang. Cast: *Chen Xing, Henry Yue Young, Charley Chiang, Linda Ling.* Dir: Chiang Hung. Pro: Jimmy L. Pascual. Screenplay: Kwok Teng Hung. (Empire–Cinema-Center–Miracle.) Rel: Floating. Colour. 90 Mins. Cert. X.

Lacombe Lucien
Louis Malle's slow, rather ambiguous, story of a bovine young French peasant who, after a casual attempt to get into the Resistance and their refusal to take him, drifts into helping the Germans root out his more patriotic fellows and ends up dead, shot as a traitor when the war ends. Beautifully wrought, as usual, but a new and not entirely happy departure for the director. Cast: *Pierre Blaise, Aurore Clement, Holger Lowenadler, Therese Gieshe, Stephane Bouy, Loumi Iacobesco, Rene Bouloc, Pierre Decazes, Jean Rougerie, Cecile Ricard, Jacqueline Staup, Pierre Saintons, Gilberte Rivet, Jacques Rispal, Jean Bousquet.* Dir & Pro: Louis Malle. Screenplay: Louis Malle & Patrick Modiano. (NEF/UPF, France–Vides Films, Rome–Hallelujah, Munich–Fox–Rank.) Rel: Floating; first shown at the Curzon, June 1974. Colour. 137 Mins. Cert. AA.

Lady Caroline Lamb
Writer Robert Bolt's first film as a director turns out to be a lavish, superbly produced, conventionally handled, rather overlong but sumptuously entertaining glimpse of high life in the reign of George IV. With *Jon Finch* excellent as Mr Lamb (later P.M. Lord Melbourne) suffering the whims and affairs of his silly, flighty and headstrong wife Caroline (played rather oddly by *Sarah Miles*), whose blatant affair with Lord Byron (*Richard Chamberlain*) nearly brings his political career to an end. Fine performances, too, by *Laurence Olivier* as Wellington, *Ralph Richardson* as the King, *John Mills* and *Sonia Dresdel*. Rest of cast: *Margaret Leighton, Pamela Brown, Silvia Monti, Peter Bull, Charles Carson, Nicholas Field, Felicity Gibson, Robert Harris, Richard Hurndall, Paddy Joyce, Bernard Kay, Janet Key, Mario Maranzana, Robert Mill, Norman Mitchell, John Moffatt, Trevor Peacock, Maureen Pryor, Fanny Rowe, Stephen Sheppard, Roy Stewart, Ralph Truman, Michael Wilding.* Dir & Written: Robert Bolt. Pro: Franco Cristaldi. (GEC/Pulsar/Vides–MGM–EMI.) Rel: July 29. Colour. 122 Mins. Cert. A.

Lady Ice
Donald Sutherland as a Private Eye hired by a group of American Insurance Companies to throw a very big legal wrench into the increasing and successful activities of a gang of jewel thieves. A "chase" film with romantic trimmings. And, say the producers, all based on truth, too. Rest of cast: *Jennifer O'Neill, Robert Duvall, Patrick Magee, Eric Braeden, Jon Cypher, Buffy Dee, Perry Lopez, Charles J. Swepeniser, Edward Biagianti, Evee Scooler, Sol Frieder, Berenice Clayre.* Dir: Tom Gries. Pro: Harrison Starr. Screenplay: Alan Trustman & Harold Clemens. (Tomorrow Entertainment–National General Pictures–Fox–Rank.) Rel: April 28. Colour. 93 Mins. Cert. AA.

Lady Sings the Blues
Screen newcomer *Diana Ross* (late of *The Supremes* pop group) giving a – quite deservedly – Oscar-nominated performance as the late, tragic jazz star Billie Holiday in a largely factual but, apparently part fictional, biographical film about her rise to fame (a Carnegie Hall concert) and her losing fight against drugs. Some fine support, too, from *Billy Dee Williams* as her faithful lover and *Richard Pryor* as her piano man. Rest of cast: *James Callahan, Paul Hampton, Sid Melton, Virginia Capers, Yvonne Fair, Scatman Crothers, Robert L. Gordy, Milton Selzer, Ned Glass, Paulene Myers, Tracee Lyles, Norman Bartold.* Dir: Sidney J. Furie. Pro: Jay Weston & James S. White. Screenplay: Terence McCloy, Chris Clark & Suzanne de Passe. (Motown/Weston/Furie–Paramount–CIC.) Rel: July 15. Colour. 125 Mins. Cert. X.

The Last American Hero
Another version of the Great American Dream, for although here the background is the Stock Car Race Track it is basically the story of a tough, independent youngster who fights the system as he aims to get to the top through his own and only his own efforts. All very competently done; exciting and well acted by *Jeff Bridges* as the "Hero". Rest of cast: *Valerie Perrine, Geraldine Fitzgerald, Ned Beatty, Gary Busey, Art Lund, Ed Lauter, William Smith II, Gregory Walcott, Tom Ligon, Ernie Orsatti, Erica Hagen, James Murphy, Lane Smith.* Dir: Lamont Johnson. Pro: William Roberts & John Cutts. Screenplay: William Roberts. (Wizan/Rojo–Fox–Rank.) Rel: Dec. 9. Colour. 95 Mins. Cert. AA.

The Last Chapter
Denholm Elliott as the best-selling writer stirred, plagued and made to look into himself by a pretty teenager who initially sets out to seduce him by taking off her sweater but turns testy when he refuses her. Rest of cast: *Susan Penhaligon, Geraldine Moffatt, Grace Arnold.* Dir & Screenplay: David Tringham. Pro: John Dark. (Cassius–Fox–Rank.) Rel: Feb. 24. Colour. 29 Mins. Cert. X.

The Last Detail
Highly salty story of a couple of American tars who, assigned to escort a young law-breaker from Virginia to a New Hampshire jail, decide to show him something of the kind of "living" he's missed before they deliver him to start his sentence. Cast: *Jack Nicholson, Otis Young, Randy Quaid, Clifton James, Carol Kane, Michael Moriarty, Luana Anders, Don McGovern, Kathleen Miller, Nancy Allen, Gerry Salsberg, Pat Hamilton, Michael Chapman, Jim Henshaw, Derek McGrath, Gilda Radner, Jim Horn, John Castellano.* Dir: Hal Ashby. Pro: Gerald Ayres. Screenplay: Robert Towne, from the novel by Darryl Ponicsan. (Acrobat–B.P. Associates–Columbia–Warner.) Rel: May. 103 Mins. Cert. X.

The Last Man on Earth
It turns out to be *Vincent Price*, disguised as scientist Robert Morgan, only completely human survivor of some American holocaust, now reduced to fighting a losing battle against the encroaching mutated zombies. Shown in the USA in 1964 but only just released here. Rest of cast: *Franca Bettoia, Emma Danieli, Giacomo Rossi Stuart, Umberto Rau, Christi Courtland, Tony Corevi.* Dir: Sidney Salkow. Pro: Robert L. Lippert. Screenplay: Logan Swanson & William P. Leicester, based on the novel *I Am Legend* by Richard Matheson. (Associated Producers/La Regina–Golden Era.) Rel: Floating. 86 Mins. Cert. X.

Last of the Red Hot Lovers
Adaptation of the Neil Simon stage comedy success which makes no bones about its derivation. *Alan Arkin* as the fiftyish man who suddenly gets that itch and makes three – all abortive – attempts at seduction in his mother's town flat while she's away at work. Nicely amusing though never uproariously funny. Rest of cast: *Sally Kellerman, Paula Prentiss, Renee Taylor, Bella Bruck, Sandy Balson, Frank Loverde, Burt Conroy, Charles Woolf, Ben Freedman, Buddy Lewis, Mousey Garner, Bernie Styles, John Batiste, Lois Aurino, Sully Boyar, J. J. Barry, Paul Larson, Ruth Jaroslow, Oliver Steindecker, Leonard Parker, Liesha Gullisson.* Dir: Gene Saks. Pro: Howard W. Koch. Screenplay: Neil Simon. (Paramount–CIC.) Rel: Floating. Colour. 98 Mins. Cert. X.

The Last of Sheila
Complicated but reasonably fair mystery thriller set largely on and around a yacht in the South of France

where during a "game" the owner sorts out the suspects of the kill-and-run murder of his wife, and offers the audience all the clues so that they can pick the guilty one out for themselves. Cast: *Richard Benjamin, Dyan Cannon, James Coburn, Joan Hackett, James Mason, Ian McShane, Raquel Welch, Yvonne Romaine, Pierro Rosso, Serge Citon, Robert Rossi, Elaine Geisinger, Elliot Geisinger, Jack Pugeat, Martial, Maurice Crosnier.* Dir & Pro: Herbert Ross. Screenplay: Stephen Sondheim & Anthony Perkins. (Columbia–Warner.) Rel: Sept. 9. Colour. 124 Mins. Cert. AA.

Last Tango in Paris
The highly controversial, censor-battered Bertolucci film about an American (very un-Kelly-like one) in Paris who runs a seedy little hotel and lives, one gathers, on his wealthy wife until she escapes by razoring herself to death. After which, meeting a warm and willing little slut in an apartment they are both viewing, he violently makes love to her and starts an affair which, purely animal, leads to disaster and death. Not at all erotic in spite of the many and highly explicit sex scenes; in fact rather sad. Not a great film, but some fine scenes and moments along with the flaws. Cast: *Marlon Brando, Maria Schneider, Jean-Pierre Leaud, Darling Legitimus, Catherine Sola, Mauro Marchetti, Dan Diament, Peter Schommer, Catherine Allegret, Marie-Helene Breillat, Catherine Breillat, Stephane Kosiak, Gerard Lepennec, Maria Michi, Veronica Lazare, Luce Marquand, Michel Delahaye, Laura Betti, Massimo Girotti, Giovanna Galetti, Armand Ablanalp, Gitt Magrini, Rachel Kesterber, Mimi Pinson, Ramon Mendizarai.* Dir: Bernardo Bertolucci. Pro: Alberto Grimaldi. Screenplay: B. Bertolucci & Franco Arcalli. (Pea/Artistes Associés–UA.) Rel: Floating. Colour. 129 Mins. Cert. X.

The Law Enforcer – see La Polizia Ringrazia

Layout for 5 Models
The largely sexual adventures of five fashion and photographic models. Cast: *Hedger Wallace, Erica Gene, Simon Kent, Louisa Livingston, Maggie Stride, Christopher Williams, Gil Barber, Hilary Lebow, Mark Jones, Tim Pearce, Alan Lake, Mina Bird, Carol Catkin, Sally Faulkner, Vicki Hodge, John Andre, Leo Kharibian.* Dir: John Gaudioz. Pro: Sergei Seiffe. Screenplay: Peter Stafford & John Stewart. (Playgirl–Amanda.) Rel: Floating; first shown at the Classic, Charing Cross Road, Nov. Colour. 76 Mins. Cert. X.

The Legend of Hell House
Polished and nicely acted thriller about an investigation carried out by a physicist (*Clive Revill*) and his team of mental medium (*Pamela Franklin*) and a physical one (*Roddy McDowall*) into the ghostly manifestations at the Belasco Mansion, scene twenty years previously of another investigation which led to the death or mental or physical destruction of nearly all concerned! And in spite of modern electromagnetic aids, history considerably repeats itself. Rest of cast: *Gayle Hunnicutt, Roland Culver, Peter Bowles.* Dir: John Hough. Pro: Albert Fennell & Norman T. Herman.

Screenplay: Richard Matheson. (James H. Nicholson–Academy–Fox–Rank.) Rel: Nov. 18. Colour. 94 Mins. Cert. X.

The Legend of Nigger Charley
A black Western! *Fred Williamson* as the escaped slave who finally, with his pals, stops the running and fights back, first against a band of professional slave catchers and then against a group of outlaws led by a self-styled Reverend Gentleman! Rest of cast: *D'Urville Martin, Don Pedro Colley, Gertrude Jeanette, Marcia McBroom, Alan Gifford, John Ryan, Will Hussung, Mill Moor, Thomas Anderson, Jerry Gatlin, Tricia O'Neil, Doug Rowe, Keith Prentice, Tom Pemberton, Joe Santos, Fred Lerner.* Dir: Martin Goldman. Pro: Larry G. Spangler. Screenplay: Larry G. Spangler & Martin Goldman. (Spangler/Paramount–CIC.) Rel: Floating. Colour. 95 Mins. Cert. X.

Legion of No Return – see Quel Maledetto Sull'Elba

Les Liaisons Particulières – Any Time Anywhere
A young French girl's sexual adventures in the big city where she becomes mixed up with lesbians and homosexuals, and the like, but survives to happily settle into a normal married life. Cast: *Astrid Frank, Nicole Debonne, Yves Vincent, Frédérik Sakiss, Bruno Balp, Kim Camba, Saint-Bris, Michel Vocoret, Michel Charrel.* Dir & Pro: Max Pecas. Screenplay: Michèle Ressi (Les Films du Griffon–Cinecenta.) Rel: Floating: first shown at Centa Cinema, February 1974. Colour. 79 Mins. Cert. X.

Let the Good Times Roll
Rolling and Rocking musical with such experts as *Chuck Berry, Little Richard, Fats Domino, Chubby Checker, Bo Diddley, 5 Satins, The Shirelles, The Coasters, Danny and the Juniors, Bill Haley and the Comets.* Dir & Screenplay: Sid Levin & Bob Abel. Pro: Gerald I. Isenberg. (Cinema Associates/Richard Nader–Metromedia–Columbia–Warner.) Rel: Oct. 21. 99 Mins. Cert. A.

The Lion at World's End
The story of Christian, the Devon-born lion, who after time at a Store Zoo and a Chelsea furniture store, becomes a problem child and is taken back to Africa, thanks to those screen lion-lovers *Virginia McKenna* and husband *Bill Travers.* Rest of cast: *Anthony Bourke, John Rendall, George Adamson, Terence Adamson, and, of course, Lions Christian, Biy and Katania.* Dir, Pro & Screenplay: Bill Travers & James Hill. (Morning Star Productions–EMI.) Rel: April 21. Colour. 48 Mins. Cert. U.

Live and Let Die
Somewhat mechanical, but lavishly produced, neatly directed James Bond opus with new Saintly 007 *Roger Moore* decimating the top echelon of a black power organisation who plan to flood the world with dope and through this attain their evil ends! Rest of cast: *Yaphet Kotto, Jane Seymour, Clifton James, Julius W. Harris, Geoffrey Holder, David Hedison, Gloria Hendry,*

Bernard Lee, Lois Maxwell, Tommy Lane, Earl Jolly Brown, Roy Stewart, Lon Satton, Arnold Williams, Ruth Kempf, Joie Chitwood, Madeline Smith, Michael Ebbin, Kubi Chaza, B. J. Arnau. Dir: Guy Hamilton. Pro: Harry Saltzman & Albert R. Broccoli. Screenplay: Tom Mankiewicz, based on the Ian Fleming story. (UA.) Rel: Sept. 9. Colour. 121 Mins. Cert. A.

The Lolly-Madonna War
Grim account of a feud between two American families over the meadow which lies between their properties and which one owns and the other feels should belong to them. Cast: *Rod Steiger, Katherine Squire, Scott Wilson, Timothy Scott, Ed Lauter, Randy Quaid, Jeff Bridges, Robert Ryan, Tresa Hughes, Paul Koslo, Kiel Martin, Gary Busey, Joan Goodfellow, Season Hubley.* Dir: Richard C. Sarafian. Pro: Rodney Carr-Smith. Screenplay: R. Carr-Smith & Sue Grafton, based on the novel of the same title by the latter. (MGM–EMI.) Rel: Feb. 3. Colour. 105 Mins. Cert. X.

The Long Goodbye
Detection thriller based, and that's about the right word, on a Raymond Chandler novel with the hero, Private Eye Philip Marlowe, changed into a mumbling kind of male slut and the whole thing updated to today. It's all about Marlowe's distrust of the cops' case that his pal has killed himself after slaying his wife and his final discovery that his suspicions are only partly justified. Cast: *Elliott Gould, Nina van Pallandt, Sterling Hayden, Mark Rydell, Henry Gibson, David Arkin, Jim Bouton, Warren Berlinger, Jo Ann Brody, Steve Coit, Jack Knight, Pepe Callahan, Vince Palmieri, Pancho Cordoba, Enrique Lucero, Rutanya Alda, Tammy Shaw, Jack Riley, Ken Sansom, Jerry Jones, John Davies, Rodney Moss, Sybil Scotford, Herb Kerns.* Dir: Robert Altman. Pro: Jerry Bick. Screenplay: Leigh Brackett, based on the novel by Raymond Chandler. (Elliott Kastner–UA.) Rel: Dec. 2. Colour. 111 Mins. Cert. X.

Lost Horizon
A re-make of the 1937 Frank Capra film of the James Hilton story about Conway's discovery of a Utopian lost world in the Himalayas, where life and love convert him and send him back there to lead the community in its perfect existence. Now given the vaster screen, music, colour – but little else, so that any comparison does indeed become odious. All the same in its light, fluffy, *South Pacific*-ish way, the new *Lost Horizon* has a certain appeal which non-comparers may find captivating. Cast: *Peter Finch, Liv Ullmann, Sally Kellerman, George Kennedy, Michael York, Olivia Hussey, Bobby Van, James Shigeta, Charles Boyer, John Gielgud.* Dir: Charles Jarrott. Pro: Ross Hunter. Screenplay: Larry Kramer, based on the James Hilton novel. (Ross Hunter–Columbia.) Rel: Oct. 21. Colour. 143 Mins. Cert. U.

Lost in the Desert
The adventures of a small (nine-year-old) boy (*Dirkie Hayes*) and his dog as they strive to reach safety after surviving a plane crash in the Kalahari Desert; filmed entirely on location in the desert. Rest of cast: *Jamie*

Hayes, Lady Frolic of Belvedale, Wilhelm Esterhuizen, Sue Burman, Jan Bruijns, Pieter Haupteleisch, Johan du Plooy, Bill Brewer, Jaques Loois, Heinrich Marnitz, Eugene Erasmus. Dir, Pro & Written: Jamie Hayes. (Mimosa–Columbia–Warner.) Rel: April 7. 84 Mins. Cert. U.

Louise
(French title *Chère Louise*.) Polished, romantic and sympathetic re-telling of the story of the middle-aged, lonely divorcée who meets a charming – if childishly feckless – young man (young enough to be her son) and takes him into her house, her bed and her heart and, intelligent enough to realise the impossibility of the situation, cannot control it or herself when he finally leaves her. Cast: *Jeanne Moreau, Julian Negulesco, Didi Perego, Yves Robert, Pipo Starnazza*. Dir: Philippe de Broca. Pro: Georges Dancigers & Alexandre Mnouchkine. Screenplay: Jean-Loup Dabadie, based on the short story by Jean-Louis Curtis. (Ariane/PECF/Champion–Columbia–Warner.) Rel: Floating. Colour. 98 Mins. Cert. A.

Love and Pain and the Whole Damn Thing
A sometimes painful, leisurely little tragi-comedy about two unfortunate people, shy, inhibited, afflicted, who meet during a tour of Spain, fall in love – whereupon it is revealed the woman is doomed to die soon from a fatal disease! *Maggie Smith* and *Timothy Bottoms* do their considerable best to make something of it, too. Rest of cast: *Don Jaine de Mora y Aragon, Charles Baxter, Margaret Modlin, May Heatherley, Lloyd Brimhall, Elmer Modlin, Andres Monreal*. Dir & Pro: Alan J. Pakula. Screenplay: Alvin Sargent. (Gus–Columbia–Warner.) Rel: July 15. Colour. 109 Mins. Cert. A.

Love-Hungry Girls
About the man in the attic who dominates the two girls downstairs until the situation becomes explosive, and then impossible. . . . Cast: *Jackie Lombard, Alain Saury, Marika Pica, Alain Tissier*. Dir: Jack Angel. Screenplay: Paul Plade. (Makifilms/Elektra–English Film Co.) Rel: Floating; first shown at the Classic, Windmill, Feb., 1974. Colour. 70 Mins. Cert. X.

The Lovemakers
A comedy about a big businessman who marries a sweet young girl and finds on the wedding night that he has become impotent, a situation which causes the girl's mother extreme fury! Cast: *Lando Buzzanca, Katia Christina, Alfredo Rizzo, Ira Firstenberg, Françoise Prevost*. Dir & Screenplay: Gianni Grimaldi. (Titan Films.) Rel: Floating. Colour. 80 Mins. Cert. X.

Love-Making – Hot Style
French-made story of a poor little secretary bird who meets a high-powered pressman, is conned by him into bed and then left as he dashes off to another assignment. Cast: *Paul Guers, Geneviève Grad, Bernard Lavalette, François Blanc, Willy Braque, Mac Piot, Josy Andrieux, Ariel Moyer, Tobias Engel, Gérard Klein, Michel Droit,*

Eric Charden, Catherine Robbe-Grillet, Claude Nougaro, Denise Glaser, Manitas de Plata, Nancy Holloway. Dir, Pro & Screenplay: Jean-Marie Pontiac. (Pyramides–English Film Co.) Rel: Floating; first shown at Oscars, Oct., 1973. Colour. 72 Mins. Cert. X.

Love Me Gently
A German-made story of some very complicated (abberative and normal) love affairs which culminates with a murder on the wedding night! Cast: *Mascha Rabben, Gabi Larifari, Ulli Lommel, Rolf Zacher, Heidy Bohlen*. Dir: Robert Van Ackeren. (Von Ackeren–Butcher's.) Rel: Floating; first shown at the Classic, Piccadilly, April 1974. Colour. 83 Mins. Cert. X.

Love, Passion and Pleasure
They're all here, in an Italian-made movie in which prostitutes, nuns and cuckolders all take a part. Cast: *Dado Crostarosa, Malisa Lonco, Orchidea De Santis, Claudia Bianchi, Renato Rinaldi*. Dir: Walter Pisani. Pro: Giacomo Rizzo. Screenplay: Antonio Racioppi. (Corinzia–Mark Associates.) Rel: Floating; first shown at the Classic, Charing Cross Road, Jan., 1974. Colour. 87 Mins. Cert. X.

The Lovers!
Rather delightful little comedy about two young people who keep telling each other they are not suited but find it difficult to keep uninvolved! Cast: *Richard Beckinsale, Paula Wilcox, Susan Littler, Nikolas Simmonds, Anthony Naylor, Rosalind Ayres, Joan Scott, Stella Moray, John Comer, Pamela Moiseiwitch, Bruce Watt, Paul Greenwood, Bernard Latham, Karen Ford, James Snell, Mary Henry, Serena, Maggie Flint, Ian Gray*. Dir: Herbert Wise. Pro: Maurice Foster. Screenplay: Jack Rosenthal. (Gildor–British Lion.) Rel: Oct. 14. Colour. 89 Mins. Cert. A.

Love Thy Neighbour
Yet another TV series brought to the larger screen, this one all about two neighbours – one couple white, the other West Indian – who are close, bickering, friends. Cast: *Jack Smethurst, Rudolph Walker, Nina Baden-Semper, Bill Fraser, Kate Williams, Charles Hyatt, Keith Marsh, Tommy Godfrey, Patricia Hayes, Melvyn Hayes, Azad Ali, Arthur English, Clifford Mollison, Lincoln Webb, Andria Lawrence, Norman Chappell, Dan Jackson, Anna Dawson, John Binden, Lesley Goldie, Bill Pertwee, George Tovey, Berry Cornish, Pamela Cundell, Annie Leake, Patrick Durkin, Horace James, Damaris Hayman, George Roderick, Nosher Powell, Isobel Hurll, Princess Tamara, Siobhan Quinlan, James Beck, Michael Sharvell-Martin, Kubi Chaza, Venicia Day, Corinne Skinner, Fred Griffiths*. Dir: John Robins. Pro: Roy Skeggs. Screenplay: Vince Powell & Harry Driver. (Hammer–MGM–EMI.) Rel: Aug. 26. Colour. 85 Mins. Cert. A.

Love, Vampire Style
German, English-dubbed, sex comedy about a young deputy mailman in Munich whose delivery excites all the females on his round and also excites the hatred

of the local psycho-analyst who finds his list of sex-repressed female patients diminishing day by day. But finally defeated, he hands over his practice to his enemy and then proceeds – as a Vampire risen from his grave – to try and even the score! Cast (includes): *Eva Renzi, Patrick Jordan, Amadeus August*. Dir & Pro: Anthony Baker. Screenplay: Martin Roda Becher & Helmut Fornbacher. (Rebel Films.) Rel: Floating. Colour. 81 Mins. Cert. X.

The Lusty Wives of Canterbury – I Racconti di Canterbury N.2
One of the flock of Italian medieval sex-fun films that followed Pasolini's "Canterbury" package: this one comprising six episodes all centred on sexual desire. Cast: *Mariangela Giordano, Mario Brega, Claudia Bianchi, Fortunato Cecilia, Dada Gallotti, Marcello Di Falco, Riki Marie Odile*. Dir: Lucio Dandolo. Pro: Gabriele Grisanti & Luigi Nannerini. Screenplay: Luigi Russo. (CG–Cinecenta.) Rel: Floating; first shown at Cinecenta, Jan., 1974. Colour. 88 Mins. Cert. X.

The Mackintosh Man
Pretty intricately plotted, rather confusing espionage thriller with *Paul Newman* the successful jewel thief "shopped" by a mysterious telephone caller, jailed, offered the chance of escape along with an incarcerated spy, again betrayed and then on the run . . . but all most ably directed and slickly paced by director John Huston. Rest of cast: *Dominique Sanda, James Mason, Harry Andrews, Ian Bannen, Nigel Patrick, Peter Vaughan, Donald Webster, Hugh Manning, Roland Culver, Leo Genn, Michael Poole, Eric Mason, Percy Herbert, Jenny Runacre, John Bindon, Ronald Clarke, Antony Viccars, Dinny Powell, Douglas Robinson, Jack Cooper, Marc Boyle, Michael Hordern, Keith Bell*. Dir: John Huston. Pro: John Foreman. Screenplay: (Newman/Foreman–Warner.) Rel: Nov. 11. Colour. 99 Mins. Cert. AA.

McQ
John Wayne leaves the West for something of a type-casting holiday as the city Cop when he decides to take things into his own hands when his great pal is murdered. Rest of cast: *Eddie Albert, Diana Muldaur, Colleen Dewhurst, Clu Gulager, David Huddleston, Jim Watkins, Al Lettieri, Julie Adams, Roger E. Mosley, Joe Tornatore, Richard Kelton, Richard Eastham, Dick Friel, Fred Waugh*. Dir: John Sturges. Pro: Jules Levy & Arthur Gardner. Screenplay: Lawrence Roman (also co-producer). (Batjac–Levy–Gardner–Columbia–Warner.) Rel: March 3. Colour. 116 Mins. Cert. AA.

La Maffia – Mafia
Argentinian film about murder and mayhem organised by the Mafia in that country in 1928, the power struggle which waxed and then waned when the police are finally forced into taking decisive action. Cast: *Alfredo Alcón, Thelma Biral, José Slavin, China Zorrilla, Hector Alterio, José María Gutierrez*. Dir & Pro: Leopoldo Torre Nilsson. Screenplay: Beatriz Guido, L. P. Estrada, R. Mortola, J. Torre and Torre

Nilsson. (Litoral–Columbia–Warner.) Rel: Floating; first shown at the Classic, Piccadilly, June, 1973. Colour. 98 Mins. Cert. X.

Magnum Force
A demoted "Dirty Harry" (the nickname of the detective who gave the original film its title) becomes closely involved in a series of mysterious killings of San Francisco's vice-ring top-brass, all done, as we know, by motor-cycle cops. A laconic, blood-spattered, brutal but highly efficient and well-made cops and robbers piece, with *Clint Eastwood* repeating the role of the taciturn, fast-drawing, ruthless cop. Rest of cast: *Hal Holbrook, Mitchell Ryan, David Soul, Felton Perry, Robert Urich, Kip Niven, Tim Matheson, Christine White, Richard Devon, Tony Giorgio, Albert Popwell, John Mitchum, Margaret Avery, Jack Kosslyn, Clifford A. Pellow, Adele Yoshioka*. Dir: Ted Post. Pro: Robert Daley. Screenplay: John Milius & Michael Cimino, from a story by the former based on the characters created by Harry Julian and Rita M. Fink. (Malpaso–Columbia–Warner.) Rel: Jan. 20. Colour. 122 Mins. Cert X.

La Maison sous les Arbres – The Deadly Trap
René Clément film about a family threatened both from within and without: the wife's bad memory and the plot to recruit the husband into a spy ring. Hardly credible but often fascinating to watch, with its imaginative, mood-setting photography. Cast: *Faye Dunaway, Frank Langella, Barbara Parkins, Michèle Lourié, Patrick Vincent, Karen Blanguernon, Maurice Ronet, Gérard Buhr, Raymond Gérôme, Louise Chevalier, Tener Eckelberry, Massimo Farinelli*. Dir: René Clément. Pro: Robert Dorfman & Georges Casati. Screenplay: Sidney Buchman & Eleanor Perry; based on the novel *The House Under the Trees* by Arthur Cavanaugh. (Corona/Pomereu/Oceania–Columbia–Warner.) Rel: Floating. Colour. 95 Mins. Cert. A.

Malizia
Italian film set in Sicily and relating the story of a rather unusual relationship between a fourteen-year-old boy with his pretty, new young stepmother-to-be, a relationship that ends with her seducing him and so solving the problem before the wedding to his father! Cast: *Laura Antonelli, Turi Ferro, Alessandro Momo, Tina Aumont, Lilla Brignone, Pino Caruso, Angela Luce, Stefano Amato, Gianluigi Chirizzi, Grazia Di Marza, Massimiliano Filoni*. Dir: Salvatore Samperi. Pro: Silvio Clementelli. Screenplay: Ottavio Jemma, Salvatore Samperi & Alessandro Parenzo. (Clesi–Columbia–Warner.) Rel: Floating. Colour. 97 Mins. Cert. X.

Man at the Top
John Braine's *Room at the Top* "hero" Joe Lampton pushes ruthlessly on, upward, always power, sex and money-greedy. Cast: *Kenneth Haigh, Nanette Newman, Harry Andrews, John Quentin, Mary Maude, Danny Sewell, Paul Williamson, Margaret Heald, Angela*

Bruce, Charlie Williams, Anne Cunningham, William Lucas, John Collin, Norma West, Clive Swift, Jaron Yalton, Tim Brinton, John Conteh, Nell Brennan, Patrick McCann, George Francis, Verne Morgan. Dir: Mike Vardy. Pro: Peter Charlesworth & Jock Jacobsen. Screenplay: Hugh Whitemore. (Hammer–MGM–EMI.) Rel: Sept. 16. Colour. 87 Mins. Cert. X.

The Man Called Noon
Strictly in the *Man With No Name* tradition of brutal, sadistic action Westerns against superb backgrounds, *Richard Crenna* plays the Man With No Memory trying, in a two-way stream of flying lead, to find out who he is and why he's involved in wiping out an army of unshaven badmen. *Stephen Boyd* happily helps him and *Rossanna Schiaffino* fills the feminine gap in his life. Rest of cast: *Farley Granger, Patty Shepard, Angel Del Pozo, Howard Ross, Aldo Sambrell, Jose Jaspe, Charley Bravo, Ricardo Palacios, Fernando Hilbeck, Jose Canalejas, Cesar Burner, Julian Ugarte, Barta Barri, Adolfo Thous, Bruce Fischer*. Dir: Peter Collinson. Pro: Euan Lloyd. Screenplay: Scott Finch, based on the novel by Louis L'Amour. (Frontier/Montana/Finarco–Scotia–Barber.) Rel: Oct. 28. Colour. 95 Mins. Cert. AA.

Man of La Mancha
Film of the stage musical of the same title which in turn was based on the old Don Quixote classic about the mad and brave old knight who went tilting at windmills! With *Peter O'Toole* as the Don giving a delicious performance. Rest of cast: *Sophia Loren, James Coco, Harry Andrews, John Castle, Brian Blessed, Ian Richardson, Julie Gregg, Rosalie Crutchley, Gino Conforti, Marne Maitland, Dorothy Sinclair, Miriam Acevedo, Dominic Barto, Poldo Bendandi, Peppi Borza, Mario Donen, Fred Evans, Francesco Ferrini, Paolo Gozlino, Teddy Green, Peter Johnston, Roy Jones, Connel Miles, Steffen Zacharias, Lou Zamprogna*. Dir & Pro: Arthur Hiller. Screenplay: Dale Wasserman. (PEA–UA.) Rel: Floating. Colour. 132 Mins. Cert. U.

Man of the East
Italian comedy Western about the British milord tenderfoot who goes Way Out West and comes up against some pretty hard-fisted facts of life but then, thanks to the tutorage of three not such bad badmen friends of his late paw, makes good and defeats the real villain and wins the girl . . . and it is all very mildly amusing. Cast: *Terence Hill, Yanti Somer, Gregory Walcott, Harry Carey, Dominic Barto, Riccardo Pizzuti*. Dir & Screenplay: E. B. Clucher. Pro: Alberto Grimaldi. (PEA/Artistes Associés–UA.) Rel: Dec. 15. Colour. 125 Mins. Cert. A.

Maniac at Large
Italian–Spanish, English-speaking whodunit. Watching for her lover's arrival, a girl sees a murder across the way, and this starts off the investigation, which leads to the guilty musician whose antidote to personal failure in his art is to periodically kill off some unfortunate member of the public who comes into

contact with him. Cast (includes): *Robert Hoffman, Susan Scott*. Dir: Maurizio Pradeaux. Screenplay: Arpad de Riso, Maurizio Balcazar, Alfonso Balcazar & George Martin. Pro: Francisco Balcazar. (Rebel Films.) Rel: Floating. Colour. 96 Mins. Cert. X.

Massage Parlour
The search of a young journalist for the lovely masseuse who steals his heart during one night of massage love! It's a search that leads through a number of highly variable massage parlours. Cast: *Lukas Ammann, Astrid Boner, Elisabeth Volkmann*. Dir: Eberhard Schroeder. Screenplay: Werner P. Zibaso. (Transatlantic–Hemdale.) Rel: Floating. Colour. 77 Mins. Cert. X.

Mean Streets
Convincing picture of the Little Italy section of New York today; the need to survive in a mean and dirty world, where vice and crime rub shoulders happily and there's an almost fatal fascination in it. Cast: *Harvey Keitel, Robert de Niro, Amy Robinson, Robert Romanus, David Proval, George Memmoli, Cesare Danova, David Carradine, Robert Carradine, Martin Scorsese*. Dir & Written: Martin Scorsese. Pro: Jonathan T. Taplin. (Taplin-Perry-Scorsese Production–Columbia–Warner.) Rel: Floating. Colour. 110 Mins. Cert. X.

Millhouse, A White Comedy
Emile de Antonio, with television and newsreel clips, having bitter fun with *President Nixon* by assembling some cruelly revealing extracts from his speeches. Dir, Pro & Screenplay: Emile de Antonio. (White–VPS.) Rel: Floating. 92 Mins.

Mr Hercules Against Karate
A new angle on the current unarmed combat flood: this time a giant of an Australian accepts an assignment to go to Hong Kong, defeat the Kung Fu fighters there who are holding the small son of a Chinese restaurant owner, and does it without benefit of any training in the arts of unarmed combat. Cast: *Tom Scott, Fred Harris, Chai Lee, George Wang*. Dir: Anthony M. Dawson. Pro: Carlo Ponti. Screenplay: Luciano Vincenzoni & Gianni Simonelli. (Laser–Champion–UA.) Rel: Floating. Colour. 104 Mins. Cert. A.

Mistress Pamela
Film of the old Samuel Richardson novel *Pamela, or Virtue Rewarded*, with Miss P. rollicking around (and in) beds while trying to preserve her virtue till the legal knot is tied. Cast: *Julian Barnes, Anna Quayle, Dudley Foster, Anthony Sharp, Rosemarie Dunham, Ann Michelle, Jolina Mitchell, Jessie Evans, Ken Parry, Fred Emney, Frederic Abbott, Marianne Stone, Barbara Hickmont, Betty Turner, Dickie Graydon, Terry Plummer*. Dir, Pro & Screenplay: Jim O'Connolly. (Merlot–MGM–EMI.) Rel: March 24. Colour. 91 Mins. Cert. X.

The Mole – see El Topo

Mon Oncle Benjamin – The Amorous Adventures of Uncle Benjamin

1969 French film: a period romp – *circa* 1750 – largely tailored to the talents of Belgian political singer *Jacques Brel*, whose adventures are considerably sexual. Rest of cast: *Claude Jade, Rosy Varte, Lyne Chardonnet, Paul Frankeur, Bernard Alane, Bernard Blier, Armand Mestral, Alfred Adam, Robert Dalban, Paul Préboist, Daniela Surina, Carlo Alighiero.* Dir: Edouard Molinaro. Pro: Roger Debelmas. Screenplay: Andre Couteaux & Jean-François Hauduroy; based on the book by Claude Tillier. (SNE Gaumont/Euro International–Golden Era.) Rel: Floating, from July, 1973. Colour. 91 Mins. Cert. X.

Nada

A new departure for Claude Chabrol; a violent, fast-paced, bloody and exciting political thriller about a few human misfits (calling themselves the group of the title) who plan to raise money for their future programme of assassination by abducting the American Ambassador in Paris and holding him for ransom, a plot which fails and brings the French police in force to their hide-out to wipe them all out, the Ambassador by now having become an accepted sacrifice! To balance the picture of the stupid, aimless left-wingers in NADA, Chabrol draws a devastating picture of the equally ruthless and callous methods employed by the authorities, both sides completely ignoring the rights of the individual as they brutally battle it out. Cast: *Fabio Testi, Mariangela Melato, Maurice Garrel, Michel Duchaussoy, Michel Aumont, Didier Kaminka, Lou Castel, André Falcon, Lyle Joyce, Viviane Romance.* Dir: Claude Chabrol. Screenplay: Jean-Patrick Manchette, based on his own book of the same title. (Les Films la Boétie, Paris; Italian International–Connoisseur.) Rel: Floating, first shown at Academy Two, April 1974. Colour. 134 Mins. Cert. X.

The Naked World of Harrison Marks

Marks, the man famous for his nude photographs of gorgeous girls, shown working at his – lovely – job! With *Pamela Green, June Palmier, Chris Williams, Annette Johson, Jutka Goz, Chris Bromfield, Ken Hayes, Derek Nichols, David Roberts.* Dir & Pro: George Harrison Marks. (Gala.) Rel: Floating. Colour. 84 Mins. Cert. X (London).

Naughty Nun – see Bella Antonia Prime Monica e Poi Dimonia

Necronomicon, Geträumte Sünden – Succubus

The title means "a female devil who appears in men's dreams to consort with them sexually". And that about sums it up, too: a mixture – from Germany – of "erotic dreams and erotic reality" set against a background of night life in Lisbon. Cast: *Janine Reynaud, Jack Taylor, Howard Vernon, Nathalie Nort, Michel Lemoine, Pier A. Caminneci, Adrian Hoven, Americo Coimbra, Lina de Wolf, Eva Brauner.* Dir: Jesus Franco. Pro: Adrian Hoven. Screenplay: Pier A. Caminneci. (Aquila–Border.) Rel: Floating; first shown at the Jacey Tatler, Nov., 1973. Colour. 81 Mins. Cert. X.

The Neptune Factor – An Undersea Odyssey

First-rate, conventional thriller about the search by one specialised small submarine craft for another which has been buffeted and crippled by an undersea earthquake. Tremendously gripping, wonderfully photographed, ably acted. Cast: *Ernest Borgnine, Walter Pidgeon, Yvette Mimieux, Ben Gazzara, Chris Wiggins, Donnelly Rhodes, Ed McGibbon, Michael J. Reynolds, David Yorston, Stuart Gillard, Mark Walker, Kenneth Pogue, Frank Perry, Dan MacDonald, Leslie Carlson, David Renton, Joan Gregson, Dave Mann, Kay Fujiwara, Richard Whelan.* Dir: Daniel Petrie. Pro: Sanford Howard. Screenplay: Jack DeWitt. (Conquest of the Deeps–Quadrant–Bellevue Pathe–Fox–Rank.) Rel: Aug. 5. Colour. 98 Mins. Cert. U.

A Nest of Gentlefolk

Very literary Russian adaptation of the Turgenev novel about a young nobleman searching for his identity, and a truer way of life than the decadent existence of Parisian High Society in which he has been spending his time. The gentle, melting photography beautifully captures the elegant, stifling atmosphere and the characters and the film become increasingly fascinating in the latter part of the story. Cast: *Irina Kupchenko, Beata Tyszkiewicz, V. Sergachov, A. Kostomolotsky, V. Kochurikhin, Nikita Mikhalkov, N. Terenteva, Dasha Semenova, Leonid Kulagin, T. Chernova, Vassili Markurev, M. Durasova, S. Nikonenko, Nikolai Gubenko, Z. Rupasova, Nadia Podgomova.* Dir: Andrei Mikhalkov-Konchalovsky. Screenplay: Valentin Yezhov & Konchalovsky. (Mosfilm–Contemporary.) Rel: Floating; first shown at the Paris-Pullman, Oct., 1973. Colour. 106 Mins. Cert. U.

The New One-Armed Swordsman

Another of Run-Run Shaw's popular melodramas made in Hong Kong. This one is about a swordsman who cuts off his own arm when he loses a duel, but later comes back into the fight business to revenge a brave anti-thuggist killed by a gang leader. Cast: *Li Ching, David Chiang, Ti Lung, Ku Feng, Chen Hsing, Wang Chung, Cheng Lei, Liu Kang, Wang Kuang Yu, Wang Ching-Ho, Huang Pei-Chi, Cheng Kang Yeh, Shen Lao, Wu Chi-Chin, Tang Yen-Tsan, Lan Wei-Lieh, Hu Wei, Liang Shan Yun.* Dir: Chang Cheh. Pro: Run-Run Shaw. Screenplay: I Kuang. (Shaw Bros.–MGM–EMI.) Rel: July 1. Colour. 86 Mins. Cert. X.

Nickel Queen

Rough-hewn Australian comedy about a woman ghost-town pub owner who becomes the innocent centre of a large-scale con trick, spends the cash and ends up after her Perth spree sadder and wiser. Cast: *Googie Withers, John Laws, Alfred Sandor, Ed Devereaux, Peter Gwynne, Joanna McCallum, Ross Thompson, Tom Oliver, Doreen Warburton, Eileen Collacoft, Maurice Ogden, Ross Lightfoot, Joan McGrath, Des Sambo, Mas Masters, Sue Hartley, Christine Mearing, Tasma Michael, Jenny Tuurenhout, Eleanor Proud, David Sarll, Doug Farley, John Hudson, Nancy Nunn, Poole Johnson, George Maw, Ken Johns, Harry Argus, Richard Argus, David Tuck, Dave Broadfield, Harriet Pace, Ossie Sanderson, Ric Rogers, Tricia Phillips, Jan Olding, Molly Hungerford, Shirley Gershon, Carol Minear, Peta Maitland, Vanyo Geddes, Geoff Jacoby, Norman Jones, Sam Harris, Ron McGuire, Bill Ward, Norman Jackson, Charles Lee Steere, Jenny Cullen, Peter Rankin, Graham Bowra, Roy Toby, Charles Brown, Charles Harper, Sir David Brand, Hon. Charles Court and the Hon. Arthur Griffith.* Dir: John McCallum. Pro: Bob Austin & Lee Robinson. Screenplay: Henry C. James, John McCallum & Joy Cavill; from a story by Henry and Anneke James. (Woomera–Fox–Rank.) Rel: Floating. Colour. 89 Mins. Cert. A.

Night Watch

Well-made but routine thriller with some neat twists at the end which not many in the audience will foresee. *Elizabeth Taylor* – in film-stealing form – is the wife, being deceived by her best friend, who sees a murdered man and then a dead girl in the old and empty house opposite, a story nobody will credit. Rest of cast: *Laurence Harvey, Billie Whitelaw, Robert Lang, Tony Britton, Bill Dean, Michael Danvers-Walker, Rosario Serrano, Pauline Jameson, Linda Hayden, Kevin Colson, Laon Maybanke.* Dir: Brian G. Hutton. Pro: Martin Poll, George W. George & Barnard Straus. Screenplay: Tony Williamson; based on the play by Lucille Fletcher. (Brut–Avco Embassy.) Rel: Nov. 4. Colour. 98 Mins. Cert. A.

Les Noces Rouges – Blood Wedding

Claude Chabrol thriller set in a quiet small Loire Valley town where suddenly passion takes over two people whose greedy desire for each other leads them rather needlessly into murdering their legal partners and then – after appearing to get away with it – are revealed to the police. Technically superb, finely acted. Cast: *Claude Piéplu, Stéphane Audran, Eliana de Santis, Michel Piccoli, Clotilde Joano, François Robert, Daniel Lecourtois, Pipo Merisi, Ermano Casanova.* Dir & Written: Claude Chabrol. Pro: André Genoves. (Les Films la Boétie/Canaria Film–Connoisseur.) Rel: Floating; first shown at Academy Two, Sept., 1973. Colour. 90 Mins. Cert. X.

No Sex Please – We're British

Screen version of the long-running stage farce by Anthony Marriott and Alastair Foot about some bank employees who become innocently involved with a large quantity of pornographic material delivered to them in error and whose efforts to surreptitiously dispose of it embrace all the classic ingredients of this kind of farce-comedy. Cast: *Ronnie Corbett, Beryl Reid, Arthur Lowe, Ian Ogilvy, Susan Penhaligon, Michael Bates, Cheryl Hall, David Swift, Deryck Guyler, Valerie Leon, Margaret Nolan, Gerald Sim, Michael Robbins, Frank Thornton, Michael Ripper, Lloyd Lamble, Mavis Villiers, Sydney Bromley, John Bindon, Stephen Greif, Brian Wilde, Eric Longworth, Edward Sinclair, Fred Griffiths, Lucy Griffiths, Bart Allison, Robin Askwith, John Scott Martin, Joe Reah.* Dir: Cliff Owen. Pro: John R. Sloan. Screenplay:

202   Anthony Marriott, Johnnie Mortimer & Brian Cooke. (John Woolf/BHP–Columbia–Warner.) Rel: Aug. 26. Colour. 91 Mins. Cert. AA.

Not Now Darling
Farce along the usual lines of misunderstandings, embarrassing situations and final happy sorting out of the many problems. Cast: *Leslie Phillips, Ray Cooney, Moira Lister, Julie Ege, Joan Sims, Derren Nesbitt, Barbara Windsor, Jack Hulbert, Cicely Courtneidge, Bill Fraser, Jackie Pallo, Trudi Van Doorn*. Dir: Ray Cooney & David Croft. Pro: Peter J. Thompson & Martin C. Schute. Screenplay: John Chapman, based on the stage play by Ray Cooney. (LMG.) Rel: January. Colour. 97 Mins. Cert. AA.

La Nuit Américaine – Day for Night
François Truffaut's superbly made, definitive film about the making of a film: the story of the filming of *Pamela*, both on and off the set, with Truffaut himself playing the patient, sleepless, worried director starting out with the idea of making a masterpiece but reduced gradually by the snags that crop up to hoping he'll just finish the film! Always amusing, and human and deeply perceptive; something of a quiet masterpiece. Rest of cast: *Jacqueline Bisset, Valentine Cortese, Dani, Alexandra Stewart, Nike Arrighi, Nathalie Baye, David Markham, Bernard Menez, Gaston Joly, Zanaide Rossi, Jean-Pierre Aumont, Jean Champion, Jean-Pierre Leaud*. Dir: Francois Truffaut. Pro: Marcel Berbert. Screenplay: Truffaut, Jean-Louis Richard & Suzanne Schiffman. (Les Films du Carosse/PECF/PIC–Columbia–Warner.) Rel: Floating; first shown at ABC1, Shaftesbury Avenue. Colour. 116 Mins. Cert. AA.

Nurses on the Job
The love lives of a group of assorted nurses. German-made, English-dubbed. Cast: *Doris Arden, Karin Heske, Rosl Mayr, Gernot Mohner, Frank Nossack, Emily Rever, Barbara Stanek, Ingrid Steeger, Claud Tinney, Elisabeth Volkman*. Dir: Walter Boos. Screenplay: Werner P. Zibaso. (New Realm.) Rel: Floating. Colour. 71 Mins. Cert. X.

Oh, Calcutta
American film of the American version of the notorious nude stage show. Cast: *Raina Barrett, Samantha Harper, Bill Macy, Gary Rethmeier, Nancy Tribush, Mark Dempsey, Patricia Hawkins, Mitchell McGuire, Margo Sappington, George Welbes*. Dir: Jacques Levy. Pro: Guillaume Martin Aucion. Original stage play by Kenneth Tynan. (Tigon.) Rel: Floating, first shown at the Classics, Victoria and Piccadilly, May 1974. 101 Mins. Cert. X. (London.)

Oklahoma Crude
Stanley Kramer's "love story" (with a difference!) set against the rough and ruthless struggle for oil in Oklahoma in the early part of the century: *Faye Dunaway* as the determined women's-lib-inclined driller fighting the brutal takeover methods of the big companies, and eventually capitulating to her forceful partner *George C. Scott*; two grand performances, as also the one by *John Mills* as the lady's daddy. And beneath all the exciting superficial incident all sorts of hinted and then abandoned themes such as the situation of the loner against the Organisation, women's position in man's society and the futile greed for wealth. It all adds up to first-rate screen entertainment. Rest of cast: *Jack Palance, William Lucking, Harvey Jason, Ted Gehring, Cliff Osmond, Rafael Campos, Woodrow Parfrey, John Hudkins, Harvey Parry, Bob Herron, Jerry Brown, Jim Burk, Henry Wills, Hal Smith, Cody Bearpaw, James Jeter, Larry D. Mann, John Dierkes, Karl Lukas, Wayne Storm, Billy Varga*. Dir & Pro: Stanley Kramer. Screenplay: Marc Norman. (Columbia–Warner.) Rel: Nov. 25. Colour. 111 Mins. Cert. AA.

O Lucky Man!
Critically highly acclaimed Lindsay Anderson film which brilliantly takes pokes at such topics as police corruption, crooked politics, big business and man's general inhumanity to man. And a fine performance by *Malcolm McDowell*, making a kind of inverted Pilgrim's Progress. Rest of cast: *Ralph Richardson, Rachel Roberts, Arthur Lowe, Helen Mirren, Dandy Nichols, Mona Washbourne, Graham Crowden, Peter Jeffrey, Philip Stone, Mary MacLeod, Wallas Eaton, Vivian Pickles, Michael Medwin, Michael Bangerter, Jeremy Bulloch, Warren Clark, Geoffrey Palmer, Anthony Nicholls, Geoffrey Chater, Bill Owen, Ben Aris, Edward Judd, Christine Noonan, Brian Glover, John Barrett, Patricia Healey, Glen Williams, David Daker, Brian Pettifer, Paul Dawkins, Hugh Thomas, James Bolam, Peter Scofield, Edward Peel, Adele Strong, Kymoke Debayo, Patricia Lawrence, Constance Chapman*. Dir: Lindsay Anderson. Pro: Michael Medwin & Lindsay Anderson. Screenplay: David Sherwin. (Memorial/Sam–Columbia–Warner.) Rel: Sept. 30. . Colour. 165 Mins. Cert. X.

On the Game
Voyeurish, strip-cartoon-style history of prostitution through the ages, from Messalina to Keeler, with lots of frontal and backward nudity from a rota of well-favoured, ripe damsels. Cast: *Pamela Manson, Charles Hodgson, Suzy Bowen, Nicola Austine, Allen Morton, Peter Duncan, Louise Pajo, Allan McClelland, Eva, Val Penny, Francis Batson, Fiona Victory, David Brierley, Mandy Murfitt, Natalie Shaw, June Palmer, Lloyd Lamble, Gloria Walker, Olive McFarland, Carmen Silvera, Pat Montgomery, Heather Chasen, Mildred Mayne, James Mellor, Flanagan, John Molloy, Lucienne*. Dir: Stanley Long. Pro: Stanley Long & Barry Jacobs. Screenplay: Suzanne Mercer. (Eagle.) Rel: Floating; first shown at the Classic, Charing Cross Road, Jan., 1974. Colour. 87 Mins. Cert. X.

The Optimists of Nine Elms
Strongly atmosphered, gentle piece about an ex-Music Hall star, now living in a derelict factory by the Thames (in the district of the title) with his beloved dog companion, who is adopted by a couple of lively cockney kids. One of *Peter Sellers'* best performances for a long time in a film which has a character entirely its own. Rest of cast: *Donna Mullane & John Chaffey (the kids), David Daker, Marjorie Yates, Katyana Kass, Patricia Brake, Don Crown, Michael Graham Cox, Bruce Purchase, Bernie Searl, Tommy Wright, Pat Becket, Daphne Lawson, Candyce Jane Brandl*. Dir: Anthony Simmons. Pro: Adrian Gaye & Victor Lyndon. Screenplay: Tudor Gates & Anthony Simmons. (Cheetah–Sagittarius–Scotia–Barber.) Rel: May 26. Colour. 107 Mins. Cert. A.

The Other
Intricate, not to say somewhat confusing at times, story about identical twin boys, one of whom is good and the other is not so much horrid as a public danger! And it is all very creepily set against a background of a small Connecticut river town in the summer of '35. Cast: *Uta Hagen, Diana Muldaur, Chris Udvarnoky, Martin Udvarnoky, Norma Connolly, Victor French, Loretta Leversee, Lou Frizzell, Portia Nelson, Jenny Sullivan, John Ritter, Jack Collins, Ed Bakey, Clarence Crow*. Dir & Pro: Robert Mulligan. Screenplay: Thomas Tryon, based on his own novel. (Rex/Benchmark–Fox.) Rel: Floating. Colour. 100 Mins. Cert. X.

The Other Canterbury Tales – see Gli Altri Racconti di Canterbury

The Outfit
Robert Duvall as the released convict whose one aim in life is to revenge his brother's murder by The Syndicate. Rest of cast: *Karen Black, Robert Ryan, Joe Don Baker, Timothy Carey, Richard Jaeckel, Sheree North, Felice Orlandi, Marie Windsor, Jane Greer, Henry Jones, Joanna Cassidy, Tom Reese, Elisha Cook, Bill McKinney, Archie Moore, Anita O'Day, Tony Young, Emile Meyer, Roy Jenson, Roland LaStarza, Edward Ness, Philip Kenneally*. Dir: John Flynn. Pro: Carter De Haven. Screenplay: John Flynn, based on the novel by Richard Stark. (De Haven/MGM–CIC.) Rel: Mar. 17. Colour. 103 Mins. Cert. AA.

The Outside Man
Professional killer *Jean-Louis Trintignant* in Los Angeles to settle his client's score, having done the job, finds himself the target of a mysterious group of killers who are out to get him before he can get back to France. Rest of cast: *Ann-Margret, Roy Schneider, Angie Dickinson, Georgia Engel, Felice Oriandi, Carlo De Mejo, Michel Constantin, Umberto Orsini, Carmine Argenziano, Rice Cartani, Ted Corsia, Edward Greenberg, Jackie Haley, Philippa Harris, John Hillerman, Jon Korkes, Connie Kreski, Ben Piazza, Alex Rocco, Talia Shire, Lionel Vitrant*. Dir: Jacques Deray. Pro: Jacques Bar. Screenplay: Jean-Claude Carrière, Jacques Deray & Ian McLellan Hunter. (Jacques Bar–UA.) Rel: April 28. Colour. 103 Mins. Cert. AA.

Paper Moon

A minor classic; an example of the American film at its best. A wonderfully convincing picture of a place – the hard, windy, sunny plains of the American Midwest – and a time – the 1930s, the years of the Depression – and two people: the handsome, easy-going travelling con man (selling bibles to the recently bereaved) and the nine-year-old girl (whose mother he "knew") who more or less blackmails him in to taking her along with him, and the development and deepening of the at first abrasive and always undemonstrative relationship between them. A fine performance by *Ryan O'Neal* as Moses Pray, the man, and a magnificent one by his small daughter *Tatum* as the child – she won an Oscar for it! And a great deal of subtle background authenticity added by producer–director Peter Bogdanovich. Rest of cast: *Madeline Kahn, John Hillerman, P. J. Johnson, Jessie Lee Fulton, Jim Harrell, Lila Waters, Noble Willingham, Bob Young, Jack Saunders, Jody Wilbur, Liz Ross, Yvonne Harrison, Ed Reed, Dorothy Price, Eleanor Bogart, Dorothy Forster, Lana Daniel, Herschel Morris, Dejah Moore, Ralph Coder, Harriet Ketchum, Desmond Dhooge, Kenneth Hughes, George Lillie, Burton Gilliam, Floyd Mahaney, Gilbert Milton, Randy Quaid, Tandy Arnold, Vernon Schwanke, Dennis Beden, Hugh Gillin, Art Ellison, Rosemary Rumbley.* Dir & Pro: Peter Bogdanovich. Screenplay: Alvin Sargent, based on the novel *Addie Pray* by Joe David Brown. (Directors Company–Paramount–CIC.) Rel: April 28. 103 Mins. Cert. A.

Pat Garrett and Billy the Kid

Yet another movie about this notorious young bad man of the old West, made by Sam Peckinpah as a mixture of fact and legend but leaning heavily on the legend by making Billy older and less villainous than in reality he was. Visually fine, however, if verbally muddy, and with a good, taciturn performance by *James Coburn,* as sheriff Pat Garrett, Billy's erstwhile pal who has now jumped over the other side of the law and order fence and whose sense of duty makes him first warn, then pursue and finally kill Billy. With lots of lovely little cameos from old-timers like *Chill Wills, Jack Elam, Slim Pickens,* etc. Rest of cast: *Kris Kristofferson* (as Billy), *Bob Dylan, Richard Jaeckel, Katy Jurado, Jason Robards, R. G. Armstrong, Luke Askew, John Beck, Richard Bright, Matt Clark, Rita Coolidge, Jack Dodson, Emilio Fernandez, Paul Fix, L. Q. Jones, Jorge Russek, Charlie Martin Smith, Harry Dean Stanton, Rutanya Alda.* Dir: Sam Peckinpah. Pro: Gordon Carroll. Screenplay: Rudolph Wurlitzer. (MGM–EMI.) Rel: Oct. 14. Colour. 106 Mins. Cert. X.

Payday

Surprisingly good and deep story about a young Country and Western artist whose ambition to get to the top, taking everything that life can offer on the way, hides a basic desire to be both loved and to be loving. And there's a fine restraint, sympathy and technical polish in the way this basically familiar material is handled. Cast: *Rip Torn, Ahna Capri, Elayne Heilveil, Michael C. Gwynne, Jeff Morris, Cliff Emmich, Henry O. Arnold, Bobby Smith, Dallas Smith, Richard Hoffman, Walter Bamberg, Eleanor Fell, Clara Dunn, Linda Spatz, Frazier Moss, Winton McNair, Earle Trigg, Mike Edwards, Gene Cody, Bill Littleton, Philip Wende, Ed Neeley, Sonny Shroyer, Cliff Hillerby.* Dir: Daryl Duke. Pro: Martin Fink. Screenwriter (& co-producer): Don Carpenter. (APFC–Fantasy–Fox-Rank.) Rel: June 23. Colour. 103 Mins. Cert. X.

Penelope

French sex film about a couple of young lesbians who arrive in a small fishing village in the winter and soon raise the temperature as they are converted to more normal forms of sensual passion. Cast: *Janine Reynaud, Nyl Clottu, Cathy Reghin, Philippe Gaste, Jacques Insermini, Georges Guéret, René Bernan, Théo Fouquet, Sean O'Neil.* Dir: Martial Berthot. Screenplay: Alain Magron. (Bassan–Cinecenta.) Rel: Floating; first shown at Centa Cinema, Aug., 1973. Colour. 75 Mins. Cert. X.

Penny Gold

Routine whodunit about murder and other mayhem seen against the background of the rare stamp business and complicated by the old gimmick of having two identical twins involved, one very good, one very bad. Cast: *Francesca Annis, James Booth, Nicky Henson, Una Stubbs, Joseph O'Conor, Richard Heffer, Joss Ackland, Sue Lloyd, George Murcell, Marianne Stone.* Dir: Jack Cardiff. Pro: George H. Brown. Screenplay: David Osborn & Liz Charles-Williams. (Fanfare/Scotia–Barber.) Rel: July 15. Colour. 90 Mins. Cert. A.

La Pension du Libre Amour – Hotel of Free Love

How the advent of a handsome young Norwegian at the hotel of the very respectable Madame Robert turns the place into a hothouse of wild passions! Cast: *Colette Mareuil, Gérard Maro, Christine Locquin, Michael Nelz, Sara Sterling, Tania Brusselier.* Dir: Jack Angel. Screenplay: Justin Lenoir & Paul Blade. (Makifilms.) Rel: Floating. Colour. 80 Mins. Cert. X.

Les Pétroleuses – The Legend of Frenchie King

Comedy Western about a family feud between four brothers and four sisters, who dress as men and carry on a highly criminal business. Cast: *Brigitte Bardot, Claudia Cardinale, Michael J. Pollard, Georges Beller, Emma Cohen, Henry Czarniak, Oscar Davis, Raoul Delfosse, France Dougnac, Teresa Gimpera, LeRoy Haynes, Valery Inkijinoff, Jacques Jouanneau, Clément Michu, Patrick Prejean, Denise Provence, Ricardo Salvino, Patty Shepard.* Dir: Christian-Jaque. Pro: Raymond Eger & Francis Cosne. Screenplay: Guy Casaril & Daniel Boulanger. (Francos/Vides/Copercines–Hemdale.) Rel: Floating; first shown at the Classic, Victoria, Dec., 1973. 96 Mins. Cert. A.

Pianorama

The episodic story of an upright piano from its initial purchase in 1902, to grace an Edwardian drawing-room, through periods as a silent cinema pit piano, theatre rehearsal and ragtime recording instrument, down to its present battered but still very lively performance in a cinema commercial. Cast: *Christopher Gable, Una Stubbs, Neal Arden, Eleanor Bron, Fiona Curzon, Paul Dawkins, Alex Dore, Donald Eccles, Tommy Godfrey, Vanda Godsell, Margie Lawrence, Alan Murley, Richard Owens, Danny Rae, John Rapley, Bernie Searle, Bernard Severn, James Snell, Alan Whitehead.* Dir & Screenplay: Richard Taylor. Pro: Jack Saward. (Tara–EMI.) Rel: Feb. 24. Colour. 22 Mins. Cert. U.

Plot – see L'Attentat

The Policeman

Gentle little Israeli comedy about a Jaffa Cop who because of his humanity is pretty ineffective and is about to be compulsorily retired when his pals, the local crooks, stage a crime and arrest for which he will get the credit! Cast: *Shay K. Ophir, Zaharira Harifai, Avner Hezkeyahu, Itzko Rachamimov, Josef Shiloach, Nitza Shaul.* Dir, Pro & Written: Ephraim Kishon. (Ephi–Monarch.) Rel: Floating; first shown at the Classic, Hendon, Feb., 1974. Colour. 87 Mins. Cert. U.

Polizia Ringrazia – The Law Enforcers

The thankless task of a Rome Police Inspector who under pressure from all sides as the crime wave mounts in volume, battles against his politically motivated superiors as well as the crooks and ends up in the morgue, with the dossier so carefully collected in the hands of a superior who for the best reason in the world, his own involvement, will obviously destroy it! Cast: *Enrico Maria Salerno, Mariangela Melato, Mario Adorf, Franco Fabrizi, Cyril Cusack, Laura Belli, Jurgen Drews, Corrado Gaipa, Giorgio Piazza, Ezio Sancrotti.* Dir: Stefano Vanzina. Pro: Roberto Infascelli. Screenplay: Lucio de Caro & Steno. (Primex Italiana/Dieter Geissler–Eagle.) Rel: May 13, 1973. Colour. 98 Mins. Cert. X.

The Porn-Brokers

A "Report" on the pornography scene in and out of Britain; the good pickings to be made from the trade. And with plenty of titillating illustrations. Dir & Pro: John Lindsay & Laurie Barnett. Commentary: Roger Heathcot. (Elmside–Target International.) Rel: Floating. Colour. 86 Mins. Cert. X.

Port of Desire – see Quai du Désir

Prison Girls

The amorous weekend of pretty prisoner advised by the prison psychologist to spend her time out of jail in sexual adventures. Cast: *Robin Whitting, Maria Arnold, Angie Monet, Lisa Ashbury, Tracy Handfuss, Ushie Digard, Jamie McKenna, Ilona Lukas, Carol Peters, Claire Bow, Lois Darst.* Dir: Thomas de Burton. Pro: Nick Grippo & Burton Gershfeld. Screenplay: Burton Gershfeld. (New Realm.) Rel: Floating. Colour. 77 Mins. Cert. X.

204

Private Parts
Sex and fear in a strange hotel with peep-holes in the bedrooms, murders, and girls who dress as, and pretend to be, men! Cast: *Ayn Ruymen, Lucille Benson, John Ventantonio, Laurie Main, Stanley Livingstone, Charles Woolf, Ann Gibbs, Len Travis, Dorothy Neumann, Gene Simms, John Lupton, Patrick Strong.* Dir: Paul Bartel. Pro: Gene Corman. Screenplay: Philip Kearney & Les Rendelstein. (Penelope–MGM–EMI.) Rel: Nov. 23. Colour. 82 Mins. Cert. X.

Quai du Désir – Port of Desire
1969 French film (not hitherto shown here). A story about a released jailbird gangster whose first job when out, a smuggling caper, ends in disaster for all concerned. Cast: *Alex le Gaston, Michel Charrel, Nikita Harris, Nathalie Nort, Laura Hilden, Bepi Fontana, Jean Maley, François Jaubert, Alexandre Mincer.* Dir: Jean Maley. Pro: Bepi Fonata. Screenplay: J. Cabain & H. Fontaine. (Welp–Golden Era.) Rel: Floating, from July, 1973. Colour. 91 Mins. Cert. X.

Quel Maledetto sull'Elba – The Legion of No Return
1968 Spanish–Italian film (not previously released here) story of a bloody, finally successful – at great cost – mission by a small group of American soldiers to blow up a bridge across the Elbe and so delay any Russian advance beyond the river! Cast: *Tab Hunter, Howard Ross, Erika Wallner, Claude Triumph, Rosanna Yanni, Oscar Pellicer, Angel Del Pozo, Indio Gonzales, Daniele Vargas, Alfonso de la Vega, José Guardiola, Antonio Cintado.* Dir: Leon Klimowsky. Pro: Ugo Guerra & Elio Scardemaglia. Screenplay: Adriano Bolzoni & Antonio Fos; based on a story by Lou Carrigan. (Daiano/Leone–Golden Era.) Rel: Floating, from July, 1973. Colour. 90 Mins. Cert. X.

Quelq'un derrière la Porte – Two Minds for Murder
Anthony Perkins as a devious doctor who to gain revenge on his faithless wife (well, her infidelity is really his fault: he's been neglecting her lately!) slyly goes to work on one of his patients and persuades him to remove the lover. It's the perfect crime . . . nearly! Rest of cast: *Jill Ireland, Charles Bronson, Henri Garcia, Adriano Magistretti, Agathe Natanson, André Penvern, Viviane Everly, Carl J. Studer, Colin Mann, Denise Peronne, Isabelle del Rio, Silvana Blase, Yves Elliot.* Dir: Nicolas Gessner. Pro: Raymond Danon. Screenplay: Marc Behm, Nicolas Gessner & Jacques Robert; based on the last's novel. (Lira/Comacico/SNC/Medusa–Miracle.) Rel: May 13, 1973. Colour. 94 Mins. Cert. AA.

Quiet Days in Clichy
Danish film based (somewhat vaguely!) on the Henry Miller book about his adventures in Paris; a sort of triple-decker sandwich of aimless Parisian wanderings interspersed with grimly erotic sequences in which our hero grinds and bumps his way to passing sexual satisfaction. Cast: *Paul Vajean, Wayne John Rodda, Louise White, Ulla Lemvigh-Muller, Avis Sagild, Susanne Krage, Elsebeth Reingahrd, Petronella.* Dir & Screenplay: Jens Jorgen Thorsen. (Miracle.) Rel: Floating. 90 Mins. Cert. X.

Ramparts of Clay
Franco-Algerian semi-documentary about a remote village in Southern Tunisia and the clash of the past and present obliquely presented through the actions of a teenage girl who accepts the futility and the necessity of her life as she visits the well each day. Cast: *Leila Schenna (as the girl) and the people of the Algerian village of Tehouda.* Dir: Jean-Louis Bertuccelli. Screenplay: Jean Duvignaud. (Contemporary.) Rel: Floating, first shown at Paris-Pullman, May 1974. Colour. 87 Mins. Cert. U.

Ransom for a Dead Man
A bored wife's "perfect" plan for her husband's murder comes unstuck as an intelligent police inspector gradually adds up the clues to the correct solution. Cast: *Peter Falk, Lee Grant, John Fink, Harold Gould, Patricia Mattick, Paul Carr, Jed Allan, Charles Macaulay, Henry Brandt, Jeane Byron, Richard Roat, Norma Connolly, Harlan Warde, Bill Walker, Timothy Carey, Judson Morgan, Richard O'Brien, Celeste Yarnell, Lisa Moore, Lois Battle, Reginald Fenderson.* Dir: Richard Irving. Pro & Screenplay: Dean Hargrove (from a story by Richard Levinson & William Link). (Universal–CIC.) Rel: April 28. Colour. 95 Mins. Cert. U.

Red Hot Zorro
Jean-Michel Dhermay as the dashing and amorous outlaw who in mid-nineteenth-century California stands up against the tyrannical Governor. Rest of cast: *Evelyne Scott, Alice Arno, Rose Kiekens, Christine Chantel, Ghislaine Kay, Evelyne Galou, Martine van Liden, Marie-Therese Lecomble, Helene Machefel, Madeline Revardy, Valerie Jalain, Sylvie Picot, Christine Casalonga, Arlette Bontemps, Louise Petit, Antoine Fontaine, Johnny Weissler, Darton.* Dir: William Russell. Pro: Pierre Querut. Screenplay: Henri Bral de Boitselier. (Cinecenta.) Rel: Floating. Colour. 72 Mins. Cert. X.

Le Rempart des Béguines
French. Pretty little *Anicée Alvina* as the teenager who falls in love with her father's mistress and, when the latter decides for social reasons to marry the dad, is suitably desolated at the end of her first love affair. Rest of cast: *Nicole Courcel, Venantino Venantini, Jean Martin, Ginette Leclerc, Harry-Max, Yvonne Clech, Elisabeth Tessier, Nadia Barentin, Axelle Abbadie.* Dir: Guy Casaril. Pro: Robert & Raymond Hakim. Screenplay: Guy Casaril & Françoise Mallet-Joris; based on the Françoise Mallet-Joris novel. (Paris/Antheo–Fox–Rank.) Rel: Floating; first shown at the Bloomsbury Cinema, Oct., 1973. 91 Mins. Cert. X.

The Return
Half-hour thriller about a murderer who in Edwardian England returns to the scene of his crime, a desolate and boarded-up house, and there confronts the ghost, a confrontation that leads to his death. Cast: *Peter Vaughan, Rosalie Crutchley.* Dir: Sture Rydman. Pro: Elizabeth McKay. Screenplay: Brian Scobie & Sture Rydman; based on stories by A. M. Burrage and Ambrose Bierce. (Jocelyn Films–MGM–EMI.) Rel: Floating. Colour. 31 Mins. Cert. A.

Return of Sabata
Sabata (*Lee Van Cleef*) and his old side-kick Clyde (*Reiner Schöne*) join forces to clean up the town – and at the same time clean up the gold, too! Italian Western. Rest of cast: *Annabella Incontrera, Gianni Rizzo, Gianpiero Albertini, Pedro Sanchez, Nick Jordan.* Dir: Frank Kramer. Pro: Alberto Grimaldi. Screenplay: Renato Izzo & Gianfranco Parolini. (PEA/Artistes Associés–UA.) Rel: Dec. 9. Colour. 89 Mins. Cert. X.

Run, Cougar, Run
Disney film about a Cougar family in the remote Red Mesa country, Utah, and the hunter who relentlessly tracks one of them down, in spite of all that the gentle shepherd can do to defend her. Cast: *Stuart Whitman, Frank Aletter, Lonny Chapman, Douglas V. Fowley, Harry Carey, Jr., Alfonso Arau and Seeta, the mountain lion.* Dir: Jerome Courtland. Pro: James Algar. Screenplay: Louis Pelletier. (Disney.) Rel: April 14. Colour. 75 Mins. Cert. U.

Santee
Glenn Ford as a dedicated bounty hunter whose heart isn't all that hard, so when he kills a boy's badman father he more or less adopts the lad as his own son and with him faces up to the gang whose murder of the ex-lawman Santee's own son initially set him on his path of revenge! Rest of cast: *Michael Burns, Dana Wynter, Jay Silverheels, Harry Townes, John Larch, Robert Wilke, Bob Donner, Taylor Lacher, Lindsay Crosby, Charles Courtney, X Brand, John Hart, Russ McCubbin, Robert Mellard, Boyd Morgan, John Bailey, Ben Zeller, Brad Merhege.* Dir: Gary Nelson. Pro: Deno Paoli & Edward Platt. Screenplay: Tom Blackburn. (American Video–Cinema–Vagabond Productions Columbia Warner.) Rel: March 24. Colour. 91 Mins. Cert. AA.

The Satanic Rights of Dracula
The bad old Baron gets cracking again (in the inevitable person of *Christopher Lee*) only to fail in his plan to kill off the world's population by a new and more virulent strain of bubonic plague, thanks to the intervention of scientist-enemy *Peter Cushing*. And a good old gory time is had by all. Rest of cast: *Michael Coles, William Franklyn, Freddie Jones, Joanna Lumley, Richard Vernon, Patrick Barr, Barbara Yu Ling, Richard Mathews, Lockwood West, Maurice O'Connell, Valerie Van Ost.* Dir: Alan Gibson. Pro: Roy Skeggs. Screenplay: Don Houghton. (Hammer–Columbia–Warner.) Rel: Mar. 24. Colour. 87 Mins. Cert. X.

Save the Tiger

Jack Lemmon as a rich but unsatisfied American businessman who wakes up one day to the realisation of his situation and who then proceeds to break the law in order to save his firm from going broke, while fully aware of his own desire to be an old American hero-type. Rest of cast: *Jack Gilford, Laurie Heineman, Norman Burton, Patricia Smith, Thayer David, William Hansen, Harvey Jason, Liv Von Linden, Lara Parker, Eloise Hardt, Janina, Ned Glass, Pearl Shear, Biff Elliott, Ben Freedman, Madeline Lee.* Dir: John G. Avildsen. Pro & Screenplay: Steve Shagan. (Filmsways/Jalem/Cirandinha–Paramount.) Rel: July 15. Colour. 101 Mins. Cert. AA.

Scarecrow

Moving story of an odd friendship between two men who never quite fit into the pattern of society: the tough, quick-tempered Max (*Gene Hackman*, a superb performance) who's just out of prison after a stretch for assault, and the contrasting small and peace-seeking Lion (*Al Pacino*), home from the sea after a six-year succession of voyages. Their high hopes and the smashing of them makes a sad yet reassuring human story. Rest of cast: *Dorothy Tristan, Ann Wedgeworth, Richard Lynch, Eileen Brennan, Penny Allen, Richard Hackman, Al Cingolani, Rutanya Alda.* Dir: Jerry Schatzberg. Pro: Robert M. Sherman. Screenplay: Garry Michael White. (Columbia–Warner.) Rel: Sept. 28. Colour. 113 Mins. Cert. X.

Scorpio

The sadness of the professional spy, when called upon to rub out his pal! In this case it's *Burt Lancaster* as an ageing C.I.A. agent, who, suspected by his bosses of being in the double-cross business is sought by hired assassin and ex-pal *Alain Delon* (the selected executioner) and Soviet spy *Paul Scofield*, who liking his long-time enemy and knowing the score, seeks to persuade him to cross the Rubicon. Conventional; violent; exciting. Rest of cast: *John Colicos, Gayle Hunnicutt, J. D. Cannon, Joanne Linville, Melvin Stewart, Vladek Sheybal, Mary Maude, Jack Colvin, James Sikking, Burke Byrnes, William Smithers, Samuel Rodensky, Howard Morton, Celeste Yarnall, Sandor Eles, Frederick Jaeger, George Mikell, Robert Emhardt.* Dir: Michael Winner. Pro: Walter Mirisch. Screenplay: David W. Rintels & Gerald Wilson. (Scimitar–Mirisch–UA.) Rel: Oct. 7. Colour. 114 Mins. Cert. X.

La Scoumoune – The Hit Man

Italian film about the lives, and deaths, of some gangsters in Marseilles between the thirties and the mid-forties. Cast: *Jean-Paul Belmondo, Claudia Cardinale, Michel Constantin, Michel Pareyton, Aldo Bufi Landi, Luciano Lorcas, Enrique Lucero, Alain Mottet, Marie-Claude Mestral, Philippe Brizard, Jacques Respel, Marc Eyrand, Dominique Zardi, Pierre Collet, Pierre Dany, Jean-Claude Michel, Henri Vilbert, Paul Beauvay, A. Augier, Bruno Balp, Hervé Sand.* Dir & Screenplay: José Giovanni, based on his own novel *L'Excommunié.*

Pro: Raymond Danon. (Lira/Praesidens–Miracle.) Rel: May 5. Colour. 96 Mins. Cert. X.

Scream

Spine-tingler about a mysterious threat of vengeance made to a woman whose evidence has resulted in the sentencing to death of several members of a fanatical religious order guilty of having crucified a more normal sort of preacher. Cast: *Jeanne Crain, Alex Nicol, Daniel Spelling, Michael Sugich, Barbara Hancock, Dawn Cleary, Gary Morgan, Stewart Bradley, James Sikking, Corinne Conley, Miller Petitt, Richard Smedley, Jack Sheppard, James Waring, Terry Pratt.* Dir: Lee Madden. Pro: Ed Carlin & Gil Lasky. Screenplay: Gil Lasky. (Lasky–Carlin–DUK.) Rel: Floating; first shown at Oscar Cinema, Dec., 1973. Colour. 85 Mins. Cert. X.

Secrets of a Door to Door Salesman

Somewhat flat British erotic story of an innocent from the West Country who comes to London and finds the sexual side of the city too much for him. Cast: *Brendan Price, Graham Stark, Chic Murray, Bernard Spear, Felicity Devonshire, Sue Longhurst, Jean Harrington, Johnny Briggs, Elizabeth Romilly, Jacqueline Logan, Victoria Burgoyne, Noelle Finch, Geraldine Hart, Valerie Bell.* Dir: Wolf Rilla. Pro: David Grant. Screenplay: Joseph McGrath & Roy Nicholas. (Oppidan–New Realm.) Rel: Floating; first shown at the Classic Moulin, Oct., 1973. Colour. 80 Mins. Cert. X.

Seduction

Italian sex drama about the great lover who moves in with an old flame and also becomes involved with her daughter – a tricky *ménage à trois* that is finally resolved with a well-placed bullet. Cast: *Lisa Gastoni, Maurice Ronet, Ornella Muti, Jenny Tamburi, Pino Caruso.* Dir: Fernando Di Leo. (Cineproduzioni Daunia 70 Roma–Gemini.) Rel: Floating, first shown at the Classic, Moulin, April 1974. Colour. 92 Mins. Cert. X.

The Serpent

Well (English–French) made, long and leisurely espionage drama based on the famous Philby spy case: the story of a Russian KGB defector who comes prepared to exchange a list of names of European spies working for the Soviets in high places in exchange for asylum. Cast: *Yul Brynner, Henry Fonda, Dirk Bogarde, Philippe Noiret, Michel Bouquet, Martin Held, Farley Granger, Virna Lisi, Guy Trejan, Marie Dubois, Elga Andersen, Robert Alda, Natalie Nerval, André Falcon, Paola Pitagora, François Maistre, Luigi Diberti, William Sabatier, Robert Party, Larry Dolgin.* Dir & Pro: Henry Verneuil. Screenplay: H. Verneuil & Gilles Perrault, based on a novel by Pierre Nord. (Euro/Rialto Films La Boétie–MGM–EMI.) Rel: Feb. 24. Colour. 122 Mins. Cert. A.

Serpico

A brilliantly directed, most ably acted, hard-hitting movie which beneath the superficial story – based on truth – about an honest, dedicated young New York

cop whose steadfast refusal to join in his fellows' graft and corruption leads to his being nearly killed – and a, belated, official enquiry – is a strong piece of propaganda for cleaning-up and keeping clean the police force. Cast: *Al Pacino, John Randolph, Jack Kehoe, Biff McGuire, Barbara Eda-Young, Cornelia Sharpe, Tony Roberts, John Medici, Allan Rich, Norman Ornellas, Ed Grover, Al Henderson, Hank Garrett, Damien Leake, Joe Bova, Gene Gross, John Stewart, Woodie King, James Tolkin, Ed Crowley, Bernard Barrow, Sal Carollo, Mildred Clinton, Nathan George, Gus Fleming, Richard Foronjy, Alan North, Lewis J. Stadlen, John McQuade, Ted Benaides, John Lehne, M. Emmet Walsh, George Ede, Charles White.* Dir: Sidney Lumet. Screenplay: Waldo Salt & Norman Wexler, from the book by Peter Maas. (Dino de Laurentis–Paramount–CIC.) Rel: May 12. Colour. 130 Mins. Cert. X.

1776

Jack L. Warner's personal, large-scale screen version of the very successful (in America) stage musical of the same title, which relates the events, and arguments, in Congress in that year to get through the bill which will make America free from the increasingly irritating British yoke. A number of tuneful if never memorable musical numbers, some nice performances, slight humour. Cast: *William Daniels, David Ford, Howard da Silva, Donald Madden, Emory Bass, Ken Howard, Ron Holgate, Rex Robbins, Peter Forster, Frederic Downs, Howard Caine, John Myhers, Richard McMurray, John Cullum, Gordon de Vol, William H. Bassett, Jonathan Moore, William Engle, Barry O'Hara, William Hansen, Ray Middleton, Leo Leyden, Patrick Hines, Heber Jentzsch, Andy Albin, Charles Rule, Jack de Mave, Jordan Rhodes, Roy Poole, James Noble, Richard O'Shea, Fred Slyter, Daniel Keyes, John Holland, Ralston Hall, Stephen Nathan, William Duell, Mark Montgomery, Blythe Danner, Virginia Vestoff.* Dir: Peter H. Hunt. Pro: Jack L. Warner. Screenplay: Peter Stone, based on the musical play of the same title for which he wrote the book. (Columbia–Warner.) Rel: Floating. Colour. 142 Mins. Cert. A.

The Seven-Ups

New York cops and robbers again, with the unconventional detective group of the title after the big-time crooks liable to be sent up for not less than a seven-year stretch when caught – hence their nickname. The unit becomes involved in some complicated inter-gang warfare which they only smash at the cost of one of their number killed. Made by the producer of *The French Connection* and showing in style and content the connection! Cast: *Roy Scheider, Victor Arnold, Jerry Leon, Ken Kercheval, Tony Lo Bianco, Larry Haines, Richard Lynch, Bill Hickman, Lou Polan, Matt Russo, Joe Spinell, Robert Burr, Rex Everhart, David Wilson, Ed Jordan, Mary Multari, Frank Mascetta, Frances Chaney, Mike Treanor, Benny Marino, Bill Funaro, Billy Longo, Ace Alagna, Sheldon Adler, Adeline Leonard, Edward Carey.* Dir & Pro: Philip D'Antoni. Screenplay: Albert Ruben & Alexander Jacobs; from a story by ex-New York cop

Sonny Grosso. (Fox–Rank.) Rel: Mar. 31. Colour. 103 Mins. Cert. X.

Sex at the Olympics
German film about the sexual and other dangers which lie in wait for young and ambitious girls who pour into Munich. Cast: *Elfriede Payer, Gunther Möhner, Christina Lindberg, Ulrike Butz*. Dir: Walter Boos. Pro: Wolf C. Hartwig. Screenplay: Günther Heller. (Rapid–Film–Gemini Films.) Rel: Floating. Colour. 71 Mins. Cert. X.

La Sexe Nu – Naked Sex
French sex film. Cast: *Alain Tissier, Valérie Boisgel, Chantral Arondel, Nathalie Zeiger, Dany Danyel, Loïc Porzier, Frederika Page*. Dir & Screenplay: José Bénazeraf. Pro: Simon Bénazeval. (Productions du Chesne–Cinecenta.) Rel: Floating, first shown at the Cinecenta, March, 1974. Colour. 74 Mins. Cert. X.

Sex Farm
British effort along familiarly titillating lines; with two wives and husbands spending separate sexy weekends and returning to each other refreshed and ready for their partner's attentions. Cast: *Hilary Labow, Amber Kammer, Kim Alexander, Tristan Rogers, Gordon Whiting, Claire Gordon, Max Mason, Ray Edwards, Tommy Wright, Barry Rohde, Steve Patterson, Sui Lin, Sue Glanville, Sonya Stevens, Patrick Tull, Mark York, Pamelo Sholto, Elsie Winsor, Marjorie Summerville, Liz Mitchell, Gillian Brown*. Dir: Arnold. Miller. Pro: Arnold & Sheila Miller. Screenplay: Alan L. Pas from an original idea by Arnold Miller. (Global–Queensway–Monarch.) Rel: Floating; first shown at Oscar Two, Mar., 1974. Colour. 84 Mins. Cert. X (London).

Sex is the Name of the Game – see Intimidades de Una Prostituta

Sex Life in a Convent
German film about the precocious pupils in a convent school having more than a fair share of sex problems; rather dreary in content but titillatory in presentation. Cast: *Doris Arden, Ulrich Beiger, Astrid Bohner, Felix Francky, Ellen Frank*. Dir: Eberhard Schroeder. Screenplay: Werner Zibasco. (TV 13–Grand National.) Rel: Floating; first shown at Oscars, Oct., 1973. Colour. 73 Mins. Cert. X.

Sex of Their Bodies
About a cold couple who find a renewal of physical passion during a visit to magical Hong Kong. Cast: *Beba Loncar, Ugo Pagliai, Zeudi Araya, Giacomo Rossi Stuart*. Dir: Luigi Scattini. (Aquila/Atlas Consorziate–English Film Co.) Rel: Floating; first shown at the Classic, Windmill, Feb., 1974. Colour. 83 Mins. Cert. X.

Sex or Bust
Sex, gangsters, the Mafia and a lot else in a story about a crook from Sicily who wants to trade a million dollars worth of stolen jewels for hard New York cash!

Cast: *Frank Corsentino, Haji, Charles Knapp, Michael Finn*. Dir & Pro: Art Lieberman. (Titan Films.) Rel: Floating. Colour. 70 Mins. Cert. X.

The Sex Shop
Claude Berri – starring under his own direction! – as the little Paris bookseller who to boost his profits launches into pornography and tries hard to live the sort of life suggested by his wares, but finally fails of course. Rest of cast: *Juliet Berto, Nathalie Delon, Jean-Pierre Marielle, Francesca Romana Coluzzi, Catherine Allégret, Béatrice Romand, Jacques Martin, Claude Piépla, Luisa Colpeyn, Grégoire Aslain, Juliette Mills, Jean Tissier, Jacques Legras, Ada Lonati, Elisabeth Volkmann, Isabelle Enni, Thomas Waintrop, Julien Langmann, Xavier Fonti, Jimmy Perrys, Jean Valmont, Sabine Glaeser, Appelt, Herbert Fux, Jean Gruault, Georges Staquet, Hélène Dieudonné, Pierre Louki*. Dir & Screenplay: Claude Berri. (Renn/Artistes Associés/Regina/PEA–Gala.) Rel: Floating; first shown in June, 1973. Colour. 94 Mins. Cert. X.

The Sex Thief
Sex crime melo about a irresistibly handsome young jewel thief who exchanges himself for the jewels he takes so that the robbed victim will not co-operate in the police's effort to apprehend him! Cast: *Jenny Westbrook, David Warbeck, Henry Rayner, Gerald Taylor, Michael Armstrong, Terence Edmond, Diane Keen, Christopher Neil, Harvey Hall, Gloria Walker, Christopher Biggins, Christopher Mitchell, Eric Deacon, Susan Glanville, Linda Coombes, David Landor, James Aubrey, David Pugh, Brenda Rae, Anthony May, Derek Martin, Val Penny, Dave Carter, Neville Barber, Michael Hannah, Carlotta Barrow, Veronica Doran*. Dir: Martin Campbell. Pro: Michael Style & Teddy White. Screenplay: Edward Hyde. (Ocarina/Drumbeat/Rainbow–LMG.) Rel: Floating. 89 Mins. Cert. X.

The Sexy Darlings
Comedy about a man who – very sensibly – prefers living on a desert island to civilisation. But, of course, he has a nubile quartet of girls to share his lonely (!) existence. Cast: *Anne Libert, Andrea Rau, Inge Steinbach, Yuda Barkan, Paul Muller, Ruth Gassman, Irene D'Astrea, Howard Vernon*. Dir: Jess Franco. Pro: Karl H. Mannchen. Screenplay: Art Bernd. (Telecine–Comptoir–Anthony Balch.) Rel: Floating. Colour. 82 Mins. Cert. X.

Shadow of the Werewolf
Spanish–West German co-production: about some grisly goings on in which people are killed, come back to life, turn into werewolves and revert to human beings . . . and love has a say in all this, too. Cast: *Paul Naschy, Gaby Fuchs, Barbara Capell, Patty Shepard, Andres Mesino, José Marco, Julio Pena, Barta Barri, Yelena Samarina*. Dir: Leon Klimovsky. Pro: No name given. Screenplay: Jacinto Molina & Hans Munkel. (Hifi Stereo 70/Plata–Butcher's.) Rel: Floating, from June, 1973. Colour. 86 Mins. Cert. X.

Shaft in Africa
Black thick-ear Private Eye Shaft – in the person of *Richard Roundtree* – doing his thing again, this time in Africa, where he is taken in order to persuade him to assist in breaking into and breaking up a modern variation on the old slave trade. Rest of cast: *Frank Finlay, Vonetta McGee, Neda Arneric, Debebe Eshetu, Spiros Focas, Jacques Herlin, Jho Jhenkins*. Dir: John Guillermin. Pro: Roger Lewis. Screenplay: Stirling Silliphant. (MGM–EMI.) Rel: Sept. 23. Colour. 109 Mins. Cert. X.

Shoot Out
Gregory Peck comes out of prison after a seven-year stretch for bank robbery determined to get even with the partner who betrayed him. Rest of cast: *Pat Quinn, Robert F. Lyons, Susan Clark, Donald Moffat, James Gregory, Rita Gam, Dawn Lyn, Pepe Serna, John Chandler, Nicholas Beauvy, Paul Fix, Arthur Hunnicutt*. Dir: Henry Hathaway. Pro: Hal B. Wallis. Screenplay: Marguerite Roberts; based on the Will James novel *The Lone Cowboy*. (Universal–Rank.) Rel: Floating. Colour. 94 Mins. Cert. AA.

Showdown
Minor but well-made Western about the unwilling confrontation of a Sheriff with his erstwhile pal, now turned train robber and outlaw. Cast: *Rock Hudson, Dean Martin, Susan Clark, Donald Moffat, John McLiam, Charles Baca, Jackson Kane, Ben Zeller, John Richard Gill, Philip L. Mead, Rita Rogers, Vic Mohica, Raleigh Gardenhire, Ed Begley, Jr., Dan Boydston*. Dir & Pro: George Seaton. Screenplay: Theodore Taylor; based on a story by Hank Fine. (Universal–CIC.) Rel: Floating. Colour. 99 Mins. Cert. A.

Siddhartha
Adaptation of the Nobel Prize novel by Herman Hesse about a young Brahmin and his search for a meaning to existence during a long life in India some twenty-five centuries ago. Made in India and full of charm and philosophic shades. Cast: *Shashi Kapoor, Simi Garewal, Romesh Sharma, Pincho Kapoor, Zul Vellani, Amrik Singh, Shanti Hiranand, Kunal Kapoor*. Dir, Pro & Screenplay: Conrad Rooks. (Rooks–Columbia.) Rel: Floating, first shown at the Bloomsbury Cinema, April 1974. Colour. 88 Mins. Cert. A.

The Silent One
Rather overlong and generally pretty unexciting French thriller about a French scientist persuaded to work for the Russians who on an official trip to England is kidnapped by MI5 who blackmail him into revealing the name of the Russian agents working in London and then set him free to be chased unendingly by the Soviet snipers, and finally finished off high in the Alps. Dubbed into English. Cast: *Lino Ventura, Leo Genn, Robert Hardy, Lea Massari, Suzanne Flon, Pierre-Michel le Conte, Bernard Dheran*. Dir: Claude Pinoteau. Pro: Alain Poire. Screenplay: Jean-Loup Dabadie & Claude Pinoteau, based on the novel *Drôle*

de Pistolet by Francis Ryck. (Variety Film Distributors.) Rel: Floating. Colour. 113 Mins. Cert. A.

Sleeper
Woody Allen as the jazz player and part-owner of a Greenwich Village health-food store who goes into a New York hospital for a minor ailment in 1973 and wakes up in 2173 to find that he's spent the intervening couple of centuries as a deep-frozen body! But he quickly finds the old familiar scene: the dictator-ruled, rigidly controlled people and the revolutionary underground, to which Woody, and the pretty girl he picks up along the way, gravitate. The usual mixture of wit, wisecrack and slapstick but with more form than some of Allen's previous film efforts. Rest of cast: *Diane Keaton, John Beck, Mary Gregory, Don Keefer, Don McLiam, Bartlett Robinson, Chris Forbes, Marya Small, Peter Hobbs, Susan Miller, Lou Picetti, Brian Avery, Spencer Milligan, Spencer Ross.* Dir & co-Scripted (with Marshall Brickman): Woody Allen. Pro: Jack Grossberg. (Jack Rollins/Charles H. Joffe–UA.) Rel: June 2. Colour. 88 Mins. Cert. A.

Sleuth
Finely performed and adapted screen version (by the author) of the brilliantly contrived detective thriller play by Anthony Shaffer: the story of a cruel duel of wits, which leads to ultimate tragedy, between a successful writer of crime-fiction (a wonderful performance by *Laurence Olivier*) and the young hairdresser neighbour (*Michael Caine*, also at his best) whom he invites to a drink and then reveals he knows is having an affair with his wife. No other cast! Dir: Joseph L. Mankiewicz. Pro: Morton Gottlieb. Screenplay: Anthony Shaffer. (Palomar–Fox–Rank.) Rel: Jan. 27. Colour. 138 Mins. Cert. AA.

Slither
Off-beat, whimsical comedy-thriller with many satirical allusions about a quartet of crooks in search of a cached, embezzled fortune along the highways and by-ways of the Californian coast, pursued by a couple of menacing black vans: ending on a quizzically limp note as the air of threatening mystery is suddenly deflated into normality. Cast: *James Caan, Peter Boyle, Sally Kellerman, Louise Lasser, Allen Garfield, Richard B. Shull, Alex Rocco, Alex Henteloff, Garry Goodrow, Len Lesser, Seaman Glass, Wayne Storm, William Noland, James Joseph, Diana Darrin, Stuart Nisbet, Edwina Goff, Virginia Sale.* Dir: Howard Zieff. Pro: Jack Sher. Screenplay: W. D. Richter. (MGM–EMI.) Rel: July 22. 96 Mins. Cert. AA.

SSSSnake
A pretty far-fetched thriller about a famous ophiologist who finds a way of turning people into his favourite reptiles but comes to a bad end – at the forked tongue of one of his pets! Cast: *Strother Martin, Dirk Benedict, Heather Menzies, Richard B. Shull, Tim O'Connor, Jack Ging, Kathleen King, Reb Brown, Ted Grossman, Charles Seel, Ray Ballard, Brendan Burns, Rick Beckner, James Drum, Ed McCready, Frank

Kowalski, Ralph Montgomery, Michael Masters, Charlie Fox, Felix Silla, Nobel Craig, Bobbi Kiger, J. R. Clark, Chip Potter. Dir: Bernard L. Kowalski. Pro & Story: Dan Striepeke. Screenplay: Hal Dresner. (Zanuck/Brown–Universal–CIC.) Rel: Nov. 25. Colour. 99 Mins. Cert. X.

Soft Beds, Hard Battles
Mildly amusing little Boulting Brothers comedy about a French brothel's contribution to the war effort; apparently mainly concerned in giving *Peter Sellers* the opportunity to present a number of highly diversified characters, from a Japanese Prince to an old French General, a cheerful British ass of an officer to Hitler himself! Rest of cast: *Lila Kedrova, Curt Jurgens, Beatrice Romand, Jenny Hanley, Françoise Pascal, Gabriella Licudi, Rula Lenska, Daphne Lawson, Carolle Rousseau, Hylette Adolphe, Rex Stallings, Timothy West, Patricia Burke, Thorley Walters, Philip Madoc, Vernon Dobtcheff, Windsor Davies, Neil Rhoden, Tony Sympson, Alan Rebbeck, John Abineri, David Toguri, Stanley Lebor, Gertan Klauber, Barry J. Gordon, Nicholas Loukes, Stephen Grief, Ian McCulloch, Bruce Purchase, Don Fellows, Michael Sheard, Basil Dignam, Andrew Lodge, Douglas Nottage.* Dir: Roy Boulting. Pro: John Boulting. Screenplay: Leo Marks & Roy Boulting. (Charter–Fox–Rank.) Rel: Mar. 3. Colour. 107 Mins. Cert. X.

Sounder
Charmingly simple, delightfully entertaining and thoroughly credible film about a devoted Negro family in the American Deep South during the Depression. With some delicious performances. A sadly undervalued and underexposed movie of – minor – classical proportions. Cast: *Cicely Tyson, Paul Winfield, Kevin Hooks, Carmen Mathews, Taj Mahal, James Best, Yvonne Jarrell, Eric Hooks, Sylvia "Kuumba" Williams, Janet MacLachan, Teddy Airhart, Rev. Thomas N. Phillips, Judge William Thomas Bennett, Inez Durham, Spencer Bradford, Myrl Sharkey.* Dir: Martin Ritt. Pro: Robert B. Radnitz. Screenplay: Lonne Elder III, based on the novel by William H. Armstrong. (Radnitz/Mattel–Fox.) Rel: Floating. Colour. 105 Mins. Cert. U.

Soylent Green
A gloomy look into the future, A.D. 2022 in fact, when New York is over-populated, over-polluted and living largely off processed plankton, which is now running out. Tracking down the killer of one of the directors of the manufacturers of the meal, tough cop *Charlton Heston* stumbles on the ghastly secret: after processed plankton, it is going to be processed bodies as a staple diet.... A prognosticating thriller of sorts with some remarkable machinic creations. Rest of cast: *Leigh Taylor-Young, Edward G. Robinson, Chuck Connors, Joseph Cotten, Brock Peters, Paula Kelly, Stephen Young, Mike Henry, Lincoln Kilpatrick, Roy Jenson, Leonard Stone, Whit Bissell, Celia Lovsky.* Dir: Richard Fleischer. Pro: Walter Seltzer & Russell Thacher. Screenplay: Stanley R. Greenberg; based on

a novel by Harry Harrison. (MGM–EMI.) Rel: July 8. Colour. 97 Mins. Cert. AA.

Spring Into Summer
A classical French film from Thomas Pascal which draws a wonderfully sensitive portrait of a small French town, a family that lives there and, more particularly, of the plump and pretty teenage daughter who in a few warm weeks of summer loses her innocence and never lets it become more than a passing incident. Superbly photographed and very finely acted by a small, well-chosen cast, all adding a breadth of reality not normally found in films from any source. Cast: *Annie Cole, Christiane Chameret, Daniel Ceccaldi, Frederic Duru, Alain Perceau, Jean Carnet, Helène Dieudonné, Claudine Paringaux, Bernard Menez, Isabelle Ganz, Friquette.* Dir: Thomas Pascal. Pro: Michel Choquet. Screenplay: Thomas Pascal, Roland Duval & Suzanne Schiffman. (Gala.) Rel: Floating, first shown at the Curzon, May, 1974. Colour. 117 Mins. Cert. X.

State of Siege
Dedicated political thriller by Costa-Gavras, the director who made *Z*: the story of a mysterious American kidnapped in a South American State and held for ransom, against the release of the State-held political prisoners. The confrontation between government and revolutionaries is climaxed by the arrest of a number of known guerrillas and the killing of the American, revealed as an important right-wing figure. Cast: *Yves Montand, Renato Salvatori, O. E. Hasse, Jacques Weber, Jean-Luc Bideau, Evangeline Peterson, Maurice Teynac, Yvette Etiévant, Nemesio Antunes, Harald Wolff, André Falcon, Mario Montilles, Jerry Brouer, Jean-François Gobbi, Eugenio Guzman, Maurice Jacquemont, Roberto Navarette, Gloria Lass, Alejandro Cohen, Martha Contreras.* Dir: Costa-Gavras. Pro: Jacques Perrin. Screenplay: Franco Solinas & Costa Gavras. (Reggane/Unidis–Euro International/Dieter Geissler–Hemdale.) Rel: Floating; first shown at the Curzon, July, 1973. Colour. 120 Mins. Cert. X.

Steelyard Blues
All about three odd-ball characters who live in a used car junk yard and there attempt to rebuild an old World War II airplane: a business which leads them into conflict with the society and the cops to whom they are opposed. Cast: *Donald Sutherland, Peter Boyle, Jane Fonda, Garry Goodrow, Howard Hesseman, John Savage, Richard Schaal, Melvin Stewart, Morgan Upton, Roger Bowen, Howard Storm, Jessica Myerson, Dan Barrows, Nancy Fish, Lynn Bernay, Edward Greenberg.* Dir: Alan Myerson. Pro: Tony Bill, Michael & Julia Phillips. Screenplay: David S. Ward. (Columbia–Warner.) Rel: Sept. 9. Colour. 93 Mins. Cert. X.

Steptoe & Son Ride Again
Another – the second – feature film based on the popular TV series about the junk-man team of *Wilfrid Brambell* and *Harry H. Corbett*, who in this episode

buy a dud greyhound, try a little insurance swindling and end up with a new horse and a half of another! Rest of cast: *Diana Dors, Milo O'Shea, Neil McCarthy, Bill Maynard, George Tovey, Sam Kydd, Yootha Joyce, Olga Lowe, Joyce Hemson, Henry Woolf, Geoffrey Bayldon, Frank Thornton, Eamonn Boyce, Hilda Barry, Richard Davies, Joan Ingram, Rafiq Anwar, Siobhan Quinlan, Peter Thornton, Stewart Bevan, Grazina Frame, Peter Newby*. Dir: Peter Sykes. Pro: Aida Young. Screenplay: Ray Galton & Alan Simpson. (Associated London/MGM–EMI.) Rel: May 19. Colour. 98 Mins. Cert. A.

The Stewardesses
A story about a group of air hostesses, who appear to be a mixed bunch of perverts, lesbians, prostitutes and other straight and narrow path strayers . . . and all this is 3-D Stereo Vision, which means, roughly speaking, that the busts come busting out almost all over you! You'll need the special glasses though. Cast: *Christina Hart, Paula Erikson, Angelique deMoline, Kathy Ferrick, Janet Wass, Donna Stanley, Patricia Fein, Beth Shields, Monica Gayle, Michael Garret, William Basil, Jerry Litvinoff, Robert Keller, Andy Roth, John Barcado, Gordon White, Barry Schoenborn, Alicia Taggart, Linda Francis, Cindy Hopkins, Barbara Caron, Lynn Harris, Candy Stokes, Brenda Morrison, Mindy Baker, Phyllis Stengle, Ann Reynolds, Nancy O'Gorman, Karen Sherman, Nancy Ison, Babbette Cartier*. Dir & Written: Alf Silliman. Jr. Pro: Louis K. Sher. (David Grant–Sherpix–Border.) Rel: Floating; first shown at the Jacey, Charing Cross Road, Dec., 1973. Colour. 69 Mins. Cert. X.

The Sting
Intricate crookery and double dealing, *circa* 1936, among the Chicago gangsters with *Paul Newman* and *Robert Redford* considerably involved. Very slick, amusing and highly entertaining. Rest of cast: *Robert Shaw, Charles Durning, Ray Walston, Eileen Brennan, Harold Gould, John Heffernan, Dana Elcar, Jack Kehoe, Dimitra Arliss, Robert Earl Jones, James J. Sloyan, Charles Dierkop, Lee Paul, Sally Kirkland, Avon Long, Arch Johnson, Ed Bakey, Brad Sullivan, John Quade, Larry D. Mann, Leonard Barr, Paulene Myers, Joe Tornatore, Jack Collins, Tom Spratley, Ken O'Brien, Ken Sansom, Ta-Tanisha, William Benedict*. Dir: George Roy Hill. Pro: Tony Bill, Michael & Julia Phillips. Screenplay: David S. Ward. (Universal–CIC.) Rel: April 7. Colour. 129 Mins. Cert. A.

The Stone Killer
Conventional, violent cops and robbers piece about a dedicated New York detective whose methods of dealing with suspects have become a little suspect (fire first and ask questions afterwards!) but who persuades his superiors to let him play a hunch that a big underworld war is in the offing. He proves right, too, but can't stop the Mafia inter-family revenge holocaust. Cast: *Charles Bronson, Martin Balsam, Ralph Waite, David Sheiner, Norman Fell, Eddie Firestone, Walter Burke, David Moody, Charles Tyner, Paul Koslo, Stuart Margolin, John Ritter, Byron Morrow, Jack Colvin,*

Frank Campanella, Alfred Ryder, Gene Woodbury, Harry Basch, Jan Arvan, Lisabeth Hush, Mary Cross, Kelly Miles, Tom Falk, Robert Emhardt. Dir & Pro: Michael Winner. Screenplay: Gerard Wilson, based on the John Gardner book *A Complete State of Death*. (Winner–Dino de Laurentis–Columbia–Warner.) Rel: Mar. 24. Colour. 96 Mins. Cert. X.

Stork
Another film from "Down Under," all about an Aussie drop-out whose favourite pastimes are drinking beer, eating prawns and talking revolution: all very comic strip-ish. Cast: *Bruce Spence, Graham Blundell, Sean McEuan, Helmut Bakaitis, Jacki Weaver, Peter Green, Madeleine Orr, Peter Cummins, Michael Duffield, Alan Finney*. Dir & Pro: Tim Burstall. Screenplay: David Williamson. (Burstall/Bilcock & Copping– LMG.) Rel: Floating; first shown at the Classic, Victoria, Oct., 1973. Colour. 90 Mins. Cert. X.

Summer Wishes, Winter Dreams
Wholly convincing, psychologically sound, simple story about a middle-aged couple who are shaken out of their routine into realisation of themselves and the lives they lead by the sudden death of the wife's mother and the trip to Europe that follows, culminating in a cathartic return by the husband to the spot in France where during the Battle of the Bulge he suffered the greatest, most disturbing and terrifying experience of his life. An unexpected gem of a film and in its own way something of a major classic. Magically acted by *Joanne Woodward* and *Martin Balsam*. Rest of cast: *Dori Brenner, Ron Rickards, Sylvia Sidney, Tresa Hughes, Helen Ludlam, Win Forman, Peter Marklin*. Dir: Gilbert Cates. Pro: Jack Brodsky. Screenplay: Stewart Stern. (Rastar–Columbia–Warner.) Rel: Floating; first shown at the Academy, Jan., 1974. Colour. 88 Mins. Cert. AA.

Sunstruck
Welsh immigrant teacher *Harry Secombe* in Australia's back of beyond, tames his little charges, knocks them into a competition choir and wins homespun beauty *Maggie Fitzgibbon*. Rest of cast: *John Meillon, Dawn Lake, Peter Whittle, Bobby Limb, Norman Erskine, Jack Allen, Lornal Wilde, Roger Cox, Tommy Mack, John Armstrong, Stuart Wagstaff, Jeff Ashby, Max Brouggy, Benita Collings, Charles McCallam, Dennis Jordan, Donald Houston, Derek Nimmo*. Dir: James Gilbert. Pro: Jack Neary & James Grafton. Screenplay: Stan Mars. (Immigrant–Anglo EMI–MGM–EMI.) Rel: Aug. 26. Colour. 92 Mins. Cert. U.

Super Dick
Ribald, rough and coarse sex comedy about a paunchy Private Eye whose investigations are always strongly sexual and who never tires of proving his boasted virility. A script peppered with four-letter words and simulated sexual exercises. Cast: *Alan Garfield, Madeleine Le Roux, David Kirk, Devin Goldenberg, Deborah Morgan, Nancy Salmon, Maureen Byrnes, Sean Walsh, Bruce Pecheur*. Dir: John Avildsen. Pro:

David Jay Disick. Screenplay: David Odell, from a novel by Michael Brett. (Cry Uncle–Eagle.) Rel: Floating. Colour. 77 Mins. Cert. X.

Swallows and Amazons
A charming, rather rambling, fairly uneventful but quite entertaining children's film largely acted by children: a story of four youngsters holidaying in the Lake District and their adventures as they picnic, feud in a friendly way, and recover some stolen loot. Cast: *Virginia McKenna, Ronald Fraser, Simon West, Sophie Neville, Zanna Hamilton, Stephen Grendon, Kit Seymour, Lesley Bennett, John Franklyn-Robbins, Jack Woolgar, Mike Pratt, David Blagden, Brenda Bruce*. Dir: Claude Whatham. Pro: Richard Pilbrow. Screenplay: David Wood, based on the book by Arthur Ransome. (Theatre Projects–EMI.) Rel: April 21. Colour. 92 Mins. Cert. U.

Swastika
Documentary about the rise and fall of Nazi Germany in general and Hitler in particular and including some hitherto never seen home-movies of the German dictator at home and off duty! Dir: Philippe Mora. Pro: Sanford Lieberson & David Puttnam. Written: P. Mora & Lutz Becker. (Visual Programme Systems.) Rel: Floating; first shown at the Odeon, Haymarket, Jan., 1974. Colour. 113 Mins. Cert. A.

The Swinging Stewardesses
The love life of a number of air-line stewardesses. Cast: *Evelyne Traeger, Ingrid Steeger, Margrit Siegel*. Dir: Michael Thomas. Pro: Erwin C. Dietrich. Screenplay: Manfred Gregor. (VIP–Miracle.) Rel: Floating. Colour. 65 Mins. Cert. X.

Take Me High
Cheery British musical with *Cliff Richard* as successful junior Merchant Banker who goes to Birmingham, meets a pretty girl on the barge-home next to his own and with her introduces that great new British food dish, The Brumberger! Rest of cast: *Debbie Watling, George Cole, Hugh Griffith, Anthony Andrews, Richard Wattis, Moyra Fraser, Ronald Hines, Jimmy Gardner, Graham Armitage, Madeline Smith, Shane Rimmer, Polly Williams, Noel Trevarthen, Elisabeth Scott, Peter Marshall, John Franklyn-Robbins, Karen Boyes*. Dir: David Askey. Pro: Kenneth Harper. Screenplay: Christopher Penfold, based on an original idea by Kenneth Harper. (Anglo EMI–MGM–EMI.) Rel: Jan. 6. Colour. 90 Mins. Cert. U.

Tales of Erotica
Four-part Italian film set in the year 1550 and concerning four young women defending themselves against charges of various offences against the opposite sex, and the way the quartet try to guide the course of justice! Cast: *Femi Benussi, Shirley Corrigan, Rosemarie Lindt, Tony Kendall, Angela Covello, Orchidea de Santis*. Dir & Screenplay: Piero Regnoli. Pro: Enzo Boetani & Giuseppe Collura. (Parf–Border.) Rel: Floating. Colour. 88 Mins. Cert. X.

The Tall Blond Man With One Black Shoe

An amusing French, English-dubbed, comedy along crazy lines about a Secret Service chief whose assistant is so ruthlessly intent on climbing into his chair that the boss sets up a complicated trap to ruin him: choosing a man at random and letting the climber think he's an ace agent. It is all rather thin and meandering but manages to be consistently amusing nevertheless, and *Mireille Darc* looks gorgeous as the final feminine weapon to break down the "spy's" diabolical – innocence! Rest of cast: *Pierre Richard, Bernard Blier, Jean Rochefort, Jean Carmet, Colette Castel, Paul le Person, Jean Obe, Robert Castel, Robert Caccia, Robert Dalban, Jean Saudray, Arlette Balkis, Yves Robert.* Dir & co-Pro (with Alain Poire) & co-Scripted (with Francis Verber): Yves Robert. (Gaumont International–La Gueville–Madeleine Films–Fox–Rank.) Rel: Floating. Colour. 89 Mins. Cert. AA.

Tarot

A film featuring the Flower People and starring *Jimi Hendrix.* Cast: *Charlotte Blob, Nuana Davis, Pat Hartley, Miss Mercy, Melinda Merr weather, Patricia O'Higgins, Teresa Pinter, Clara Schuff, Dindy Sussman, Hawaiian Suzanne, Maureen Thronton, Bob Amicer, Barron Bingen, Dr Emmanuel Bronner, Paul Gebauer, Chris Green, Benny Harris, Luke Hynes, Mike Hynson, David Nuuiwha, Leslie Potts, David de Prendergast, Alan Shuben, Steve Sutherland, Chuck Wein.* Dir: Chuck Wein. Pro: Barry de Prendergast. (Transvue Pictures.) Rel: Floating, first shown at Times, June, 1973. Colour. 90 Mins. Cert. A.

Techniques of Love

German film about teenage love affairs, centred on a Dancing School where the pupils are taught various dance routines – some of them sensually erotic. Cast: *Natascha Verell, Sandro Castell, Marlies Petersen, Birgit Zamulo, Frank Sommer.* Dir: John Weeran. Pro: Wolfgang Bellenbaum. Screenplay: John Weeran & Henry Vulpin. (City–Film–Gemini.) Rel: Floating, first shown at the Classic Moulin, April, 1974. Colour. 70 Mins. Cert. X.

Ten Fingers of Steel

Hong Kong action melo about a young Chinese seeking to revenge his bandit-raped village and tracking his quarry to Japan, where he kills the leader by a dazzling display of unarmed combat! Cast: *Wang Yu, Chang Chin Chin, Kan Kai, Tze Lan, Lun Fei, Lou Pin.* Dir: Kien Lun. Pro: Chan Wein Chien & Che Tsao Shin. Screenplay: Wang Pi Jen. (King Hwa–Ember.) Rel: Floating; first shown at Oscar One, Nov., 1973. Colour. 95 Mins. Cert. X.

Terror in the Wax Museum

In fact some shuddery goings-on in Madame Tussaud's Chamber of Horrors, where some of the villains are live and the others waxen! Cast: *Ray Milland, Broderick Crawford, Elsa Lanchester, Maurice Evans, Shani Wallis, John Carradine, Louis Hayward, Patric Knowles, Mark W. Edwards, Lisa Lu, Steven Marlo, Ben Wright, Matilda Calnan, Peggy Stewart, Leslie Thompson, Nicole Shelby, Don Herbert, Judy Wetmore, Jo Williamson, George Farina, Diane Wahrman, Rosa Huerta, Ben Brown, Rickie Weir, Paul Wilson, Ralph Cunningham, Don Williamson, Evelyn Reynolds.* Dir: Geoeg Fenady. Pro: Andrew J. Fenady. Screenplay: Jameson Brewer. (Charles A. Pratt–BCP–NationWide Film Distributors.) Rel: Floating. Colour. 95 Mins. Cert. X.

That Man Bolt

He's black, and a courier, and he's got the job of taking a million dollars from a Hong Kong bank to Mexico City and trying to stop the crooks from taking it from him *en route!* Cast: *Fred Williamson, Bryon Webster, Miko Mayama, Teresa Graves, Satoshi Nakamura, John Orchard, Jack Ging, Ken Kazama, Vassili Lambrinos.* Dir: Henry Levin & David Lowell Rich. Pro: Bernard Schwartz. Screenplay: Quentin Werty & Charles Johnson. (Universal–CIC.) Rel: Mar. 10. Colour. 103 Mins. Cert. X.

Theatre of Blood

Thriller with a twinkle in its eye: about the macabre revenge enacted on a bunch of critics by infuriated actor *Vincent Price* when they vote him out of the Award he feels is his by right: he systematically wipes them out by various horrible Shakespearean ways (and that makes some very gory sequences, too). Rest of cast: *Diana Rigg, Ian Hendry, Harry Andrews, Coral Browne, Robert Coote, Jack Hawkins, Michael Hordern, Arthur Lowe, Robert Morley, Dennis Price, Milo O'Shea, Eric Sykes, Madeline Smith, Diana Dors, Joan Hickson, Renee Asherson, Bunny Reed, Peter Thornton, Charles Sinnickson, Brigid Erin Bates, Tutte Lemkow, Stanley Bates, Eric Francis, Sally Gilmore, John Gilpin, Joyce Graeme, Jack Maguire, Declan Mulholland.* Dir: Douglas Hickox. Pro: John Kohn & Stanley Mann. Screenplay: Anthony Greville-Bell. (Cineman–UA.) Rel: June 24–July 1, 1973. Colour. 104 Mins. Cert X.

They Call Me Trinity

Light-hearted Italian Western about two brothers, *Terence Hill* and *Bud Spencer*, who step between a greedy gang of outlaws and the local Mormon farmers and restore law and order before moving on to new adventures.... Rest of cast: *Farley Granger, Steffen Zacharias, Dan Sturkie, Gisela Hahn, Elena Pedemonte, Ezio Marano.* Dir & Screenplay: E. B. Clucher. Pro: Italo Zingarelli. (Levine–Avco Embassy.) Rel: Feb. 22. Colour. 93 Mins. Cert. A.

They Only Kill Their Masters

Quite excellent if minor whodunit with *James Garner* as the pleasant Police Chief whose underlying shrewdness solves the crime of the murdered girl. Rest of cast: *Katharine Ross, Hal Holbrook, Harry Guardino, June Allyson, Christopher Connelly, Tom Ewell, Peter Lawford, Edmond O'Brien, Arthur O'Connell, Ann Rutherford, Art Metrano, Harry Basch, Jenifer Shaw, Jason Wingreen, Robert Nichols, Norma Connolly, David Westberg, Lee Pulford, Roy Applegate, Alma Lenor Beltran.* Dir: James Goldstone. Pro: William Belasco. Screenplay: Lane Slate. (MGM–EMI.) Rel: July 15. Colour. 98 Mins. Cert. AA.

Three

About a couple of Americans vacationing in Europe meeting a girl who eventually splits the friends up. Based on the Irwin Shaw novel, *When We Were Three.* Cast: *Charlotte Rampling, Robie Porter, Sam Waterston, Pascale Roberts, Edina Ronay, Gillian Hills, Mario Cotone, Patrizia Giammei, Franca Tasso, Roberto Scheiber, Alfredo Rizzo.* Dir & Screenplay: James Salter. Pro: Bruce Becker. (Salter–UA.) Rel: March 10. Colour. 95 Mins. Cert. A.

Thumb Tripping

A new, neat label for hitch-hiking, and this American film by a young director – his first movie – is the story of such a trip by a couple of casually met youngsters who make what in fact is a psychological voyage of discovery into the more depressing facts of life and end by splitting up. Cast: *Michael Burns, Meg Foster, Mariana Hill, Burke Burns, Mike Conrad, Bruce Dern, Larry Hankin, Joyce Van Pattern, Nevada Spencer, Sundown Spencer.* Dir: Quentin Masters. Pro: Robert Chartoff & Irwin Winkler. Screenplay: Don Mitchell, based on his own novel. (Avco–Embassy.) Rel: Nov. 4. Colour. 94 Mins. Cert. X.

Tiffany Jones

Lots of girlie glamour and slick light comedy thrills in the first screen adventures of the popular strip-cartoon model heroine. She becomes caught up in a Zirdanian left-wing underground movement, gangster gun-sellers and the nice Crown Prince . . . constantly losing her clothes or otherwise stripping down for action! Cast: *Anouska Hempel, Ray Brooks, Susan Sheers, Damien Thomas, Eric Pohlmann, Richard Marner, Ivor Salter, Lynda Baron, Martin Benson, Alan Curtis, John Clive, Geoffrey Hughes, Bill Kerr, Martin Wyldeck, Nick Zaran, Walter Randall, Kim Alexander, Sam Kelly, Rose Hill, Tony Simpson, Pearl Hackney, Tom Mennard, Derek Royle, Maggie Walker, David Hamilton.* Dir & Pro: Peter Walker. Screenplay: Alfred Shaughnessy. (Peter Walker–Hemdale.) Rel: Floating. Colour. 90 Mins. Cert. X.

Till Sex Do Us Part

Vilgot Sjoman's (Swedish) sex comedy about a wife who won't let her husband make love to her because she is obsessed by the thought that if he does she'll die! And how she finally decides she'll die then! Cast: *Solveig Ternstrom, Borje Ahlstedt, Margaretha Bystrom, Frej Lindqvist.* Dir & Written: Vilgot Sjoman. (Eagle Films.) Rel: Floating, first shown at the Classic, Piccadilly, April 1974. Colour. 96 Mins. Cert. X.

'Tis Pity She's a Whore

Screen version of the John Ford play, a story of a destroying physical passion between a brother and sister which leads to a bloody end when he forestalls the husband's revenge by killing his sister, cutting her heart out and serving it up on a platter and himself suffering ritual death. Strong stuff indeed, interestingly filmed. Cast: *Charlotte Rampling, Oliver Tobias, Fabio Testi, Antonio Falsi, Rik Battaglia, Angela Luce, Rino Imperio*. Dir: Giuseppe Patroni Griffi. Pro: Silvio Clementelli. Screenplay: G. P. Griffi, Alfio Valdarnini & Carlo Carunchio, based on the play by John Ford. (Clesi Cinematografica–Miracle.) Rel: Floating; first shown at the Swiss Centre Cinema, Aug., 1973. Colour. 102 Mins. Cert. X.

Tom Sawyer
A most engaging screen adaptation as a musical of Mark Twain's famous story about a boy and his friends living along the Mississippi; pleasing melodies, lovely backgrounds, delightful performances by *Celeste Holm, Warren Oates* and *Jeff East*, and a wholly winning one by tow-headed *Johnny Whitaker* as Tom. Rest of cast: *Jodie Foster, Lucille Benson, Henry Jones, Noah Keen, Dub Taylor, Richard Eastham, Sandy Kenyon, Joshua Hill Lewis, Susan Joyce, Steve Hogg, Sean Summers, Kevin Jefferson, Page Williams, James A. Kuhn, Mark Lynch, Jonathan Taylor, Anne Voss, Kunu Hank.* Dir: Don Taylor. Pro: Arthur P. Jacobs. Screenplay: Robert B. Sherman & Richard M. Sherman. (Apjac International–Reader's Digest–UA.) Rel: Aug. 12. Colour. 103 Mins. Cert. U.

Tombs of the Blind Dead
Macabre thriller about a deserted village where the tombs (of the Templars) open from time to time and the corpses come out to carry on killing . . . Cast: *Cesar Burner, Lone Fleming, Helen Harp, Joseph Thelman.* Dir & Screenplay: Amando de Ossorio. (Plata/Interfilme–Butcher's.) Rel: Floating. Colour. 85 Mins. Cert. X.

Top of the Heap
Christopher St John as the Negro cop in Washington, D.C., who because he's straight and tries to keep a fair balance between black and white, is despised by both, so escapes periodically into a private fantasy world. And Mr St John wrote, directed and produced the film. Rest of cast: *Tim Smyth, J. J. Johnson, Barry Thomas, Paula Kelly, Florence St Peter, Leonard Kuras, John Alderson, Patrick McVey, Ingeborg Sorensen, Ron Douglas, Almeria Quinn, Beatrice Webster, Essie McSwine, Jerry Jones, Willie Harris, Tiger Joe Marsh, John McMurtry, Raymond O'Keefe, Brian Cutler, Hedgemon Lewis, Kenneth Norton, Damu King, Ji-Tu Cumbuka, Marilyn Wirt, Angela Seymour, Joe Tornatore, Ann Mason, Maria Lennard, Mayrita Varna, Dan Roth, Arnold Dover, June Fairchild, Cliff Emmich, Pamela Whorf, Allen Garfield, Richard M. Dixon.* Dir, Pro & Screenplay: Christopher St John. (Fanfare/St John Unlimited–Doverton.) Rel: Floating. Colour. 88 Mins. Cert. X.

A Touch of Class
Classy, polished and amusing comedy-romance about the affair between an American husband on the make in London and the cool English divorcée who, thrown into his company by coincidence, coolly accepts his proposal that they go away together for a short holiday –

which starts as a comical disaster but leads to love and, finally, to the inevitable parting. Superbly acted by (especially) *Glenda Jackson, George Segal* and *Paul Sorvino*. Rest of cast: *Hildegard Neil, Cec Linder, K. Callan, Mary Barclay, Michael Elwyn, Samantha Weyson, Michael McVey, Edward Kemp, Lisa Vanderpump, Ian Thompson, Donald Hewlett, John Sterland, David Healy.* Dir & Pro: Melvin Frank. Screenplay: Melvin Frank & Jack Rose. (Joseph E. Levine & Brut Productions–Avco–Embassy.) Rel: Sept. 23. Colour. 106 Mins. Cert. AA.

Tout Va Bien
Another complicated, far left-leaning, political document from Godard in which he repeats some old ideas about class warfare while endeavouring to present some new ones! The stuff to give the addicts. Cast: *Yves Montand, Jane Fonda, Vittorio Caprioli, Jean Pignol, Pierre Oudry, Elizabeth Chauvin, Eric Chartier, Yves Gabrielli, Bugette, Castel Casti, Michel Marot, Huguette, Miéville, Marcel Gassouk, Anne Wiazemski, René Defleurieu, Didier Gaudron, Luce Marneux, Nathalie Simon, Louise Rioton.* Dir: Jean-Luc Godard & Jean-Pierre Gorin. (Anouchka/Vicco/Empire–The Other Cinema.) Rel: Floating. Colour. 95 Mins. Cert. X.

Treasure Island
Routine re-make of the famous R. L. Stevenson story for boys: about a small boy thrown into contact with the roaring pirates in general and Long John (*Orson Welles*) Silver in particular. Rest of cast: *Kim Burfield, Lionel Stander, Walter Slezak, Angel Del Pozo, Rik Battaglia, Maria Rohm, Paul Muller, Jean Lefebvre, Michael Garland, Aldo Sambrell, Alibe, Chinchilla.* Dir: John Hough. Pro: Harry Alan Towers. Screenplay: Wolf Mankowitz & Orson Welles. (Massfilms/FDL/CCC Filmkunst/Eguiluz–MGM–EMI.) Rel: Aug. 5. Colour. 95 Mins. Cert. U.

Trinity is Still My Name
Second in the series of light-hearted Italian "Trinity" Westerns, with *Terence Hill* and *Bud Spencer* as the two brothers trying hard, but failing, to live up to their dying dad's wish that they go out and become notorious bandits. Somehow they always end up as the good guys! Rest of cast: *Harry Carey, Jr., Yanti Somer, Jessica Dublin, Gerald Landry, Enzo Tarascio, Pupo De Luca, Dana Ghia, Emilio Delle Piane, Enzo Fiermonte, Tony Norton, Franco Ressel, Jean Louis, Adriano Mercantori.* Dir & Screenplay: E. B. Clucher. Pro: Italo Zingarelli. (West Film–Avco–Embassy). Floating. Colour. 121 Mins. Cert. U.

Trip to Kill
Heroically throwing himself on top of a hand-grenade in the Vietnam War, the hero relives in the moments before it goes off his involvement with drugs and gangsters in Hollywood! (The film is known in America as *Clay Pigeon*.) Cast: *Tom Stern, Telly Savalas, Robert Vaughn, Jeff Corey, Peter Lawford, Marilyn Akin, John Marley, Marlene Clark, Burgess Meredith, Belinda Palmer, Ivan Dixon, Mario Alcade,*

James Dobson. Dir: Tom Stern & Lane Slate. Pro: Frank Avianca & Ronald Buck. Screenplay: Ronald Buck, Buddy Ruskin & Jack Gross, Jr. (Tracom–Doverton Films.) Rel: Floating. Colour. 91 Mins. Cert. X.

Trouble Man
Fast-paced, violent gangster piece about trouble-shooter Mr T and the efforts of a couple of nasty characters to frame him for the gang killing which they do in order to move in on a new stretch of rival-held territory. And it is quite incidental that the "hero" and many of the characters are black. Cast: *Robert Hooks, Paul Winfield, Ralph Waite, William Smithers, Paula Kelly, Julius Harris, Bill Henderson, Wayne Storm, Akili Jones, Vince Howard, Stack Pierce, Larry Cook, Virginia Capers, Rick Ferrell, James "Texas Blood" Brown, Tracy Reed, Felton Perry, Jita Hadi, John Crawford, Howie Steindler.* Dir: Ivan Dixon. Pro: Joel D. Freeman. Screenplay: John D. F. Black. (JDF/B Productions–Fox–Rank.) Rel: Sept. 30. Colour. 99 Mins. Cert. X.

Tuo Vizio E una Stanza Chiusa e Solo lo ne ho la Chiave – Excite Me
Interesting if finally not anything like completely successful Italian attempt to bring Edgar Allan Poe's horror story *The Black Cat* to the screen: with the lovely wife the villainess who tries to drive her husband into fearing he's insane and is certainly prepared to do murder to prove it! Cast: *Edwige Fenech, Anita Strindberg, Luigi Pistilli, Angela La Vorgna, Enrica Bonaccorti, Daniela Giordano, Ermelinda de Felice, Marco Mariani, Carla Mancini, Bruno Boschetti, Franco Nebbia.* Dir: Sergio Martino. Pro: Luciano Martino. Screenplay: Ernesto Gastaldi, Adriano Bolzoni & Sauro Scavolini: based on the Edgar Allan Poe story *The Black Cat.* (Lea–Border Films.) Rel: Floating; first shown at the Jacey, Trafalgar Square, June, 1973. Colour. 96 Mins. Cert. X.

Ultimo Tango a Zagarol – The Last Italian Tango
Well, that's what he dances after leaving his brothel-keeping wife, falling for a prostitute and, revolted when he learns what she is, tries to avoid her as she pursues him. Cast: *Franco Franchi, Martine Beswick, Gina Rovere, Nicola Arigliano, Franca Valeri, Loudona Mongiordini, Franzia Di Mariza, Ugo Fancoreggi, Carlo Mancini, Bruno Bossio.* Dir: Nando Cicero. Pro: Mario Mariani. Screenplay: Marino Onorati. (Cinemar–Border Films.) Rel: Floating. Colour. 95 Mins. Cert. X.

Up the Sandbox
Lightly amusing little comedy about a wife and mother who is constantly fantasising her actually rather unexciting family life. Cast: *Barbara Streisand, David Selby, Ariane Heller, Terry & Gary Smith, Jane Hoffman, John C. Becher, Jacobo Morales, Paul Benedict, George Irving, Jane House, Pitt Herbert, Janet Brandt, Pearl Shear, Carl Gottlieb, Marina Durell, Barbara Rhodes, Ji-Tu Cumbuka, Paul Dooley, Conrad Bain, Jane Betts, Efrain Lopez Neris.* Dir: Irvin Kershner. Pro: Irwin

Winkler & Robert Chartoff. Screenplay: Paul Zindel; based on the novel by Anne Richardson Roiphe. (First Artists–Barwood–Chartoff/Winkler–Cinerama.) Rel: Floating. Colour. 98 Mins. Cert. AA.

Vault of Horror
Companion film to *Tales from the Crypt* with a similar situation of a group of characters marooned together below earth level – in this case taken there by a tower-block lift which doesn't stop at the basement button – who are then encouraged to tell each other their respective "nightmares" – are they in fact just nightmares, or experiences, or . . .? Incredible, of course, affronting commonsense, but done with some style and quite a lot of polish, raising the film well above the normal crude chiller. Casts – Midnight Mass: *Daniel Massey, Anna Massey, Michael Pratt, Erik Chitty, Jerold Wells;* The Neat Job: *Terry-Thomas, Glynis Johns, Marianne Stone, John Forbes-Robertson;* This Trick'll Kill You: *Curt Jurgens, Dawn Addams, Jasmina Hilton, Ishaq Bux;* Bargain in Death: *Michael Craig, Edward Judd, Robin Nedwell, Geoffrey Davies, Arthur Mullard;* Drawn and Quartered: *Tom Baker, Denholm Elliott, Terence Alexander, John Witty.* Dir: Roy Ward Baker. Pro: Max J. Rosenberg & Milton Subotsky. Screenplay: Milton Subotsky; based on stories by Al Feldstein & Bill Gaines. (Cinerama–Fox–Rank.) Rel: Nov. 18. Colour. 85 Mins. Cert. X.

Visions of Eight
Eight famous international directors each provide a kind of filmic essay on one aspect of the last Olympic Games as follows: John Schlesinger on "The Longest" (The Marathon); Milos Forman on "The Decathlon"; Mai Zetterling on "The Strongest" (Weightlifters); Kon Ichikawa on "The Fastest" (The Sprinters); Juri Ozerov on "The Beginning"; Arthur Penn on "The Highest" (Pole Vaulters); Michael Pfleghar on "The Women"; and Claude Lelouch on "The Losers". Best and most amusing contribution from Forman; most moving from Lelouch; shiniest from Schlesinger; most intimately searching from Ichikawa; in all, a fascinating rather than illuminating record. Pro: Stan Margulies. (David Wolper–MGM–EMI.) Rel: Floating. Colour. 110 Mins. Cert. U.

Visit to a Chief's Son
A simple father and son relationship drama set against a background of the Kenyan jungles, where Dad is an American anthropologist on safari and his son unintentionally keeps on bringing the expedition to the edge of disaster. Cast: *Richard Mulligan, Johnny Sekka, Phillip Hodgson, Jesse Kinaru, Jock Anderson, Chief Lo Moiro and the Masai Tribespeople.* Dir: Lamont Johnson. Pro: Robert Halmi. Screenplay: Albert Ruben. (UA.) Rel: June 2. 92 Mins. Cert. A.

Voices
Rather slow, and oddly unsympathetic ghost thriller based on a play by Richard Lortz: about a somewhat quarrelsome young couple who have lost their only child in the river while they were making love (an accident which gives the wife such a shock she spends

the next two years in an asylum) celebrating their reunion by visiting a large old country house left them by the wife's aunt, on the way to which they run into thick fog and in which they hear voices and see visions and the next morning discover the horrible truth of their situation. Cast: *David Hemmings, Gayle Hunnicutt, Lyn Farleigh, Russell Lewis, Eva Griffiths, Adam Bridge, Peggy Ann Clifford.* Dir: Kevin Billington. Pro: Roberts Enders. Screenplay: George Kirgo & Robert Enders; from the stage play by Richard Lortz. (Hemdale.) Rel: Floating. Colour. 91 Mins. Cert. AA.

Walking Tall
Based-on-facts story about an ex-wrestler who decides to settle down to become a farmer in the McNairy County, Tennessee, but immediately comes into conflict with the gamblers, pimps and whores who have taken over the town; is beaten, knifed and left for dead, but recovers and, as elected sheriff, fights back against the racketeers and, though losing his wife and almost his own life, battles on to finally win the war. A frightening tale of corruption and ineffectiveness in the ranks of law and order and a frightening lesson that only by using even more violence than the crooks can some sort of honest life be restored. Cast: *Joe Don Baker, Elizabeth Hartman, Gene Evans, Noah Beery, Brenda Benet, John Brascia, Bruce Glover, Arch Johnson, Felton Perry, Richard X. Slattery, Rosemary Murphy, Lynn Borden, Ed Call, Sidney Clute, Douglas V. Fowley, Don Keefer, Sam Laws, Pepper Martin, John Myhers, Logan Ramsey, Kenneth Tobey, Lurene Tuttle, Wanea Wes, Leif Garrett, Dawn Lyn, Dominick Mazzie, Russell Thorson, Gil Perkins, Carey Loftin, Warner Venetz, Gene Lebell, Del Monroe, Lloyd Tatum, Vaudie Plunk, Pearline Wynn, Ted Jordan, Red West, Andrew J. Pirtle.* Dir: Phil Karlson. Pro & Screenplay: Mort Briskin. (BCP–MGM–EMI.) Rel: Feb. 10. Colour. 99 Mins. Cert. X.

A Warm December
A kind of black *Love Story*, in that this sad and sentimental little story about a hopeless love has the heroine dying of an incurable disease. The man is Doctor *Sidney Poitier* from Washington, in London with his small daughter on holiday, and the girl is an Ambassador's daughter from one of the new African States. They meet, they love and they part, because of her nearing death and national obligations! Rest of cast: *Esther Anderson, Yvette Curtis, George Baker, T. P. McKenna, Johnny Sekka, Earl Cameron, Hilary Crane, John Beardmore, Milos Kirek, Anthony Stamboulieh, Dennis Chin, Tommy Eytle, Ann and Stephanie Smith, Letta Mbulu.* Dir: Sidney Poitier. Pro: Melville Tucker. Screenplay: Lawrence Roman. (First Artists–National General–Cinerama.) Rel: July 8. Colour. 100 Mins. Cert. A.

The War Between Men and Women
Amusing comedy made on a less than comic theme: about a cartoonist who is going blind, and in fact finally does so. Based on the writings and cartoons of James

Thurber. *Jack Lemmon* superb as the cartoonist who is more or less pushed into marriage by the girl who he would prefer to keep as a mistress and then has all the worries of a ready-made family along with his other problem of fading sight. An equally good performance by *Barbara Harris,* the two keeping the film away from the sticky sentimentality it could otherwise have drifted into. Rest of cast: *Jason Robards, Herb Edelman, Lisa Gerritsen, Moosie Drier, Severn Darden, Lisa Eilbacher, Lucille Meredith, Ruth McDevitt, Joey Faye, Alan De Witt, John Zaremba, Rick Gates, Lea Marmer, Janya Brannt, Olive Dunbar, Margaret Muse, William Hickman, Dr Joyce Brothers.* Dir: Melville Shavelson. Pro: Danny Arnold. Screenplay: Melville Shavelson & Danny Arnold. (Cinema Center–Fox.) Rel: Floating. Colour. 105 Mins. Cert. A.

Wattstax
The film record of a black concert given in the summer of '72 as part of the annual Watts Festival in Southern California, with *Isaac Hayes, The Staple Singers, Luther Ingram, Johnnie Taylor, The Emotions, Rufus Thomas, Carla Thomas, Albert King and others.* Dir & Screenplay: Mel Stuart. Pro: Al Bell & David L. Wolper. (Stax/Wolper–Columbia–Warner.) Rel: Floating. Colour. 102 Mins. Cert. X.

The Way of the Dragon
The late *Bruce Lee* not only starred in this story of the innocent in the big city but also wrote and directed it. Set in Rome, the story is about the young man from Hong Kong coming to Italy to help a Chinese restaurant-owner relative who is being harassed by gangsters. Rest of cast (includes): *Chuck Norris, Nora Miao.* Dir & Screenplay: Bruce Lee. Pro: Raymond Chow. (Golden Harvest–Cathay Films.) Rel: June 16. Colour. 98 Mins. Cert. X.

The Way We Were
A real throwback to the time of its life, the late thirties and early forties, in that, basically a tender romance along "Woman's Weepie" lines, it has the style, the mood and atmosphere as well as the story of the period. *Barbara Streisand,* looking lovelier than ever previously on the screen, gives the performance of her life as the dedicated, left-wing causes agitator who falls in love with the handsome and thoroughly conventionally minded and motivated college sports ace (and, later, naval officer) *Robert Redford* with whom she has a long but always basically uneasy relationship which, quite inevitably, breaks up in the end. Slow, sad, romantic and beautifully made. Rest of cast: *Bradford Dillman, Lois Chiles, Patrick O'Neal, Viveca Lindfors, Allyn Ann McLerie, Murray Hamilton, Herb Edelman, Diana Ewing, Sally Kirkland, Marcia Mae Jones, Don Keefer, George Gaynes, Eric Boles, Barbara Peterson, Roy Jenson, Brendan Kelly, James Woods, Connie Forslund, Robert Gerringer, Susie Blakely, Ed Power, Suzanne Zenor, Dan Seymour.* Dir: Sydney Pollack. Pro: Ray Stark. Screenplay: Arthur Laurents. (Rastar–Columbia–Warner.) Rel: Mar. 17. Colour. 118 Mins. Cert. A.

Westworld

A very unusual Western! It's all set in a luxury holiday resort in the desert where every whim of the wealthy visitors is catered for by life-like robots, who can be abused, seduced and even killed by the guests . . . until things start to go wrong and the robots decide to stick up for themselves! Cast: *Yul Brynner, Richard Benjamin, James Brolin, Norman Bartold, Alan Oppenheimer, Victoria Shaw, Dick Van Patten, Linda Scott, Steve Franken, Michael Mikler, Terry Wilson, Majel Barrett, Anne Randall, Julie Marcus, Sharyn Wynters, Anne Bellamy, Chris Holter, Charles Seel, Wade Crosby.* Dir & Written: Michael Crichton. Pro: Paul N. Lazarus III. (MGM–EMI.) Rel: Mar. 17. Colour. 89 Mins. Cert. AA.

What?

Roman Polanski's pretty crazy sex comedy set in a villa on the Riviera and apparently concerned with nothing in particular as it relates the exploits of our rape-escape heroine who never wears more than a pyjama top and often sheds that! And in the role, a most promising performance by newcomer *Sydne Rome*. Rest of cast: *Marcello Mastroianni, Hugh Griffith, Romolo Valli, Guido Alberti, Gianfranco Piacentini, Roger Middleton, Roman Polanski.* Dir: Roman Polanski. Pro: Carlo Ponti. Screenplay: Gerard Brach & Roman Polanski. (International Film Theatre–Gala.) Rel: Floating, first shown at the Curzon, April, 1974. Colour. 133 Mins. Cert. X.

Who Killed Mary Whats'ername?

The rather strange murder investigation carried out by a former boxing champion, now diabetic, who coming out of hospital is horrified to read about on the unsolved murder mystery of a prostitute and on the spot decides that he himself will uncover the guilty killer. Cast: *Red Buttons, Alice Playten, Sylvia Miles, Sam Waterston, Dick Williams, Conrad Bain, Norman Rose, David Doyle, Ellen Gurin, Ron Carey.* Dir: Ernie Pintoff. Pro: George Manasse. Screenplay: John O'Toole. (Cannon–Gala.) Rel: Floating; first shown at Berkeley One, June, 1973. Colour. 90 Mins. Cert. AA.

White Lightning

Amusing enough to offset the violence, the story concerns bootlegger *Burt Reynolds'* revenge on the sheriff who callously drowned his younger brother in a mangrove swamp, a revenge condoned by the U.S. Treasury Dept. who suspect the Sheriff of being involved in an illegal whisky racket. Rest of cast: *Jennifer Billingsley, Ned Beatty, Bo Hopkins, Matt Clark, Louise Latham, Diane Ladd, R. G. Armstrong, Conlan Carter, Dabbs Greer, Lincoln Demyan, John Steadman, Iris Korn, Stephanie Burchfield, Barbara Muller, Robert Ginnaven, Fay Martin, Richard Allin, Bill Bond, Sherry Boucher, Glenn Wilder, Dick Ziker, Buddy Joe Hooker, Cathy Finley.* Dir: Joseph Sargent. Pro: Arthur Gardner & Jules V. Levy. Screenplay: William Norton. (Levy–Gardner–Laven–UA.) Rel: Nov. 11. Colour. 101 Mins. Cert. X.

Wicked, Wicked

Conventional whodunit about the mysterious vanishings of a number of blondes, a mystery separately investigated by the cops and the private eye of the hotel where it all happens. All this in "Duo-Vision", which appears to be another name for the split-screen technique which is used for almost the entire length of the movie. Cast: *David Bailey, Tiffany Bolling, Randolph Roberts, Scott Brady, Ed Byrnes, Diane McBain, Roger Bowen, Madeleine Sherwood, Indira Danks, Arthur O'Connell, Jack Knight, Patsy Garrett, Robert Nichols, Kirk Bates, Maryesther Denver.* Dir, Pro & Screenplay: Richard L. Bare. (United National–MGM–EMI.) Rel: Oct. 14. Colour. 95 Mins. Cert. X.

The Wicker Man

Thriller set on a small and enclosed island community off the coast of Scotland, to which comes a young policeman to investigate the disappearance of a twelve-year-old girl. But he soon finds that he is up against deep pagan undercurrents which frighten and confuse him. Cast: *Edward Woodward, Britt Ekland, Diane Cilento, Ingrid Pitt, Christopher Lee, Lesley Mackie, Walter Carr, Irene Sunters, Lindsay Kemp, Ian Campbell, Kevin Collins, Aubrey Morris, Russell Waters, Donald Eccles, Geraldine Cowper.* Dir: Robin Hardy. Pro: Peter Snell. Screenplay: Anthony Shaffer. (British Lion.) Rel: Floating. 86 Mins. Cert. X.

Wife By Night – see Bella di Giorno, Moglie di Notte

The Winners

The final thwarting, ironically enough by his own heavily indoctrinated family, of the ruthless business and sporting ambitions of one Will Maddox! Cast: *Joe Stewardson, Richard Loring, Marie Du Toit, Tony Jay, Madeleine Usher, John Higgins, Ken Leach, Diane Ridler, Jenny Meyer, Gregorio Fiascanaro, Ian Yule, Clive Scott.* Dir: Emil Nofal & Roy Sargeant. Pro & Screenplay: Emil Nofal. (Nofal–Scotia–Barber.) Rel: Nov. 4. 107 Mins. Cert. A.

Wonder Women

Minor fantasy-thriller about a private eye's investigation of some mysteriously missing athletes, which leads him to a small island ruled over by a sort of Lady Dr Fu Manchu who needs the abductees for her horrid human transplant experiments! Cast: *Nancy Kwan, Ross Hagen, Maria de Aragon, Roberta Collins, Tony Lorea, Sid Haig, Vic Dias, Claire Hagen, Shirley Washington, Gail Hansen, Eleanor Siron, Bruno Punzalon, Jonee Gamboa, Rick Reveke, Rudy de Jesus, Wendy Greene, Leila Benitez, Ross Rival.* Dir: Robert O'Neil. Pro: Ross Hagen. Screenplay: Lou Whitehill. (General Films–Target International.) Rel: Dec. 1. Colour. 81 Mins. Cert. X.

The World's Greatest Athlete

Typical Walt Disney "family" comedy: about young Tarzan type found in the African jungle who, brought back by an American college coach whose team has gone from bad to worse, immediately wins every sporting event in sight! Cast: *Tim Conway, Jan-Michael Vincent, John Amos, Roscoe Lee Browne, Dayle Haddon, Billy De Wolfe, Nancy Walker, Danny Goldman, Vito Scotti, Don Pedro Colley, Clarence Muse, Howard Cosell, Bud Palmer, Bill Toomey, G. T. The Tiger.* Dir: Robert Scheerer. Pro: Bill Walsh. Screenplay: Gerald Gardner & Dee Caruso. (Walt Disney.) Rel: Aug. 19. Colour. 92 Mins. Cert. U.

Yellow Dog

Not unamusing hybrid story, originally written in Japanese, from an idea by Terence Donovan, then put into screenplay form by Shinobu Hashimoto, translated into English by Prof. Alan Turney with additional dialogue by John Bird! And the result is a spy thriller about a Japanese agent in Britain who is the target for police distrust and even more active dislike by sundry other agents and it is all pretty confusing, quite amusing and generally lightly entertaining. Cast: *Jiro Tamiya, Robert Hardy, Carolyn Seymour, Joseph O'Conor, Hilary Tindall, Jonathan Newth, Keith Drinkel, Madge Ryan, Gay Singleton, Angela Thorne, Annabel Lord, Rupert Lord, Geoffrey Lumsden, Belinda Carroll, John M. Bray, Harvey Hall, Graham Mallard, Richard Pendrey, Harold Innocent, Noel Davis, Jerome Willis, Hugh Sullivan, John Welsh, Michael Godfrey, Brian Hall, Esmond Knight, Eric Mason.* Dir & Pro: Terence Donovan. Screenplay: Shinobu Hashimoto. (T. Donovan–Akari–Scotia–Barber.) Rel: Floating. Colour. 101 Mins. Cert. X.

Zardoz

Gloomy predictions about the world to come in a not always clearly defined picture about a small élite living in a plastic-bag world outside of which the miserable survivors of the non-élite are ridden down and killed or forced into slave labour by the God-chosen Exterminators. Well, that's a little like some of the content of this cleverly presented (it is an Effects Man's dream) science-fiction film. *Sean Connery*, as the ace exterminator who turns on his God, turns the ordered way of this living into chaos and then starts a brand new line of humans with the help of *Charlotte Rampling*. Rest of cast: *Sara Kestelman, Sally Anne Newton, John Alderton, Niall Buggy, Boscoe Hogan, Jessica Swift, Barbara Dowling, Christopher Casson, Reginald Jarman.* Dir, Pro & Screenplay: John Boorman. (Fox–Rank.) Rel: June 30. Colour. 105 Mins. Cert. X.

INDEX

Numbers in italics indicate pictorial reference

WALT DISNEY PRODUCTIONS'
The ISLAND at the TOP of the WORLD
U
Starring
DONALD SINDEN · DAVID HARTMAN · JACQUES MARIN
MAKO · DAVID GWILLIM · AGNETA ECKEMYR
Screenplay by JOHN WHEDON
Based on "The Lost Ones" by IAN CAMERON
Music by MAURICE JARRE
Produced by WINSTON HIBLER
Directed by ROBERT STEVENSON · TECHNICOLOR®
© WALT DISNEY PRODUCTIONS
FOR CHRISTMAS 1974

GREAT STARS in GREAT ENTERTAINMENT

CALIFORNIA SPLIT
George Segal,
Elliott Gould.

BITE THE BULLET
Gene Hackman,
Candice Bergen,
James Coburn,
Ben Johnson,
Jan-Michael Vincent,
Ian Bannen.

BREAKOUT
Charles Bronson,
Robert Duvall,
Jill Ireland,
Randy Quaid.

THE FORTUNE
Stockard Channing,
Jack Nicholson,
Warren Beatty.

THE BLACK BIRD
(...or The Maltese Falcon
Rides Again)
George Segal,
Stephane Audran,
Lee Patrick, Lionel Stander,
Elisha Cook Jnr.

BUSTER AND BILLIE
Jan-Michael Vincent,
Pamela Sue Martin,
Clifton James,
Robert Englund,
Joan Goodfellow.

FUNNY LADY
Barbra Streisand,
James Caan,
Omar Sharif,
Roddy McDowall,
Ben Vereen, Carole Wells.

OPEN SEASON
Peter Fonda,
Cornelia Sharpe,
John Phillip Law,
Richard Lynch,
Albert Mendoza,
William Holden.

SHAMPOO
Warren Beatty,
Julie Christie,
Goldie Hawn, Tony Bill,
Jack Warden, Lee Grant.

THE ODESSA FILE
Jon Voight,
Maximilian Schell,
Mary Tamm,
Maria Schell.

THE WIND AND THE LION
Sean Connery,
Brian Keith.

OLIVER!
Ron Moody, Oliver Reed,
Harry Secombe,
Shani Wallis,
Jack Wild, Mark Lester.

THE SEX SYMBOL
Connie Stevens,
Shelley Winters,
Don Murray.

From COLUMBIA PICTURES
A Division of
Columbia Pictures
Industries, Inc.